D1278462

TRACE ELEMENTS IN NUTRITION OF CHILDREN—II

The Twenty-third Nestlé Nutrition Workshop, Trace Elements in Nutrition of Children—II, *was held in Marrakech, Morocco, May 24–27, 1989.*

Workshop participants *(left to right from bottom row):* First row—K. Bergmann, R. Bergmann, I. Lombeck, T. Lahrech, N. Hajji, R.K. Chandra, L. Khouri-Dufour, S. Zlotkin, W. Mertz, P. Aggett. Second row—V.E. Negretti de Brätter, P. Brätter, M. Anke, B. Exl, K. Dörner, M. Gabr, M. Hambidge, F.Z. Sebti, B. Lönnerdal, P. Krasilnikoff. Third row— F. Haschke, O. Rachid-Tahri, M. Ouazzani, B. Leroux, B. Teo Siew Eng, H. Singh, B. Chhaparwal, A. Marini, P. Goyens. Fourth row—M. Sbihi, P. Lubeck, H. von Stockhausen, W. Baumann, O. Oster, P. Pharoah, A. Nkhili, L. Chabraoui.

Trace Elements in Nutrition of Children—II

Editor

Ranjit Kumar Chandra, M.D.

Professor of Pediatric Research, Medicine and Biochemistry
Memorial University of Newfoundland
Janeway Child Health Center
St. Johns, Newfoundland, Canada

Nestlé Nutrition
Workshop Series
Volume 23

NESTLÉ NUTRITION

RAVEN PRESS ■ NEW YORK

Nestec Ltd., Avenue Nestlé 55, CH-1800 Vevey, Switzerland
Raven Press, Ltd., 1185 Avenue of the Americas, New York,
New York 10036

Made in the United States of America

Library of Congress Cataloging-in-Publication Data

Trace elements in nutrition of children. II / editor, Ranjit Kumar
  Chandra.
      p.   cm.—(Nestlé Nutrition workshop series; v. 23)
    Proceedings of the 23rd Nestlé Nutrition workshop held in
  Marrakech, Morocco, May 24–27, 1989.
    Includes bibliographical references.
    Includes index.
    ISBN 0-88167-741-8
    1. Trace element deficiency diseases in children—Congresses.
  2. Trace elements in nutrition—Congresses.   3. Infants—Nutrition—
  Congresses.   4. Children—Nutrition—Congresses.   5. Trace
  elements—Toxicology—Congresses.   I. Chandra, Ranjit Kumar.
  II. Nestlé Nutrition S.A.   III. Series.
      [DNLM: 1. Child Nutrition—congresses.   2. Infant Nutrition—
  congresses.   3. Trace Elements—congresses.   W1 NE228 v. 23 / QU
  130 T758271 1989]
  RJ399.T7T732 1991
  618.92'39—dc20
  DNLM/DLC
  for Library of Congress   90-9012

9 8 7 6 5 4 3 2 1

Preface

The phenomenal increase both in fundamental and applied knowledge of trace elements continues to surprise scientists and clinicians alike. Advances in biochemistry, molecular biology, analytical chemistry, and immunology have enriched the field of trace element research. Much of the basic information obtained in the last decade has already found application in the revised formulation of infant nutrition products and parenteral solutions. It is now recognized that subclinical deficiencies of several trace elements occur commonly, more often in some populations than in others, more often in some age groups than in others. Moreover, such deficits can affect the function of almost all organ systems, some more than others. This awareness is slowly permeating to the general pediatrician.

When we concluded the 8th Nestlé Nutrition Workshop in Munich in 1984, it was agreed unanimously that the continuing pace of research in the field of trace elements warranted a second workshop within 5 years. The proceedings of the 23rd Nestlé Nutrition Workshop in this volume validate that hope. The choice of some new participants was deliberate, so that new perspectives and thoughts could enrich the conference. The range and depth of topics covered in the workshop are varied. The common thread was the basic knowledge that has supported and strengthened clinical observations. The high quality of the presentations by a panel of international scientists and clinicians with expertise in a variety of fields is reflected in the chapters of this book. Incisive discussion that followed the formal presentations was a highlight of the workshop, excerpts of which follow the chapters. It is to be hoped that both academic and practicing pediatricians will find useful material in this volume.

I wish to express my personal gratitude to all the participants for their contributions and to Dr. Pierre Guesry of Nestec for sponsoring this workshop. Dr. Laila Dufour was the moving force before, during and after the workshop, to ensure that everything went off smoothly. The local Moroccan hospitality of Mr. Nkhili Abbes of SOMIPA was greatly appreciated by all the participants.

Only time will tell if another workshop in 1994 would be justified. The scope of increasing knowledge in this field during the last 5 years strongly indicates that a future workshop will be justified, if not essential.

RANJIT KUMAR CHANDRA

Foreword

This is the second volume in the Nestlé Nutrition Workshop series on the theme of Trace Minerals. It would, however, be incorrect to assume that repetition of the same subject means that we are running out of new ideas; on the contrary, our Workshop program is fully booked until 1993 with new and exciting topics.

At the first "Trace Mineral" Workshop in 1984, lack of time forced us to set aside a certain number of topics, particularly relating to the risks of excess of certain trace minerals, so we made plans at that time for another workshop in 1989. The proof of the decision about a second meeting has subsequently been fully justified by the multitude of developments in this field which have occurred in the five year interval.

We consider that this volume not only updates and completes the first one but, of even greater importance, it gives the basis for reasoning when considering trace mineral requirements, deficiency and excess. It will therefore give the reader an invaluable tool for assessing pleas in favor of some of the new ultratrace minerals, where we are under the impression that fashion sometimes plays a greater role than science.

PIERRE R. GUESRY, M.D.
Medical and Scientific Director
Nestec Ltd.
Vevey, Switzerland

Contents

Contributors

Peter J. Aggett
Department of Child Health
University of Aberdeen
Polwarth Building
Foresterhill
Aberdeen AB9 2ZD, Scotland, UK

Marvin Ament
Division of Pediatric Gastroenterology
Marion Davies Children's Clinic
10833 Leconte Avenue
Los Angeles, California 90024, USA

Manfred Anke
Karl-Marx Universität Leipzig
Sektion Tierproduktion und
*   Veterinärmedizin*
Wissenschaftsbereich
*   Tierernährungschemie*
Dornburger Strasse 24
6900 Jena, German Democratic Republic

A. Balafrej
Service de Pediatrie II
Hôpital d'Enfants
Pédiatrie 2
Rabat, Morocco

A. Baroudi
Hôpital d'Enfants
Pédiatrie 2
Rabat, Morocco

Karl E. Bergmann
Federal Health Office
Division of Public Health and Statistics
Thielallee (POB 330013)
W-1000 Berlin 33, Federal Republic of
*   Germany*

Renate L. Bergmann
Free University Berlin
Department of Pediatrics
University Hospitals
Heubnerweg 6
W-1000 Berlin 19, Federal Republic of
*   Germany*

Peter Brätter
Hahn-Meitner-Institute Berlin
Department of Trace Elements Research
Glienicker Strasse 100
1000 Berlin 39, Federal Republic of
*   Germany*

Doris M. Campbell
Department of Obstetrics and Gynecology
University of Aberdeen
Aberdeen Maternity Hospital
Foresterhill
Aberdeen AB9 2ZA, Scotland, UK

L. Chabraoui
Laboratoire de Biochimie
Hôpital d'Enfants
Rabat, Morocco

Ranjit Kumar Chandra
Janeway Child Health Centre
Department of Immunology
Memorial University of Newfoundland
St. Johns, Newfoundland, Canada
*   A1A 1R8*

Alan B. Gruskin
Children's Hospital of Michigan
Detroit Medical Center
3901 Beaubien Boulevard
Detroit, Michigan 48201, USA

K. Michael Hambidge
Department of Pediatrics
University of Colorado
Health Sciences Center
4200 East 9th Avenue
Box C233
Denver, Colorado 80262, USA

T. Lahrech
Hôpital d'Enfants
Pédiatrie 4
Rabat, Morocco

M. Lahrichi
Laboratoire de Biochimie
Hôpital d'Enfants
Rabat, Morocco

Bo Lönnerdal
Department of Nutrition
University of California at Davis
Davis, California 95616, USA

Walter Mertz
Beltsville Human Nutrition Research
* Center*
US Department of Agriculture, ARS
Beltsville, Maryland 20705, USA

V. E. Negretti de Brätter
Hahn-Meitner-Institute Berlin
Department of Trace Elements Research
Glienicker Strasse 100
1000 Berlin 39, Federal Republic of
* Germany*

Kenneth R. Page
Department of Physiology
University of Aberdeen
Marischal College
Aberdeen AB1 4AS, Scotland, UK

Peter Pharoah
Department of Public Health
University of Liverpool
P.O. Box 147
Liverpool L69 3PY, United Kingdom

U. Rösick
Hahn-Meitner-Institute Berlin
Department of Trace Element Research
Glienicker Strasse 100
1000 Berlin 39, Federal Republic of
* Germany*

Martti A. Siimes
Pediatric Hematology Division
Children's Hospital
University of Helsinki
Stenbäckinkatu 11
SF-00290 Helsinki, Finland

H. B. von Stockhausen
University Children's Hospital
Josef-Schneider Strasse 2
8700 Würzburg, Federal Republic of
* Germany*

Stanley H. Zlotkin
Division of Clinical Nutrition
Suite 8511
Hospital for Sick Children
555 University Avenue
Toronto, Ontario, M5G 1X8, Canada

Invited Attendees

W. Baumann/*Mainz, Federal Republic of Germany*
K. Bergmann/*Berlin, Federal Republic of Germany*
B.C. Chhaparwal/*Indore, India*
K. Dörner/*Kiel, Federal Republic of Germany*
M.K. Gabr/*Cairo, Egypt*
P. Goyens/*Brussels, Belgium*
N. Hajji/*Rabat, Morocco*
F. Haschke/*Vienna, Austria*
P.A. Krasilnikoff/*Hiellerup, Denmark*
P.O. Lubeck/*Karlstad, Sweden*
B. Leroux/*Reims, France*
I. Lombeck/*Düsseldorf, Federal Republic of Germany*
A. Marini/*Milan, Italy*
O. Oster/*Mainz, Federal Republic of Germany*
A.M. Ouazzani/*Casablanca, Morocco*

F.Z. Sebti/*Casablanca, Morocco*
M. Seip/*Oslo, Norway*
H. Singh/*Kuantan, Malaysia*
R.O. Tahri/*Rabat, Morocco*

B. Teo Siew Eng/*Kusing, Malaysia*
H.B. von Stockhausen/*Würzburg, Federal Republic of Germany*

Nestlé Participants

B.M. Exl
Nestlé Deutschland
Munich, Germany

L. Dufour-Khouri
Nestec Ltd.
Vevey, Switzerland

Nestlé Nutrition Workshop Series

Trace Elements in Nutrition of Children—II,
edited by Ranjit K. Chandra, Nestlé Nutrition
Workshop Series, Vol. 23, Nestec Ltd.,
Vevey/Raven Press, Ltd., New York 1991.

General Considerations Regarding Requirements and Toxicity of Trace Elements

Walter Mertz

Beltsville Human Nutrition Research Center, United States Department of Agriculture, ARS, Beltsville, Maryland 20705, USA

Every nutrient or non-nutrient that we ingest or inhale is toxic when present in excess. For most of the thousands of substances in food and the environment, toxicity is the only concern related to human health. The answer for modern societies is to set and enforce limitations on exposure. For a second, much smaller group of substances, the essential nutrients (including the essential trace elements), there are additional concerns: they must be present in the organism at a certain level of concentration in order to maintain life; anything less than that level results in impaired function, disease and, ultimately, death. Thus, every essential nutrient has its special range of tissue concentrations and of intakes compatible with adequate physiological and biochemical functions and good health (1). To define this range of intakes that is safe from toxicity and adequate to meet the requirement as accurately as possible and to design and implement diet patterns that provide this range in good balance of all nutrients is the main objective of human nutrition research.

TRACE ELEMENT REQUIREMENTS

It is important to distinguish between the *absolute* (or physiological) and the *dietary* requirement. Absolute describes the average daily amount that must be absorbed over several days to maintain the specific, element-dependent functions. A dietary requirement is the average amount of the element that must be ingested over several days to provide the absolute requirement.

Absolute Requirement

Absolute requirement must be complemented by a definition of the "normal, healthy nutritional status" achieved when the requirement is fully met. That state is one in which element-specific functions do not improve with additional intake of the element. This definition comprises all element-dependent functions, clinical and physiological, including cognitive and immune functions. It does not include full saturation of specific transport proteins and it does not necessarily include maximal activity of all element-specific enzymes. The interpretation of enzyme activities as criteria for requirement setting is controversial because many enzyme activities are not limiting in the overall metabolism and, in order to obtain maximal activity, inordinate and unphysiological intakes of the nutrient would be required. Many animal experiments and several studies in humans have shown that the various functions depending on a particular nutrient have different requirements: they do not decline simultaneously in response to a reduction of intake, some being more sensitive to marginal intakes than others. A reduction in reproductive performance of animals is an extremely sensitive indicator of a marginal trace element deficiency, whereas anatomical lesions or clinically detectable diseases usually appear only in response to severe and protracted deficiencies (2).

Early signs of mild deficiencies are difficult to detect because they show little or no specificity for the deficient element (3). Proof for a tentative diagnosis of a specific trace element deficiency comes retrospectively from a supplementation trial: if an element-specific function is restored to normal by supplementation of the specific element in physiological amounts, the prior existence of a deficiency can be accepted.

These considerations lead to two conclusions of some practical importance:

1. Diagnostic methodology in most fields of the life sciences has helped to include additional functions among the criteria for nutritional adequacy. These functions were unaccessible for study a few decades ago, for example, cognitive and immune functions, homeostasis in the face of environmental imbalances, and so forth. To cite one example, it has been demonstrated that copper intakes which meet the requirement for growth of experimental animals do not maintain optimal antibody production. Intakes three times higher are required (4). Refinement of diagnosis often results in an increase of the estimated requirements, almost never in a decrease.

2. The retrospective diagnostic trial discussed above makes it possible to define the normal nutritional status for trace elements. The terms normal versus average nutritional status have been confounded in the past until Hambidge showed in the early 1970s that young children and infants living in good surroundings with free access to an abundant food supply, then considered healthy and normal, were limited in their growth rates by a suboptimal intake of zinc (5). Similar observations were made more than a decade later in China (6). These experiences strongly suggest that traditional standards of performance should neither be accepted as normal nor attributed to genetic influences until nutritional deficiencies have been ruled out. The secular changes in body stature in many countries of Asia during the past half century most certainly can be ascribed to improved nutritional status.

Dietary Requirement

Dietary requirement is defined as the daily intake of an element, averaged over several days, that allows the absorption and utilization from the diet of the absolute requirement. These two terms would be identical in the hypothetical case of an element that is completely absorbed. The dietary requirement is only slightly greater than the absolute requirement for trace elements that are highly available, but the two terms can differ by a factor of ten or more for elements of poor biological availability. Elements present in small, anionic form such as the halogens, selenite, and molybdate are rapidly and efficiently absorbed, but even for those elements there are differences in the biological availability, depending on their food sources.

The rest of the trace elements occur mainly in cationic form; they are incompletely absorbed and subject to many influences from the chemical form in which they are bound and from interactions with other nutrients. For example, absorption efficiency for dietary iron can range from less than 1% to more than 30% of the amount present in the intestines, depending on chemical form and the composition of the diet. Absorption efficiency of zinc may vary from between less than 10% to 40% (7). The chemical mechanisms responsible for these differences are not well understood, but it is reasonable to assume that a chemical structure that keeps an element in solution at the alkaline pH of the intestines until it reaches the site of absorption will result in high bioavailability. This is the case when iron is part of the heme structure which is known to be absorbed intact. Hundreds of known and suspected interactions with other dietary factors also affect biological availability of trace elements. Only one of those has been described quantitatively: the interactions of non-heme iron with ascorbic acid and the yet unidentified "meat factor" (8). The interaction of zinc with dietary fiber and phytate, of paramount importance for children in many developing countries because it determines their zinc status, is not well quantified. Because of these interactions the estimation of dietary requirements requires thorough knowledge of the dietary habits of the target groups. It is only logical, therefore, that estimates of dietary requirements should be different for different countries, each with its own dietary practices (7).

The preceding considerations were restricted to the requirements of individuals, as experimentally determined on the basis of specific functions, body size and composition, climate, dietary patterns, and so forth. Requirements are specific for each individual and vary widely. Thus, dietary recommendations set for large populations must be high enough to cover the needs of most, including those with high requirements. The Recommended Dietary Allowances of the United States National Academy of Sciences promise to cover the need of practically all healthy people (9). Statistical considerations involved in that process have been discussed (10); they give a firm scientific foundation to recommendations when they can be applied to adequate data. Unfortunately, data on the requirement for the great majority of trace elements, except perhaps iron, are not yet adequate for a thorough statistical treatment and judgment must compensate for lack of scientific precision.

Because dietary recommendations cover the need of practically all healthy persons, they must be set in excess of the true requirements of most. It is therefore wrong to use dietary recommendations as a standard to assess the nutritional adequacy of a diet of individuals. Recommendations for trace elements do not have enough precision to allow even an estimate of that point below the recommendation at which an intake becomes unsatisfactory; to determine a limit at two thirds or one half of the recommended intake is, for trace elements at least, arbitrary and without scientific foundation.

Criteria for Trace Element Requirements

Many criteria have been used to set dietary recommendations for individual nutrients. The most logical ones, resulting in the most scientific approach, apply to nutrients for which adequate information on requirements and intakes is available, such as protein. In that case the recommended allowance is set at such a level that it covers the requirement of all but the extreme 2% of the population. This is usually accomplished by adding to the mean requirement two standard deviations of the mean.

For most trace elements there is not enough information available on individual requirements to use this scientific approach. Studies in which a deficiency has been experimentally induced are few; also, they are becoming more and more difficult to perform. Their results usually define inadequate intakes and then therapeutic intakes to overcome the deficiency once it has been induced. The results, based on a few data from a few subjects, must serve as an approximate basis for estimates when no other data are available. In that case no statistical treatment of variance is possible and a large safety factor must be included to arrive at a figure that can serve as a recommended intake. A second method, much used in the past, has taken advantage of various balance methods. Conventional balance studies, measuring the intake and output of a nutrient, do not determine a person's requirement as defined above; they specify the intake that maintains a person's existing nutritional status (11). Thus, balance studies performed in a population of poor nutritional status will show lower obligatory losses and therefore lower ''requirements'' to compensate for these losses than studies performed in a population with adequate status. Such differences have led to widely different estimates among nutrient requirements, especially for calcium (12). The use of more sophisticated methods, for example, determinations of true absorption or of intestinal re-excretion of absorbed nutrient do not give much more information of a requirement than the conventional balance studies, because their results, too, depend on the prevailing nutritional status.

A third method that can be used quite appropriately under certain circumstances is the determination of the habitual intake of a nutrient by a population. The routine conduct of national production and consumption surveys in several countries has furnished reasonably adequate data for all age groups large enough for statistical treatment. If health surveys also demonstrate adequate nutritional status with regard to the nutrient in question, the habitual intake can be accepted as satisfactory to meet the needs of the population and can serve as a basis for recommendations, without an additional safety factor included.

In the setting of dietary recommendations for trace elements many assumptions have to be made for lack of adequate data, and subjective judgment must often be substituted for scientific logic. The very first step, for example, the definition of a "requirement", relies on judgment as to which functional criteria should be accepted for the definition. Because signs and symptoms of marginal deficiencies are less specific and less quantifiable than those of the more severe stages, they are considered as "soft" by some and rejected (3). Depending on that judgment, requirements as defined can vary substantially. The next step, evaluation of a population distribution, is based on the assumption that distribution characteristics typical for other nutrients are also valid for trace elements.

The translation of absolute requirement estimates into those of dietary requirements demands thorough knowledge of the dietary factors that influence biological availability of trace elements. Such knowledge is reasonably satisfactory and quantifiable only for one trace element, iron; for all other trace elements an estimate of bioavailability must rest on extrapolation from few data and, again, on subjective judgment.

Finally, in the translation of dietary requirements to recommendations, judgments will have to be made to define the proportion of a population to be covered by the recommendations. Is it justifiable under certain circumstances not to take into account the needs of 3% or 5% of the population with very high needs? Omitting the high requirements of these outliers results in lower recommendations and increases the probability that the recommendations can be met by a national diet. On the other hand, it increases the risk of deficiency for those whose high requirements are not taken into account. These considerations clearly demonstrate that dietary recommendations for trace elements are not strictly scientific documents but entail much personal judgment by those who are involved in setting the allowances.

Depending on the relation of the recommended allowances to the intake distribution of the nutrient in question, some proportion of population will consume less and another proportion will consume more than the recommended intake. Quantitative aspects have been discussed by Beaton (10). By definition, intakes below the recommended allowances are not necessarily "deficient" but increase the number of individuals in a population at risk of deficiency.

What happens when intakes are increased over and above the recommendations? That question is of some practical interest in areas of high environmental exposure, or where self-supplementation has become fashionable. By definition, all known health-related functions are at their optimal level when a requirement of their specific nutrient is met. It follows from this definition that an increase over and above the requirement (and recommended intake) does not confer any known health benefit: an optimal function does not become "superoptimal". A vicarious benefit of higher intakes than recommended could come from the assumption that yet unidentified, nutrient-specific functions may increase the requirement. Many users rely on their supplements as an insurance against this possibility.

A real effect of exceeding required and recommended intakes of trace elements is the increase in the pool size of the element in the body. Optimization of all health-related functions is associated with a certain pool size, which also protects the organism against periods of inadequate intakes. Superadequate intakes, then, would increase the time during which normal functions are protected against inadequate supply by increasing the reserves. Over a certain range of intakes, specific for each trace element, superadequate intakes are properly metabolized, by diminished absorption, higher saturation of transport proteins, increased excretion, and the induction of special storage proteins which act as sinks for excesses (1).

At some point of excessive intakes these mechanisms gradually become ineffective and result in adverse health effects. Thus there is a range of intakes for each trace element that, on the basis of present knowledge, can be considered to be adequate to meet the requirement and to be safe from adverse effects. By definition, all intakes within that range are equivalent as far as their health effect is concerned. The intakes below that range are associated with increased risk for deficiency; those above with increased risk for toxicity. As stated before, the exact definition of the range of safe and adequate intakes for population groups and different age categories among those is the ultimate goal of human nutrition research.

TOXICITY

The toxicology of the essential trace elements is different from the toxicology of other, nonessential substances (13). Both categories of substances pose the challenge to the toxicologist of determining mechanisms of toxic action, metabolism, and the dose levels at which such actions occur. When this has been accomplished, the approaches and even the basic philosophies of toxicologists and nutritionists diverge. The classical toxicological approach has as its aim to determine a no effect dose level and exposure, that is, concentrations in the environment, including human foods, that can be tolerated by man without any adverse health effects. Even in this one approach there are considerable uncertainties and differences of scientific opinion relating, for example, to the shape of the dose-response curve at very low exposures. This translates into the question whether there really is a "no effect" exposure.

That uncertainty has led in the past to the postulate of "zero tolerance levels" which is practically unenforceable because it depends on the state of analytical sensitivity at any given time. A practical compromise emerged from this scientific dilemma which is now much applied: When the most sensitive biological methods in animal tests have defined an apparent "no effect" level of a substance, an arbitrary safety factor usually of 100 is applied and the resulting lower concentrations are assumed to be safe for human exposure.

The approach to the toxicology of essential trace elements is basically different, because the "no effect level" or "zero tolerance" is as incompatible with health and life as any toxic concentration. Therefore the toxicological dose-response curve must be complemented by the biological dose-response curve which represents the physiological response of the organism to an essential nutrient.

In analogy to the physiological part of the dose-response curve, mild overexposure to an essential nutrient results in marginal signs and symptoms. Marginal overexposure is as difficult to define and to diagnose as marginal deficiency, and the diagnosis depends on the state of sophistication of biochemical, immunological, and behavioral tools. Although the signs and symptoms of mild overexposure and the organism's defense mechanisms differ for each element, two categories can be delineated. These have considerable practical importance worldwide. Homeostatic controls to maintain the physiological *milieu interieur* are relatively weak for those essential elements occurring in small anionic form, including the halogens and the high oxidation states of some cationic elements such as selenites, selenates, molybdates, and chromates; they are much stronger for the rest of the essential elements present in their natural cationic form. Environmental exposure to excesses of the former group is readily reflected in tissue concentrations and pathological consequences as evidenced by the endemic occurrence of fluorosis, selenosis, and molybdenosis, and of industrial chromate poisoning in the past (1).

Both anionic and cationic elements respond to overexposure with increased excretion, some of them also with decreased intestinal absorption efficiency. Because small anionic species of trace elements penetrate membranes relatively easily, any excesses that cannot be excreted find their ways into parenchymal tissues. The fluoride ion, for example, has a high affinity for bone, which acts as a sink until toxic concentrations are reached and pathological reactions, such as exostoses, occur. Chromates easily penetrate into the nucleus of the cells where they react with nucleic acids, unless they are reduced somewhere along the way to the cationic trivalent form.

The cationic elements, on the other hand, are subject to much stricter homeostatic control. Specific transport mechanisms control intestinal absorption and even excretion by the intestinal mucosal cells, transport proteins bind the elements once they appear in the circulation, and storage proteins stand ready to absorb excesses. These defense mechanisms effectively protect the parenchymal cells of the organism against a wide range of overexposures. When the defenses of the intestinal mucosa are overcome the transport proteins, normally little saturated, become more saturated, and at the same time the synthesis of specific storage proteins is induced. Only after the capacity of the latter is overcome does an excess of cationic elements spill over into vulnerable parenchymal tissues.

Although there is no consensus on that definition, the first stage of marginal toxicity of a cationic element could be described as an oversaturation of the transport proteins. This can lead to undesirable interactions with other trace elements as has been demonstrated for the iron-carrying transport protein, transferrin. Transferrin carries not only iron but other elements as well, one of them chromium. Saturation of transferrin with iron displaces chromium and results in an impairment of chromium-dependent functions (e.g., glucose tolerance). Similar situations are well known for metallothionin, which acts as a ''sink'' for at least three elements, copper, zinc, and cadmium. The adverse prognostic significance of transferrin oversaturation with iron is well established for the survival of malnourished Jamaican children (14) and for the chromium status and glucose tolerance of patients with hemochromatosis (15). The adverse effects of overexposures of zinc on immune reactions (16) and on lipoprotein metabolism (17) may possibly be mediated by similar mechanisms.

The end stage of the toxicity of cationic elements, the invasion and destruction of parenchymal tissue, is rare and almost always conditioned by genetic deficiencies, as in hemochromatosis and Wilson's disease.

THE TOTAL BIOLOGICAL DOSE-RESPONSE CURVE

The preceding discussion has examined how essential nutrients become toxic in excess. Conversely, developments during the past three decades have identified essential elements once considered only as toxic. This was shown 30 years ago for selenium and chromium and, more recently, for nickel, arsenic, and, possibly, lead and cadmium. Other elements less prominent in toxicological concern, silicon, lithium, and boron, have been postulated to be essential. All these elements have in common that their requirement is far below, by several orders of magnitude, the levels of concern to the environmental toxicologists. Therefore there need not exist any controversy between the nutritionist who is concerned about adequate intakes and the toxicologist who wants to assure safe exposure levels. The common goal of both must be the definition of the safe and adequate range of exposure. The width of this range depends on the nature of the elements: it is smaller for anionic species than for cationic elements. It also depends on the nature of the environment, particularly on the composition of the habitual diet. For example, selenium is more biologically available from plant foods than from animal and marine sources; on the other hand, most cationic elements are better available from animal than from plant foods. Table 1 expresses the opinion of the author and is, most certainly, subject to future

TABLE 1. *Estimated ranges of adequate intakes*[a]

Element	Absolute requirement	Availability	Dietary requirement	Interactions
Fe	1–1.5 mg	< 1–25%	6–150	Vit C, "meat factor", Ca
Zn	2–3 mg	< 10–40%	5–30	Phytate, fiber, Ca
Cu	0.1–0.4 (?) mg	25–70%	< 1–5 (?)	Zn, Mo, Vit C
Se	0.03 (?) mg	50–90%	< 0.04–0.08	Plant *vs* animal sources
Cr	0.001 (?) mg	1–25% (?)	.004–0.1 (?)	

[a]The figures in the table are intended only to demonstrate the wide range of intakes that could be considered adequate in the context of different diets including those of extremely low and of extremely high bioavailability. They do not suggest dietary recommendations; those must be set on the basis of regional food habits on which bioavailability depends.

TABLE 2. *Concerns with toxicity*

Element	Effect
Fe	Poor excretion efficiency
	Genetic defects of regulation
Zn	Strong interactions with Cu
Cu	Genetic defects of transport
Se	Strong environmental influences
Cr	Hexavalent toxic when inhaled
Mn	Toxic when inhaled
F	Strong environmental influences

changes as our methods of diagnosis of marginal deficiencies and toxicities increase.

In general, trace element intakes four- to fivefold the requirement can be considered safe from even marginal toxicity; with higher intakes the risk of adverse interactions with other nutrients and of marginal toxicity increases (Table 2).

Thus, an intake of a trace element that is barely adequate under certain dietary conditions can become toxic under others. These considerations stress the need for better understanding of the mechanisms that determine biological availability of trace elements.

REFERENCES

1. Underwood EJ, Mertz W. Introduction. In: Mertz W, ed. *Trace elements in human and animal nutrition*, 5th ed, vol. I. San Diego: Academic Press, 1987.
2. Anke M, Krause U, Groppel B. The effect of arsenic deficiency on growth, reproduction, life expectancy and disease symptoms in animals. In: Hemphill DD, ed. *Trace substances in environmental health XXI*. Columbia, Mo: University of Missouri, 1987:533–50.
3. Buzina R, Bates CJ, van der Beek J, et al. Workshop on the significance of mild-to-moderate malnutrition. *Am J Clin Nutr* 1989;50:172–6.
4. Failla ML, Babu U, Seidel KE. Use of immunoresponsiveness to demonstrate that the dietary requirement for copper in young rats is greater with dietary fructose than dietary starch. *J Nutr* 1988;118:487–96.
5. Hambidge KM, Hambidge C, Jacobs MA, Baum JD. Low levels of zinc in hair, anorexia, poor growth and hypogensia in children. *Pediatr Res* 1972;6:868–74.
6. Chen XC, Yin TA, He JS, Ma RY, Han ZM, Li LX. Low levels of zinc in hair and blood, pica, anorexia, and poor growth in Chinese preschool children. *Am J Clin Nutr* 1985;42:694–700.
7. WHO Expert Committee. *Trace elements in human nutrition*. WHO Technical Reports Series No 532. Geneva: WHO, 1973.
8. Monsen E, Hallberg L, Layrisse M, et al. Estimation of available dietary iron. *Am J Clin Nutr* 1978;31:134–41.
9. Committee on Dietary Allowances. *Recommended Dietary Allowances*, 10th ed. Washington, DC: National Academy Press, 1989.
10. Beaton GH. Nutrient requirements and population data. *Proc Nutr Soc* 1988;47:63–78.
11. Mertz W. Use and misuse of balance studies. *J Nutr* 1987;117:1811–3.
12. Committee, I-5, International Union of Nutritional Sciences. Recommended dietary intakes around the world. *Nutr Abstr Rev Clin Nutr* (A) 1983;53:539–1015.

13. Mertz W. Essentiality and toxicity of heavy metals. In: Schmidt EHF, Hildebrandt AG, eds. Health evaluation of heavy metals in infant formula and junior food. Berlin: Springer, 1983:47–56.
14. Golden MHN, Golden BE, Bennett FI. High ferritin values in malnourished children. In: *Trace elements in man and animals*. Commonwealth Agricultural Bureaux Farnham Royal, UK: TEMA-5, CAB, 1985:775–9.
15. Sargent T III, Lim TH, Jenson RL. Reduced chromium retention in patients with hemochromatosis, a possible basis of hemochromatotic diabetes. *Metabolism* 1979;28:70–9.
16. Chandra RK. Excessive intake of zinc impairs immune responses. *JAMA* 1984;252:1443–6.
17. Hooper PL, Visconti L, Garry PJ, Johnson GE. Zinc lowers high-density lipoprotein-cholesterol levels. *JAMA* 1980;244:1960–1.

DISCUSSION

Dr. Haschke: The absorption of iron can be improved by ascorbic acid (up to fivefold by increasing the ascorbic acid/iron ratio from 1 to 5). Therefore there is a tendency to increase the ascorbic acid content of infant formulas in most countries. Are there interactions between ascorbic acid and copper and selenium?

Dr. Mertz: Copper reacts easily *in vitro* with ascorbic acid in a 1:1 or a 1:2 molar ratio but as far as I know the latter has always been given in large excess over copper in *in vivo* studies. Ascorbic acid also reacts with selenite in stoichiometric proportions to reduce it to biologically inert elemental selenium. Here again, a large excess of the vitamin has been fed in animal studies. This not only neutralized the protective effect of selenium against experimental cancer, but it also appeared to increase tumor incidence above that of controls (1). Although the chemical reactions between Cu/Se and ascorbic acid are straightforward, the mechanisms of the interactions *in vivo* are still poorly understood. So far as the practical implications are concerned, we do not know how far we can extrapolate these observations to the much lower amounts of vitamin C that we would get from the diet. Personally I do not believe that interactions between these three nutrients are of biological importance under normal circumstances.

Dr. Aggett: Interactions between vitamin C and copper can occur when both micronutrients are ingested simultaneously. Studies in both rats and humans suggest that systemic disturbances of copper metabolism may result from high intakes of vitamin C. For example, in young men ascorbic acid (500 mg three times a day with meals for 64 days) lowered plasma copper and ceruplasmin concentrations, though the values remained within the reference range and increased to earlier levels when the ascorbic acid was stopped (2). Similar interactions have been shown in rats (3). The significance of these findings is uncertain since it is at present impossible to measure copper turnover effectively due to lack of suitable radioisotopes.

Dr. Chandra: In our work related to nutrient intake and immune responses, we have found that vitamin C intakes of more than 2 g per day (amounts that some people do consume) impair both lymphocyte and neutrophil function. In an attempt to understand the underlying mechanism we have measured the activity of various enzymes in neutrophils, including superoxide dismutase, myeloperoxidase, and ribonucleotidyl reductase, and found them to be subnormal. I do not know if this is a reflection of changes in concentrations of certain trace elements.

Dr. Zlotkin: Could Dr. Mertz elaborate on his comments on the use of balance studies for determining requirements? If I understood him correctly, he said that the body adapts in different ways to varying intakes. For example, in the case of iron, as the intake decreases and as iron stores decrease in the body, one gets an adaptive response in the direction of increased absorption to maximize the body supply of iron. Ultimately however, if one had the ability to do accurate studies of intake and excretion, the adaptation would not be sufficient to deal with an inadequate intake. So it is not simply a problem of the quality of our collections.

Dr. Mertz: In my view, the quality of balance studies is far from perfect and we still have many difficulties to overcome. The use of stable isotopes has helped and holds promise for the future. As to the interpretation of balance studies, we must realize that there is no single obligatory loss. Losses are proportional to the nutritional status: they will be greater in a person in a good state of nutrition than in one in a poor state. This is certainly true for zinc, chromium, and manganese. The dependence of the obligatory losses on the body pool of an element means that a negative balance, leading eventually to a smaller body pool, will also result in a diminished obligatory loss. The new amount of loss and the intake resulting in negative balance will at some time reach equilibrium. The equilibrium is established at a reduced size of the body pool, meaning that there are reduced reserves of the element but not necessarily a deficiency. This model is valid for reduced intakes but not for zero or near-zero intakes of an element.

Dr. Zlotkin: I do not entirely agree with the ultimate long-term effect you have described. If what you are saying is true, then we would not have deficiency states for any metal. We know, however, that iron deficiency is perhaps the most common nutrient deficiency in the pediatric population around the world. If there was perfect adaptation and obligatory losses came down to zero then we should never see deficiencies, and of course this is not the case.

Dr. Mertz: As I said before, we cannot apply this model to zero or near zero intakes. At some point the size of an element's pool in the body must become inadequate to support the specific functions of the element.

Dr. Gruskin: In terms of your reasonable intake and the variation in pool size, is the explanation that a change in absorption accounts for the difference necessarily true for all elements, or might the differences be explained by changes in excretion or in excretion and absorption combined?

Dr. Mertz: This varies with each element. Homeostasis of iron, for example, is controlled mainly by regulation of absorption; of manganese by control of excretion. Turnlund et al (4) reported increases in absorption efficiency and decreases in endogenous excretion of copper when copper intake was reduced to something like 0.7 mg/day. For that element the homeostasis is achieved by control of absorption *and* excretion.

Dr. Lombeck: We have started to define recommendations for intakes of different trace elements in Europe, but we have difficulty in making recommendations that are valid in both north and south Europe. Dietary habits are very different in people living in different regions and with different ethnic backgrounds. We feel we cannot definitively say that we recommend 3 or 10 mg of zinc; we must clearly define for which group of people and in which distinct area of the world we are making this recommendation.

Dr. Mertz: I agree with you that recommendations have to be adjusted according to national dietary conditions; I am convinced, for example, that the bioavailability of zinc in the diet is likely to be lower in some Mediterranean countries than in northern Europe.

Dr. Chandra: I should like to emphasize the distinction between absolute requirement and dietary requirement. The former will perhaps be the same universally, whereas the latter will vary between countries and between populations within a country. The bioavailability of some nutrients may vary from 5% or 10% to as much as 80% or 90%.

Dr. Gabr: In developing countries there may be factors involved in different dietary requirements other than variations in dietary intake and possible nutrient interactions. For example, there may be genetic differences in trace-element-dependent enzymes, and there will be a higher proportion of children and pregnant women in the population, who are more vulnerable to toxic effects. A future workshop of this type on trace element nutrition should be aimed at helping developing countries to determine their own standards in the light of these variables. Furthermore, most developing countries cannot carry out the necessary studies locally without outside help.

Dr. Mertz: I agree. It should be possible to organize studies on human requirements in developing countries with the assistance of people from developed countries who have had "hands on" experience, such as those in the present workshop. Such studies should aim to produce solid data on requirements under specified regional conditions, which would help to develop policies for further action.

Dr. Dufour: This suggestion is precisely within the remit of the Nestlé Nutrition Research Grant Program, which encourages collaboration between researchers from developed and developing countries. The award of grants is made annually by an independent committee and applications need to be submitted by December of each year.

Dr. Zlotkin: I should like to make a comment on toxicity. There are certain groups of infants who are more at risk of toxicity than others, (e.g., preterm infants and those receiving intravenous nutrition). In order to determine toxicity, we need to turn to novel approaches to assess when and if toxicity is a problem. The use of manganese in preterm intravenously fed babies is a good example. Manganese homeostasis is primarily regulated via gastrointestinal absorption, and once manganese is in the body, very little is excreted. Thus in intravenously fed infants, where absorptive control is bypassed and little or no stool is passed, excretion is minimal. Suggested doses for TPN are largely empirical and may be incorrect. Intravenous infusion may well result in altered tissue distribution, while the blood-brain barrier is immature and likely to be more permeable to potentially toxic substances (5). Finally, there are in the case of many of the minerals neither the necessary clinical studies nor good functional measures available to look at outcome.

Dr. Chapparwal: Dietary intakes may be different in different parts of the world, but when you compare serum levels of trace elements they are not very different.

Dr. Mertz: Let me clarify that statement. There are two classes of trace elements. In the case of the cationic trace elements (zinc, copper, iron, chromium, manganese) your statement is correct. On the other hand, for the anionic elements (fluorine, iodine, selenium, molybdenum) there are very large differences. In the case of selenium, for example, there are 100-fold differences in blood selenium levels between people in the Keshan district areas and those in the selenosis areas just a few hundred miles away. The anionic elements penetrate easily into our system from the environment in contrast to the cationic elements.

Dr. Aggett: It is clear that neither the compositional nor the functional assays that we have at the moment are ideal for assessing requirements for trace elements. As yet we cannot identify the vital pools which are most sensitive to depletion. Nonetheless these are probably the pools that are protected by systemic adaptation or homeostatic regulation. Should we now encourage more research on the metabolism of these elements, with a view to characterizing more clearly the systemic factors that regulate their metabolism?

Dr. Mertz: I agree. One can only hope that in the future we shall be able to identify and measure these specific vital pools. We still have to use too much judgment in setting our recommendations.

REFERENCES

1. Jacobs MM, Griffin AC. Effects of selenium on chemical carcinogenesis: Comparative effects of antioxidants. *Biol Tr Element Res* 1979;1:1–13.
2. Jacob RA, Kala JH, Omayue ST, Turnlund JR. Effect of varying ascorbic acid intakes on copper absorption and ceruplasmin levels of young men. *J Nutr* 1987;117:2109–15.
3. Johnson MA, Murphy CL. Adverse effects of high dietary iron and ascorbic acid on copper status in copper-deficient and copper-adequate rats. *Am J Clin Nutr* 1988;47:96–101.
4. Turnlund JR, Keyes WR, Anderson HL, Acord LL. Copper absorption and retention in young men at three levels of dietary copper by use of stable isotope ^{65}Cu. *Am J Clin Nutr* 1989;49:870–8.
5. Zlotkin SM, Buchanan BE. Manganese intakes in intravenously fed infants. Dosages and toxicity studies. *Biol Tr Element Res* 1986;9:271–80.

Trace Elements in Nutrition of Children—II,
edited by Ranjit K. Chandra, Nestlé Nutrition
Workshop Series, Vol. 23, Nestec Ltd.,
Vevey/Raven Press, Ltd., New York © 1991.

Aluminum Toxicity in Infants and Children

Alan B. Gruskin

Department of Pediatrics, Wayne State University School of Medicine, and Children's Hospital of Michigan, Detroit, Michigan 48201, USA

As methodology for accurately measuring trace metals improves, the role of aluminum (Al) as a cause of childhood disease has become progressively clearer; however, many issues remain unclear. This report has several objectives: to review Al metabolism; to discuss the role of Al in causing disease with a focus on childhood disease; and finally, to consider the impact of the nutrient of Al on growing children.

ALUMINUM METABOLISM

Physiology of Aluminum

Renal clearances of Al range from 2% to 50% of the glomerular filtration rate (1). The renal clearance of Al is low because Al is highly and tightly protein bound; consequently, Al also is not readily dialyzable. Increasing levels of serum Al progressively saturate Al-binding sites and therefore result in higher concentrations of "free" Al in serum. This progressive increase in unbound Al leads to an increased filtered load of Al, to an increased urinary Al/creatinine ratio, and to an increased rate of excretion of Al in the urine.

Balance studies in adults indicate that 0.02% to 0.1% of ingested Al is retained. Urinary Al excretion can increase from 15 mg/day to 350 mg/day in normal adults ingesting Al-containing phosphate binders (ACPB) (2). Al retention approaches 10% of the ingested dose in adults given large oral loads of antacids. Umbilical cord blood levels of Al are similar to normal adult and infant blood levels of Al (3).

In dogs given 1.0 mg/kg of elemental Al, plasma half-life is 276 minutes; up to 21% of the infused Al was excreted within 150 minutes (4). In animals, intravenously administered Al is not excreted in significant quantities into bile or into the intestine (5). In humans, fecal Al losses are small when the source of Al is parenteral nutrition (5). Al has been shown to be excreted into the large intestine in rats preloaded with Al (6). This study also demonstrated that Al uptake by the duodenum is passive and that some of the metal is sequestered within the gut mucosa and shed when the mucosa cells are shed.

Tissue Aluminum Levels

In normal adults, mean tissue levels of Al in heart, brain, spleen, liver, muscle, bone, skin, and brain gray matter are less than mean normal plasma Al levels; the latter were 7.0 ± 1.0 µg/liter (7). The only tissue in normal adults found to contain elevated Al levels was lung. These data suggest that in normal adults, minimal, if any Al is accumulated in tissues other than the lung and that most absorbed Al is not stored in tissues but is excreted. Furthermore, it is not known whether the Al found in adult lungs is naturally concentrated in lung after it is ingested, or if it is deposited after being inhaled. Two facts explain the failure of normal adults to accumulate significant quantities of Al. First, less than 0.5% of ingested Al is absorbed. Second, individuals with normal renal function can excrete significant quantities of Al which are naturally ingested.

ALUMINUM RELATED DISEASES

Aluminum Related Diseases

The most extensively studied Al-related disorder is the Al intoxication syndrome which develops in patients with renal failure (8). Clinical features of Al intoxication include encephalopathy, aluminum bone disease (ABD), and an iron-resistant microcytic hypochromic anemia. The clinical problems associated with Al toxicity in patients with normal renal function are summarized in Table 1. Two significant Al-related diseases occur in children: Al intoxication in association with renal failure, and possibly Al intoxication in association with parenteral nutrition. The latter problem will be discussed in the section dealing with the impact of the nutrient intake of Al on growing children.

TABLE 1. *Features of aluminum toxicity in patients with normal renal function*

Clinical features	Source of aluminum
Granuloma	Antiperspirants, medications, vaccines
Osteomalacia	Parenteral nutrition
Phosphate depletion syndrome	Excessive antacid ingestion
Contact dermatitis	Al-precipitated allergens
Acute/chronic encephalopathy	Occupational exposure
Acute/chronic pulmonary disease	Occupational exposure

Aluminum Intoxication Associated With Renal Insufficiency

In patients with reduced renal function (particularly anuric patients) absorbed or intravenously infused Al is not excreted. Thus, in patients exposed to Al, the body burden of Al progressively increases over time. Sources of Al in uremic patients include Al-containing oral drugs (particularly aluminum-containing phosphate binders), intravenous salts, intravenous albumin, and Al-containing dialysate. The intestinal absorption of Al may be increased when hyperparathyroidism or low serum calcium levels exist and when 1,25-dihydroxyvitamin D_3 is administered.

Postmortem tissue levels of Al are increased in all tissues in adults dying after being on dialysis or from dialysis encephalopathy. The highest levels of Al are found in liver, spleen, lung, and bone; increased concentrations of Al are found in heart, muscle, skin, and brain. Compared to controls, brain levels of Al are increased twofold, fourfold, and tenfold in nondialyzed patients, dialyzed patients, and dialyzed patients with encephalopathy, respectively (7). Plasma levels of Al do not positively correlate with tissue levels of Al in uremic adults who do not develop dialysis encephalopathy. Tissue levels of Al which are increased in adults who develop encephalopathy tend to correlate positively with blood levels. Measurements of Al in cerebrospinal fluid are usually normal in uremic patients.

Encephalopathy in patients with renal failure has been described in three clinical settings and in "epidemic" numbers in a fourth clinical setting. Encephalopathy has been reported in patients on dialysis; in renal failure patients not yet on dialysis and who are exposed to large quantities of Al; and in patients after renal transplantation. Also, encephalopathy in "epidemic" numbers has occurred in hemodialysis units where large numbers of patients were exposed to dialysate solutions with high concentrations of Al. In these patients, Al intoxication occurred because ionized Al readily crossed dialysis membranes and accumulated within the body. Encephalopathy has also occurred sporadically in dialysis populations undergoing both hemodialysis or peritoneal dialysis. The sources of Al have included dialysate and drugs, primarily aluminum-containing phosphate binders.

Initially, renal associated encephalopathy in children was described in children with congenital forms of renal disease before treatment with dialysis was indicated (8). They had been given large quantities of aluminum containing phosphate binders to treat renal osteodystrophy. Subsequently, there were reports of Al intoxication developing in children undergoing hemodialysis and peritoneal dialysis. The clinical features observed in children who develop Al encephalopathy are summarized in Table 2. It has also been suggested that chronic Al intoxication in children with renal insufficiency may result in mental retardation.

A few adults and some children have developed an acute deterioration of neurological function within the first few weeks after receiving a renal transplant. Etiological significance has been attributed to a rapid mobilization of Al stored in tissue; the rapid mobilization may be related to either the administration of corticosteroids or an enhanced ability by the transplanted kidney to excrete Al.

Aluminum bone disease is the most consistent feature of Al intoxication in chil-

TABLE 2. *Progression of neurological changes in children developing aluminum encephalopathy in association with progressive renal failure*[a]

Stage 1
  Ataxia, mild
  Dysmetria
  Failure to develop new motor skills
  Hyperreflexia
  Plantar extensor signs
  Tremors
Stage 2
  Ataxia, marked
  Hypotonia
  Myoclonic seizures, extremities and facial
  Regression in cognitive and motor function
  Saccadic ocular movements
Stage 3
  Absent response to auditory and visual stimuli
  Absent swallowing with intact gag reflex
  Hypotonia, marked
  Hyperreflexia
  Myoclonus, generalized
  No volitional movements

[a]Adapted from Foley CM, et al. (17).

dren as well as adults. Al affects bone by altering mineralization at the site where bone osteoid undergoes calcification; by suppressing parathyroid function; and, by altering osteoblastic function. Histological features of aluminum bone disease include: a positive staining of bone for Al; a reduced rate of bone mineralization as measured by double tetracycline labelling; an increased quantity of osteoid; and a decreased number of osteoblasts and osteoclasts. In general, children with elevated blood levels of Al have increased amounts of bone Al. However, children with similarly elevated levels of plasma Al may have a marked variation in their bone Al. Since aluminum bone disease is characterized by a reduced rate of new bone formation, children with this condition may be expected to grow at a significantly slower rate. Increased stores of bone Al can be demonstrated by the desferrioxamine (DFO) infusion test. A positive DFO test is one in which blood Al levels increase significantly after infusing DFO. A positive DFO test has been used as an indicator of Al overload and as evidence that chelation therapy is needed in order to lower body Al content.

Al intoxication leads to a microcytic hypochromic anemia, which can be produced experimentally in animals (8). Anemia often predates the onset of encephalopathy. An inverse correlation can be demonstrated between the mean corpuscular volume (MCV) and both serum Al levels and red blood cell Al content. No correlation can be demonstrated between serum Al levels or red blood cell Al content and serum ferritin levels. Also, Al accumulation may be associated with an increased left ventricular mass (9).

Al intoxication in children is best treated by prevention (8). During the past few years, the use of Al-free dialysate has become routine; calcium carbonate has been successfully substituted for aluminum-containing phosphate binders; and the routine monitoring of blood Al levels has become possible. The combined use of these modalities has been shown to prevent the accumulation of Al. In children with excessive Al stores, chelation therapy with DFO has been shown to partially reverse encephalopathy and to improve bone histology. Also, DFO has been shown to improve Al-related anemia in adults undergoing chronic dialysis.

NUTRIENTS AS A SOURCE OF ALUMINUM

Children are exposed to Al from a variety of sources including orally ingested foods, cookware and intravenous preparations. This section discusses the implications and possible consequences of Al exposure during early childhood.

Sources of Aluminum

During various nutritional processes, children are exposed to Al in five ways: 1) in water used for drinking and for preparing intravenous agents; 2) in food prepared in Al cookware; 3) in natural foods where it accumulates ecologically; 4) in Al-containing additives used in manufacturing foods; and 5) in salt and protein additives used in the preparation of parenteral nutritional solutions.

Aluminum in Drinking Water

The Al content of water is variable. It is affected by acid rain, the Al content of soil, and by water treatment processes. For example, the Al content of water significantly increases when alum, $[Al_2(SO_4)_3]$, is added to drinking water as a flocculent. The Al concentration of municipal water supplies may exceed 1000 μg/liter. Water containing a high concentration of Al may be unknowingly used to produce many commercial foods, infant formulas, and additives for parenteral nutrition. Therefore, the Al concentration of such preparations might be significantly increased. Also, because alum is often used at irregular intervals by municipalities, the Al content of water changes in an unpredictable and unknown manner. The concentration of Al is less than 50 μg/liter in sterile water and dextrose water preparations (10).

Aluminum Added to Food Cooked or Stored in Aluminum Containers

The Al content of many foods increases when prepared in Al cookware (11). Acidic foods, such as tomatoes and apple sauce tend to accumulate more Al than other foods. This is especially true when acidic foods are cooked more than 15 minutes. The food is not the source of the Al because Al is not added when the same foods are cooked in stainless steel cookware. In practical terms, the amount of Al added to foods through cooking is generally minimal. When cooked in Al cookware, a 100-g serving of fresh meat, peas, rice or pasta contains less than 0.1 mg of added Al, while 0.3 to 0.7 mg Al is added by a 100-g serving of cabbage or apple sauce. However, a 100-g serving of tomato sauce cooked for 180 minutes in Al cookware contains up to 5.7 mg of added Al. Frozen foods stored in Al containers accumulate minimal additional quantities of Al. Most Al cans currently used in the USA contain a plastic inner liner; thus food does not come in contact with the metal.

Aluminum Content in Naturally Grown Foods and Seasonings

Major sources of Al in the daily diet include: grains, processed cheese, seasonings prepared with Al-containing additives and flavorings (herbs, salts), and tea. Spices, flavorings, and tea naturally concentrate Al (12). Plants may accumulate Al at rates that reflect the acid-base status and Al content of soil. Soybeans may be a significant source of the high Al content found in soy-based infant formulas. The median concentrations of Al in human milk and cow's milk are 14 μg/liter and 27 μg/liter, respectively. A report from the USSR stated that the Al content of mature human milk in the USSR varies from 250 to 2400 μg/liter; these values are similar or higher than those found in infant formulas in the USA and are higher than those reported in human milk in the USA (13). Additional studies are needed to ascertain whether these differences are real or technical. In adults, the normal dietary intake of Al is 40 to 50 μg/kg/day.

Aluminum in Infant Formulas

The Al content of infant formulas varies significantly according to its preparation (14). The range of reported values for Al in various preparations used to feed infants is summarized in Table 3. The Al concentration in infant formulas varies from one batch to another when prepared by the same manufacturer. When the Al content of different classes of formula (standard, premature, soybean, and special formulas for inborn errors of metabolism) are measured, the Al content is quite similar and independent of the manufacturer. In North America and Western Europe, all infant formulas contain more Al than that found in either human or cow's milk. There are multiple sources of Al in infant formulas. These sources include: Al contained in cow's milk; Al contained in soybeans; Al in additives, such as calcium gluconate and phosphate salts; and Al in the container in which the formula is stored. The nature of the storage container affects the Al concentration of "humanized" cow's milk formulas. Al concentrations of infant formulas are highest when the formula is stored in glass containers, lower in steel cans and lowest in powder form.

TABLE 3. *Aluminum content of solutions used for feeding infants*[a]

Preparation	Aluminum content range (μg/liter)
Whole milk	
Human	< 5–45
Cow's	24–40
Infant formula	
Standard	14–565
Preterm	289–811
Soy-based	455–2346
Products for specific diseases	295–1594
Water	
Sterile, 5% dextrose	< 5–39
Electrolyte in water	63–81

[a]Adapted from Gruskin AB (8), Koo WWK, et al. (10), and Koo WWK, et al. (14).

Additives Used to Prepare Parenteral Nutrition Solutions

A number of compounds and products used to prepare peripheral alimentation solutions contain significant quantities of Al (10). High concentrations (greater than 1500 μg/liter) are found in calcium and phosphate salts. Some salt products, such as calcium gluconate obtained from different manufacturers, have high concentrations of Al. These data suggest that some naturally occurring salts contain significant Al as a natural phenomenon or that all manufacturers utilize similar procedures to prepare the salt. Other salts, such as sodium phosphate obtained from different manufacturers, contain variable quantities of Al. This suggests that different processes are used to prepare these salts or that the naturally occurring products have been exposed to different amounts of Al. A major source of Al is the Cohn fractionation process used to prepare proteins for hyperalimentation. Altering the Cohn fractionation process can lower the Al concentration of the resulting salt. Some intravenous vitamin preparations (aquamephyton, ascorbic acid, and B_{12}) have Al concentrations that exceed 1000 μg/liter; other multivitamin preparations have insignificant concentrations of Al.

Neonatal Exposure to Aluminum

In one study of a group of 20 infants (ages 29 to 41 weeks) who received Al from intravenous parenteral nutrition, the mean urinary Al/creatinine ratio increased threefold; serum concentrations of Al ranged from normal to levels exceeding 300 μg/liter; and, serum Al levels remained fairly constant for a given neonate (15). In another study, two groups of ten infants were given parenteral nutrition solutions containing a mean Al concentration of 306 μg/liter and 144 μg/liter, respectively (15). Less than 50% of the infused Al was eliminated by both groups. The urinary Al/creatinine ratio was significantly higher in the infants who received the higher concentration of Al. Serum Al levels exceeded the upper limits of normal (41 μg/liter reported by these investigators) in 11 of the 20 infants studied. It was concluded that when full-term and preterm infants are presented with similar loads of Al, both have similar abilities to excrete the Al load.

The urinary Al/creatinine ratio in normal bottle-fed infants is approximately six times higher than that observed in adults (3). Two possible explanations for the high ratio exist. First, the neonates have been exposed to higher quantities of Al in their food. Second, as with lead, the neonate may absorb a greater fraction of ingested Al than the adult. Data to explain this observation are lacking.

There are few data defining how long the urinary Al excretion remains elevated after intravenous Al loading in newborns. In a study of 18 premature and eight normal newborns, four of the 18 infants who had received parenteral nutrition continued to have elevated urinary Al/creatinine ratios for at least 13 days after discontinuing the intravenous infusion (3). The fact that blood Al levels were in the normal range while the rate of urinary excretion of Al was elevated provides evidence that Al stored in tissue can be mobilized. The amount of administered Al which is ultimately retained within the body remains unknown (3).

In one report of two infants who died, postmorten examination revealed Al in their vertebrae (16). In another study, bone Al content in six premature infants who died after having received parenteral nutritional infusions for 3 weeks was increased tenfold when compared to infants who had not received Al containing infusions. The mean bone Al values of the exposed and control infants was 20.2 and 1.98 mg/kg dry weight, respectively (3). It has been suggested that the osteomalacia observed in premature infants is related, in part, to exposure to Al. Histologic criteria, however, for diagnosing osteomalacia in premature infants are not precise. Also, meaningful data on bone histology in prematures are lacking.

Since intravenously administered Al remains in the body, it is reasonable to suggest that chemicals and drugs with the lowest possible concentration of Al should be used when peripheral alimentation is given. Appropriate alternative agents are available with the exception of calcium gluconate salts.

PRACTICAL CONSIDERATIONS

As regards the exposure of newborns to Al, the critical issue to consider is the degree of harm from Al contained in parenteral alimentation and orally administered food. It is known that parenteral nutritional preparations containing high concentrations of Al contribute to Al being deposited in tissue, particularly bone. Consequently, the acute and chronic effects of Al exposure are real. Long-term effects, however, remain to be demonstrated. The effects on growth and neurological development, particularly cognitive function, remain to be defined. While awaiting new data, it appears reasonable to suggest that solutions and salts used to prepare parenteral solutions should have the lowest possible Al content.

Another important issue is whether Al exposure from prepared oral infant formulas is harmful. I have not been able to find any data that suggest or prove that the quantities of Al orally fed to full-term infants with age-appropriate normal renal function are either harmful or accumulate in tissues. Noteworthy is that Al intake of infants increases significantly when "solids" are added to their diet. Also noteworthy is that Al is virtually nondetectable in bone obtained from normal adults. However, because the newborn is known to have an increased absorption of macromolecules and toxins such as lead, neonates and infants may be at increased risk for absorbing and retaining Al. Additional studies are needed before concluding that permanent damage results from Al in orally used infant formulas and foods. Although it is reasonable to suggest that the Al content of infant foods ought to be reduced, changes in manufacturing processes are costly. Nevertheless, given that Al accumulation can be toxic, it is reasonable to suggest that the infant food industry gradually attempt reduction of Al content of their products.

REFERENCES

1. Recker RR, Blotcky AJ, Leffler JA, Rack EP. Evidence for aluminum absorption from the gastrointestinal tract and bone deposition by aluminum carbonate ingestion with normal renal function. *J Lab Clin Med* 1977;90:810–5.
2. Kaehny WD, Hegg AP, Alfrey AC. Gastrointestinal absorption of aluminum from aluminum containing antacids. *N Engl J Med* 1977;296:1389–90.
3. Sedman AB, Klein GL, Merritt RJ, et al. Evidence of aluminum loading in infants receiving intravenous therapy. *N Engl J Med* 1985;312:1337–43.
4. Henry DA, Goodman WG, Nudelman RK, et al. Parenteral aluminum administration in the dog: I. Plasma kinetics, tissue levels, calcium metabolism, and parathyroid hormone. *Kidney Int* 1984; 25:362–9.
5. Klein GL, Ott SM, Alfrey AC, et al. Aluminum as a factor in the bone disease of long-term parenteral nutrition. *Trans Assoc Am Physicians* 1982;95:155–64.
6. Rumbelow B, Bletas A, Goddard G, Cochran M. Absorption and excretion of aluminum by the rat intestine. *Kidney Int* 1989;35:210A.
7. Alfrey AC. Aluminum metabolism in uremia. *Neurotoxicology (Park Forest II)* 1980;1:43–53.
8. Gruskin AB. Aluminum: A pediatric overview. *Adv Pediatr* 1988;35:281–330.
9. London GM, de Vernejoul M-C, Fabiani F, et al. Association between aluminum accumulation and cardiac hypertrophy in hemodialyzed patients. *Am J Kidney Dis* 1989;13:75–83.
10. Koo WWK, Kaplan LA, Horn J, Tsang RC, Steichen JJ. Aluminum in parenteral nutrition solution—sources and possible alternatives. *J Parenter Enter Nutr* 1986;10:591–5.
11. Greger JL, Goetz W, Sullivan D. Aluminum levels in foods cooked and stored in aluminum pans, trays, and foil. *J Food Protection* 1985;48:772–7.
12. Pennington JAT. Aluminium content of foods and diets. *Food Addit Contam* 1987;5:161–232.
13. Wells JCK. Aluminum contamination of intravenous pharmaceuticals, nutrients, and blood products. *Lancet* 1986;ii:(letter) 380.
14. Koo WWK, Kaplan L, Krug-Wispe SK. Aluminum contamination of infant formulas. *J Parenter Enter Nutr* 1988;12:170–3.
15. Koo WWK, Kaplan LA, Bendon R, et al. Response to aluminum in parenteral nutrition during infancy. *J Pediatr* 1986;109:877–83.
16. Koo WWK, Kaplan LA. Aluminum and bone disorders: With specific reference to aluminum contamination of infant nutrients. *J Am Coll Nutr* 1988;7:199–214.

17. Foley CM, Polinsky MS, Gruskin AB, Baluarte HJ, Grover WD. Encephalopathy in infants and children with chronic renal disease. *Arch Neurol* 1981;38:656–8.

DISCUSSION

Dr. Haschke: We measured aluminum concentration in 61 infant formulas from 17 European countries. Formulas that are recommended from birth to 4 months (''whey formulas'') tend to have higher aluminum concentrations than ''follow-up'' formulas (5–12 months), which are unsophisticated formulas. We cannot therefore rule out the possibility that infant formulas are contaminated during the manufacturing process. The technique of aluminum determination should be improved and standardized. One way to do this is to organize aluminum analysis quality control surveys. Nestec organized such a survey in 1987 and it should be repeated in the near future.

With regard to aluminum toxicity in preterm infants, we know that rickets of prematurity is related to low phosphorous (and calcium) supply with human milk or unsupplemented formulas, but we also know that a high aluminum load causes bone disease. Very low-birth-weight infants have a good chance of receiving a high aluminum load during prolonged parenteral nutrition and with contaminated calcium and phosphorous salts that are used as supplements. Are there any studies looking at the influence of high aluminum load on bone disease in such infants?

Dr. Gruskin: Other than a few measurements of aluminum in vertebrae from children who have died, I am not aware of anyone doing bone biopsies, or even looking at growth plates in autopsy specimens from children who died after developing prematurity rickets or osteopenia.

This is certainly something worth doing, although most people would probably hesitate to do bone biopsies in neonates. It is reasonable to imagine that there could be a relationship between aluminum intake and bone disease in preterm infants since the amount of aluminum given has been high. Changes in bone can clearly be shown in children with renal disease given aluminum-containing formulas.

So far as oral feeding in the newborn is concerned, aluminum is potentially toxic and therefore it is in our best interests to reduce the aluminum content of all formulas. However, after speaking to people in the industry, it is clear that is not easily done and is an expensive undertaking, although careful attention to containers and to the types of filter used can certainly reduce aluminum content. With regard to premature infants, bone disease during growth is an important pediatric question and it would make sense to further study this area.

Dr. Lombeck: If semisynthetic diets given during pregnancy are high in aluminum, is anything known about prenatal aluminum accumulation or brain damage?

Dr. Gruskin: I do not know of any study of this in humans. There have been studies of aluminum toxicity in growing animals that indicate that the brain is more resistant to aluminum in younger animals than in older ones.

This may be a reflection of the fact that the lipid content of the brain is not complete in the developing animal.

Dr. Oster: Serum aluminum is routinely used in dialysis patients in control of therapy to avoid heavy aluminum intoxication. Do you think that the serum of preterm infants or children on parenteral nutrition should be regularly monitored for aluminum in order to detect intoxication, and would you suggest recommendations for the aluminum content of parenteral nutrition solutions or baby foods?

Dr. Gruskin: The problem of monitoring aluminum in preterm infants is the same as in patients with chronic renal disease, that is the lack of widespread availability of suitable methods. Where these methods are available, it makes sense to use them. However, it would be expensive to monitor all preterm infants. Until the role of aluminum in causing neonatal disease is more fully understood, I would not recommend routine widespread monitoring of blood aluminum in neonates.

So far as recommendations about aluminum content of foods are concerned, my view is that as much as possible should be done to reduce the aluminum content of parenteral solutions from the present levels, and that the content of oral feeds should be reduced where possible to values found in human milk.

I believe that if breast milk contains something, we should be very careful before we simply discard it. This is not to say that the milk does not contain aluminum because the mother ingests it, but its concentration is low and whenever we deviate from the composition of breast milk in providing food for newborns it often rebounds on us in some way or other.

Trace Elements in Nutrition of Children—II,
edited by Ranjit K. Chandra, Nestlé Nutrition
Workshop Series, Vol. 23, Nestec Ltd.,
Vevey/Raven Press, Ltd., New York © 1991.

The Metabolism of Trace Elements in Pregnancy

Peter J. Aggett, *Doris M. Campbell, and †Kenneth R. Page

*Departments of Child Health, *Obstetrics and Gynecology, and †Physiology, University of Aberdeen, Polwarth Buildings, Foresterhill, Aberdeen AB9, 2ZD, Scotland, UK*

The detrimental effects of trace element deficiencies on conception and fetal development in animal models have been studied extensively, in particular by the late Professor L. Hurley and the team which she created at the University of California, Davis. Tables 1 through 3 summarize these effects with respect to zinc, copper, and manganese (1–9). Understandably much interest has focused on the possibility that such deficiencies may also jeopardize human pregnancy, and that during pregnancy extra supplies of these trace elements should be provided to reduce this risk. However, in the evaluation of any presumed needs for extra nutrient intakes, altered metabolism of nutrients induced by pregnancy is an important consideration. This chapter outlines these interactions and the resultant difficulties in determining the metabolic requirement for trace elements during pregnancy, and in detecting any impending deficiency. Most of this discussion will focus on zinc because it is the trace element studied most extensively. Some of these aspects have been considered

TABLE 1. *Defects arising from prenatal deficiency of zinc[a]*

Impaired implantation
Embryonic and fetal death and resorption
Congenital abnormalities
Cleft lip and palate, micro- or anophthalmia
Anencephaly, hydrocephaly, neural tube defects
Spina bifida, syndactyly
Urogenital defects, cardiac malformations
Pulmonary malformations, altered surfactant
Endocrine and exocrine pancreatic insufficiency
Immune defects
Delayed ossification, reduced bone density
Low birth weight, (increased birth weight)
Inefficient labor, prolonged bleeding
Abnormal postnatal behavior in mother and offspring

[a]Adapted from refs. 1–9.

TABLE 2. *Defects arising from prenatal deficiency of copper*[a]

Fetal and early neonatal death
Neurological abnormalities, fits, defective myelin synthesis, cerebral and/or cerebellar
  hypotrophy
Cardiovascular; aneurysms, varicosities, vascular fragility
Skeletal matrix defective (collagen and elastin)
Altered metabolism of energy and phospholipid
Impaired growth

[a]Adapted from Hurley LS (1).

TABLE 3. *Defects arising from prenatal manganese deficiency*[a]

Altered mucopolysaccharides
Chondrodystrophy, short bowed (thick) long bones, epiphyseal dysplasia
Ataxia: absent or abnormal otoliths
Susceptibility to convulsions

[a]Adapted from Hurley LS (1).

in an earlier workshop (9,10) and, since it is still relevant, some of that material will be repeated.

Table 4 shows the estimated daily nutritional burdens caused by pregnancy in various species (11,12). The daily demands on rodents are obviously much more than those in women or, to give additional perspective, the blue whale. At the end of gestation in women the weight of the products of conception expressed as a percentage of the mother's preconceptional weight is 4% to 6%, compared with 40% in the mouse, 25% in the rat, and 9% in the rhesus monkey. Possibly many erroneous as-

TABLE 4. *Mean gain in weight before birth of the young of 5 species related to weight of the mother*[a]

Species (wt)	Weight of mother	Total weight of young (number in litter)		Length of gestation (days)	Mean gain per day (g)	Mean gain per day as % of mother's weight
Mouse (g)	25	10	(8)	20	0.5	2.0
Rat (g)	205	50	(10)	22	2.3	1.11
Rhesus monkey (kg)	5.3	0.47	(1)	167	2.8	0.053
Woman (kg)	56	3.4	(1)	280	12.1	0.021
Blue whale (kg)	79,000	2,000	(1)	365	540	0.00068

[a]Adapted from Leitch I (11) and Widdowson EM (12).

sumptions about human nutritional requirements during pregnancy have been reached on the basis of extrapolation from laboratory models without appropiate allowance for the different relative metabolic burdens or for the degree of maternal adaptation that can be achieved.

METABOLIC ADAPTATION

The metabolic changes that occur during pregnancy include: increased intestinal absorption of some nutrients (e.g., calcium); expansion of the plasma volume; altered metabolism of protein, carbohydrate, calcium, and bone; increased renal blood flow and glomerular filtration rate with alterations in tubular reabsorption; and alterations in the blood cell numbers along with altered proportions of the circulating subsets (13). Most, if not all, of these changes are anticipatory in that they occur before the products of conception would be large enough to impose any appreciable nutrient demand. These metabolic changes distort the customary indices of nutrient "status", including those of the trace elements. Unfortunately, these perturbations have often been erroneously interpreted as evidence of altered "nutritional status" and, in particular, of an increased risk of trace element deficiency.

ZINC DEPRIVATION MODELS IN PREGNANCY

Both sustained and transient zinc deficiency in rats, mice, guinea pigs, domestic livestock, and subhuman primates cause a wide spectrum of reproductive failure.

The model closest to humans is the rhesus monkey (3–7,9). Pregnant rhesus monkeys fed diets containing 4 mg of zinc per kg developed features of zinc deficiency. They had an increased rate of abortions, stillbirths, neonatal deaths, and abnormal deliveries; their offspring, particularly males, had reduced plasma zinc concentrations, immune dysfunction, reduced bone density, lower weights, and shorter crown-rump lengths than those from mothers fed diets containing 100 mg zinc per kg. Because reproductive failure also occurred in pair-fed animals, however, the effects may not be due directly or solely to zinc deficiency.

Additionally, the earlier caution about extrapolation from animal models to women also applies to the studies in rhesus monkeys. Here the difficulty arises from a consideration of the zinc content of the experimental (4 ppm) and control (100 ppm) diets. Relative to energy or dry matter these would correspond, in women, to daily zinc intakes of 2 to 3 mg and 50 to 60 mg, respectively. The lower intake is much less than that of most pregnant women (furthermore in the monkey this low intake is supporting a relatively larger metabolic burden), and the higher intake reflects a much larger intake than has been recorded in women. Nonetheless, these studies have provided information relevant to the better understanding of the metabolism of zinc in human pregnancy.

Important examples of the effects of severe zinc deficiency on human pregnancy can be seen in women with acrodermatitis enteropathica (AE), in which there is a defect in the intestinal absorption of the metal (14). Before the use of zinc supplements the only effective treatment of AE was the use of chelating agents, of which diiodohydroxyquin (5,7-diiodo-8-hydroxyquinoline) (DIH) was used most often.

Fourteen pregnancies have been reported in women with AE untreated with zinc. One untreated woman had an achondroplastic dwarf but when treated with DIH, had three normal infants (15). Another had a relapse during pregnancy and needed more DIH; she, herself, was growth retarded and had a caesarean section and delivered a 2.52 kg infant because of cephalopelvic disproportion! (16). A third mother had a spontaneous abortion and later delivered an anencephalic stillbirth despite having been treated with DIH (17). A fourth untreated woman experienced severe relapses throughout her four pregnancies; the first two had normal outcomes, but during the next two her symptoms were so severe that she had therapeutic terminations (18); her symptoms resolved immediately following the end of each pregnancy.

A fifth woman also endured a severe deterioration during her first pregnancy which produced a normal boy. Her symptoms resolved but were so severe during her next pregnancy that she had a termination, after which she had an immediate remission. In the last week of her third pregnancy, her plasma zinc concentration was 2.8 μmol/liter and the diagnosis of AE was made. Zinc therapy was immediately beneficial, and, despite her previous symptomatic zinc depletion, this woman had a healthy boy weighing 3.06 kg (19). The successful outcomes of pregnancies in women with AE treated with zinc supplements (20) show the efficacy of zinc in managing pregnancy in AE.

Women with AE represent the most severe and distinct form of zinc deficiency and these case reports raise several points: (i) earlier zinc deficiency may impair growth such that physical factors jeopardize delivery; (ii) zinc deficiency may be teratogenic in human pregnancy; (iii) the exacerbation of zinc deficiency by pregnancy may represent changes in the systemic metabolism of zinc which affect all women; and, fascinatingly, (iv) women with severe zinc deficiency can still have normal infants. The last two aspects are of particular relevance to pregnancy in general.

The birth of apparently normal infants to zinc-deficient women could be explained by the protective transfer to the fetus of zinc released adventitiously from maternal tissues which are being catabolized either as a result of pregnancy or as a direct or indirect result of zinc deficiency. Pregnant rats deprived of zinc can actually accumulate more zinc in their products of conception than they eat during pregnancy (21–23). The extra zinc is derived from the dams' bones and muscle; however, if calcium and energy intakes were maintained in these models, thereby minimizing nutritional causes of tissue breakdown, reproductive abnormalities characteristic of zinc deficiency occcur.

A similar phenomenon probably occurred in some zinc-deprived pregnant rhesus monkeys which showed a negative correlation between food intake during the third trimester of pregnancy and their infants' birthweight; the mothers were anorexic, they lost weight and had a smaller fall in plasma zinc content than those who ate normally (4); this may thus represent the release of zinc from catabolized maternal tissue increasing the circulating zinc and its availability to the feto-placental unit.

METABOLIC DEMAND FOR ZINC IN PREGNANCY

Although in normal rats most fetal zinc comes from the maternal diet, as much as 30% may still derive from maternal tissues (22). It is not known in women how much maternal zinc is transferred to the fetus or how pregnancy influences zinc turnover but the fact that this happens is suggested strongly by the experience in AE outlined above.

All published recommended dietary intakes of zinc (Table 5) allow for an increased intake of zinc during pregnancy (24,25); however, few pregnant women achieve even the lowest recommendations (Table 6) (26–32). Most intakes hardly differ from those of nonpregnant women, and as yet no problems can be attributed reliably to failure to achieve any of the recommendations (33). To some extent estimates of dietary intakes alone are unhelpful; one also needs to consider the efficiency with which the dietary zinc is absorbed by the intestine; this is a function of intestinal adaptation and of the nature of the diets.

The possibility that dietary zinc deficiency might affect human pregnancy should

TABLE 5. *Estimated zinc dietary requirements during pregnancy and lactation (mg/day)*

	Some national recommendations		
	Nonpregnant	Pregnant	Lactating
Australia	14	18.5	20
Canada	10	13	17
Czechoslovakia	8	16	18
FDR	12	13–16	25
USA	12	15	19

	World Health Organization Expert Committee		
	Total needed	Required intake assuming bioavailability of zinc is:		
		10%	20%	40%
Nonpregnant	2.2	22	11	5.5
Pregnant				
0–20 weeks	2.55	25.5	12.8	6.4
20–30 weeks	2.9	2.9	14.5	7.3
30–40 weeks	3.0	30	15	7.5
Lactation	5.45	54.5	27.3	13.7

TABLE 6. *Some reported daily zinc and copper intakes during pregnancy*[a]

Population (stage in pregnancy)	Zinc (mg)	Copper (mg)	Energy (MJ)	Protein (g)	Method	Reference
USA						
Navajo (mid)[b]	12(6.9)	1.57(0.7)	10.2(3.7)	95(41)	24 h recall	26
Middle income (37 weeks)						
Subsequent lactators	9.8(0.6)	—	8.5(0.3)	80 (3)	3 day dupli-cate diet	27
Nonlactators	7.9(0.5)	—	6.8(0.4)	63 (4)		
Denver (throughout)[b]	11.3(4.1)	—	8.5(2.1)	85(25)	1 day recall and 3 day record	28
Hispanics (mid)[b]	9.7(5.0)	1.39(1.7)	6.9(2.5)	68(30)	1 day recall	29
Vegetarian (37 weeks)	12.6(0.9)	2.80(0.3)	10.2(0.6)	93 (7)	3 day recall	30
Nonvegetarian (37 weeks)	14.4(0.6)	2.10(0.4)	8.4(0.6)	97 (5)		
Nonpregnant vegetarian	6.4(0.8)	1.30(0.2)	5.6(0.6)	51 (6)		
UK						
Aberdeen (30 weeks)[b]	9.1(2.0)	1.51(0.3)	8.4(1.9)	72(14)	7 day weighed intake	31
London (mid)[b]						
Asian						
Vegetarian	7.5(2.1)	1.53(0.7)	8.2(2.2)	57.3(16)	7 day recall	32
Nonvegetarian	10.2(3.0)	1.80(0.8)	9.1(1.9)	75 (19)		
European	11.6(2.8)	1.50(0.3)	8.5(1.1)	80 (20)		

[a]Data in parentheses are standard errors of mean or [b]standard deviation

not be too readily dismissed, however. Mexican women with daily intakes of less than 8 mg of zinc have been noted to have particularly low plasma zinc concentrations during pregnancy, as well as other biochemical abnormalities consistent with zinc deficiency (34): this could be a subpopulation worthy of closer investigation, as could a similar group of North London women who had an daily intake of less than 5 mg of zinc (32).

CALCULATED ZINC REQUIREMENTS

The extra net requirement during pregnancy can be calculated on the basis of the extra tissue components arising. Thus, if one allows for the zinc content of amniotic fluid (35), increased blood components and plasma volume (31), the accretion of lean tissue by the mother (13) and the placenta (36,37), and of zinc by the fetus (38), the derived requirements for zinc over the last trimester of pregnancy are approximately 7.5 to 9.5 μmole per day; a similar figure (9 μmol/day) has been calculated by Swanson and King (33) and by Sandstead (39). If such a factorial analysis is applied to the four 10-week intervals of pregnancy, the calculated daily extra maternal requirement of zinc during these quarters are 0.08, 0.24, 0.53, and 0.73 mg (33). Values calculated from the accumulation of protein during pregnancy are very similar at 0.07, 0.24, 0.61, and 0.78 mg (40). If these estimates are added to the likely basal daily requirement of 2.0 mg (41), the respective requirements during pregnancy are 2.1, 2.2, 2.5 to 2.6, and 2.7 to 2.8 mg zinc daily. At absorptive efficiencies of 20% to 50%, the requirements of late pregnancy could be met by dietary intakes of 14.0 to 5.6 mg Zn/day. These figures match most observed intakes. If extra zinc is needed to sustain pregnancy then, perhaps, it is met by metabolic adaptation. The extra requirements could be achieved by enhanced intestinal absorption of zinc or systemic metabolic adaption or both.

Some evidence of adaptative changes in the metabolism of zinc during pregnancy has been noted in rats (42) and sows (43); these included increased intestinal uptake of zinc, an accumulation of zinc in the liver but not in other tissues, and hypozincemia (44).

Even if the intestine of pregnant women extracted from the diet all the extra zinc thought to be needed, the amounts involved would be so small that the increases in absorption would be difficult to measure by conventional chemical balance techniques. Nonetheless these have been used to assess the metabolism of zinc during pregnancy. Unfortunately, most studies have used intakes corresponding to recommended intakes and therefore have been greater than the observed customary intakes of women. Thus the reported negative balances on daily intakes of 26 to 32 mg of zinc observed in teenagers (45) may only represent homeostatic adjustments to such high intakes.

At more representative daily zinc intakes of 8.9 (SD 3.2) mg, women showed, at mid pregnancy, a retention of 1.9 (SD 3.4) mg zinc (46); with supplementation to 23 mg of zinc, the retention was not altered substantially, at 2.3 (SD 7.6) mg; the large variability may represent homeostatic influences. Balance studies of 15 days duration using semisynthetic diets providing 20 mg of zinc per day found a mean increased daily zinc retention of 1.3 mg in pregnant compared with nonpregnant women; this could represent an adapatation to pregnancy (47); however, no such differences were found in mid-term pregnant women on meat- or vegetable-based diets providing 16 mg of zinc daily (48).

In our studies on 10 women eating self-selected diets providing about 10 mg of zinc daily, there was a net intestinal loss (-0.64 mg) of the metal in the mid trimester, and a net intestinal absorption (0.86 mg) per day during late pregnancy (40). However, although these data suggest an increased intestinal uptake of zinc later in pregnancy, there was considerable variance in the data and the differences were not statistically significant; much larger numbers would be needed to avoid a type II error in interpreting such data.

The urinary excretion of zinc is slightly lower in the first two trimesters than in nonpregnant women or in later pregnancy (28); the physiological basis and importance of this is unclear.

In the overall economy of zinc during pregnancy the amount no longer being lost with menstruation is relatively small; it is estimated to be 0.48 ± 0.37 mg (range 1.36–0.09) (49), or 0.23 ± 0.2 (SD) mg (range 0.64–0.06) (50) per period.

POSSIBLE INDICES OF "ZINC NUTRITURE" IN PREGNANCY

Plasma and Serum Zinc

During pregnancy, plasma or serum zinc concentrations fall by 0.07 µg/dl (0.01 µmol/liter) daily; this starts in very early pregnancy and continues until about 36 weeks (28,51). This is probably due to a number of factors. The importance of the dilution effect of the expansion of plasma volume was shown in a longitudinal study of primigravidas whose total plasma zinc contents, calculated from serial simultaneous determinations of plasma volume and zinc concentrations, were constant throughout pregnancy despite a steady fall in plasma zinc concentrations (Table 7) (31). However, this is probably not the only explanation since plasma zinc concentrations are reduced early in pregnancy before there is any appreciable increase in plasma volume (51). This early change is accompanied by an increase in plasma copper concentrations; it probably results from a redistribution of zinc induced by estrogen, cortisol, and the other endocrine changes and it is not prevented by supplementing daily intakes to 20 mg (28) and 30 mg (29) of zinc, although unphysiological supplements of 90 mg daily during the latter half of pregnancy did manage to do so (52).

The plasma volume increases by around 1.0 liter during pregnancy and achieves a maximal plateau about the middle of the last trimester; an increase of this order occurs in all women irrespective of their size (13). Thus, the relative increase in plasma volume and the associated potential dilution effect on plasma constituents is greater in small women than in larger women. This observation may explain why

TABLE 7. *Plasma volume, intravascular zinc mass and intravascular albumin mass in normal human pregnancy[a]*

Period of gestation (weeks)	No of subjects	Plasma volume (ml)		Zinc mass (µmol)		Albumin mass (g)	
		Mean	SD	Mean	SD	Mean	SD
14	29	2918	441	36.4	6.17	104.4	17.25
20	28	3202	377	37.2	8.01	112.9	13.45
25	32	3464	398	38.1	5.76	119.8	14.79
30	33	3642	328	39.4	5.71	123.5	12.94
35	31	3793	448	40.6	8.69	127.3	16.45

[a]Adapted from Tuttle S (31).

larger falls (40%) of plasma zinc concentrations have been reported in pregnant Indian (53) and Hong Kong Chinese women (54) than in North Americans or Aberdonians (20–25%) (28,31). Larger increases in plasma volume also occur with multiple pregnancies and multiple parities, and smaller ones accompany poor fetal growth and other clinical problems (13).

This could explain the weak inverse correlations which have been noted between mid-pregnancy plasma zinc and infant birthweight (53,55–59). Otherwise, with normal pregnancies no relationships between plasma, or serum zinc, and eventual birthweight (28,31,32,60–62) or the duration of labor have been found. However, mid-trimester hypozincemia may accompany pre-eclamptic toxemia, vaginitis, intrapartum hemorrhage, postmaturity, and threatened and spontaneous abortions (56,58,59,62,63).

Those who have not found any fall in plasma zinc during healthy pregnancies (52,64) have argued that, when found, such falls represent possible zinc depletion. However, since serum or plasma zinc concentrations are depressed by trauma, infections and corticosteroids, as well as by estrogens, even in nonpregnant individuals, they are unreliable indicators of zinc "status". The probability should always be remembered that associations between low plasma and serum zinc levels with abnormal pregnancies, deliveries, and fetuses, may arise from separate systemic reactions to stress rather than from zinc deprivation, and more extensive studies have found other altered biochemical indicators of "nutriture" in abnormal pregnancies as well as hypozincemia (59). Thus, although low plasma zinc content may have some predictive value in human pregnancy, it does not necessarily indicate zinc deficiency or a reason to presume that zinc supplements could be beneficial.

Plasma zinc concentrations also fall physiologically at delivery and thus complicate the interpretation of values gained at this time. In one study, normal and pre-eclamptic pregnant women delivering infants with normal birthweight had lower plasma zinc levels than pre-eclamptics who had low birthweight babies (65); in another study, a positive correlation between plasma zinc at delivery and infant birthweight has been found (54).

It has been speculated that the prevalence of anencephaly in some areas of the Middle East may be related to endemic zinc deficiency because mothers of anencephalic infants had lower serum, red cell, and hair zinc concentrations at term than those having normal babies (64,66). It is possible that abnormal zinc metabolism may occur in mothers of anencephalic fetuses because of abnormal fetal adrenal architecture and biochemistry which conceivably would alter the maternal endocrine milieu of pregnancy appreciably (67). On the other hand, low maternal plasma zinc values occur also with less extensive neural tube defects (68). However, such results may also indicate secondary changes in zinc metabolism as is suggested by the increased hair zinc content in mothers of infants with spina bifida (69). Why low plasma zinc concentrations were found in Ireland, in women up to 24 months after delivery of infants with congenital defects (70) is unknown.

There are probably many reasons for the various associations outlined above. Isolated zinc deficiency is rare, and since there are many possible nutritional and metabolic causes of hypozincemia in pregnancy, the apparent inconsistencies need not be contradictory; they may represent different pathogeneses and different effects on the metabolism of zinc. Unfortunately, few studies allow for, or provide information on, the many independent factors which affect plasma zinc levels or fetal birthweight in normal and abnormal pregnancies.

Hair Zinc

Although in some circumstances occipital hair zinc content may provide evidence of inadequate zinc intake, its value is limited (71). If hair growth is impaired by malnutrition (72), or, in animals, by zinc deprivation (73), its zinc content may actually be increased. A progressive fall in hair zinc during pregnancy has been found in some (29,58,68) but not all studies (28), and in the absence of an adequate understanding of the factors influencing hair growth and zinc metabolism during pregnancy, such values are uninterpretable. For example, if spina bifida or neural tube defects are attributable to zinc deficiency, presumably early in pregnancy, the precise relevance of the zinc content of the proximal 2 to 3 cm of hair at delivery is hard to evaluate unless it represents a persistent zinc deprivation which is not otherwise evident.

One study that determined the zinc content of serial, distal to proximal, sections of hair shafts showed a steady decline in mothers with normal pregnancies and infants, but a constant zinc concentration along the hair of mothers of infants with spina bifida. This probably illustrates, as the authors suggest, altered zinc metabolism (68).

Interpretive difficulties arise also from an association of neural tube defects with an elevated hair zinc in affected infants, but with low hair zinc in their mothers (66); this may reflect abnormal maternal zinc metabolism and contamination of fetal hair by amniotic fluid zinc which has been shown to be elevated in association with such defects (74). Certainly, it is impossible to reconcile these findings with fetal or maternal zinc deficiency without further characterization of hair growth in pregnancy.

Leukocyte Zinc Content

The problems of interpreting plasma and hair zinc concentrations have stimulated a search for more effective and less equivocal, compositional or functional indicators of zinc "status", and attention has focused on blood cells.

The red cell zinc content increases during normal pregnancy. It has been reported that lower maternal erythrocyte zinc is associated with the delivery of small for gestational age babies and of anencephalics (64); apart from this no association of red cell zinc with either birthweight (54,60) or abnormal labor or pregnancy (63) has been found.

Epidemiological studies have monitored leukocyte composition and "bioactivities'' as indices of nutriture during pregnancy (57). More recently, leukocyte zinc content has been used as an indicator of an individual's risk of developing zinc deficiency. During pregnancy the zinc content of mixed leukocytes falls, and lower values have been observed in women with growth retarded fetuses (75), but this decline has been questioned (65,76). A direct correlation has been shown between the zinc content of leukocytes taken at the start of the third trimester (77), or shortly after delivery (60), with birthweight and, in particular, intrauterine growth retardation (78); furthermore, growth-retarded infants themselves have reduced zinc content in cord blood leukocytes (79).

Some difficulties in interpreting findings based on the zinc content in mixed leukocytes arise from changes in the relative proportion of leukocyte subsets during pregnancy and in labor, and the differing zinc content of these subsets. The neutrophil count rises from 45 days postovulation and becomes constant during the last trimester, with a further increase at the onset of and during labor. The degree of leukocytosis increases with subsequent pregnancies. Although there is a moderate increase in eosinophils during pregnancy, their relative proportion falls; at the onset of labor their numbers fall and by delivery they are virtually absent. In contrast, the mononuclear cells such as the lymphocytes and the relative proportion of T- and B-cells do not alter during pregnancy. Usually by 6 days after delivery, the white cell count has returned to nonpregnant levels (13). Because neutrophils have a lower zinc content than other polymorphs and mononuclear cells (80), their increased proportion would reduce the zinc content of total mixed leukocytes, and any further change in their number caused by factors associated with abnormal pregnancy would have to be considered before accepting reduced mixed leukocyte zinc content as possible evidence of deficiency or altered metabolism of zinc.

Some potential confusion can be avoided or minimized by determining either the zinc content of leukocyte subsets, or specific zinc-dependent functions in leukocytes, or both. Such analyses should be less ambiguous.

Lower polymorphonuclear (PMN) and mononuclear (MN) cell zinc content has been found 24 to 48 hours after delivery in mothers who have had growth-retarded babies (81). But other studies measuring granulocyte zinc found no relationship at term between their zinc content and birth weight (76,80). Functional abnormalities of white cell prostaglandin metabolism were also found: PGE_2: $F_{2\alpha}$ ratios, and $PGF_{2\alpha}$ production correlated with the cellular zinc content although total prostaglandin production was not altered (81). The clinical implications of these findings are unclear, but in zinc-deprived rats, abnormally prolonged labor is normalized by treatment with $PGF_{2\alpha}$ (82)

SUPPLEMENTATION STUDIES

The monitoring of the clinical and biochemical response to zinc supplementation is probably the only effective way of diagnosing zinc-responsive states and this is probably the best means of discovering if zinc supply is adequate during pregnancy.

However, the design and conduct of such a study is difficult. Most of those reported have been small, and were not controlled adequately for other influences on the outcome of pregnancy, such as social class, general nutritional intake, parity, alcohol intake, smoking, and maternal size and weight gain. Evidently, if any effect on malformations is to be examined, zinc would need to be started very early in pregnancy, if not before conception.

Supplements of 90 and 45 mg of elemental zinc have been reported to reduce the incidence of postmaturity, the duration and incidence of abnormal labor, and maternal blood loss at delivery (52). These are hard criteria to define and such studies merit substantiation. In a double-blind study of Hispanic women in Los Angeles, a daily supplement of 20 mg of zinc reduced the number of women at term with serum concentrations of zinc below 8.1 μmol/liter (29,83,84) and the incidence of preeclamptic toxemia in adult women (83), but not in teenagers (84); however, the overall outcome of pregnancy was not altered (83,84). Interestingly, women with plasma zinc concentrations below 8.1 μmol/liter had some biochemical abnormalities consistent with inadequate zinc supply (83).

In ten Denver women extra zinc (average 11.1 mg/day) increased hair and saliva zinc, and serum alkaline phosphatase activity, but had no effect on serum zinc concentrations or on the outcome of pregnancy (28); a larger study using 20 mg of zinc daily only in the latter half of pregnancy (85) found that unsupplemented mothers had babies with a marginally lower mean birthweight (3236 g, SD 661) compared with those on supplements (3318 g, SD 483), and a higher proportion of premature or abnormal labor, and of small or large for gestational age infants. The last observation seems a little incongruous, but it is consistent with a report of increased weights in the offspring of rats which were deprived of zinc only in late gestation (86). Ideally, future studies should contain sufficient data to enable the identification and characterization of those groups of women who may benefit from supplements, and who would therefore merit further study.

METABOLIC INTERACTIONS AFFECTING ZINC METABOLISM IN PREGNANCY

As well as disturbances induced by normal or abnormal pregnancy, the metabolism of zinc may also be upset by nutritional supplements (e.g., iron and folate), alcohol, and smoking.

Two-week courses of folate (350 μg) with or without iron (50 mg) impaired the apparent absorption of zinc as assessed by "oral tolerance tests" using 25 mg of the element (87), and large iron supplements (range 164–395 mg daily) given in "practice" altered zinc metabolism (88) as evidenced by reduced plasma zinc concentrations; however, serum alkaline phosphatase activity, and neutrophil (PMN) and mononuclear leukocyte (MN) zinc contents were not effected. Sheldon et al. (89) did not even find any change in plasma zinc concentrations in patients on 78 mg of iron and 200 μg folic acid daily; Hambidge and colleagues (88) surmised that the data of Sheldon and coworkers showed a steeper decline in plasma zinc levels in women who were receiving iron than in those who were not. It is also worth noting that the women in Sheldon's study were considered to need iron whereas Hambidge's population were on "prophylactic" supplements. Mechanisms of mineral interactions probably differ in anemic and nonanemic states, or more specifically iron-replete and iron-deficient states. Therefore it is interesting that another study of "prophylactic iron" found that women given vitamins and iron (47-mg elemental iron as ferrous sulphate) for 22 weeks from 16 weeks gestation had lower plasma zinc concentrations than those on vitamins alone; their placental alkaline phosphatase activity increased more slowly than in a group not supplemented with iron, but leukocyte zinc contents were similar in both groups (90). It is evident, therefore, that iron supplements can, in some circumstances, interfere with zinc metabolism, but, as yet the clinical significance of this interaction is unknown.

Maternal smoking reduces the birthweight of infants, and has been associated with reduced zinc content of polymorphonuclear cells and to a lesser, and statistically insignificant, extent, of mononuclear cells (60). Smoking increases the body burden of cadmium and this metal is a potent antagonist of zinc metabolism (91). Interestingly the zinc to cadmium ratio in placentas is inversely related to maternal age and smoking (37). Mothers who smoke, compared with nonsmokers, have higher placental concentrations of both cadmium and zinc (92,93), and their infants have lower plasma zinc levels and lower birthweights (36,93). Thus a cadmium: zinc interaction in the placenta may compromise zinc supply to the fetus and, perhaps, contribute to growth retardation *in utero*.

Disturbed zinc metabolism may also contribute to the pathogenesis of fetal alcohol syndrome (94). In alcoholic mothers plasma zinc concentrations at delivery have been claimed to correlate with the number of malformations in their offspring (95), but, as has been explained above, the use of plasma zinc values gained during the stress of labor as evidence of zinc deprivation during pregnancy is contentious and should be regarded cautiously. However, relative hypozincemia and hyperzincuria in the offspring of alcoholic mothers (96) indicate that disturbances of zinc metabolism may have been initiated *in utero*. In rats even brief exposure to alcohol impairs the placental uptake and transfer of zinc as it does that of other nutrients (97), and this defect is not overcome by zinc supplementation (98).

Placental Transfer of Zinc

Clearly the crucial factor in gauging the effect of maternal zinc metabolism on the fetus is the placental transfer of the element. Little is known of this process. It is not known if zinc crosses the placenta bound to a specific carrier. Contractor and Eaton (99) reported that α-2-macroglobulin complexed with trypsin was taken up by the perfused human placenta and, since α-2-macroglobulin binds zinc, they suggested that this complex could mediate the placental uptake of the metal. It has also been proposed that zinc crosses membranes when associated with amino acids (100). Placental tissues bind zinc avidly (101) and contain low molecular weight, cysteine-rich, metal-binding proteins which could also be involved in zinc transport (102).

The maternal aspect of the placenta could be the principal barrier to materno-fetal transport of zinc. In studies on the guinea pig such transfer occurred against a concentration gradient and when placental zinc levels exceeded those in fetal and maternal plasma (101). The maternal surface appeared to be rate controlling and it was concluded that zinc may be taken up by active transport at the maternal surface of the placenta and released across the fetal surface by diffusion.

In the isolated dually perfused human placental lobule, uptake of zinc from physiologically appropriate zinc concentrations in the maternal circulation perfusate may be carrier mediated (103). Zinc was accumulated in the placental tissue whence it passed by diffusion into the fetal perfusate. The translocation of zinc from maternal to fetal perfusates was independent of any differential protein binding. There is no evidence yet that the placental uptake of zinc is energy dependent. Neither is it known how these processes are affected by smoking or alcohol, but such information would help in discovering if maternal zinc supplements could overcome these insults.

COPPER

About 75 μg (1.2 μmol) of elemental copper is needed daily to meet the requirements of pregnancy (104). The calculated daily copper accumulation by a fetus is 51 μg (0.8 μmol)/kg bodyweight/day (105), and at term the total amount of copper in the fetus and placenta may be as much as 17% of that in the nonpregnant woman (12) which represents an accretion of about 45 mg of copper throughout pregnancy at an increased daily retention of 4%. If the maternal accumulation of copper is related to that estimated for protein, the overall extra copper acquired during pregnancy is 31 mg and the extra daily requirements for the four quarters of pregnancy are 17.0, 61.0, 160.0, and 200.0 μg (0.27, 0.96, 2.5, and 3.2 μmol) respectively (40). Daily intakes of copper shown in Table 6 are less than the USA estimated safe and adequate range of 2 to 3 mg/day (106). Although, as with zinc, this comparison is of little value in assessing any individual woman's risk of deficiency, one recent report suggests that mid-term pregnant women need 3 mg of copper daily to achieve a reliable copper retention (46). However, balance studies of women eating animal- and plant-based diets supplying respectively 1.4 and 2.5 mg of copper found marginally higher intestinal absorption of copper in pregnant compared with nonpregnant women (104).

Plasma or serum copper and ceruloplasmin concentrations increase steadily throughout pregnancy (31,51), and, after delivery, return rapidly to nonpregnant levels. Concentrations at mid-pregnancy do not correlate with neonatal birthweight or the outcome of pregnancy, but reduced concentrations have been seen in placental insufficiency (107), intrauterine death (108), and threatened abortion (109), and high concentrations accompany infection and toxemia. Anecdotal reports of reduced hepatic copper in pregnant women who have died in road traffic accidents (110) or with late toxemia (111) support the probability that the increased plasma pool arises from mobilization of this depot.

As yet there have been no descriptions of maternal copper deficiency affecting human pregnancy, but abnormalities have occurred in the offspring of two women, one with cystinuria and the other with Wilson's disease, who were being treated with the chelating agent penicillamine (112,113). Both of the involved children had hernias, and cutis laxa; one infant had hypotonia, hyperflexibility of the joints, vascular anomalies, and an overwhelming *Candida* septicemia. Before attributing these phenomena entirely to copper deficiency, one should remember that penicillamine can chelate other trace elements and nutrients.

The concentration of copper in the maternal plasma exceeds that in the fetal circulation (114), but the significance of this gradient on the materno-fetal transfer of copper is unknown.

SELENIUM

Pregnant women have been estimated to accumulate 3.5 to 5 μg of selenium daily (115). Increased maternal retention of selenium during pregnancy was evident in a study of women consuming 150 μg of selenium daily: pregnant women retained 34 (SD 2) μg compared with 11 (SD 2) in nonpregnant women. This was achieved by a progressive decrease in urinary loss of selenium and is suggestive of some adaptive mechanism which is, as yet, uncharacterized (115).

Plasma concentrations of selenium fall during pregnancy whereas erythrocyte concentrations are unaltered (116,117); maternal plasma content exceeds that in cord blood (116). An intriguing recent observation was that plasma and red blood cell selenium levels were lower during late pregnancy in women who planned to breast feed than those in women who had decided not to breast feed (118). This difference was maintained during lactation although the dietary intakes of selenium were higher in the lactators both before and after parturition, even after allowance was made for different energy intakes.

INTERFERENCES OF METABOLISM OF TRACE ELEMENTS CAUSING FETAL DEFECTS

In humans 2% to 5%, and 4% of neonates respectively have major or minor congenital malformations, most of these arise in early pregnancy, during organogenesis, and thus before any period of possible increased nutrient demand. It is, however, conceivable that many teratogens may operate by interfering with either the metabolism of trace elements or with mechanisms which are dependent on them. With such interactions, a marginally adequate trace metal supply may act as coteratogen. In animal models zinc deprivation exacerbates the teratogenicity of

EDTA, vitamin A deficiency, 6-mercaptopurine, thalidomide (1), and alcohol (94). In rats antenatal penicillamine exacerbated the adverse effects of low maternal copper intakes on the fetuses (1). The analogous clinical experience in women being treated with penicillamine has been mentioned earlier; however, in general, no abnormalities have been associated with women being treated with penicillamine for Wilson's disease (119). Perhaps the larger amount of copper in the latter patients prevented any significant interference by penicillamine with the use of copper and, possibly, other metals by the feto-placental unit.

These examples demonstrate the important possibility that agents may adversely affect the outcome of pregnancy by altering the metabolism of trace metals independently of any nutritional deprivation.

CONCLUSION

Reliable, convenient, and ethical means are needed to monitor the metabolism of trace elements in human pregnancy. The role of maternal adaptation in ensuring an adequate supply of trace metals for the fetus has not been fully elucidated. Only when this has been achieved would it be possible to devise means of detecting deficiencies of these minerals and the effects of such deficiencies on reproductive efficiency. It would then be possible to develop more accurate strategies to assess the requirements of pregnant women for trace elements.

ACKNOWLEDGMENTS

We thank the Scottish Home and Health Department, The Rank Prize Funds, The Jules Thorne Trust, and the Nuffield Trust for financial support.

REFERENCES

1. Hurley LS. Teratogenic aspects of manganese, zinc, and copper nutrition. *Physiol Rev* 1981; 61:249–97.
2. Beach RS, Gershwin ME, Hurley LS. Gestational zinc deprivation in mice: Persistence of immunodeficiency for three generations. *Science* 1982;218:469–71.
3. Golub MS, Gershwin ME, Hurley LS, Baly DL, Hendrickx AG. Studies of marginal zinc deprivation in rhesus monkeys. I. Influence on pregnant dams. *Am J Clin Nutr* 1984;39:265–80.
4. Golub MS, Gershwin ME, Hurley LS, Baly DL, Hendrickx AG. Studies of marginal zinc deprivation in rhesus monkeys: II. Pregnancy outcome. *Am J Clin Nutr* 1984;39:879–87.
5. Golub MS, Gershwin ME, Hurley LS, Saito WY, Hendrickx AG. Studies of marginal zinc deprivation IV. Growth of infants in the first year. *Am J Clin Nutr* 1984;40:1192–202.
6. Leek JC, Vogler JB, Gershwin ME, Golub MS, Hurley LS, Hendrickx AG. Studies of marginal zinc deprivation in rhesus monkeys. V. Fetal and infant skeletal defects. *Am J Clin Nutr* 1984; 40:1203–12.
7. Haynes DC, Gershwin ME, Golub MS, Cheung ATW, Hurley LS, Hendrickx AG. Studies of

marginal zinc deprivation in rhesus monkeys. VI. Influence on the immunohaematology of infants in the first year. *Am J Clin Nutr* 1985;42:252–62.
8. Apgar J. Zinc and reproduction. *Annu Rev Nutr* 1985;5:43–68.
9. Hurley LS. Trace elements in prenatal and neonatal development: Zinc and manganese. In: Chandra RK, ed. *Trace elements in nutrition of children.* New York: Raven Press/Vevey: Nestlé Nutrition, 1985:121–35.
10. Aggett PJ. Trace elements in human pregnancy and lactation. In: Chandra RK, ed. *Trace elements in nutrition of children.* New York: Raven Press/Vevey: Nestlé Nutrition, 1985:137–55.
11. Leitch I, Hytten FE, Billewicz WZ. The maternal and neonatal weights of some mammalia. *Proc Zool Soc Lond* 1959–60;133:11–28.
12. Widdowson EM. The demands of the fetal and maternal tissues for nutrients, and the bearing of these on the needs of the mother to "eat for two". In: Dobbing J, ed. *Maternal nutrition in pregnancy—eating for two.* London: Academic Press, 1981:1–19.
13. Hytten FE, Chamberlain G, eds. *Clinical physiology in obstetrics.* Oxford, UK: Blackwell Scientific Publications, 1980:193–233.
14. Aggett PJ. Acrodermatitis enteropathica. *J Inherited Metab Dis* 1983;6 (suppl 1):39–43.
15. Epstein S, Vedder JS. Acrodermatitis enteropathica persisting into adulthood. *Arch Dermatol Syph* 1960;82:189–90.
16. Verburg DJ, Burd LI, Hoxtell EO, Merrill LK. Acrodermatitis enteropathica and pregnancy. *Obstet Gynecol* 1974;44:233–7.
17. Neldner KH, Hambidge KM. Zinc therapy of acrodermatitis enteropathica. *N Engl J Med* 1975;292:879–92.
18. Olholm-Larson P. Untreated Acrodermatitis enteropathica in adults. *Dermatologica* 1978;156:155–66.
19. Bronson DM, Barksky R, Barsky S. Acrodermatitis enteropathica: Recognition at long last during a pregnancy. *J Am Acad Dermatol* 1983;9:140–4.
20. Brenton DP, Jackson MJ, Young A. Two pregnancies in a patient with acrodermatitis enteropathica treated with zinc sulphate. *Lancet* 1981;2:500–2.
21. Masters DG, Keen CL, Lonnerdal B, Hurley LS. Zinc deficiency teratogenicity: The protective role of maternal tissue catabolism. *J Nutr* 1983;113:905–12.
22. Masters DG, Keen CL, Lonnerdal BO, Hurley LS. Release of zinc from maternal tissues during zinc deficiency on simultaneous zinc and the pregnant rat. *J Nutr* 1986;116:2148–54.
23. Record IR. Zinc deficiency and the developing embryo. *Neurotoxicology* 1987;8:369–78.
24. International Union of Nutritional Sciences. A report of committee 1/5 on recommended dietary intakes around the world. *Nutr Abstr Rev Clin Nutr, Series A* 1983;53:1109–10.
25. World Health Organization Expert Committee. *Trace elements in human nutrition.* World Health Organization Technical Reports Series No 532. Geneva: World Health Organization, 1973.
26. Butte N, Calloway DH, Van Duzen JL. Nutritional assessment of pregnant and lactating Navajo women. *Am J Clin Nutr* 1981;34:2216–28.
27. Moser PB, Reynolds RD. Dietary zinc intake and zinc concentrations of plasma, erythrocytes, and breast milk in antepartum and postpartum lactating and non-lactating women: A longitudinal study. *Am J Clin Nutr* 1983;38:101–8.
28. Hambidge KM, Krebs NF, Jacobs MA, Favier A, Guyette L, Ikle DN. Zinc nutritional status during pregnancy: A longitudinal study. *Am J Clin Nutr* 1983;37:429–42.
29. Hunt IF, Murphy NJ, Cleaver AE, et al. Zinc supplementation during pregnancy: zinc concentrations of serum, and hair from low income women of Mexican descent. *Am J Clin Nutr* 1983;37:572–82.
30. King JC, Stein T, Doyle M. Effect of vegetarianism on the zinc status of pregnant women. *Am J Clin Nutr* 1981;34;1649–55.
31. Tuttle S, Aggett PJ, Campbell D, Macgillivray I. Zinc and copper nutrition in human pregnancy: A longitudinal study in normal primigravidae and in primigravidae at risk of delivering a growth retarded baby. *Am J Clin Nutr* 1985;41:1032–41.
32. Campbell-Brown M, Ward RJ, Haines AP, North WRS, Abraham R, McFadyen IR. Zinc and copper in Asian pregnancies—is there evidence for a nutritional deficiency? *Br J Obst Gynaecol* 1985;92:875–85.
33. Swanson CA, King JC. Zinc and pregnancy outcome. *Am J Clin Nutr* 1987;46:763–71.
34. Hunt IF, Murphy NJ, Martner-Hewes PM, et al. Zinc, vitamin B-6, and other nutrients in pregnant women attending prenatal clinics in Mexico. *Am J Clin Nutr* 1987;46:563–9.

35. Gardiner PE, Rosick E, Rosick U, Bratter P, Kynast G. The application of gel filtration immuno-nephelometry and electrothermal atomic absorption spectrometry to the study of the distribution of copper-, iron-, and zinc-bound constituents in human amniotic fluid. *Clin Chim Acta* 1982;120: 103–17.

36. Kuhnert PM, Kuhnert BR, Erhard P, Brashear WT, Groh-Wargo SL, Webster S. The effect of smoking on placental and fetal zinc status. *Am J Obstet Gynecol* 1987;157:1241–6.

37. Kuhnert BR, Kuhnert PM, Zarlingo TJ. Associations between placental cadmium and zinc and age and parity in pregnant women who smoke. *Obstet Gynecol* 1988;71:67–70.

38. Shaw JCL. Trace elements in the fetus and young infant: Zinc. *Am J Dis Child* 1979;133:1260–8.

39. Sandstead HH. Zinc nutrition in the United States. *Am J Clin Nutr* 1973;26:1251–60.

40. Armstrong J. *Trace element metabolism in human pregnancy*. Aberdeen: Robert Gordon's Institute of Technology, 1985. M Phil Thesis.

41. Hess FM, King JC, Margen S. Zinc excretion in young women on low zinc intakes and oral contraceptive agents. *J Nutr* 1977;107:1610–20.

42. Williams RB, Davies NT, McDonald I. The effects of pregnancy and lactation on copper and zinc retention in the rat. *Br J Nutr* 1977;38:407–16.

43. Schwarz FJ, Kirchgessner M, Sherif SY. Zur intestinalen Absorption von Zink wahrend der Graviditat und Lactation. *Res Exp Med Berl* 1981;179:35–42.

44. Kirchgessner M, Sporl R, Roth-Maier DA. Exkretion in Kot und Schienbare Absorption von Kupfer, Zink, Nickel, und Mangan bei Nichtgraviden und Graviden Sauen nach unterschiedlicher. Spurenelement-versorgung. *Z Tierphysiol, Tierernahrg u Futtermitrelkde* 1980;44:98–111.

45. Schraer KK, Calloway DH. Zinc balances in pregnant teenagers. *Nutr Metab* 1974;17:205–12.

46. Taper LJ, Oliva JT, Ritchey SJ. Zinc and copper retention during pregnancy: The adequacy of prenatal diets with and without dietary supplementation. *Am J Clin Nutr* 1985;41:1184–92.

47. Swanson CA, King JC. Zinc utilization in pregnant and nonpregnant women fed controlled diets providing the zinc RDA. *J Nutr* 1982;112:697–707.

48. Swanson CA, Turnland JR, King JC. Effect of dietary sources and pregnancy on zinc utilisation in adult women fed controlled diets. *J Nutr* 1983;113:2557–67.

49. Greger JL, Buckley S. Menstrual blood loss of zinc, copper, magnesium and iron by adolescent girls. *Nutr Rep Int* 1977;16:639–47.

50. Umoren J, Kies C. Menstrual blood losses of iron, zinc, copper and magnesium in adult female subjects. *Nutr Rep Int* 1982;26:717–26.

51. Breskin MW, Worthington-Roberts BS, Knopp RH, et al. First trimester serum zinc concentrations in human pregnancy. *Am J Clin Nutr* 1983;38:943–53.

52. Jameson S. Zinc and pregnancy. In: Nriagu JO, ed. *Zinc in the environment, II. Health effects.* New York: J. Wiley and Sons, 1979:183–97.

53. Prema K. Predictive value of serum copper and zinc in normal and abnormal pregnancy. *Indian J Med Res* 1980;71:554–60.

54. Ghosh A, Fong LYY, Wan CW, Liang ST, Woo JSK, Wong V. Zinc deficiency is not a cause for abortion, congenital abnormality and small for gestational age infant in Chinese women. *Br J Obstet Gynaecol* 1985;92:886–91.

55. Crosby WH, Metcoff J, Costiloe, JP. Fetal malnutrition: An appraisal of correlated factors. *Am J Obstet Gynecol* 1977;128:22–31.

56. McMichael AJ, Dreosti IE, Gibson GT, et al. A prospective study of serial maternal serum zinc levels and pregnancy outcome. *Early Hum Dev* 1982;7:59–69.

57. Metcoff J, Costiloe JP, Crosby W, et al. Maternal nutrition and fetal outcome. *Am J Clin Nutr* 1981;34:708–21.

58. Vir SC, Love AHG, Thompson W. Zinc concentration in hair and serum of pregnant women in Belfast. *Am J Clin Nutr* 1981;34:2800–7.

59. Mukherjee MD, Sandstead HH, Ratnaparkhi MV, Johnson LK, Milne DB, Stelling HP. Maternal zinc, iron, folic acid, and protein nutriture and outcome of human pregnancy. *Am J Clin Nutr* 1984;40:496–507.

60. Simmer K, Thompson RPH. Maternal zinc and intrauterine growth retardation. *Clin Sci* 1985; 68:395–9.

61. Turnlund JR, King JC, Wahbeh CJ, Ishkanian I, Tannous RI. Zinc status and pregnant outcome of pregnant Lebanese women. *Nutr Res* 1983;3:309–15.

62. Cherry FA, Bennett EA, Bazzano GS, Johnson LK, Fosmire GJ, Batson HK. Plasma zinc in hy-

pertension/toxemia and other reproductive variables in adolescent pregnancy. *Am J Clin Nutr* 1981; 34:2367–75.

63. Lazebnik N, Kuhnert BR, Kuhnert PM, Thompson KL. Zinc status, pregnancy complications, and labor abnormalities. *Am J Obstet Gynecol* 1988;158:161–6.
64. Cavdar AO, Arcasoy A, Baycu T, Himmetoglu O. Zinc deficiency and anencephaly in Turkey. *Teratolgy* 1980;22:141.
65. Adeniyi FAA. The implications of hypozincemia in pregnancy. *Acta Obstet Gynecol Scand* 1987;66:579–82.
66. Cavdar AO, Bahceci M, Akar N, et al. Zinc status in pregnancy and the occurence of anencephaly in Turkey. *J Trace Elem Electrolytes Health Dis* 1988;2:9–14.
67. Gray ES, Abramovich DR. Morphological features of the anencephalic adrenal gland in early pregnancy. *Am J Obstet Gynecol* 1980;137:491–5.
68. Buamah PK, Russell M, Bates G, Milford Ward A. Maternal zinc status: A determination of control nervous malformation. *Br J Obstet Gynaecol* 1984;91:788–90.
69. Bergman KE, Makosch G, Tews K-H. Abnormalities of hair zinc concentration in mothers of newborn infants with spina bifida. *Am J Clin Nutr* 1980;33:2145–50.
70. Soltan MH, Jenkins DM. Maternal and foetal plasma zinc concentrations and fetal abnormality. *Br J Obstet Gynaecol* 1982;89:56–8.
71. Hambidge KM. Hair analyses: Worthless for vitamins, limited for minerals. *Am J Clin Nutr* 1982;36:943–9.
72. Erten J, Arcasoy A, Cavdar AO, Cin S. Hair zinc levels in healthy and malnourished children. *Am J Clin Nutr* 1978;31:1172–4.
73. Pallauf J, Kirchgessner M. Zink konzentration des rattenhaares be: Zink depletion und repletion. *Zbl Vet Med A* 1973;20:100–9.
74. Nevin NC. Prevention of neural tube defects in an area of high incidence. In: Dobbing J, ed. *Prevention of spina bifida and other neural tube defects*. London: Academic Press, 1983:127–53.
75. Meadows NJ, Ruse W, Smith MF, et al. Zinc and small babies. *Lancet* 1981;2:1135–7.
76. Jepsen LV, Clemmensen K. Zinc in Danish women during late normal pregnancy and pregnancies with intrauterine growth retardation. *Acta Obstet Gynecol Scand* 1987;66:401–5.
77. Wells JL, James DK, Luxton R, Pennock CA. Maternal leucocyte zinc deficiency at start of third trimester as a predictor of fetal growth retardation. *Br Med J* 1987;294:1054–6.
78. Patrick J, Dervish C, Gillieson M. Zinc and small babies. *Lancet* 1982;1:169–70.
79. Meadows N, Ruse W, Keeling PWN, Scopes JW, Thompson RPH. Peripheral blood leukocyte zinc depletion in babies with intrauterine growth retardation. *Arch Dis Child* 1983;58:807–9.
80. Goode HF, Kelleher J, Walker BE. Zinc concentrations in pure populations of peripheral blood neutrophils, lymphocytes and monocytes. *Ann Clin Biochem* 1989;26:89–95.
81. Simmer K, Punchard NA, Murphy G, Thompson RPH. Prostaglandin production and zinc depletion in human pregnancy. *Pediatr Res* 1985;19:697–700.
82. Bunce GE, Wilson GR, Mills CF, Klopper A. Studies on the role of zinc in parturition in the rat. *Biochem J* 1983;210:761–7.
83. Hunt IF, Murphy NJ, Cleaver AE, et al. Zinc supplementation during pregnancy: Effects on selected blood constituents and on progress and outcome of pregnancy in low income women of Mexican descent. *Am J Clin Nutr* 1984;40:508–21.
84. Hunt IF, Murphy NJ, Cleaver AE, et al. Zinc supplementation during pregnancy in low income teenagers of Mexican descent: Effect on selected blood constituents and on progress and outcome of pregnancy. *Am J Clin Nutr* 1985;42:815–28.
85. Kynast G, Saling E. Effect of oral zinc application during pregnancy. *Gynecol Obstet Invest* 1986;21:117–23.
86. Southon S, Fairweather-Tait SJ, Williams CM. Fetal growth, glucose tolerance, and plasma insulin concentration in rats given a marginal-zinc diet in the latter stages of pregnancy. *Br J Nutr* 1988;59:315–22.
87. Simmer K, James C, Thompson RPH. Are iron-folate supplements harmful? *Am J Clin Nutr* 1987;45:122–5.
88. Hambidge KM, Krebs NF, Sibley L, English J. Acute effects of iron therapy on zinc status during pregnancy. *Obstet Gynecol* 1987;70:593–6.
89. Sheldon WL, Aspillaga MO, Smith PA, Lind T. The effects of oral iron supplementation on zinc and magnesium levels during pregnancy. *Br J Obstet Gynaecol* 1985;92:892–8.

90. Bloxam DL, Williams NR, Waskett RJD, Pattison-Green PM, Morarji Y, Stewart SG. Maternal zinc during oral iron supplementation in pregnancy: a preliminary study. *Clin Sci* 1989;76:59–65.
91. Stacey NH, Klaassen CD. Zinc uptake by isolated rat hepatocytes. *Biochim Biophys Acta* 1981;640:693–7.
92. Ward NI, Watson R, Bryce-Smith D. Placental element levels in relation to fetal development for obstetrically "normal" births: A study of 37 elements. Evidence for effects of cadmium, lead and zinc on fetal growth, and for smoking as a source of cadmium. *Int J Biosoc Res* 1987;9:63–81.
93. Kuhnert BR, Kuhnert PM, Debanne S, Williams TG. The relationship between cadmium, zinc, and birth weight in pregnant women who smoke. *Am J Obstet Gynecol* 1987;157:1247–51.
94. Anonymous. Zinc and fetal alcohol syndrome: Another dimension. *Nutr Rev* 1986;44:359–60.
95. Flynn A, Miller SI, Martier SS, Golden NL, Sokol RJ, del Villano BC. Zinc status of pregnant alcoholic women: A determinant of fetal outcome. *Lancet* 1981;1:572–5.
96. Assadi FK, Ziai M. Zinc status of infants with fetal alcohol syndrome. *Pediatr Res* 1986;20:551–4.
97. Ghishan FK, Patwardham R, Greene HL. Fetal alcohol syndrome: inhibition of placental transport of zinc as a potential mechanism for fetal growth retardation. *J Lab Clin Med* 1982;100:45–52.
98. Gishan FK, Greene HL. Fetal alcohol syndrome: Failure of zinc to reverse the effect of ethanol on placental transport of zinc. *Pediatr Res* 1983;17:529–31.
99. Contractor SF, Eaton BM. Uptake of alpha-2-macroglobulin and its trypsin complex by the perfused human placenta. *J Physiol* 1987;386:32P.
100. Giroux EL, Henkin RI. Competition for zinc among serum albumin and amino acids. *Biochim Biophys Acta* 1972;273:64–72.
101. Simmer K, Dwight J, Brown IMH, Thompson RPH, Young M. Placental handling of zinc in the guinea pig. *Biol Neonat* 1985;48:114–21.
102. Waalkes MP, Poisner AM, Wood GM, Klaassen CD. Metallothionein-like proteins in human placenta and fetal membranes. *Toxicol Appl Pharmacol* 1984;74:179–84.
103. Page KR, Abramovich DR, Aggett PJ, Todd A, Dacke CG. The transfer of zinc across the dually perfused human placental lobule. *Quart J Exp Physiol* 1988;73:585–93.
104. Turnland JR, Swanson CA, King JC. Copper absorption and retention in pregnant women fed diets based on animal and plant proteins. *J Nutr* 1983;113:2346–52.
105. Shaw JCL. Trace elements in the fetus and young infant: copper, manganese, selenium and chromium. *Am J Dis Child* 1980;134:74–81.
106. Committee on Dietary Allowances, Food and Nutrition Board. *Recommended dietary allowances*, 9th ed. Washington, DC: National Academy of Sciences, 1980.
107. Freidman S, Bahary C, Eckerling B, Gans B. Serum copper levels as an index of placental function. *Obstet Gynecol* 1969;33:189–94.
108. Schenker JG, Jiengies E, Polishiek WZ. Serum copper levels in normal and pathological pregnancies. *Am J Obstet Gynecol* 1969;105:933–7.
109. O'Leary JA, Novalis GS, Vosburgh GJ. Maternal serum copper concentrations in normal and abnormal gestations. *Obstet Gynecol* 1966;28:112–7.
110. Mirzakarimov MG. Blood copper of women during pregnancy. *Akush Ginekol* 1953;1:55–85.
111. Rasuli ZM. Copper metabolism in toxaemia of late pregnancy. *Akush Ginekol* 1963;39:63–6.
112. Linares A, Larranz JJ, Rodriguez-Aluscon J, Diaz-Perez JL. Reversible cutis laxa due to maternal D-penicillamine treatment. *Lancet* 1979;2:43–4.
113. Mjolnerod OK, Rasmussen K, Dommerad SA, Gjeraldsen ST. Congenital connective tissue defect due to D-penicillamine treatment during pregnancy. *Lancet* 1971;1:673–5.
114. Henkin RI, Marshall JR, Meret S. Maternal fetal metabolism of copper and zinc at term. *Am J Obstet Gynecol* 1971;103:320–44.
115. Swanson CA, Reames DC, Veillon C, King JC, Levander OA. Quantitative and qualitative aspects of selenium utilization in pregnant and nonpregnant women: An application of stable isotope methodology. *Am J Clin Nutr* 1983;38:169–80.
116. Rudolph N, Wong SL. Selenium and glutathiane peroxidase in maternal and cord plasma and red cells. *Pediatrics* 1978;12:789–92.
117. Behne D, Wolters W. Selenium content and glutathiane peroxidase activity in the plasma and erythrocytes of nonpregnant women. *J Clin Chem Clin Biochem* 1979;17:133–5.
118. Levander OA, Moser PB, Morris VC. Dietary selenium intake and selenium concentrations of plasma, erythrocytes, and breast milk in pregnant and postpartum lactating and nonlactating women. *Am J Clin Nutr* 1987;46:694–8.
119. Walshe JM. Pregnancy in Wilson's disease. *Q J Med* 1977;46:73–83.

DISCUSSION

Dr. Lönnerdal: We have been interested in studying the effects of marginal zinc deficiency on zinc absorption during pregnancy and lactation using a primate model. In the rhesus monkey with very mild zinc deficiency the only disturbance we found was a slight impairment of immune function. Zinc stores appeared normal and everything else was identical in the control group and the marginal deficiency group. However, when we looked at zinc absorption, as assessed by ^{65}Zn whole-body counting, there was a highly significant increase in absorption in the marginally deficient group. Thus it was clear that a compensatory increase in absorption was occurring under these circumstances.

Dr. Aggett: Rhesus monkey studies have contributed greatly towards our understanding of zinc nutrition in pregnancy. These data show how effectively pregnant females adapt. It seems reasonable to suppose that these adaptive changes have evolved to ensure adequate zinc supply for the fetus, and it may be that in the presence of such adaptation zinc supplementation in pregnancy is superfluous. This does not mean that we should not be looking for ways to ensure that women are adequately nourished between pregnancies.

Dr. Chandra: A relationship between low plasma zinc during pregnancy and increased incidence of neural tube defects and other congenital malformations has been shown in some suburbs of Beijing, China, where there is a high incidence of zinc deficiency in pregnant women and preschool children. A zinc supplementation trial is being planned.

Dr. Zlotkin: I was interested in the comments you made on the effect of smoking on transplacental transfer of zinc. These data showed higher zinc content in the placentas of smoking women, and higher cadmium intakes. One of the most potent stimulators of metallothionein synthesis is cadmium, so one may postulate that the reason for the increase in zinc in the placenta was the stimulation of metallothionein synthesis preventing the transfer of zinc across the placenta. Do you think there is a relationship between the low birthweight of infants of smoking mothers and the effect of cadmium on metallothionein synthesis and increased placental zinc?

Dr. Aggett: That is possible. However, as well as inducing metallothionein, we should also accept the possibility that smoking and perhaps the increased cadmium burden could have adverse effects on placental metabolism and on energy-dependent transport processes.

Dr. Mertz: I am as impressed as you are with the adaptability of zinc metabolism in relation to marginal intakes or increased requirements. One practical question, however, is what to recommend to pregnant women in the United States, who get a very substantial iron and folic acid supplement. Both of these are believed to interfere with the utilization of zinc under certain circumstances. In addition, our recommendations that energy intakes should be increased in pregnancy will result in a diet with diluted zinc content unless extra zinc is provided.

Dr. Aggett: Recommendations have to make sense in terms of observed experience. If recommendations for one nutrient are not consonant with those for other nutrients, then we cannot expect them to be taken seriously, no matter how careful one is to to emphasize what the recommendations mean, and how they were defined and determined. Certainly we must be aware that the use of substantial iron and folic acid supplements may interfere with the absorption and systemic metabolism of zinc, but we are far from certain that this makes any difference to the transfer of zinc to the fetus. Even if transfer is affected, this is not necessarily an indication to increase the intake of zinc. It might be more appropriate to examine critically the need for iron and folate supplements.

Dr. Hambidge: Do you think that absorption is likely to be a significant factor in adaptation if there is a high phytate content in the diet?

Dr. Aggett: I believe that systemic adaptation involves more than just absorption. Professor Hurley's group in Davis has shown that in pregnant rats fed adequately, 30% of the fetal zinc is derived from maternal tissue and bone. This must represent a tremendous turnover. Obviously, for the reasons I have explained, we cannot necessarily extend this information to women but it highlights the point that we should be exploring the possibility of systemic adaptation in zinc metabolism in pregnancy.

Dr. Hambidge: I would like to suggest that adaptation is still only hypothetical. It has not been proven in the pregnant human. Urine excretion of zinc is actually higher during pregnancy.

Dr. Aggett: At the same time we still have a general phenomenon that women are sustaining normal pregnancies on similar intakes to those in the nonpregnant state, while there are nutritionists who recommend that pregnant women take 15 to 20 mg zinc per day, which, as you have pointed out, is difficult to achieve without substantial modification to diets.

Dr. Hambidge: I think there is a level of zinc intake during pregnancy below which it is undesirable to go. This level is unknown. Even if no adverse effects can be detected from an intake that is too low to meet the demands of the conceptus and maintain maternal balance, there is no reason to wait until after the pregnancy to make up the deficit.

Dr. Aggett: That is correct, and of course pregnancy is the time when one has access to the mother. But the reason for supplementing is not that there is an extra requirement for dietary intake during pregnancy, but that additional zinc may be required for other purposes later on.

Dr. Singh: What are the effects of intestinal parasites on the absorption of zinc?

Dr. Aggett: This probably depends on the nature of the parasite, how big the intestinal burden is, and where it is located. We have explored the interactions between intestinal helminthiasis and zinc metabolism in an animal model. Under such experimental circumstances, increased turnover of a ^{65}Zn-labeled endogenous pool was found in the presence of apparently unaffected intestinal zinc absorption. This may well be because the intestinal lesions were located proximally, whereas fairly effective zinc absorption can occur in the distal intestine. This mirrors what has been observed for other nutrients, namely that intestinal reserve can compensate for potentially adverse effects of intestinal parasitism.

Dr. Chandra: A number of recent studies are addressing this question. It has been found that there is no strict correlation between malabsorption of other nutrients and zinc in specific parasitic diseases, for example ascariasis. Secondly, there is good evidence that zinc deficiency does alter the immune status, and some immune responses are useful for defense against parasites. Thirdly, zinc deficiency alters the balance of different types of T lymphocytes and this in part determines the IgE-mediated responses which may be important in many parasitic diseases. Finally, recent studies are examining the effect of zinc supplements on parasite loads in populations where these infections are endemic, and the effect of zinc supplementation on growth in the absence of antiparasitic medication.

Trace Elements in Nutrition of Children—II,
edited by Ranjit K. Chandra, Nestlé Nutrition
Workshop Series, Vol. 23, Nestec Ltd.,
Vevey/Raven Press, Ltd., New York © 1991.

Assessment of Trace Element Requirements (Zinc) in Newborns and Young Infants, Including the Infant Born Prematurely

Stanley H. Zlotkin

Departments of Nutritional Sciences and Pediatrics, University of Toronto and the Research Institute and Division of Clinical Nutrition, Hospital For Sick Children, Toronto, Ontario, Canada M5G 1X8

Special emphasis should be placed on the title and intent of this chapter. Because the title includes the word assessment, this chapter apparently addresses the issue of assessment of trace metal status. That is not the intent of this chapter. The focus is on the assessment of *requirements* for trace elements, using zinc as an example of a nutritionally essential trace element.

ESTABLISHING DIETARY REQUIREMENTS

Trace mineral requirements can be defined as the amount of an individual mineral that *must be absorbed* to replace body losses, maintain levels in tissues or stores in the body, and provide for normal accretion rates during the growth process. This is a definition of *physiological requirements* as distinct from *dietary requirements.* The latter must normally take into account the bioavailability of the mineral from the diet. Because the requirement as defined above includes a component for the maintenance (or repletion) of tissue stores, it is higher than the intake which would be needed to prevent a specific nutrient deficiency from developing.

It is important to note that requirements for nutrients vary among individuals of comparable body size, physical activity, age, sex, and so forth. Thus, in calculating a dietary requirement, individual variability must be considered. The requirement of a group of similar individuals, therefore, will show a range that is either wide or narrow depending on the nutrient and the population being considered.

The physiological requirements for most nutrients have been established using a factorial method. Using the factorial approach, the obligatory losses of a nutrient from the body are measured when the subject is ingesting none of that particular nutrient. The components that must always be considered when establishing a physiological requirement using the factorial approach include losses from feces and urine, as well as sweat and skin desquamation. Losses in menstrual fluids are also considered in women of childbearing age; losses in milk in lactating women, and so forth. Having measured obligatory losses, an estimate of the amount needed for maintenance (or repletion) of stores is added on, and in infants, children, and adolescents, a component for tissue growth is also calculated. The total is an estimate of the factorial *physiological requirement*. In calculating the *dietary requirement,* absorption is then factored in.

Using dietary requirements for iron as an example, for an infant between the ages 13 to 24 months, obligatory losses are estimated to be 0.24 mg/day; growth needs are estimated at 0.16 mg/day; accretion of stores are estimated to be 0.1 mg/day (1). Therefore, the average physiological needs (excluding a factor for individual variability) are 0.5 mg/day. To determine the dietary requirement, an estimate of absorption must be made. Of course accurate estimates of absorption are very difficult to make because absorption depends not only on the source of iron in the diet and the other food components of the diet (e.g., heme iron is much better absorbed than non-heme iron; ascorbic acid enhances absorption, while phytate blocks absorption), but also the iron status of the individual (e.g., iron-depleted individuals absorb much more iron than iron-replete individuals). Therefore, the dietary iron requirement may be 5 mg/day assuming 10% absorption, or 2.5 mg/day if 20% absorption is assumed. In most countries which have published recommended dietary allowances, an average figure of about 10% absorption for iron has been assumed (2).

In theory, calculation of the physiological and dietary nutrient requirement of the newborn and young infant is no different from that described above. Infants also have obligatory excretion of nutrients and needs for maintenance, storage, and growth. In practice, however, because the diet of the infant is optimally limited to a single food, human milk, and because human milk is considered to be the optimal food for the infant, the nutrient content of human milk has been used to define dietary requirements for infants in the first months of life.

Zinc Requirements

Human milk contains zinc at 2.5 mg/liter at 1 month after birth (3). If average milk intake is 700 ml/day when the infant is 1 month of age (4), then the zinc intake would be 1.75 mg/day (Table 1). The zinc concentration of human milk decreases as postpartum time increases, while the volume of milk ingested slowly increases. Thus at age 3 months, with a milk zinc concentration of 1.1 mg/liter and an average intake of 750 ml/day, the zinc intake would be 0.83 mg/day. If we assume for an individual infant that there is an appropriate match between the content of zinc in the infant's own mother's milk and the volume ingested and the infant's specific requirement (obligatory losses plus needs for storage and growth), then the zinc intake from human milk would equal the dietary requirement for zinc (for the human milk-fed infant).

TABLE 1. *Estimate of zinc intake (the dietary requirement) from breast milk at four, 12 and 24 weeks after birth*

Age (weeks)	Zinc[a] content (mg/liter)	Milk[b] intake (ml/day)	Zinc[c] intake (mg/day)
4	2.5	700	1.75
12	1.1	750	0.83
24	0.5	790	0.40

[a]The mean zinc content of milk, adapted from Vuori E, Kuitunen P. (3).
[b]The mean volume of intake of human milk, adapted from Neville MC et al. (4).
[c]Zinc intake calculated as zinc content of milk (mg/l) × milk intake (ml/day), expressed as mg/day.

To test whether zinc intake from human milk is adequate, one must look at the zinc status of infants who are receiving human milk. Until recently, the answer would have been that infants receiving an adequate volume of human milk were indeed receiving an adequate intake of zinc (i.e., that their physiological requirement was being met). Recently, however, at least five cases of exogenous zinc deficiency due to low levels of zinc in human milk were described *in full term infants* (5–7) (Table 2). All of the infants described were well at birth and were totally breast fed. An acrodermatitis-like rash developed between 10 to 20 weeks after birth accompanied by low serum zinc levels. In all cases, the content of zinc in the infants' mothers' milk was lower than expected. As shown in Table 3, the zinc content of the milk ingested by the infants who became zinc deficient would not meet the physiological requirement even at the highest estimate of fractional absorption. Defective human mammary gland zinc secretion is a likely cause of this deficiency disorder. Other than these rare cases, it is generally believed that for the human milk-fed in-

TABLE 2. *Characteristics of fullterm infants with "zinc deficiency" due to inadequate human milk zinc content*

Birth weight (kg)	Sex	Age at onset[a] (months)	Zn content of milk (mg/l)	Reference values[b] (mg/l)
3.7[c]	Male	3.5	0.27	0.44 ± 0.2
3.7[d]	Female	4	0.03	0.75 ± 0.3
3.0[d]	Male	2	0.27	0.75 ± 0.3
—[e]	Male	2.5	0.18	1.30 ± 0.3
—[e]	Female	2.5	0.14	1.30 ± 0.4

[a]This value corresponds to the postnatal date at which the milk sample was taken.
[b]From Vuori E et al. (3).
[c]From Roberts LJ et al. (5).
[d]From Bye AME et al. (7).
[e]From Kuramoto Y et al. (6).

TABLE 3. *Estimate of zinc intake (the dietary requirement) from breast milk at 20 weeks after birth, compared to estimates of zinc intake by an infant who developed frank zinc deficiency*[a]

Age (weeks)	Zinc[b] content (mg/l)	Milk[c] intake (ml/day)	Zinc intake (mg/day)	Fractional absorption (%)	Physiologic requirement (mg/day)	Factorial estimate[d] (mg/day)
	Average human milk fed infant					
				30	0.17	
20	0.75	770	0.58	40	0.23	0.67
				50	0.29	
	Zinc deficiency infant					
				30	0.06	
20[a]	0.27	770	0.21	40	0.08	
				50	0.10	

[a]From Bye AME et al. (7).
[b]The mean zinc content of milk, adapted from Vuori E. et al. (3).
[c]The mean volume of intake of human milk, adapted from Neville MC et al. (4).
[d]Factorial estimates of zinc requirement were calculated as follows: daily obligatory zinc loss + daily accretion of zinc (for growth and storage) = zinc requirement; where obligatory loss = 90 μg/kg$^{0.75}$ and accretion = 300 μg/day.

fant, the amount of zinc in human milk defines the dietary requirement and meets the physiological requirement, at least until the infant is weaned from milk.

If we compare the physiological requirement as determined from the zinc content of human milk and the physiological requirement from factorial estimates, other than for the first 4 to 8 weeks of life, the factorial estimate is significantly higher than the estimate derived from the ingestion of human milk (Table 4). Since human milk-fed infants are usually not zinc deficient, it is likely that the factorial estimate is too high because of an overestimate of losses or estimates of zinc absorption are too low.

Not all newborn infants receive human milk; thus, the dietary requirement for zinc in infants receiving formula (cow's milk or soy bean based) must also be considered. How then does one go about determining a dietary requirement for the non-human-milk fed infant? If we look in more detail at the zinc content of human milk, we note that there is a range of "normal" values for each postnatal age range. For example, at 1 month postpartum, human milk contains zinc at 2.6 ± 0.2 mg/liter (mean $\pm$ 1 SD) (3) while infant milk intake is 700 ± 175 (550–1135) ml/day (4). At age 3 months postpartum, milk zinc concentration is 1.1 ± 0.2 mg/l (3) and intake is 750 ± 120 ml/day (4). In order to cover the intake needs of the majority of the population, it is customary when determining the physiological requirements of populations to add a value equal to 2 standard deviations to the mean value. Taking the mean plus 2 standard deviations for both milk intake and milk zinc content, the intake of zinc from human milk would be 3.88 mg/day at age one month; 1.68 at age 3 months (Table 5). From the table it becomes very clear that the zinc content of hu-

TABLE 4. *Estimate of zinc intake (the dietary requirement) from breast milk at four, 12 and 24 weeks after birth, and the physiologic requirement at three levels of fractional absorption compared to estimates of zinc requirement based on a factorial method*[a]

Age (weeks)	Zinc[b] content (mg/l)	Milk[c] intake (ml/day)	Dietary requirement (mg/day)	Fractional absorption (%)	Physiologic requirement (mg/day)	Factorial estimate[a] (mg/day)
				30	0.53	
4	2.5	700	1.75	40	0.70	0.58
				50	0.88	
				30	0.25	
12	1.1	750	0.83	40	0.33	0.67
				50	0.42	
				30	0.12	
24	0.5	790	0.40	40	0.16	0.73
				50	0.20	

[a]Factorial estimates of zinc requirement were calculated as follows: daily obligatory zinc loss + daily accretion of zinc (for growth and storage) = zinc requirement; where obligatory loss = 90 μg/kg$^{0.75}$ and accretion = 300 μg/day.
[b]The mean zinc content of milk, adapted from Vuori E et al. (3).
[c]The mean volume of intake of human milk, adapted from Neville MC et al. (4).

TABLE 5. *Estimate of zinc intake (the dietary requirement) from breast milk at the 97.5% level (mean + 2 SD), and the physiologic requirement at three levels of fractional absorption*

Age (weeks)	Zinc content (mg/l)	Milk intake (ml)	Zinc intake (mg/day)	Fractional absorption (%)	Physiologic requirement (mg/day)
				30	1.17
4	2.5 ± 0.6[a]	700 ± 175	3.88[b]	40	1.55
				50	1.94
				30	0.50
12	1.1 ± 0.3	750 ± 120	1.68	40	0.67
				50	0.84
				30	0.47
24	0.5 ± 0.5	790 ± 125	1.56	40	0.62
				50	0.78

[a]Mean ± SD.
[b]Calculated as follows: (mean zinc content + 2 SD) × (mean volume of intake + 2 SD) = zinc intake. This value represents the upper range (97.5%) of zinc intake for all infants. Only 2.5% of infants would be expected to have a higher intake.

man milk changes rapidly with time after birth. In determining the amount of zinc to include in formulas, does one choose the concentration of zinc in milk at 2, 3, or 4 months of postnatal age? Depending on which value is chosen, the dietary intake will be quite different. Also of consideration is the bioavailability of zinc from cow's-milk-based formula. If it were the same as human milk, then the content of zinc in formula would be identical to human milk. There are some data that suggest, however, that the zinc in cow's milk has a lower bioavailability than in human milk (8). There is better documentation that the zinc in soya-based formulas is not well absorbed; however, the overall data base regarding zinc absorption in human infants is limited (9).

In Canada, a Scientific Review Committee is currently reviewing and updating the recommended nutrient intakes for Canadians (2). For infants less than 5 months of age who are fed human milk, the dietary requirement is defined as the *average* amount of zinc found in breast milk when fed at an *average* volume of intake. For children older than 5 months and for non-human-milk-fed infants, the committee has concluded that ''inadequate data exist to allow for the establishment of specific dietary recommendations.'' Table 6 compares the dietary zinc requirement from human milk at age 1 month, using the mean plus 2 standard deviations, compared to the content of zinc in formula available in Canada, and the same estimate of 'milk' intake. Quite clearly, intake from formula is similar to human milk even if calculations are completed using lower fractional absorption rates for formula. The fact that no formula-fed infants have been reported to have zinc deficiency is testimony that the zinc content of formula meets the dietary requirement of the full-term infant.

TABLE 6. *Estimate of zinc intake from breast milk at the 97.5% level (mean + 2 SD) compared to zinc intake from cow's milk based formulas at a similar volume of intake*

Age (weeks)	Diet	Zinc content (mg/l)	"Milk" intake (ml/day)	Zinc intake (mg/day)	Fractional absorption (%)	Net zinc intake (mg/day)
4	Human Milk	2.5 ± 0.6[a]	700 ± 175[a]	3.88[b]	30	1.17
					40	1.55
					50	1.94
4	Formula 1	4.0	700 ± 175	4.20	30	1.26
					40	1.68
					50	2.10
4	Formula 2	5.0	700 ± 175	5.25	30	1.56
	Formula 3	5.0			40	2.10
	Formula 4	5.0			50	2.63

[a]Mean $\pm$ SD.
[b]Calculated as follows: (mean zinc content + 2 SD) × (mean volume of intake + 2 SD) = zinc intake. This value represents the upper range (97.5%) of zinc intake for all infants. Only 2.5% of infants would be expected to have a higher intake.

REQUIREMENTS FOR THE INFANT BORN PREMATURELY

There are a number of quite obvious differences in the nutrient requirements of the infant born prematurely compared to those of the full-term infant. Although the definition of nutrient requirements for both is identical (i.e., the amount of nutrient required for growth and accretion of stores, plus inevitable losses), the quantitative requirements are different because the premature infant is born with lower total nutrient stores, grows at a more rapid rate than the full-term infant and has higher obligatory losses. The requirements for zinc exemplify this difference very clearly.

A recent study was completed examining hepatic metallothionein as a source of storage zinc during the first year of life (10). Due to the smaller size of the preterm infant (including smaller livers), total zinc stores at birth in the premature compared to the full-term infant are significantly lower (11). Widdowson has estimated that two thirds of the zinc in the fetal body at term is transferred to the fetus during the last 12 to 15 weeks of gestation. Zinc is mainly stored in bone, muscle, and hepatic tissue. The major zinc binding protein of the liver is metallothionein (12). Metallothioneins are a group of structurally similar low molecular weight intracellular proteins with high content (30%) of cysteinyl residues and complete absence of aromatic amino acids and histidine. They have a high affinity for essential divalent metals such as zinc and copper and nonessential metals like cadmium and mercury. Since this protein can bind with various metals both essential and nonessential, it may have an important function in regulating the metabolism and toxicity of these metals, as well as being a storage protein (13).

We recently investigated the accumulation of metallothionein in premature and full-term infants during the first year of life (10). Forty-seven samples of human liver tissue were obtained during postmortem examination. In addition, a small number of samples of kidney were also obtained. Samples were divided into four groups based on their gestational and postnatal ages. The three study groups consisted of newborn preterm and full-term infants and infants less than 1 year of age. Infants older than 1 year were considered to be the control group. At the time of death, all premature and full-term infants were less than 2 weeks of age. The mean postnatal age of the older infants was 4.4 ± 3.7 months. By chance, more male than female subjects were included. The clinical diagnosis of the infants studied included: prematurity and respiratory distress syndrome; congenital heart disease; other congenital anomalies; birth asphyxia; sudden infant death syndrome (SIDS); and other pulmonary-related causes. The control group consisted of samples of children who died older than 1 year of age. Their cause of death was unrelated to primary hepatic, or renal pathology.

Concentrations of Metallothionein and Zinc in Hepatic Tissue

During the first week of life, there was no difference in the concentration of metallothionein either between premature and full-term infants, or between older in-

TABLE 7. *Hepatic metallothionein and zinc concentration (mean ± SD)*

	Metallothionein (µg/g wet weight)	Zinc
Premature	234.5 ± 214.6[a]	226.0 ± 85.6[b]
Fullterm	217.6 ± 218.0[a]	142.2 ± 60.8[b]
Infants	52.2 ± 47.0†	49.8 ± 14.6[b]
Controls[c]	54.9 ± 37.6†	64.2 ± 14.8

[a]$p<0.01$ (premature and fullterm vs. infants and controls).
[b]$p<0.05$ (premature vs. fullterm vs. infants vs. controls).
[c]All control subjects (n = 9) died from accidents and were older than 1 year of age (mean age was 7.9 ± 4.4 years).

fants and control values (Table 7). The concentration of metallothionein, however, was significantly lower in older infants than in newborns. The hepatic zinc concentration was significantly different in each of the three groups. The highest values were in the premature group. Interestingly, as with data for concentrations of zinc in other body tissues including plasma, the lowest levels were in the older infants, with concentrations increasing in the older control group (14,15).

The renal concentration of metallothionein (7.2±8.6 µg/g), and zinc (35.6± 11.8 µg/g) were significantly lower than corresponding hepatic levels.

Zinc, Metallothionein Correlations

There was a significant positive correlation between hepatic zinc and metallothionein concentrations ($r=0.76$, $p<0.0001$) (Fig. 1). Although data in Fig. 1 are a

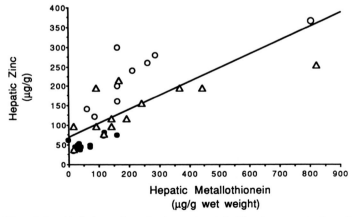

FIG. 1. The relationship between hepatic zinc and metallothionein concentrations. Each point represents an individual data measurement. Open circles (○) represent data from preterm infants; open triangles (△) from full-term infants; and, closed circles (●) from older infants. There was a significant positive correlation between hepatic zinc and metallothionein concentrations ($r=0.76$, $p<0.0001$).

combination of the three groups, the correlation remains strongly positive when each of the three groups (and the control group) is evaluated independently.

Effect of Postnatal Age on Hepatic Concentrations of Zinc and Metallothionein

During the first year of life, there was a significant negative correlation between postnatal age and hepatic metallothionein concentration, and postnatal age and hepatic zinc concentration. By plotting the graphs of postnatal age and metallothionein (and zinc), the best fit obtained was an exponential curve. The graph of postnatal age versus metallothionein is shown in Fig. 2.

In the perinatal rat liver, the great accumulation of cytosolic zinc-bound metallothionein peaks at or soon after birth (16,17). This has been interpreted as indicating that the liver is the main site of regulation of zinc metabolism (and prevention of zinc toxicity). In the human fetal liver, metallothionein concentration is extremely high with the highest levels found between 14 and 23 weeks of gestation (2500 μg/g) (18). We have determined that during the last trimester of gestation, metallothionein concentrations fall from the high fetal values, but are still elevated compared to older infants. Hepatic zinc levels, however, remained as high in the last trimester as were described in the younger fetus (18). Once again, similar to other mammalian species and to results from young human fetuses, there was a strong correlation between the concentration of zinc and metallothionein in hepatic tissue.

Despite a difference of 10 weeks in gestational age between the preterm and full-term infants included in the study, within the first week of life hepatic metallothionein concentrations were similarly high. It has been suggested that a primary role

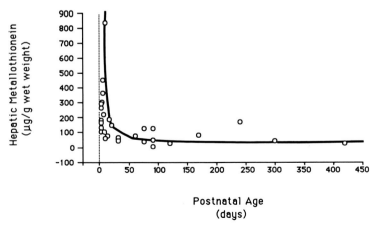

FIG. 2. The relationship between hepatic metallothionein concentration and postnatal age. Each point represents a data measurement from a single subject. A "best fitting" curve of the form y = A/x using PROC NLIN in SAS was used to generate the line.

for metallothionein is as a storage depot for zinc and that zinc bound to metallothionein can be reutilized in the body, thus protecting the body during periods of limited access to exogeneous zinc (12). Consistent with the theory that metallothionein is a storage depot for zinc is the negative zinc balance which has been described in preterm and full-term infants during the first months of life (19,20) Thus, at a time when zinc balance is negative, hepatic metallothionein/zinc levels are at their highest and are likely to be able to contribute zinc to help maintain the high rates of tissue synthesis that occur during the newborn period.

We demonstrated that full-term and preterm newborns have higher hepatic stores of metallothionein that older infants, and, as described in other species, there is a high correlation between concentrations of zinc and metallothionein in the liver. These observations are important for at least two reasons. First, because of serious concurrent illnesses, premature infants often receive few nutrients for the first 7 to 10 days of life, with little obvious detrimental effect. Stores of zinc, as zinc bound to metallothionein, are present even in the premature infant and may act to maintain zinc homeostasis even in the total absence of dietary zinc intake. In addition to the stores of cysteine from glutathione, metallothionein stores may also contribute cysteine to the infant at a time when endogenous cysteine production from methionine is limited (21). Second, premature infants often receive nutrients directly into their systemic venous circulation, bypassing the protective mechanisms present in the gut for trace metal homeostasis, with no obvious indications of toxicity. The presence of hepatic metallothionein may act to protect the infant from potentially toxic effects even when the gut is bypassed.

Unlike the situation for the full-term infant, the content of human breast milk cannot be used as a "gold standard" to establish dietary zinc requirements. For the preterm infant, requirement can be estimated by the factorial approach. Based on estimates of tissue accretion prior to 36 weeks gestation, and measurement of the zinc content of that tissue, an estimate of tissue zinc accretion of 250 μg/kg day has been made (22). We have measured "obligatory" urine zinc losses in full-term infants intravenously fed zinc-free glucose and electrolyte solutions. These losses were 62.3 ± 5.8 μg/kg/day (23). These values are somewhat higher than those reported by Hambidge and Krebs (30–40 μg/kg/day in premature infants (24). Using the above data (and ignoring sweat losses), one may calculate a requirement for net absorption of about 300 μg/kg/day. Assuming absorption of 50% (for simplicity's sake), the recommended dietary intake would be 600 μg/kg/day. This figure is higher than the usual zinc intake of breast-fed premature infants; however, fewer than ten cases of acute zinc deficiency have been described (Table 8) (25–28). Thus, the factorial estimate is probably an overestimate of requirement, absorption may be greater than 50%, or stores of zinc (as hepatic metallothionein) may release zinc slowly over the first months of life to prevent acute deficiency from occuring.

Alternatively, there may be many human-milk-fed premature infants who are zinc depleted, but without frank zinc deficiency. The clinical effects of acute frank zinc deficiency include growth failure, diminished food intake, skin lesions, poor wound healing, fetal abnormalities, hair loss, decreased protein synthesis, and depressed

TABLE 8. *Characteristics of premature infants with "zinc deficiency"*
due to inadequate human milk zinc content

Birth weight (kg)	Gestational age (weeks)	Sex	Age at onset (months)	Zn content of milk (mg/liter)	Reference values[a,b] (mg/liter)
1.05[c]	27	Male	3	0.26	0.75 ± 0.3
1.98[d]	32	Male	2	0.58	0.78 ± 0.3
1.62[e]	32	Male	2	0.30	0.95 ± 0.3
1.58[e]	32	Female	2.5	0.50	0.78 ± 0.3
0.71[f]	26	Female	6.0	0.09	0.49 ± 0.4

[a]This value corresponds to the postnatal date at which the milk sample was taken.
[b]From Vuori E et al. (3).
[c]From Weymouth RD et al. (25).
[d]From Aggett PJ et al. (27).
[e]From Zimmerman AW et al. (28).
[f]From Parker PH et al. (29).

immune function (29). Cases of severe zinc deficiency are relatively easy to diagnose because of the severity of the clinical and biochemical presentation. Patients have distinctive skin lesions, diarrhea, and growth and behavioral changes. Plasma zinc levels are usually below normal. Such cases, however, are quite rare. Patients with a milder form of zinc deficiency associated with such diverse diseases as biliary atresia (30), celiac sprue (31), sickle cell disease (32), renal disease (33), and so forth, have been more frequently reported. In these cases, there is said to be an effect of zinc deficiency on growth, with associated changes in taste acuity, diminished appetite, and some behavioral changes. Biochemical confirmation of zinc deficiency is not universally present. The only definitive method of diagnosing zinc deficiency is to note the clinical and biochemical response to zinc supplementation (34).

Friel et al. have examined longitudinally the trace element status of low birthweight preterm infants during the first year of life (outside the newborn period) (35,36). They described significantly lower values for hair zinc content from preterm compared to full-term infants at 6 months of age (81 *vs.* 144 μg/g, p<0.05). Thirty-seven percent of the preterm infants at 6 months had hair zinc concentrations below 70 μg/g, the level reported by Hambidge et al. to be indicative of zinc deficiency (37), compared to only 7% of the full-term infants at that time. Median hair zinc concentrations for the male infants (preterm and full-term) were significantly lower than corresponding female values at the same age. Dietary zinc intake was also lower in the preterm compared to the term infants. Of some relevance was the finding that length at 3 months could be best predicted (using multiple regression equations) by length at birth and dietary zinc intake. These reports, although limited, support the suggestion that zinc, which plays an important role in early growth in the preterm infant, may be limiting to growth.

PARENTERALLY FED PREMATURE INFANTS

Meeting zinc intake requirements in the parenterally fed infant is not the same as for the enterally fed infant. The main difference is that with the intravenous infusion of nutrients, all of the nutrients are "absorbed" compared to the 30% to 60% absorption estimates for the enterally fed infant. Infants receiving total parenteral nutrition (TPN) may become zinc deficient when not enough zinc is included in the parenteral formulation; when growth and zinc utilization are rapid; and when urinary losses are excessive. In addition, infants born prematurely have low stores of zinc and therefore are also at risk of zinc deficiency.

Under normal conditions, fecal loss of zinc is the major excretory route (38). Infants, however, who receive no oral nutrients and who are parenterally fed, pass little stool. Losses in the urine, therefore, for the parenterally fed infant, are the main route of zinc excretion. We recently demonstrated that about 60% of parenterally infused zinc is retained. Of the zinc not retained, 87% was excreted in the urine (23), compared to 8% in healthy breast-fed full-term infants (39).

Although the renal handling of zinc is not completely understood, significant renal ultrafiltration and increased renal zinc excretion has been observed when high amounts of zinc and specific amino acids are infused together under appropriate experimental conditions (40). In plasma, zinc is mostly bound to albumin, but other proteins such as α_2-macroglobulin, and to a lesser extent transferrin, ceruloplasmin, haptoglobin, and globulins also bind zinc (41). In addition to the amount which is protein bound, a small proportion (2–3% of total zinc) also exists as an ultrafilterable fraction, mostly bound to amino acids. In their classic experiment, Prasad and Oberleas demonstrated that amino acids compete effectively with albumin, haptoglobin, transferrin, and IgG for binding of zinc (41). Of all the amino acids tested, histidine, followed by cysteine, and to a lesser extent glutamine, threonine and lysine appeared to have zinc-binding ability (41,42). This amino-acid-bound fraction, although small, exerts a significant effect on zinc homeostasis since it is this amino-acid-bound zinc which is excreted in the urine.

As previously mentioned, urinary excretion of zinc is the major source of zinc loss in the parenterally fed infant (23). Factors that increase zincuria will, therefore, further predispose the infant to zinc deficiency. Although glutamine is not included in the amino acid formulations which are most widely used in North America, commercial amino acid formulations contain significant amounts of histidine, threonine, and lysine, three amino acids that have been shown to bind zinc and increase its renal ultrafilterability (41,43). Cysteine is also present in some amino acid formulations or is available as an additive to the parenteral formulation.

The amino acids cysteine and histidine have the strongest binding affinity for zinc (41). The effect of infusions of amino acids on the enhancement of urinary zinc excretion has been demonstrated in dogs and rats (40,44) and in man (45). Cysteine infusion in dogs results in a significant rise in the percentage of ultrafilterable zinc and in urinary zinc excretion (46). Several studies, including our own earlier on cysteine metabolism in the human neonate, demonstrated that the infusion of cysteine resulted in a large urinary excretion of total cysteine (47). We felt that it was possible, therefore, that zinc was excreted in the urine bound to cysteine. In normal volunteers, the ingestion of large doses of histidine increases urinary zinc excretion to the point where zinc depletion results (45).

In two separate studies, we recently examined the effects of infusions of varying quantities of amino acids (histidine, threonine, lysine, and cysteine) on urinary zinc excretion in the parenterally fed newborn (48,49). In the first study, the effect of the infusion of high and low lysine (206 ± 34 *vs.* 158 ± 38 mg/kg/day; $x \pm SD$), threonine (147 ± 24 *vs.* 113 ± 27) and histidine (124 ± 34 *vs.* 85 ± 15) on urinary zinc excretion, were determined in 23 newborns on TPN who received similar zinc intakes (6.8 ± 1.4 μmol/kg/day) (48). Following a 72-h adaptation period, each infant had urine collected for two 24-h periods. Despite the significant difference in amino acid intakes, mean urinary zinc excretion was identical (1.58 ± 0.73 *vs.* 1.56 ± 0.63 μmol/kg/day). Hyperzincuria, therefore, did not occur when amino acids were infused at these particular rates.

In the second study, cysteine was added to the amino acid formulation, and the dosages of histidine and zinc were somewhat higher (but still within the range used in pediatric populations) (49). The effects of the infusion cysteine or no cysteine (100 *vs.* 0 mg/kg/day) and of high and low amounts of histidine (165 *vs.* 95 mg/kg/day) on urinary zinc excretion was determined in 14 newborn infants on TPN who received similar zinc intakes (~ 7 μmol/kg/day). After a 72-h adaptation period, each infant had urine collected for two 48-h periods. Urinary zinc excretion during the high-dose histidine and cysteine infusions was significantly elevated compared to the low-dose cysteine and histidine periods.

The results of this study have practical implications. There are large differences in the histidine and cysteine content of the amino acid formulations currently commercially available in North America. For example, Trophamine (Kendall McGaw Laboratories, Irvine, CA) has 4.8 g histidine and 0.23 g cysteine per 100 g amino acids, and Aminosyn (Abbott Laboratories) has 3.0 g histidine per 100 g of amino acids and no cysteine. Parenteral amino acid intake can vary between 2.0 and 3.5 g/kg/day, so histidine and cysteine intake can also vary widely. At a total amino acid intake of 2.0 g/kg/day with Trophamine and Aminosyn, histidine intakes would be 96 and 60 mg/kg/day, respectively. If total amino acid intake were 3.5 g/kg/day with the same two formulation, the intakes of histidine would be 168 and 105 g/kg/day, respectively. Based on the results from this study, the higher intake of histidine would be enough to increase zinc excretion by 65% to 86%. In a preterm infant who is already at risk of zinc deficiency, this additional urinary loss of zinc could put the infant into negative zinc balance. However, the zinc intake in the current study was approximately 40% higher than the previous dosage recommended by the AMA and 10% higher than the currently recommended dosage for the premature infant (50). The effect of high amino acid intake combined with lower zinc intake is unknown.

CONCLUSION

In summary, a discussion of the zinc requirements of the full-term and premature infant, orally and parenterally fed, has highlighted the general problems in determining dietary intake requirements for the trace minerals in infants during the first year of life.

REFERENCES

1. Stekel A. *Iron nutrition in infancy and childhood.* Nestlé Nutrition Workshop Series, vol 4. New York: Raven Press, 1984.
2. Nutrition Recommendations: The Report of the Scientific Review Committee, Health & Welfare Canada, Ottawa 1990:141.
3. Vuori E, Kuitunen P. The concentrations of copper and zinc in human milk. *Acta Paediatr Scand* 1979;68:33-7.
4. Neville MC, Keller R, Seacat J, et al. Studies in human lactation: Milk volumes in lactating women during the onset of lactation and full lactation. *Am J Clin Nutr* 1988;48:1375-86.
5. Roberts LJ, Shadwick CF, Bergstresser PR. Zinc deficiency in two full-term breast-fed infants. *J Am Acad Dermatol* 1987;16:301-4.
6. Kuramoto Y, Igarashi Y, Kato S, et al. Acquired zinc deficiency in two breast-fed mature infants. *Acta Dermatol Venereol (Stockh)* 1986;66:359-63.
7. Bye AME, Goodfellow A, Atherton DJ. Transient zinc deficiency in a full-term breast-fed infant of normal birth weight. *Pediatr Dermatol* 1985;2:308-11.
8. Sandstrom B, Cederblad A, Lonnerdal B. Zinc absorption from human milk, cow's milk and infant formula. *Am J Dis Child* 1983;137:726-9.
9. Lonnerdal B, Bell J, Hendrickx AG, et al. Affect of phytate removal on zinc absorption from soy formula. *Am J Clin Nutr* 1988;48:1301-6.
10. Zlotkin SH, Cherian G. Hepatic metallothionein as a source of zinc and cysteine during the first year of life. *Pediatr Res* 1988;24:326-9.
11. Widdowson EM, Dauncey J, Shaw JC. Trace elements in fetal and early postnatal development. *Proc Nutr Soc* 1974;33:275-84.
12. Cousins RJ. Absorption, transport, and hepatic metabolism of copper and zinc: special reference to metallothionein and ceruloplasmin. *Physiol Rev* 1985;65:238-309.
13. Webb M. Metallothionein in regeneration, reproduction and development. In: Kagi JHR, Kojima Y, eds. *Metallothionein II.* Basel-Boston: Birkhauser Verlag, 1987:483-98.
14. Gibson RS, DeWolfe MS. Changes in serum zinc concentrations of some Canadian full-term and low birthweight infants from birth to six months. *Acta Paediatr Scand* 1981;70:497-500.
15. McMaster D, Lappin TRJ, Halliday HL, Patterson CC. Serum copper and zinc levels in the preterm infant. A longitudinal study of the first year of life. *Biol Neonate* 1983;44:108-13.
16. Mason R, Bakka A, Samarawickrama GP, Webb M. Metabolism of zinc and copper in the neonate: Accumulation and function of (Zn, Cu)-metallothionein in the liver of the newborn rat. *Br J Nutr* 1980;45:375-82.
17. Templeton DM, Banarjee D, Cherian MG. Metallothionein synthesis and localization in relation to metal storage in rat liver during gestation. *Can J Biochem Cell Biol* 1985;63:16-22.
18. Clough SR, Mitra RS, Kulkarni AP. Qualitative and quantitative aspects of human fetal liver metallothioneins. *Biol Neonate* 1986;49:241-54.
19. Cavell PA, Widdowson EM. Intakes and excretions of iron, copper and zinc in the neonatal period. *Arch Dis Child* 1964;39:496-501.
20. Dauncey MJ, Shaw JCL, Urman J. The absorption and retention of magnesium, zinc and copper by low birthweight infants fed pasteurized human breast milk. *Pediatr Res* 1977;11:991-7.
21. Zlotkin SH, Anderson GH. The development of cystathionase activity during the first year of life. *Pediatr Res* 1982;16:65-8.
22. Shaw JCL. Trace elements in the fetus and young infant. *Am J Dis Child* 1979;133:1260-7.
23. Zlotkin SH, Buchanan BE. Meeting zinc and copper intake requirements in the parenterally fed preterm and full-term infant. *J Pediatr* 1983;103:441-6.
24. Hambidge KM. Trace element requirements in premature infants. In: Lebenthal E. ed. *Textbook of gastroenterology and nutrition in infancy.* New York: Raven Press, 1989;393.
25. Weymouth RD, Kelly R, Lansdell BJ. Symptomatic zinc deficiency in a premature infant. *Aust Pediatr J* 1982;18:208-10.
26. Murphy JF, Gray OP, Rendall JR, Mann S. Zinc deficiency: A problem with preterm breast milk. *Early Human Dev* 1985;10:303-7.

27. Aggett PJ, Atherton DJ, More J, et al. Symptomatic zinc deficiency in a breast-fed, preterm infant. *Arch Dis Child* 1980;55:547–50.
28. Zimmerman AW, Hambidge KM, Lepow ML, et al. Acrodermatitis in breast-fed premature infants: Evidence for a defect of mammary zinc secretion. *Pediatrics* 1982;69:176–83.
29. Parker P, Helinek GL, Meneely RL, et al. Zinc deficiency in a premature infant fed exclusively human milk. *Am J Dis Child* 1982;136:77–8.
30. Suita S, Ikeda K, Doki T, et al. Zinc status and its relations to growth retardation in children with biliary atresia. *J Pediatr Surg* 1987;22:401–5.
31. Hurry VJ, Gibson RS. The zinc, copper, and manganese status of children with malabsorption syndromes and inborn errors of metabolism. *Bio Trace Element Res* 1982;4:157–73.
32. Abshire TC, English JL, Githens JH, Hambidge KM. Zinc status in children and young adults with sickle cell disease. *Am J Dis Child* 1988;142:1356–9.
33. Reimold EW. Changes in zinc metabolism during the course of the nephrotic syndrome. *Am J Clin Nutr* 1980;134:46–50.
34. Hendricks KM, Walker WA. Zinc deficiency in inflammatory bowel disease. *Nutr Rev* 1988; 46:401–8.
35. Friel JK, Gibson RS, Kawash G, Watts JL. Dietary zinc intake and growth during infancy. *Pediatr Gastroenterol Nutr* 1985;4:746–51.
36. Friel JK, Gibson RS, Balassa R, Watts JL. A comparison of the zinc, copper, and manganese status of very low weight preterm and full-term infants during the first twelve months. *Acta Pediatr Scand* 1984;73:596–601.
37. Hambidge KM, Hambidge C, Jacobs M, Baum JD. Low levels of zinc in hair, anorexia, poor growth and hypogeusia in children. *Pediatr Res* 1972;6:868–74.
38. Cousins RJ. Absorption, transport and hepatic metabolism of copper and zinc: special reference to metallothionein and ceruloplasmin. *Physiol Rev* 1985;65:238–309.
39. Cavell PA, Widdowson EM. Intakes and excretions of iron, copper, and zinc in the neonatal period. *Arch Dis Child* 1964;39:496–501.
40. Yunice AA, King RW Jr, Kraikitpanitch S, et al. Urinary zinc excretion following infusions of zinc sulfate, cysteine, histidine, or glycine. *Am J Physiol* 1978;235: F40–5.
41. Prasad AS, Oberleas D. Binding of zinc to amino acids and serum proteins in vitro. *J Lab Clin Med* 1970;76:416–25.
42. Giroux EL, Henkin RI. Competition for zinc among serum albumin and amino acids. *Biochim Biophys Acta* 1972;273:64–72.
43. Zlotkin SH, Stalling VA, Pencharz PB. Total parenteral nutrition in children. *Pediatr Clin N Am.* 1985;32:381–400.
44. Freeman RM, Taylor PR. Influence of histidine administration on zinc metabolism in the rat. *Am J Clin Nutr* 1977;30:523–7.
45. Henkin RI, Patten BM, Re PK, et al. A syndrome of acute zinc loss, cerebellar dysfunction, mental changes, anorexia, taste and smell dysfunction. *Arch Neurol* 1975;32:745–51.
46. Abu-Hamdan DK, Migdal SD, Whitehouse R, et al. Renal handling of zinc: effect of cysteine infusion. *Am J Physiol* 1982;241:F487–94.
47. Zlotkin SH, Bryan MH, Anderson GH. Cysteine supplementation to cysteine-free intravenous feeding regimens in newborn infants. *Am J Clin Nutr* 1981;34:914–23.
48. Zlotkin SH, Buchanan BE. Amino acid intake and urinary zinc excretion in newborn infants receiving total parenteral nutrition. *Am J Clin Nutr* 1988;48:330–4.
49. Zlotkin SH. Nutrient interactions with total parenteral nutrition: Effect of histidine and cysteine intake on urinary zinc excretion. *J Pediatr* 1989;114:859.
50. American Medical Association. Guidelines for essential trace element preparations for parenteral use. *JAMA* 1979;241:2051–9.

DISCUSSION

Dr. Lönnerdal: Although we do not have comparative absorption data for Formula 1 (F1) and breast milk in human infants, we do have such data for human adults and for infant rhesus monkeys. In the human adult, absorption of zinc from breast milk is about 12% better than from F1 (42% *vs.* 30%), while in the infant monkey it is about 20% better (60% *vs.* 40%). Translating these values to the human infant it seems to me that F1 is fairly close to the borderline for producing some form of zinc deficiency—not frank deficiency, but maybe a depletion of stores. We need more sensitive measures to explore this possibility.

Dr. Zlotkin: I cannot disagree with that. In the preterm infant in particular if we looked carefully or asked the right questions we should certainly see a large number of infants with zinc deficiency. More importantly, if we had a good way to identify the problem, we should probably find many more infants with marginal deficiency. There have been few studies in preterm survivors which have looked at marginal deficiency, but there is evidence that hair zinc is lower in the preterm population than in controls.

Dr. Lombeck: I have seen data from Professor Manz's group on 20 to 30 preterm infants with severe zinc deficiency. They had skin lesions, diarrhea, feeding difficulties, and failure to thrive. They had very low plasma zinc and decreased plasma alkaline phosphatase. After zinc supplementation they recovered quickly. In my view, we should be looking for signs of zinc deficiency more often, even in healthy infants.

Dr. Hashke: We did a prospective study on 40 preterm infants on various formulas providing between 2 and 4 mg zinc per liter. These infants were followed to 6 months of age and we did not find a single case of zinc deficiency, either clinically or biochemically, using serum and hair zinc estimations.

Dr. Zlotkin: Could Dr. Lonnerdal tell us about his studies on rhesus monkeys. What measures best reflected marginal deficiency?

Dr. Lönnerdal: Serum zinc levels and hair zinc are not satisfactory measures of marginal deficiency. It seems that stores are utilized for a prolonged period. However, we found that marginally deficient rhesus monkey infants absorbed a much higher proportion of dietary zinc than well nourished controls.

Dr. Chandra: Another index of marginal deficiency relates to immunologic function. Preterm babies normally take between 3 and 6 months to catch up immunologically with fullterm babies (measuring thymulin activity, mitogen responses, numbers of mature T cells), but when given a zinc supplement of 4 to 5 mg per day, the time period for catch up is only 4 to 8 weeks.

Dr. Marini: In relation to preterm babies, it is important to distinguish those that have intrauterine growth retardation from the remainder, because their stores are likely to be different. So far as clinical deficiency is concerned, one estimation that may be worthwhile is the liver fraction of alkaline phosphatase, which may be depressed in deficiency states. I remember a case of pronounced zinc deficiency in a surgical case in which this was the only abnormal biochemical finding. On zinc supplementation, the liver alkaline phosphatase returned to normal.

It may be that exchange between various trace element pools in the body is limited. For example the body iron content is quite large, but it seems that there is relatively poor exchange between the pools since in both experimental animals and humans with mild anemia, there may be relatively well preserved red cell iron but coexistent signs of extrahematologic iron deficiency such as depressed function of some iron-dependent enzymes.

Dr. Oster: You mentioned a drop in the zinc and selenium content of human milk with lactation time. Do you have any idea what this decrease in trace element content through lactation means? Is it an adaptation to the needs of the child, which seems unlikely, or could it be a reflection of declining maternal trace element status during lactation?

Dr. Zlotkin: I certainly don't think it is the latter. There is little evidence to suggest that the trace element status of lactating women decreases to the point where zinc content of milk falls by 75% over the lactation period. I think there is a change in the function of the mammary gland which allows this normal physiologic alteration in the amount of zinc passing into the milk, independent of the mother's nutritional status.

Trace Elements in Nutrition of Children—II,
edited by Ranjit K. Chandra, Nestlé Nutrition
Workshop Series, Vol. 23, Nestec Ltd.,
Vevey/Raven Press, Ltd., New York © 1991.

Zinc in the Nutrition of Children

K. Michael Hambidge

University of Colorado, Health Sciences Center, Denver, Colorado 80262, USA

Interest in human zinc nutriture unfolded about 30 years ago. Since then, there has been substantial progress in our understanding of the importance of zinc in human nutrition. It has become apparent that, at a molecular and cellular level, zinc has a central role at all stages of the cell cycle and in a wide variety of metabolic pathways. Human zinc deficiency has been identified or proposed in a wide range of circumstances and severe deficiency states have been reasonably well characterized. Despite these recent advances in our understanding of the role of zinc in human nutrition, however, many unanswered questions remain.

From a practical point of view, to those interested in the nutrition of children, the most tantalizing questions relate to mild zinc deficiency states. There is evidence to suggest that mild zinc deficiency occurs quite frequently in infants and children, in contrast to the relatively rare occurrence of severe, readily identified zinc deficiency states. Yet the evidence for the existence of these milder zinc deficiency syndromes is still quite slender and their clinical importance has not been well characterized. The purpose of this chapter is to undertake a review of our current understanding of mild zinc deficiency in children, with special attention to the results of research undertaken at the University of Colorado School of Medicine. Questions addressed include: Does mild zinc deficiency occur in children? If so, in what circumstances and what is the clinical significance? What are dietary zinc requirements in childhood and why does zinc deficiency occur?

TISSUE ZINC CONCENTRATIONS AND INDICES OF ZINC NUTRITIONAL STATUS

Tissue zinc concentrations change very little even in the most severe zinc deficiency states. The total body deficit in severely zinc-depleted rats has been calculated at approximately 20% (1), but they are severely growth-retarded. Although there are conflicting data on loss of zinc from bone as a result of zinc deficiency, in this study a high percentage of zinc loss was from bone, where its metabolic importance, except in the epiphyseal region, is uncertain. Most tissues, including skeletal muscle, had no measurable decline in zinc concentration in this or other studies. Jackson (2) calculated that a similar loss of zinc occurred in severe human zinc deficiency. It has also been hypothesized that there must be depletion of one or more small but physiologically important body pools of zinc which contribute relatively little to the total cell content, and the depletion of which cannot be easily detected by measurements of total body zinc. The demonstration of changes in hepatic metallothionein and corresponding changes in hepatic zinc at different stages of the life cycle that are discussed by Zlotkin in his chapter (this volume) provide support for this concept.

Partly because of the lack of marked changes in tissue zinc concentrations, laboratory indices for the detection of milder zinc deficiency states remain unsatisfactory (3). Specific, sensitive, functional indices are also lacking at present.

EVIDENCE FOR THE OCCURRENCE OF MILD ZINC DEFICIENCY IN CHILDREN

The detection of mild zinc deficiency states is complicated not only by the lack of adequate indices of zinc nutriture but also by the lack of specific clinical features. In these circumstances, the most reliable approach is usually that of a carefully designed, randomized, controlled study of dietary zinc supplementation with physiological quantities of zinc. It is preferable that the functional variables to be monitored are not affected pharmacologically by zinc. Growth velocity provides a good example. Animal studies have shown quite clearly that additional zinc beyond an optimal level of intake does not lead to an increased rate of growth (4). These same studies have shown a graded response in impairment of growth velocity when dietary zinc is progressively decreased below the minimum level required to maintain maximal growth velocity. This is an example of research in animal models that has demonstrated a spectrum of zinc deficiency depending on the severity of restriction of available zinc in the diet. This type of observation is strongly supportive of the concept of mild human zinc deficiency states.

To date, the primary focus of research in Denver and elsewhere that has been designed to detect the occurrence of mild zinc deficiency in infants and children has been on physical growth rates. Two of the earlier zinc supplementation studies involved low-income Denver preschool children who were selected on the basis of low height-for-age percentiles. In each of these randomized, controlled, and double-blind studies, zinc supplementation was associated with a modest, statistically significant increase in growth velocity over the study period of 6 months or 1 year (5–7). Growth percentiles of these young children, who were primarily Hispanic, typically started to decline in later infancy or during the second year of life. At that time they presented with a characteristic pattern of nonorganic failure to thrive with a decline in weight-for-length percentiles prior to any decline in length-for-age. The response to zinc supplementation under randomized controlled conditions in the preschool children suggested that part of the poor growth of these subjects was attributable to zinc deficiency. Thus it was hypothesized that zinc deficiency started relatively early in postnatal life and contributed to the onset of failure to thrive in infancy or during the second year. Accordingly, a further randomized, double-blind controlled study of dietary zinc supplementation was undertaken with the aim of determining whether early intervention, soon after weight-for-length percentiles started to decline, would contribute to the arrest and reversal of this decline. In this study, mean increases in weight-for-length Z scores of infants and toddlers (mean age 15 months) treated with zinc at 60 μmol (4 mg) per day were significantly greater than for the placebo-treated subjects (8). These differences were significant for the sexes combined (25 pairs of subjects) and for the males. There was a similar trend ($p = 0.056$) for the girls.

A similar growth response has recently been documented in a subgroup of school children (aged 6–8 years) in Ontario, Canada (9). These children had height-for-age below the 15th percentile. The subgroup of 16 children was identified on the basis of low hair zinc concentrations. The results of an earlier supplementation study (10) in Denver had indicated that the growth rates of normal term, formula-fed male infants are sensitive to the zinc concentration in cow's milk formulas.

The small number of participants in these studies underlines the need for caution in interpreting these data. However, the combined results do provide considerable support for the hypothesis that growth-limiting mild zinc deficiency can occur in children. Additional evidence and other effects of mild zinc deficiency will be considered in subsequent sections.

CIRCUMSTANCES IN WHICH MILD HUMAN ZINC DEFICIENCY HAS BEEN IDENTIFIED

Subjects included in the studies cited in the previous section were apparently quite normal apart from mild deviations from normal growth patterns. Thus, mild zinc deficiency appears to occur in some children in the free-living population in whom there is no evidence of other specific nutrient deficiencies apart from relatively low energy intakes. These studies have indicated that this syndrome is not limited to any one ethnic, socioeconomic, or age group between birth and adolescence. Although mild zinc deficiency has been well documented only in males, it appears probable that females can also be affected.

Supportive, although not definitive, evidence for the occurrence of this syndrome has come from other countries including Beijing, China, where a pilot study involved a relatively large number of children (11).

There is evidence that the clinical course of malnourished infants and children in less developed countries can be complicated by zinc deficiency. The most extensive studies have been in Kingston, Jamaica (12–16). Additional data have been provided by the results of a randomized controlled study of zinc supplementation in malnourished infants in Chile (17).

Apart from the studies in the Middle East which were the first to indicate that an inadequate intake of zinc may lead to human zinc deficiency (18), surprisingly few investigations of zinc nutrition in adolescents have been reported. A recent study of aboriginal children and adolescents with growth retardation failed to show any significant effects of zinc supplementation on growth velocity (19). A linear relationship has been observed between serum zinc and circulating testosterone levels in children with constitutional growth retardation (20). However, the interrelationships between testosterone, growth hormone, and zinc nutrition in the human require further study (21). There are limited data to suggest that zinc deficiency may contribute to the clinical features of anorexia nervosa (22), but more definitive, large-scale studies are needed.

Clinical Significance

The full clinical significance of mild zinc deficiency in children is not yet understood. The primary focus of attention has been on growth velocity in studies primarily designed to determine the existence of evidence for the occurrence of zinc deficiency. In one of the Denver studies (23), zinc supplementation was associated with a significant increase in calculated energy and protein intakes compared with the control (placebo) group. The increment raised average energy intakes from an undesirably low level to a recommended level over the study period. Taste perception may be impaired, but earlier observations (24) require more rigorous evaluation. Abnormalities of the immune system might reasonably be anticipated, but reports in children have been limited primarily to less developed countries. In Jamaica, topical zinc application was associated with improvement in delayed cutaneous hypersensitivity in malnourished children (13). Zinc deficiency has also been indicated as a cause of an abnormally small thymus (12). In Chile (17), zinc-supplemented children had a lower incidence of skin infections, a decrease in the incidence of anergy, and an increase in serum IgA. In non-breast-fed Amazonian infants, zinc supplementation was associated with higher salivary secretory IgA levels (25). In Denver, a study is currently in progress to determine the effects of zinc supplementation on one index of early brain development. The study group is from the same primarily low-income Hispanic population that has been the target of several of the previous Denver studies.

MILD ZINC DEFICIENCY: ETIOLOGICAL CONSIDERATIONS

The free-living children in North America who have been shown to have evidence of mild zinc deficiency were apparently quite normal apart from relatively poor growth. Although genetic factors cannot be entirely ruled out, these observations suggest that dietary zinc intake was inadequate to meet their requirements. In this section, available data on the zinc intake of these subjects will be reviewed. These data will then be evaluated in relation to what is known about dietary zinc requirements in young children. By this means, it will be determined if the concept of a mild dietary deficiency of zinc appears to be tenable in the current state of knowledge.

TABLE 1. *Calculated dietary zinc intakes of placebo-treated children participating in zinc supplementation studies*

	Reference	Age (yrs)	Dietary Zn[a] μmol/day	(mg/day)
Studies with evidence of growth response to zinc	Walravens et al. 1989 (8)	1.25 (0.75–2.0)	69 ± 15[a]	(4.5 ± 1.0)
	Walravens et al. 1983 (6)	4.30 (2–6)	70 ± 28	(4.6 ± 1.8)
	Gibson et al. 1989 (9)	6.75 (6–8)	99 ± 31	(6.5 ± 2.0)
Study with no growth response to zinc	Hambidge et al. 1979 (27)	4.90 (3–7)	96 ± 46	(6.3 ± 3.0)

[a]Mean ± 1 SD.

The inaccuracies of dietary records are well known as is the tendency to exaggerate intakes when these are poor. Furthermore, records could be obtained from only a minority of the Denver families. With these limitations in mind, calculated dietary zinc intakes of placebo-treated control subjects in the Denver and Canadian studies are given in Table 1. These intakes ranged from a calculated average of 69 μmol (4.5 mg) Zn/day for the Denver toddlers and preschool children to 100 μmol (6.5 mg) Zn/day average for the Canadian school-age children.

Approximately half of the control (placebo) group of Denver toddlers continued to have a decline in weight-for-age Z scores during the six-month study period. The other half maintained or increased their initial weight-for-age Z scores, as did virtually all of the zinc-treated subjects (8). These findings suggest that the "average basal" zinc requirement, (i.e., the level of intake that is adequate for 50% of the population) for older infants and toddlers is approximately 69 μmol (4.5 mg) Zn/day.

Table 2 includes calculations for "low-risk" requirements based on these clinical studies. These were derived from basal requirements by adding 30%. The figure of

TABLE 2. *Estimation of daily zinc requirements[a]*

	Source of Data				
	Clinical			Factorial	
Age (yrs)	μmol	mg	ref	μmol	mg
1.25	89	(5.8)	(8)	73–92	(4.8–6.0)
4.3	92	(6.0)	(6)	80–110	(5.2–7.2)
6.75	128	(8.4)	(9)	92–116	(6.0–7.6)

[a]Requirement refers to "low-risk" requirement.

30% is that used for protein with which zinc is closely associated biologically. This is also similar to the variation (2 SD) for minimal fecal losses of endogenous zinc (26).

In accord with these calculations, there was no growth response to zinc supplementation in children with an average age of 4.9 years whose mean dietary zinc intake was 9 μmol (6.3 mg) Zn/day (27) (i.e., higher than the calcuated "low-risk" requirement) (Table 1).

Is it possible to begin to assess the validity of these calculations using an independent approach? Historically, balance studies have been used to try to calculate requirements for minerals and trace elements. It is now realized that this approach is compromised for some elements including zinc by the ability of the body to adapt and thus to maintain balance in the face of widely varying dietary intakes of these elements. Despite this major limitation, it is of some interest to review published data on zinc balance in preadolescent children.

In a series of balance studies in preadolescent girls performed at the Virginia Polytechnic Institute, balance was generally near equilibrium or positive with zinc intakes ranging from 69 μmol (4.5 mg) to 223 μmol (14.6 mg) Zn/day. It was concluded (28) that an intake of 107 to 122 μmol (7–8 mg) Zn/day was adequate to meet requirements of preadolescent girls including retention required for growth. Earlier studies had indicated that 42 μmol (2.75 mg) dietary zinc was required for zero balance excluding dermal losses (29). With an allowance for sweat losses and for growth, assuming 25% absorption, this suggests a dietary requirement of about 75 μmol (5 mg) Zn/day. On the basis of the results of over 150 balance studies in infants and young children, Ziegler et al. (30) concluded that an average of 3.2 μmol (0.21 mg) Zn/kg/day was needed to achieve balance. To achieve balance in all subjects, it was calculated that an intake of 12.5 μmol (0.82 mg) Zn/kg/day was needed (not including an allowance for growth). Not surprisingly, these balance data cover a wide range. This range does bracket the estimations of requirements derived from the clinical studies and thus helps establish the credibility of the latter estimations.

Incidentally, the notable ability of the human, or at least the adult human, to adapt to an extremely wide range of zinc intake (31,32), including a very low intake, raises the question of why mild zinc deficiency states should occur. Although the answer to this is not altogether clear, several points merit consideration. First, it has not been determined if the ability of the infant and child to adapt to low zinc intake is comparable to that of the adult. If so, it would seem quite likely that the adaptive process might include a slowing of growth rates which would decrease requirements. Furthermore, it is by no means clear, even in the adult, to what extent adaptation can overcome the effects of dietary components that tend to inhibit zinc absorption. It has been shown in the case of iron absorption that there is neither short-term nor long-term adaptation capable of overcoming the inhibitory effects of dietary phytate (33).

Although a factorial approach has, to some extent, the same limitations as traditional balance techniques and is hampered by lack of adequate data, it is informative

to consider what can be learned from factorial estimates of dietary zinc requirements. Moreover, with careful acquisition of data, utilizing sophisticated stable isotope techniques, and with careful interpretation of these data, this approach has
considerable future potential. A factorial estimate of dietary zinc requirements will
first be considered for the infant, for whom information is more extensive than for
the child.

Requirements for growth are relatively high in the first 4 postnatal months (34)
but are quite modest for the older infant (Fig. 1). On a bodyweight basis, urine zinc
excretion rates have declined to the adult range of ≤0.15 μmol (10 μg) kg/day by 2
months of age even in the premature infant (Hambidge KM, Krebs NF, unpublished
data). Sweat losses in the child have not been measured adequately, but, extrapolat-
ing from the adult (35), they are likely to be very similar to or less than urine losses.
These losses, like growth requirements, are quite small. Calculated requirements for
"net" absorption are, therefore quite modest [≤ 8μmol (0.5 mg) Zn/day] in later
infancy. This may apply also to the young infant if, contrary to previous concepts,
some neonatal stores are available for postnatal use. Zlotkin's data in his chapter
(this volume) indicate that there may be a significant neonatal hepatic copper store
that could help to offset the high-growth requirements of the young infant.

In order to calculate "physiological requirements", it is also necessary to know
the quantity of endogenous zinc excreted in the feces. Information on these losses is
not yet available, apart from some approximate calculations reported for the first 6
months (36). The calculated figures for fecal excretion of endogenous zinc in this report were 1.2 μmol (78 μg) Zn/kg/day on a formula containing 15.3 μmol (1 mg)
Zn/l, and 19.7 μmol (129 μg) Zn/kg/day on a formula containing 92 μmol (6 mg)
Zn/liter. The lower of these figures has been used in Fig. 1. It can be seen from this
figure that, subject to confirmation, endogenous fecal losses of zinc have a major
impact on calculations of physiological requirements. The latter average approximately 15.3 μmol (1 mg) Zn/day throughout the first 6 months, giving a "low-risk"
physiological requirement of 20 μmol (1.3 mg) Zn/day.

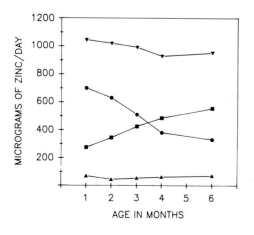

FIG. 1. Factorial estimate of physiological zinc requirements of male infants.
Growth requirements and urine and
sweat losses from Krebs NF et al. (34).
Losses of endogenous zinc in feces from
Ziegler EE et al. (36). ▲, urine and sweat
losses; ■, fecal excretion of endogenous
zinc; ●, growth requirement; ▼, estimated basal physiological requirement.

Physiological requirements have to be divided by fractional ("true") absorption in order to calculate dietary zinc requirements. Use of a figure of 0.3 (30%) for fractional absorption of zinc by formula-fed infants (37) gives an estimated "low-risk" dietary requirement of approximately 61.2 μmol (4 mg) Zn/day. Unless treated with phytase, calculated dietary zinc requirements will be considerably higher for the infant fed a soy protein formula.

This is an appropriate point to digress to the zinc intake of the fully breast-fed infant. With some exceptions, which may partly depend on maternal zinc intake (38), the zinc status of the breast-fed infant during the first 6 weeks is considered to be especially favorable (39). Yet the zinc intake of the fully breast-fed infant averages 26 μmol (1.7 mg) Zn/day at 0 to 3 months and only 13.8 μmol (0.9 mg) Zn/day at 4 to 6 months (40), that is, less than the calculated physiological requirement. These figures suggest two hypotheses: (i) the reabsorption of endogenous zinc secreted into the gastrointestinal tract is especially favorable in breast-fed infants, and results in a substantially lower fecal excretion of endogenous zinc and thus a substantially lower physiological zinc requirement; and (ii) percentage absorption of zinc by the fully breast-fed infant is considerably higher than the reported figures (averaging 40–60%) when zinc absorption from breast milk is measured in adults (37). This hypothesis is supported by other observations (41). While the zinc intake of fully breast-fed infants provided an excellent indicator of minimal dietary zinc requirements of young infants in optimal circumstances, it clearly does not provide a measure of zinc requirements of infants fed with various categories of infant formulas.

Returning to a discussion of requirements based on a factorial approach, growth requirements are relatively small throughout later infancy, childhood, and even during adolescence (Fig. 2). For adult males, average minimal endogenous losses have

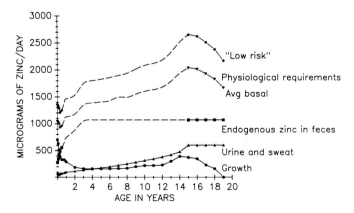

FIG. 2. Factorial estimate of physiological zinc requirements of male children. Requirements for growth calculated as follows: ≤ 10 yrs, g/day increase in lean body mass × 30 μg Zn/g; 11 to 18 years, g/day increase in body weight × 23. Estimated minimum urine and sweat losses: 6 μg Zn/kg/day each < maximum of 300 μg Zn/kg/day each. Fecal losses of endogenous zinc: infants aged 0 to 6 months from Ziegler EE et al. (36); adults from Baer MT et al. (26) (adolescents assumed to be same as adult).

been reported to be 25.5 μmol (1.67 mg) Zn/day (26), including about 16.8 μmol (1.1 mg) endogenous Zn/day in feces. This gives a calculated "low-risk" adult physiological requirement of 2.2 mg Zn/day (Fig. 2), or at 25% absorption, a calculated "low-risk" dietary zinc requirement for the adult male of 138 μmol (9 mg).

No data are available on the fecal excretion of endogenous zinc in children or infants beyond the age of 6 months. In Fig. 2 fecal losses of endogenous zinc during adolescence are assumed to be comparable to those of the adult. A very tentative estimate of fecal losses of endogenous zinc across childhood has been depicted by connecting uncertain data for the young infant and adolescent with a straight (broken) line. A corresponding dotted line depicts the tentative calculations of physiological requirements for the older infant and child. An alternative but equally feasible hypothetical estimation of fecal excretion of endogenous zinc and hence of physiological zinc requirements across childhood is depicted in Fig. 3. Calculations of "low-risk" dietary zinc requirements from these estimations of physiological requirements, assuming 25% absorption, are given in Table 2. For the two Denver studies, these figures match quite well with the corresponding figures calculated from the clinical data that have been considered earlier. The comparison is less good for the Canadian study.

The very tentative nature of these factorial calculations must be re-emphasized. With this important proviso, it is concluded that, as with balance data, these factorial calculations are reasonably compatible with the calculations based on the clinical data. Thus, the latter calculations appear to be credible pending more precise experimental data on which to base estimates of dietary zinc requirements.

The corollary to this conclusion is that, at least in the Denver studies in which zinc supplementation was associated with a growth response, the average calculated dietary zinc intakes were indeed low enough to be associated with a risk of zinc deficiency. These calculated levels of intake are not much lower than calculated intakes for apparently normal children of similar age (27). Thus, these observations

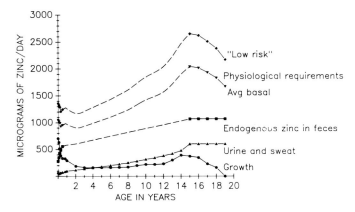

FIG. 3. Same as Fig. 2, except for alternative hypothetical pattern of change in fecal losses of endogenous zinc with age.

suggest that quite subtle variations in dietary zinc intake and/or bioavailability of dietary zinc may lead to a syndrome of mild zinc deficiency in which physical growth rates are impaired.

ZINC TOXICITY

Until recently, zinc has been regarded as a relatively nontoxic micronutrient with an extremely wide range between normal dietary intakes and a potentially toxic dose. It is now known that intakes only five times the average dietary intake in this country can lead to biochemical evidence of copper deficiency (42). Measures by which such intakes are likely to be achieved are through zinc-containing vitamin-mineral preparations or the enthusiastic consumption of zinc-fortified breakfast cereals. Any measures to prevent zinc deficiency should be undertaken with caution, using the minimum effective quantity of zinc.

CONCLUSIONS

Mild growth-limiting zinc deficiency, apparently of dietary origin, has been found to occur in some otherwise normal infants and children. Though the incidence and epidemiology of this mild zinc deficiency state is not well understood, there is evidence that its occurrence is not limted to any one socioeconomic or ethnic group. It appears to have a wide geographic distribution. Although more evident in males, it probably also occurs in females. Further research is required to determine the full extent of the clinical significance of this mild zinc deficiency state. A better insight into the etiology of these mild zinc deficiency states will depend on a clearer definition of physiological and dietary requirements for zinc in infancy and childhood.

ACKNOWLEDGMENT

The original work undertaken by the author to which reference is made in this paper was supported in part by a grant from the National Institutes of Health, NIAD-DKD, 5R22 AMI2432, and grant RR-69 from National Institutes of Health, General Clinical Research Center.

REFERENCES

1. Jackson, MR, Jones DA, Edwards RHT. Tissue zinc levels as an index of body zinc status. *Clin Physiol* 1982;2:333–43.
2. Jackson MJ. Zinc and di-iodohydroxyquinoline therapy in acrodermatitis enteropathica. *J Clin Pathol* 1977;30:284–7.
3. Hambidge KM. Assessing the trace element status of man. *Proc Nutr Soc* 1988;47:37–44.

4. Williams RB, Mills CF. The experimental production of zinc deficiency in the rat. *Br J Nutr* 1970;24:989–1003.
5. Hambidge KM,Walravens PA. Zinc supplementation of low income preschool children. In: Kirchgessner M, ed. *Trace element metabolism in man and amimals, 3*. Weihenstephan: Arbeitskreis fier tierernahrungs-forschung, 1978:296–99.
6. Walravens PA, Krebs NF, Hambidge KM. Linear growth of low-income preschool children receiving a zinc supplement. *Am J Clin Nutr* 1983;38:195–201.
7. Hambidge KM, Krebs NF, Walravens A. Growth velocity of young children receiving a dietary zinc supplement. *Nutr Res* 1985;1:306–16.
8. Walravens PA, Hambidge KM, Koepfer DM. Zinc supplementation in infants with a nutritional pattern of failure to thrive: A double-blind, controlled study. *Pediatrics* 1989;83:532–8.
9. Gibson RS, Vanderkooy PDS, MacDonald AC, Goldman A, Ryan BA, Berry M. A growth-limiting mild zinc deficiency syndrome in some Southern Ontario boys with low-height percentiles. *Am J Clin Nutr* 1989;49:1266–73.
10. Walravens PA, Hambidge KM. Growth of infants fed a zinc-supplemented formula. *Am J Clin Nutr* 1976;29:1114–21.
11. Xue-Cun C, Tai-An Y, Jin-Sheng H, Qiu-Yan M, Zhi-Min H, Li-Xiang L. Low levels of zinc in hair and blood, pica, anorexia, and poor growth in Chinese preschool children. *Am J Clin Nutr* 1989;42:694–700.
12. Golden MHN, Jackson AA, Golden BE. Effect of zinc on thymus of recently malnourished children. *Lancet* 1977;2:1057–9.
13. Golden MHN, Golden BE, Harland PSEG, Jackson AA. Zinc and immunocompetence in protein-energy malnutrition. *Lancet* 1978;1:1226–8.
14. Golden BE, Golden MHN. Plasma zinc and the clinical features of malnutrition. *Am J Clin Nutr* 1979;32:2490–4.
15. Golden BE, Golden MHN. Plasma zinc, rate of weight gain, and the energy cost of tissue deposition in children recovering from severe malnutrition on a cow's milk or soya protein based diet. *Am J Clin Nutr* 1981;34:892–9.
16. Golden MHN, Golden BE. Effect of zinc supplementation on the dietary intake, rate of weight gain, and energy cost of tissue deposition in children recovering from severe malnutrition. *Am J Clin Nutr* 1981;34:900–8.
17. Castillo-Duran C, Heresi G, Fisberg M, Uauy R. Controlled trial of zinc supplementation during recovery from malnutrition: Effects on growth and immune function. *Am J Clin Nutr* 1987;45:602–8.
18. Prasad AS. A century of research on the metabolic role of zinc. *Am J Clin Nutr* 1969;22:1215–21.
19. Smith RM, King RA, Spargo RM, Cheek DB, Field JB. Zinc, iron, and copper in the nutrition of Australian aboriginal children. In: Hurley LS, Keen CL, Lonnerdal B, Rucker RB, eds. *Trace elements in man and animals, 6*. New York: Plenum Press, 1988:163–72.
20. Castro-Magana M, Collipp PJ, Chen SY, Cheruvanky T, Maddaiah VT. Zinc nutritional status, androgens, and growth retardation. *Am J Dis Child* 1981;135:322–5.
21. Hambidge KM, Casey CE, Krebs NF. Zinc. In: Mertz W, ed. *Trace elements in human and animal nutrition*, 5th Edition, vol 2. Florida: Academic Press, 1986:1–137.
22. Katz RL, Keen CL, Litt IF, Hurley LS, Kellams-Harrison KM, Glader LJ. Zinc deficiency in anorexia nervosa. *J Adol Health Care* 1987;8:400–6.
23. Krebs NF, Hambidge KM, Walravens PA. Increased food intake of young children receiving a zinc supplement. *Am J Dis Child* 1984;138:270–3.
24. Hambidge KM, Hambidge C, Jacobs MA, Baum JD. Low levels of zinc in hair, anorexia, poor growth, and hypoguesia in children. *Pediatr Res* 1972;6:868–74.
25. Shrimpton R, Marinho HA, Rocha YS, Alencar FH. Zinc supplementation in urban Amazonian mothers: Concentrations of Zn and retinol in maternal serum and milk. *Proc Nutr Soc* 1983;42:122A.
26. Baer MT, King JC. Tissue zinc levels and zinc excretion during experimental zinc depletion in young men. *Am J Clin Nutr* 1984;39:556–70.
27. Hambidge KM, Chavez MN, Brown RM, Walravens PA. Zinc nutritional status of young middle-income children and the effects of consuming zinc-fortified breakfast cereals. *Am J Clin Nutr* 1979;32:2532–9.
28. Ritchey SJ, Korslund MK, Gilbert LM, Fay DC, Robinson MF. Zinc retention and losses of zinc in sweat by preadolescent girls. *Am J Clin Nutr* 1979;32:799–803.
29. Engel RW, Miller RF, Price NO. In: Prasad AS, ed. *Zinc metabolism*. Springfield, Illinois: Thomas, 1966:326.

30. Ziegler EE, Edwards BB, Jensen RL, Filer LJ, Fomon SJ. Zinc balance studies in normal infants. In: Kirchgessner M, ed. *Trace element metabolism in man and animals, 3.* Weihenstephan:Arbeitskreis fur Tierernahrungs forschung, 1978:292–9.
31. Jackson MJ, Jones DA, Edwards RHT. Zinc homeostasis in man: Studies using a new stable isotope-dilution technique. *Brit J Nutr* 1984;51:199–208.
32. Wada L, Turnlund JR, King JC. Zinc utilization in young men fed adequate- and low-zinc intakes. *J Nutr* 1985;115:1345–54.
33. Brune M, Rossander L, Hallberg L. Iron absorption: No intestinal adaptation to a high-phytate diet. *Am J Clin Nutr* 1989;49:542–5.
34. Krebs NF, Hambidge KM. Zinc requirements and zinc intakes of breast fed infants. *Am J Clin Nutr* 1986;43:288–92.
35. Milne DB, Canfield WK, Mahalko JR, Sandstead HH. Effect on dietary zinc on whole body surface loss of zinc: Impact on estimation of zinc retention by balance method. *Am J Clin Nutr* 1983;38:181–6.
36. Ziegler EE, Figueroa-Colon R, Serfass RE, Nelson SE. Effect of low dietary zinc on zinc metabolism in infancy: Stable isotope studies. *Am J Clin Nutr* 1987;45:849(A).
37. Sandstrom B, Cederblad A, Lonnerdal B. Zinc absorption from human milk, cow's milk, and infant formulas. *Am J Dis Child* 1983;137:726–9.
38. Krebs NF, Hambidge KM, Jacobs MA, Oliva-Rasbach J. The effects of a dietary zinc supplement during lactation on longitudinal changes in maternal zinc status and milk zinc concentrations. *Am J Clin Nutr* 1985;41:560–70.
39. Hambidge KM, Walravens PA, Casey CE, Brown RM, Bender C. Plasma zinc concentrations of breast fed infants. *J Pediatr* 1979;94:607–8.
40. Casey CE, Neville MC, Hambidge KM. Studies in human lactation: Secretion of zinc, copper, and manganese in human milk. *Am J Clin Nutr* 1989;49:773–85.
41. Zimmerman AW, Hambidge KM, Lepow ML, Greenberg RD, Stover ML, Casey CE. Acrodermatitis in breast-fed premature infants: Evidence for defect of mammary zinc secretion. *Pediatrics* 1982;69:176–83.
42. Yadrick MK, Kenney MA, Winterfeldt EA. Iron, copper, and zinc status: Response to supplementation with zinc or zinc and iron in adult females. *Am J Clin Nutr* 1989;49:145–50.

DISCUSSION

Dr. Chapparwal: A zinc deficiency state may be detected by measuring serum zinc levels. Mild zinc deficiency has been found in acute diarrhea and protein-energy malnutrition.

Dr. Hambidge: In the Denver and Canadian studies the infants, toddlers, and school-age children had normal plasma or serum zinc concentrations. I think we are talking here about a zinc deficiency state that is mild enough to escape detection by a decline in plasma or serum zinc. If the hypozincemia you mention is attributable to zinc deficiency it would suggest a more severe degree of deficiency than I have been discussing.

Dr. Zlotkin: Most of the studies which have looked for marginal zinc deficiency have been in males. Would you comment on the requirement for females, and why they should be different from males.

Dr. Hambidge: The pattern of growth response was very similar in females and males. The *p* value of 0.056 indicates a trend not quite reaching conventional significance. There is a small difference in growth rates and in increase in body mass favoring males and I think this may be enough to make males more vulnerable to marginal zinc deficiency.

Dr. Haschke: Do you have data on serum cholesterol and copper in the infants who were supplemented with zinc? Do foods records show that food intake increased on supplementation and what were the zinc intakes?

Dr. Hambidge: We looked at cholesterol and copper in our earliest supplementation study and found no difference at all in the levels. Food intake data have been difficult to obtain. We were only able to get serial records in a small proportion of the population. These were the data I have presented already and the average zinc intake was about 4.5 mg/day. We have some concern that these records may be exaggerated in this low income population. I know that, in general, records tend to give an underestimate rather than an overestimate, but I am concerned that with this population it could be the other way round. So far as the effects of zinc supplementation on food intake are concerned, we showed an increased intake in pre-school children in the previous study, but could not show a difference in the current one. However, this remains open to question because of the limitations of the data.

Dr. Mertz: There is a sad lack of diagnostic tools for exploring zinc deficiency. Do you have any experience in using serum metallothionein measurements?

Dr. Hambidge: I have had no experience with metallothionein research in Denver.

Dr. Aggett: Dr. Zlotkin has already outlined the principal characteristics of metallothionein. It is a cysteine-rich protein of relative molecular mass 6000. It has the ability to bind zinc, copper, cadmium, and some other elements. It seems that zinc is a prime inducer of metallothionein and in the absence of zinc, e.g. in pure zinc deficiency in animal models, metallothionein is not synthesized, even when the animals are exposed to high cadmium intakes. Much work on metallothionein has been done by Dr. Ian Bremner and his team at the Rowett Research Institute, Aberdeen, Scotland. In stress states they find that metallothionein is induced, and hypozincemia develops, with accumulation of zinc in the tissues in association with metallothionein, principally in the liver. Some of this hepatic metallothionein may leak into the circulation and a good correlation between circulating metallothionein and hepatic metallothionein has been shown. In contrast, with zinc deficiency, hepatic metallothionein is low; thus, the opportunity exists to distinguish the hypozincemia of stress from that of zinc deficiency. These are encouraging developments and their potential for the study of zinc metabolism in humans is obvious.

Trace Elements in Nutrition of Children—II,
edited by Ranjit K. Chandra, Nestlé Nutrition
Workshop Series, Vol. 23, Nestec Ltd.,
Vevey/Raven Press, Ltd., New York © 1991.

Selenium in the Nutrition of Infants: Influence of the Maternal Selenium Status

Peter Brätter, V. E. Negretti de Brätter, U. Rösick,
and *H. B. von Stockhausen

*Hahn–Meitner-Institut Berlin, Department of Trace Element Research; and *University
Children's Hospital, Würzburg, Federal Republic of Germany*

After delivery, the infant has to develop and maintain his or her own regulatory systems including the antioxidant system. Because selenium, as part of the enzyme glutathione peroxidase, is essential for the proper functioning of a number of cellular defense mechanisms, a sufficient supply of selenium for the infant has to be guaranteed. In this connection, the feeding practice adopted by the mother is an important factor. It is generally assumed that breast milk contains adequate amounts of trace elements to satisfy the growing demands of healthy infants. On the other hand, the selenium content of breast milk reflects the maternal selenium intake via food, so that the selenium status of the infant depends entirely on the nutritional status of the nursing mother. Presently, work data on infants' selenium supply from breast milk and formulas are given, using the infants' serum selenium concentration as an index. Furthermore, data on selenium in breast milk are presented and discussed with respect to regional variation, maternal dietary selenium intake and serum selenium concentration, and the interaction between selenium and other trace elements.

EXPERIMENTAL

Milk samples were obtained by manual pressure from the breast. The samples were directly collected into previously acid-washed polyethylene tubes and stored deep-frozen until analysis. The concentration of selenium and other trace elements including Fe, Rb, and Zn was determined by instrumental neutron activation analysis. About 200 μl of fluid were pipetted into vials of high-purity quartz and dried at 50°C. The vials were sealed using a specially designed quartz burner. All preanalytical treatment was carried out in a dust-free laboratory. The vials were irradiated for 10 days at a thermal neutron flux density of about $5.10 \, \text{n} \cdot \text{cm}^{-2} \cdot \text{s}^{-1}$ in the Berlin Research Reactor (BER II), together with the standard reference materials NBS 1577a bovine liver. After a cooling time of 2 to 3 months, selenium was determined via the long-living radionuclide Se-75 by means of high-resolution gamma ray spectrometry.

79

SELENIUM SUPPLY OF FORMULA-FED INFANTS

The selenium content of formulas based on cow's milk is much lower that that of breast milk, and hence the selenium supply of formula-fed infants is correspondingly reduced (1–5). Furthermore, regional and seasonal variation in the selenium content of infants' and young children's foodstuffs (5–8) complicate the estimation of their selenium supply. In this connection, measurement of the serum selenium levels provides a better estimate not only of the ingested quantity but also of the utilized quantity of selenium (2–3). We examined the serum selenium concentration of infants in relation to the dietary habits of their mothers (9). One hundred and forty full-term healthy infants were divided into two groups: solely breast-fed and exclusively formula-fed. After 12 to 24 weeks the concentrations of essential trace elements, including selenium, were determined in the infants' serum (Table 1). Statistically significant differences in the serum selenium levels were found by application of Wilcoxon's rank test to the results. The mean selenium concentration of the formula-fed groups was about half that of the breast-fed group. This means that their intake of about 5 to 6 μg per day is far below the recommendations (10–40 μg/day) of the Food and Nutrition Board of the National Research Council of the USA (10). However, no differences were observed between the two groups with respect to the development of the infants. Infants receiving selenium-free total parenteral nutrition (TPN) showed a marked decline in serum selenium concentration (down to 12 ng/ml after 2 months of administration) (Fig. 1) without manifestation of deficiency symptoms. In a single case the serum selenium concentration was found to be below 1 ng/ml after 21 months of TPN (11,12). At this level, selenium deficiency syndromes including erythrocyte macrocytosis, myopathy, and pseudoalbinism occurred. These were reversed by the administration of selenium in the form of Semethionine.

TABLE 1. *Selenium in serum samples (ng/g) of healthy breast-fed and formula-fed infants (age 12–14 weeks)*

Feeding	N	Mean ± SD	Range	Median	Se content of dietary source[a]
Human milk	45	58.8 ± 11.0	38–85	58.0	15.3 ± 5.7
Preterm formula 1	29	31.4 ± 5.4	21–45	31.0	5.3
Formula 2	33	30.1 ± 5.9	13–48	30.0	8.1
Formula 3	27	34.4 ± 7.4	10–49	36.0	4.6
Formula 4	17	29.9 ± 8.9	18–47	29.0	—
Preterm formula 5	6	19.8 ± 2.8	16–23	18.5	—
Home-made formula[b]	25	34.5 ± 10.9	20–58	33.0	—

[a]Figures represent ng/g wet weight.
[b]Based on cow's milk.

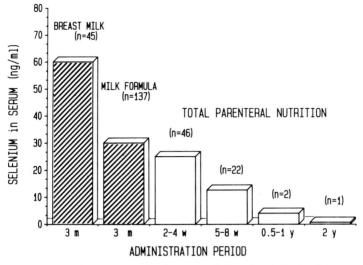

FIG. 1. Mean selenium concentration in serum of infants in relation to dietary sources.

VARIATION OF THE BREAST MILK LEVEL IN GERMANY

An average breast milk selenium concentration of 28 µg/l in West Germany was reported in 1978 by Lombeck et al. (1). Based on this level, West Germany was placed among the countries with relatively high maternal dietary selenium intakes, such as Japan (13) and the USA (14). This has also been mentioned in recent comparisons of data cited in published reports (2,15). However, a total diet study carried out in 1981 with female adults from Germany revealed an average selenium intake of 55 ± 31 µg per day (16). This is close to the lower limit of the recommended safe daily intake range for adults (50–200 µg/day) (10).

We therefore investigated whether the reported lower selenium intake for Germany in 1981 might have been reflected in lower selenium breast milk concentrations of mothers from different areas in Germany, including Berlin, Lübeck, and Würzburg. The breast milk samples of 140 mothers collected during the years 1983 to 1985 (Table 2) yielded a mean selenium concentration of 15.4 ± 4.9 µg/liter; the corresponding daily selenium intake of the infants can be estimated to be in the range of 11 to 12 µg. This level is still within the recommended safe and adequate daily intake range for infants of this age (10–40 µg), but it is close to the lower limit.

In order to be able to compare these breast milk data with other data from published reports, variations in selenium content were studied at various stages of lactation (Table 3) as well as during the nursing period. In our study, selenium decreased with advancing stages of lactation from 16.5 µg/liter at 1 to 2 weeks to 13.5 µg/liter

TABLE 2. *Selenium in breast milk of German mothers*

Location	Year	No	Mean (μg/liter)	Range (μg/liter)	Lactation stage	Reference
Nordrhein-Westfalen	1978	44	28.3	11−54	11−173 days	(1)
Berlin	1983	45	15.1	9−25	10−20 days	This work
Lübeck	1983	55	15.2	11−29	12−63 days	This work
Würzburg	1984	40	16.4	8−40	12−62 days	This work
Mainz	1986	32	17.8	12−30	11 days	(5)
Bavaria (different areas)	1987	59	16.0	—	3−11 days	(17)

TABLE 3. *Selenium in breast milk of mothers from Lübeck and Würzburg as a function of lactation stage*

Lactation stage	No	Mean ± SD (μg/liter)	Range (μg/liter)
5−11 days	29	16.5 ± 4.5	12−29
12−19 days	28	15.6 ± 6.1	10−20
20−30 days	13	14.5 ± 5.7	8−30
1−2 months	11	13.5 ± 4.1	9−20

at 2 months postpartum. For comparison, Lombeck et al. (1) reported a decline from 30.5 μg/liter to 28.3 μg/liter between days 4 and 10 and days 11 and 173 of lactation. A decline in the breast milk selenium level with advancing lactation stages has also been observed by other authors (12,18,19). In samples of mature breast milk collected at the beginning and the end of a single nursing period we found the selenium level of hindmilk to be 16 ± 6% higher than in foremilk.

Taking into account the range of variation in the selenium content in breast milk mentioned above, our results and the others from Germany (5,6) given in Table 2 suggest that the dietary selenium intake of German mothers has decreased significantly since 1978. This possibility has received support recently (1988) in a study by Oster who estimated the regional (Mainz) daily dietary selenium intake of female adults to be about 37 μg (20).

REGIONAL COMPARISONS

A comparison of data from the literature obtained from various geographic regions and in different laboratories must be viewed with caution because (a) dietary intake values are obtained by different procedures including market basket studies, selective studies of individual foodstuffs, and the duplicate portion technique, each with its own limitations (16); and (b) the trace element content of breast milk de-

TABLE 4. *Daily dietary selenium intake (µg) and selenium concentration (µg/ml) of mature human milk in various countries*

Country	Se intake	Se in breast milk	Reference
China	8.8	2.6	21
	198	40	
New Zealand	25	7.6	22,23
Finland	30	7.6	8,18
	50	11.8	8,24
Italy	43	13.8	25,26
Belgium	52	10.0	19,27
Germany (FRG)	59	15.4	9,16
Sweden	68	14	28
USA	80	20	3,14,29
Japan	88	18	2,13,30
Philippines	136	34	26
Venezuela	230	46	31,32,33
	350	60	
	500	90	

pends on several parameters which may be physiological, pathological, environmental, or analytical. Sampling procedures and necessary preanalytic treatment are especially critical steps in the analysis of a trace element.

Nevertheless, data from a number of countries on the dietary selenium intake of the population were available, together with data on the breast milk content (Table 4). Comparing the selenium levels of breast milk with the regional dietary selenium intake, a linear relationship can be observed (Fig. 2) when only data for mature

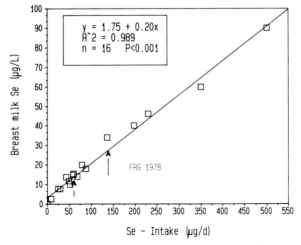

FIG. 2. Selenium in mature human milk of various populations as a function of their daily dietary selenium intake.

breast milk are used. It is remarkable that the correlation fits within a wide range of selenium concentration, from 2.6 ng/ml in selenium-deficient regions of China up to 60 ng/ml in the seleniferous areas of Venezuela. An interesting fact of this strong relationship is the possibility of estimating the selenium supply of a population via the analysis of breast milk samples or, even better, of a regional breast milk pool. This may be a helpful tool in related epidemiological studies. An application of the relationship to the data from Germany suggests that the present dietary selenium intake of German mothers has decreased to half that of the 1978 value. This marked decrease in the breast milk selenium level needs explanation. In the Federal Republic of Germany there are some signs (34) that leaching effects of the soil and/or agricultural processes (e.g., alteration in the type or composition of forage crops) may lead to a reduction in the selenium supply via the food chain.

COMPARISON OF SELENIUM IN MATERNAL SERUM AND BREAST MILK

The results of the correlation study clearly indicate that geographical variation in the selenium content of mature breast milk is associated with the estimated maternal dietary intake levels of selenium. However, contradictory observations have been reported concerning the correlation between maternal serum selenium levels and breast milk selenium content. No relationship was found by Higashi et al. (13) in Japan, and only a weak correlation was observed by Levander et al (14) for Maryland. On the other hand, strong correlations between selenium in human milk and selenium in serum were reported by Kumpulainen et al. (24) in Finland and Mannan and Picciano (35) for women living in Illinois. Williams (36) observed a strong relationship between selenium in whole blood and selenium in the breast milk of New Zealand women. Completing a previous study (31), we obtained a strong positive relationship between serum selenium content (range 2 to 10 μg/g dry weight) and the breast milk selenium content in Venezuelan women (Fig. 3). The great variation in maternal dietary selenium intake in the regions investigated was favorable for the confirmation of this relationship.

Comparing the selenium levels of maternal serum and mature breast milk, a nearly constant gradient seems to exist which is independent of the maternal selenium intake level (Fig. 4). We found the selenium content to be 6 to 7 times lower in mature breast milk at maternal serum selenium concentrations between 75 and 540 ng/liter. Similar behavior but lower gradients have been observed for copper and iron. On the other hand, as shown in Fig. 4B, several other elements (including Cs, K, Mn, Rb, and Zn) are found to be more highly concentrated in breast milk than in maternal serum (37). It might be assumed that selenium, like copper, is stored during prenatal stages of development for use in the neonatal period. Indeed, the selenium content of liver (38), erythrocytes, serum (39) and hair (40) is high at birth in the normal-term infant and declines during the first months of life. In this context we would like to stimulate discussion of the hypothesis that this property might be ex-

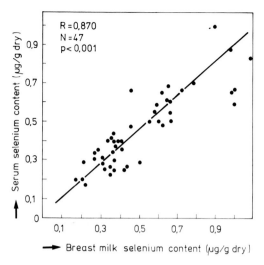

FIG. 3. Mature breast milk selenium content as a function of the maternal serum selenium content of lactating women living in Caracas and in seleniferous areas of Venezuela.

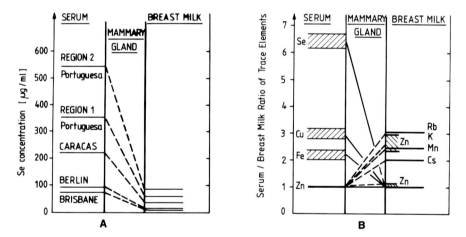

FIG. 4. **(A)** Difference between the selenium concentration in serum and breast milk at various serum levels. **(B)** Trace elements concentration ratio of serum and breast milk.

hibited by trace elements involved in the development of the regulatory systems during the neonatal period.

SELENIUM SUPPLEMENTATION DURING LACTATION

In certain geographic regions an insufficient selenium supply may cause problems in infant nutrition. In principle, the selenium supply in infancy can be increased by providing the lactating mother with selenium. The effectiveness of such a dietary concept was experimentally investigated by Kumpulainen et al. in Finland (41,42). However, in the administration of selenium supplements, the possibility of interaction with other essential nutrients has to be taken into account. In the case of high selenium intake, the breast milk levels of other essential trace elements might be influenced by interactions during their secretion into the milk. This was indicated by preliminary results of the investigation of copper, rubidium, and zinc levels in mature breast milk as a function of the dietary selenium intake of mothers living in Caracas and in seleniferous regions of Venezuela (31,33). In Fig. 5 the ratios of the mean trace element concentration in mature breast milk and maternal serum reveal a marked downward trend with increasing serum selenium level. The data were normalized to Caracas and the results of the German group investigated have been included for comparison.

Trace element levels are known to be highest in colostrum, decreasing rapidly within 1 to 2 weeks of parturition to the characteristic values of mature mammary secretion. In order to obtain fairly representative results, in Figs. 5 and 6, only breast milk samples taken between 12 days and 1 month of lactation have been compared. Furthermore, the Venezuelan mothers from Caracas and from the seleniferous areas of Portuguesa belonged to the same low socioeconomic strata. This was ensured by the use of the socioeconomic standards that had been set up for the regional populations (43). It has to be pointed out that, unlike selenium, the maternal serum values of copper and zinc showed no significant regional variation, nor did an analysis of the meals reveal any dietary deficiency of either element.

In addition to the regional mean values of Fig. 6, the data from single subjects with higher selenium status underline the fact that high selenium intake of lactating

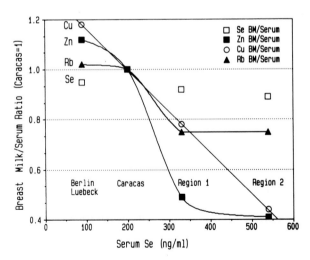

FIG. 5. Breast milk/serum ratio of trace elements as a function of the regional maternal serum selenium concentration (Caracas = 1). Region 1: Subjects from Turen and La Colonia. Region 2: Subjects from Poblado 3 and El Aji.

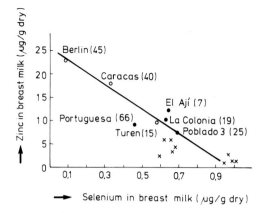

FIG. 6. Relationship between zinc and selenium content of mature human breast milk. ○, ●, regional mean values; ( ), number of subjects; X, single subjects.

women may reduce the zinc level in breast milk. The intercept corresponds to a daily dietary selenium intake of about 700 μg if the relationship in Fig. 2 is used for conversion. The interactions observed in this preliminary study must be taken into consideration when the supply of zinc and copper to the child is being assessed. Furthermore, it must not be forgotten that the populations investigated have very probably become adapted to the high selenium content in their food.

Due to lack of knowledge about the selenium requirement during infancy and the lack of information on the interactions of selenium with other nutrients, long-term selenium supplementation during pregnancy and lactation should be regarded more critically in the future.

REFERENCES

1. Lombeck I, Kasparek K, Bonnermann B, Feinendegen LE, Bremer HJ. Selenium content of human milk and cow's milk infant formulas. *Eur J Pediatr* 1978;129:139–49.
2. Hatano S, Aihara K, Nishi Y, Usui T. Trace elements (copper, zinc, manganese, and selenium) in plasma and erythrocytes in relation to dietary intake during infancy. *J Pediatr Gastroenterol Nutr* 1985;4:87–92.
3. Smith AM, Picciano MF, Milner JA. Selenium intakes and status of human milk and formula-fed infants. *Am J Clin Nutr* 1982;35:521–26.
4. von Stockhausen HB, Rösick U, Negretti de Brätter VE, Brätter P. Trace element supply in young, healthy infants as related to trace element content of diet. In: Berger H, ed. *Vitamins and minerals in pregnancy and lactation.* (Nestlé Nutrition Workshop Series Vol. 16. Nestec Ltd., Vevey) New York: Raven Press, 1988:49–50.
5. Oster O, Schmiedel G, Prellwitz W. Ein Vergleich des Selengehaltes von Säuglingsnahrung. In: Welz B, ed. *Fortschritte in der atomspektrometrischen Spurenanalytik*, vol 2. VCH-Verlagsgesellschaft mbH Weinheim: 1986:409.
6. Verlinden M, Van Sprundel M, Van der Auwera JC, Eylenbosch WJ. The selenium status of Belgian population groups II. Newborn, children, and the aged. *Biol Trace Element Res* 1983;5:103–13.
7. Watkinson JH. Changes in blood selenium in New Zealand adults with the importation of Australian wheat. *Am J Clin Nutr* 1981;34:836–42.
8. Varo P, Koivistoinen P. Annual variations in the average selenium intake in Finland: Cereal products and milk as sources of selenium in 1979/80. *Int J Vitam Nutr Res* 1981;51:79–84.

9. Brätter P, Negretti de Brätter VE, Rösick U, von Stockhausen HB. Trace element concentration in serum of infants in relation to dietary sources. In: Brätter P, Schramel P, eds. *Trace element analytical chemistry in medicine and biology*, vol 4. Berlin, New York: de Gruyter, 1987:133–43.

10. Committee on Dietary Allowances. Food and Nutrition Board National Research Council. *Recommended dietary allowances*, 9th ed. Washington, DC: National Academy Press, 1980.

11. Brätter P, Negretti de Brätter VE, Rösick U, von Stockhausen HB. Development of selenium deficiency in the total parenteral nutrition of infants. In: *Selenium in medicine and biology, Part B*. Combs Jr. GF, Spallholz JE, Levander OA, Oldfield JE, eds. New York: AVI, 1987:652.

12. Gramm H-J, Goecke J, Brätter P, Stoltenburg-Didinger G, Waldschmidt J, Eyrich K. Selenmangel-Myopathie unter langzeitparenteraler Ernährung. *Infusionstherapie* 1988;15:11–2.

13. Higashi TH, Tamari H, Kuroki Y, Matsuda I. Longitudinal changes in the selenium content of breast milk. *Acta Pedriatr Scand* 1983;72:433–6.

14. Levander OA, Moser PB, Morris VC. Dietary selenium intake and selenium concentrations of plasma, erythrocytes, and breast milk in pregnant and postpartum lactating and nonlactating women. *Am J Clin Nutr* 1987;46:694–8.

15. Neve J, Vertongen F, Molle L. Selenium deficiency. *Clin Endocrinol Metab* 1985;14:629–56.

16. Schelenz R. Intake of Zn, Mn and Se by adult females. A total diet study. In: Brätter P, Schramel P, eds. *Trace element analytical chemistry in medicine and biology*, vol 3. Berlin, New York: de Gruyter, 1984:73.

17. Schramel P, Lill G, Hasse S, Klose B-J. Mineral and trace element concentrations in human breast milk, placenta, maternal blood, and the blood of the newborn. *Biol Trace Element Res* 1988;16:67–75.

18. Kumpulainen J, Vuori E, Kuitunen P, Makinen S, Kara R. Longitudinal study on the dietary selenium intake of exclusively breast-fed infants and their mothers in Finland. *Int J Vitam Nutr Res* 1983;53:420–26.

19. Robberecht H, Roekens E, Van Caillie-Bertrand, Deelstra H, Clara R. Longitudinal study of the selenium content in human breast milk in Belgium. *Acta Paediatr Scand* 1985;74:254–58.

20. Oster O, Prellwitz W. Are Germans selenium deficient? In: Wendrel A, ed. Proceedings of the 4th International Symposium on Selenium in Biology and Medicine. Heidelberg, New York, London, Paris, Tokyo, Hong Kong: Springer, 1989:229–233.

21. Yang G. Research on Se-related problems in human health in China. In: GF Combs, JE Spallholz, OA Levander, JE Oldfield, eds. Proceedings of the 3rd International Symposium on Selenium in Medicine and Biology. Westport Conn: Avi Publishing Co. 1986:9.

22. Thomson, CD, Robinson MF. Selenium in health and disease with emphasis on those aspects peculiar to New Zealand. *Am J Clin Nutr* 1980;33:303–23.

23. Miller KR, Sheppard AD. Tocopherol and selenium levels in human and cow's milk. *N Z J Sci* 1972;15:3–15.

24. Kumpulainen J, Vuori E, Siimes MA. Effect of maternal dietary selenium intake on selenium levels in breast milk. *Int J Nutr Res.* 1984;54:251–5.

25. Clementi GF, Ingrao G, Santaroni G. The concentration of some trace elements in human milk from Italy. *Sci Total Env* 1982;24:255–65.

26. Cresta M, Allegrini M, Casadei E, Gallorini M, Lanzola E, Panatha GB. *Food Nutr* 1976;2:8–18.

27. Robberecht HJ, Deelstra HA. Dietary selenium intake in Belgium. *Z Lebensm Unters Forsch* 1984;178:266–71.

28. Abdulla M, Aly K-A, Anderson I, et al. Nutrient intake and health status of lactovegetarians: Chemical analyses of diets using duplicate portion sampling technique. *Am J Clin Nutr* 1984;40:325.

29. Welsh SO, Holden JM, Wolf WR, Levander OA. Selenium in self-selected diets of Maryland residents. *J Am Diet Assoc* 1981;79:277–85.

30. Sakurai H, Tsuchiya K. A tentative recommendation for maximum daily intake of selenium. *Environ Physiol Biochem* 1975;5:107–18.

31. Brätter P, Negretti de Brätter VE, Rösick U, Jaffe WG, Mendez C, Tovar EG. Effects of selenium intake in man at high dietary levels of seleniferous areas of Venezuela. In: Brätter P, Schramel P, eds. *Trace element analytical chemistry in medicine and biology*, vol 3. Berlin, New York: de Gruyter, 1984:29.

32. Mondragon MC, Jaffé WG. Consumo de selenio en la ciudad de Caracas en comparación con el de otras ciudades del mundo. *Arch Latinoam Nutr* 1976;26:341–50.

33. Brätter P, Negretti de Brätter VE, Rösick U, Mendez CH, Tovar EG, Jaffé WG. Zum Spurenele-

mentgehalt de Muttermilch bei hoher Selenaufnahme durch die Nahrung. Proceedings of the 5th International Symposium on Iodine and other Trace Elements, KMU Leipzig and FSU Jena, 1986:695–700.

34. Hartfiel W, Bahners N. Selenium deficiency in the Federal Republic of Germany. *Biol Trace Element Res.* 1988;15:1–12.
35. Mannan S, Picciano MF. Relationship of maternal selenium status to human milk content. Proceedings of the 69th annual meeting of the American Society for Experimental Biology, 1985;44:1855.
36. Williams MMF. Selenium and glutathione peroxidase in mature human milk. Proceedings of the University of Otago Medical School. 1983;61:20.
37. Cumming FJ, Fardy JJ, Briggs MH. Trace elements in human milk. *Obstet Gynecol* 1983;62:506–8.
38. Westermarck T. Selenium content of tissues in Finnish infants and adults with various diseases, and studies on the effects of selenium supplementation in neuronal ceroid lipofuscinosis patients. *Acta Pharmacol Toxicol* 1977;41:121–28.
39. Lombeck I, Kasparek K, Harbisch HD, Feinendegen LE, Bremer HJ. The selenium state in healthy children. I. Serum selenium concentration at different ages, activity of glutathione peroxidase of erythrocytes at different ages: Selenium content of food of infants. *Eur J Pediatr* 1977;125:81–8.
40. Musa Al-Zubaidy, Lombeck I, Kasparek K, Feinenlegen LE, Bremer HJ. Zinc status of Libyan children—a pilot study. *Z Ernährungswiss* 1983;22:1–5.
41. Kumpulainen J, Salmenperä L, Siimes MA, Koivistoinen P, Letho J, Perheentupa J. Formula feeding results in lower selenium status than breast feeding or selenium supplemented formula feeding: A longitudinal study. *Am J Clin Nutr* 1987;45:49–53.
42. Kumpulainen J, Salmenperä L, Siimes MA, Koivistoinen P, Perheentupa J. Selenium status of exclusively breast-fed infants as influenced by maternal organic or inorganic selenium supplementation. *Am J Clin Nutr* 1985;42:829–35.
43. Lopez M, de Blanco C, Landaeta de Jimenez M, Fossi de Mejia M, Mejia de Rahamut B, Alvarez ML. *El problema nutricional en Venezuela.* Caracas: FUNDACREDESA, 1983.

DISCUSSION

Dr. Chandra: Have you measured selenium-dependent enzymes and correlated them with low selenium intake and low blood selenium, particularly in relation to breast milk intake?

Dr. Brätter: We measured glutathione peroxidase in children on total parenteral nutrition but not in the course of our field study in the seleniferous areas of Venezuela. We have not examined glutathione peroxidase in relation to breast milk intake.

Dr. Lombeck: In preterm infants there is a decrease in plasma glutathione peroxidase activity in infants fed either human milk or formula. With respect to selenium stores, the selenium content of the liver is higher in the preterm than in the term infant, but because of the small liver size, the selenium store is smaller. In cord blood samples selenium values in whole blood are not so reduced as the plasma values, but blood cannot represent a large selenium store because of its small volume.

Dr. Mertz: It is a very important finding that a high selenium intake in mothers in Venezuela depresses the copper and zinc content of their milk. As I understand it, zinc content is reduced by about 50%. Did you find any evidence of zinc deficiency?

Dr. Brätter: During the field study we found that when compared to age-matched children in Caracas, the height of the children in the seleniferous areas was less, about 3 to 5 cm in boys. It was supposed that this might have been a reflection of the lower zinc intake.

Dr. Aggett: What is the explanation for the effect of selenium on milk zinc? Is there any change in the ratios between Zn, Cu, Rb, and Se during the course of lactation?

Dr. Brätter: We investigated serum and breast milk samples from mothers between 12 and

30 days of lactation. During this period a decline in trace element content is to be expected, but we found that in breast milk from mothers with high dietary selenium there was an increased rate of decline in Cu, Zn, and Rb concentrations. We want to confirm these findings by examining samples obtained at more clearly defined lactational stages.

Dr. Lönnerdal: I can think of two possibilities to explain the effect of selenium on milk zinc. The high level of selenium could impair the transfer of zinc into milk; or a low selenium level could increase zinc transfer into milk. There could of course be a combination of both.

Dr. Oster: In Germany we have found a positive correlation between selenium and zinc. There is a much lower selenium intake in Germany than that reported by Dr. Brätter, the daily dietary intake in women being about 37 mg. Under these conditions there is a clear positive correlation between the selenium content of the milk and the zinc content. We explain this positive correlation by the fact that both elements have a similar organ distribution. About 50% of the whole body selenium and 50% of whole body zinc are found in skeletal muscle.

Dr. Lombeck: In any discussion of the relationships between different elements in milk it is very important to be precise about the stage of lactation. Selenium decreases mainly during early lactation (i.e., within the first weeks, and then remains rather stable), whereas zinc continues to decrease throughout lactation. Any correlations made between different trace elements must therefore be at precisely the same stage of lactation.

Dr. Marini: Returning to the clinical problem of selenium deficiency, you said you found very low selenium concentrations with clinical manifestations in babies receiving total parenteral nutrition for 2 years. You also found low concentrations after 2 months of TPN. Was there any evidence of clinical impairment in these cases? This is very important because of the stimulant effect of selenium on antioxidant enzymes, which may be crucial for preterm babies.

Dr. Brätter: We observed macrocytosis after prolonged parenteral nutrition (> 1 year) which was reversible with selenium supplements. Using 1 to 2 μg selenium methionine per kg body weight daily in severe selenium depletion, the serum selenium and the selenoenzyme glutathione peroxidase increased and became normal after 3 weeks of treatment. There was a simultaneous rise in muscle selenium level and restoration of diminished movement.

Dr. Mertz: When you go critically into everything that has been published on selenium, you become convinced that in humans as well as in animals there is no such thing as pure uncomplicated selenium deficiency. Selenium deficiency always becomes clinically important in conjunction with a second or third factor. Of this I am reasonably convinced. Perhaps the biological explanation for that theory is the fact that there are other transferase enzymes that are not selenium dependent that can take over some of the most important functions. The big puzzle now is what are the interacting factors that make selenium a clinical problem.

Dr. Lombeck: Those patients with symptomatic selenium deficiency who have been reported from the USA and Switzerland were severely ill and were fed parenterally for long periods. Besides selenium deficiency, there may well have been other imbalances which we do not know about. I speculate that the intake of fatty acids may play a role, and particularly polyunsaturated fatty acids. I discovered recently that people from the Keshan area in China eat excess erucic acid. Parenterally fed patients get lipid infusions with different fatty acids from the usual enteral intake, and they don't pass the liver before entering the tissues.

Dr. Oster: One final point—there are reports from the Swedish scientist Dr. Plantin that during the last 10 years there has been a decrease in population serum and whole blood selenium concentrations of about 30 μg/liter. The Danish scientist Gissel-Nielsen has reported that the accumulation of selenium in plants is lower when soil is acidic. Maybe the problem of acid rain, producing an acid soil, has been influencing the selenium accumulation by plants and secondarily affecting human selenium intakes.

Trace Elements in Nutrition of Children—II,
edited by Ranjit K. Chandra, Nestlé Nutrition
Workshop Series, Vol. 23, Nestec Ltd.,
Vevey/Raven Press, Ltd., New York © 1991.

Iodine Deficiency Disorders

Peter Pharoah

Department of Public Health, University of Liverpool, PO Box 147, Liverpool L69 3BX, United Kingdom

The most important clinical abnormalities attributable to iodine deficiency are endemic goitre and endemic cretinism. In recent years, revival of interest in the latter condition has revealed a syndrome with a widespread spectrum of severity ranging from a degree of cerebral damage that is incompatible with life, through clinical neurological and other deficits, to subclinical deficits merging into normality. This complexity of abnormality led to the coining of the term iodine deficiency disorders (IDD) in 1983 to encompass the spectrum of disorder that occurs (1).

ENDEMIC GOITRE

The geographic distribution has been covered in a comprehensive world-wide review of published reports (2). Almost no country is exempt and it was estimated that 200 million people are affected. A more recent estimate confirms the earlier review and considers that 800 million world-wide are at risk of iodine deficiency disorders, with 190 million suffering from endemic goitre, and adds the new dimension of 3 million suffering overt cretinism (3).

Areas with a high prevalence are:

Mountainous regions, such as the Alps, the Andean cordillera, the Himalayas, and the mountain chain extending through southeast Asia and the countries of the South Pacific (e.g., Burma, Indonesia, Papua New Guinea, the Philippines).

Alluvial plains that have recently been the site of quaternary glaciation (e.g., the Great Lakes basin of Canada and the USA, Finland, and the low-lying Netherlands). Geochemists explain this on the basis of leaching of iodine from the soil by glaciation or flooding in the last Ice Age, with insufficient time having elapsed for replacement of the iodine from oceanic sources (4).

Hard water areas (e.g., where water supplies permeate through limestone).

It is now generally accepted that dietary iodine deficiency is the major cause of endemic goitre. Although Boussingault 150 years ago advocated the use of iodized salt for goitre prevention [quoted by Kelly and Snedden (2)] it was not until a controlled trial was carried out in which sodium iodide supplements were given to schoolgirls that the prophylactic value of iodine was convincingly demonstrated (5). Since then, other evidence has been adduced in support of the iodine deficiency hypothesis. Endemic goitre occurs in areas of low soil iodine content and an inverse relationship can often be shown between soil iodine and goitre prevalence (6). Urinary iodine excretion is low and thyroidal uptake is regularly elevated in areas of endemic goitre (7), and goitre may be produced experimentally in animals fed on a diet low in iodine (8).

Because iodine deficiency is the major component responsible for the development of endemic goitre, a frequently used measure of the severity of iodine deficiency in any region is the prevalence of goitre.

THE EPIDEMIOLOGY OF ENDEMIC GOITRE

In the past, comparison of goitre prevalence levels in different communities has been hampered by the lack of a consensus for grading of goitre. A grading now commonly recognized was originally developed by Perez, Scrimshaw and Munoz (9) and subsequently modified by the Pan American Health Organization. It is as follows:

Grade 0a   No enlargement of the thyroid.

Grade 0b   Enlargement detectable by palpation but not visible even when the neck is fully extended.

Grade 1   Gland palpable but only visible when the neck is fully extended.

Grade 2   Gland visible when head is in normal position, palpation not needed for diagnosis.

Grade 3   Very large gland which can be recognized from a distance.

Even this classification is unnecessarily complex and the distinction between Grades 0a, 0b, and 1 is subjective and liable to intra- and interobserver variation.

The highest goitre prevalence rates are to be found in those whose iodine requirements are greatest, that is, women of childbearing age and, to a lesser degree, adolescent girls or boys. Goitres may increase in size with each pregnancy and regress when childbearing ceases. In order to assess the severity of the prevailing problem, therefore, it is important to determine age and sex prevalence rates of goitre (10). Surveys in the past have often covered only certain groups, such as school children or military recruits, thus yielding a distorted picture of the true prevalence. In severely affected areas, the prevalence rate of goitre may approach 100%, with even infants being affected.

The goitrogenic action of iodine deficiency may be exacerbated by other goitrogens. The greater predisposition to goitre in hard water areas has long been appreciated. In 1769 Prosser recognized that "Derby neck" was associated with the hard water of limestone regions (11) and in 1819 it was noted that goitre was more frequent in institutions which used well water of exceptional hardness for cooking (2). Thus, a dietary iodine level that is adequate in a soft water area may prove inadequate where the water is hard. This notion is supported by the observation that calcium enhances the growth of the iodine-deprived rat thyroid (12). Other ions which have been associated with a goitrogenic effect include fluoride, magnesium, and manganese (13,14). There are probably complex interrelationships between these various ions.

The development of goitre in rabbits fed on a diet of cabbages first drew attention to the possibility that goitrogens might be present in food (15). This observation was the forerunner of the development of the antithyroid drugs. Other dietary goitrogens have since been implicated, most of which are to be found in plants of the *Brassica* and *Crucifera* families. The agent is usually a thioglucoside, which yields thiocyanates and isothiocyanates on hydrolysis. For the goitrogens to have a significant effect, either large quantities of the food must be consumed, or the goitrogen must be concentrated at some stage in the food chain. The latter mechanism was suggested as the cause of the seasonal epidemics of goitre among Tasmanian schoolchildren which could not be prevented by iodine administration. The epidemics were attributed to a goitrogen which entered cow's milk during the spring flush of goitrogen-containing weeds in pasture. Attempts to isolate the goitrogen were, however, unsuccessful (16).

Although a goitre may be cosmetically unsightly, especially if the enlargement is gross, it must be looked upon as a physiological response to iodine deficiency. The enlargement is to enable a greater efficiency in the utilization of available iodine. It is only rarely that the enlargement gives rise to obstructive symptoms arising from tracheal or esophageal compression. From the clinical standpoint, goitre is relatively unimportant. The current revival of interest in iodine deficiency stems from its relationship to the syndrome of endemic cretinism.

ENDEMIC CRETINISM

Cretinism is often considered to be synonymous with hypothyroidism, either congenital or developing early in childhood. However, the clinical features of cretinism as described in the early literature are quite different and it is apparent that there are two overlapping syndromes.

Clarification is obtained if the problem is analyzed from a historical perspective. The association between endemic cretinism and goitre was noted by Paracelsus in 1567 who wrote:

> . . . but to speak of these creatures that they perchance also have defects of the body, that is they carry growths with them such as goitres and the like: this perhaps is not a characteristic of fools but also of others, however it fits most of them (17).

Although this recognition of an association between goitre and cretinism is often attributed to Paracelsus, it was implicit in the literature prior to that time, such as the

Reuner Musterbuch of 1215 that depicts a figure with a large multilobed goitre, a stupid facial expression, and brandishing a fool's staff in one hand and ear-trumpet in the other (18). In 1220, in the encyclopedia of Jacques de Vitry, large goitres and deaf-mutism are both recorded as occurring in the Burgundy region and it was stated that "ex mutis et surdis, muti et surdi infantes procreantur" (18).

The term "cretin" first appeared in Diderot's encyclopedia of 1754 and referred to "an imbecile who was deaf and dumb with a goitre hanging down to the waist" (19).

In 1847, Norris described the cretins in Chisleborough, Somerset, dividing them into four groups. These consisted of: a) four perfect idiots; b) 17 partial idiots, all quite unable to articulate so as to be understood and walking with an unsteady step and an unsteady waddling gait; c) five deaf and dumb; and d) a majority of the whole population, namely those with an obvious deficiency of intellect and, without a single exception, affected with bronchocele (20). At that time bronchocele was the term used for goitre.

William Farr, the first Registrar-General in England, reporting on the 1851 census states:

> Cretins most of whom are deaf-mutes . . . . The disease of cretinism is also accompanied by mental imbecility in a greater or less degree (21).

In all these early descriptions of cretinism, mental retardation and deaf-mutism are invariably included and abnormalities of gait are frequently mentioned. Yet, apart from mental retardation, these clinical features are not associated with sporadic hypothyroid cretinism that is seen today. The original description of sporadic cretinism was given by Thomas Curling in 1850 when he reported on two infants and noted:

> In countries where cretinism and bronchocele prevail, it was long supposed that there is some connection between the defective condition of the brain and the hypertrophy of the thyroid . . . in the foregoing cases we have examples of an opposite condition, namely a defective brain or cretinism combined with an entire absence of the thyroid (22).

It is salutory to note that Curling was stressing the difference between the findings in his two cases and what were then the recognized signs of cretinism.

Fagge in 1871 described four further cases of sporadic cretinism and compared them with endemic cretinism. He also specifically drew attention to the comparative features of the two syndromes stating that sporadic and endemic cretinism were associated with a deficiency of the mental powers; that sporadic cretinism, instead of being associated with a goitre, appears to be attended with a wasting or absence of the thyroid gland; and that sporadic cretinism is not necessarily congenital (23).

Endemic cretinism has disappeared from the developed world and is now largely confined to developing countries. The declining prevalence has been recorded in several countries. In England, referring to the cretins of Chisleborough previously described by Norris, it was stated that "one solitary cretin now survives of about 50 years of age, the march of civilization having stamped out the disease" (24). A similar decline has been reported by several authors in Italy (25) and a steady downward trend can be observed in the statistics of the Sardinian Royal Commission of 1848 (26).

These examples all relate to foci of the disease in Europe but the downward trend has occurred in other countries also. The prevalence of deaf-mutism in the United Provinces of India decreased by a half between the censuses of 1881 and 1921 (27). Similarly, census figures for Argentina show a steady decline in the number of deaf-mutes in all provinces between the years 1869, 1895, and 1914 (28). These declines predate knowledge about etiology or any specific prophylactic measures.

Against the background of endemic cretinism disappearing from many countries are the increasingly numerous reports of sporadic cretinism. Thus, in time, the term cretinism has become synonymous with sporadic hypothyroidism. The endemic variety barely receives mention in Western textbooks of medicine, which belies its importance as a clinical entity in many countries.

There were occasional voices warning that the distinction between the two forms of cretinism should not be blurred. Gordon in 1922 and again in 1938 was very specific in distinguishing between sporadic and endemic cretinism. He suggested that "sporadic cretinism" be renamed "childhood myxedema" because "cretinism as described in Europe is a clinically distinct entity from sporadic hypothyroidism" (29,30).

The confusion over the two forms of cretinism, sporadic and endemic, has been intensified by the observation that the syndrome of endemic cretinism encompasses both a hypothyroid variety, which is essentially the same as sporadic cretinism, and a syndrome of neurological impairment where deaf-mutism, cerebral diplegia, mental retardation, and strabismus are the cardinal clinical features.

The subclassification of endemic cretinism into two types, namely, myxedematous and nervous was initially made by McCarrison in 1908 as a result of his work in the Chitral and Gilgit valleys in the Himalayas (31). His description of the clinical features of the myxedematous type was incomplete, merely stating that "it corresponds to that form of the affliction met with in Europe and is described in any textbook of medicine." His clinical description of nervous cretinism is more precise and remains a model of accuracy. The disability is described as pertaining more especially to the central nervous system. "Deaf-mutism is as a rule complete, mentality is much disordered and there is a congenital diplegia with increased knee jerks and a spastic rigidity more severely affecting the lower limbs with a characteristic gait." A coarse nystagmus and internal strabismus were noted in some cases.

The relative proportion of the two subtypes of endemic cretinism differs between countries. Reviews of the world literature indicate that the hypothyroid variety predominates in some African countries, while the nervous variety is more common in most other countries (32,33). Currently the definition of endemic cretinism includes aspects relative to its epidemiology, its clinical manifestations, and its prevention:

Epidemiology. It is associated with endemic goitre and severe iodine deficiency.
Clinical manifestations. These comprise mental deficiency together with either:
    a) predominant neurological syndrome consisting of defects of hearing and

speech, and with characteristic disorders of stance and gait of varying degree; or
b) predominant hypothyroidism and stunted growth. Athough in some regions
one of the two types may predominate, in other areas a mixture of the two syndromes will occur.

Prevention. In areas where adequate correction of iodine has been achieved, endemic cretinism has been prevented (34).

The Aetiology of Endemic Cretinism

The importance of iodine deficiency as a cause of endemic goitre and the observation that endemic cretinism is only to be found in areas where goitre is endemic in-
evitably led to the suggestion that iodine deficiency is also responsible for endemic
cretinism. Controversy over this last point centered on the fact that the prevalence
of cretinism declined in several countries prior to any specific measure of iodine
prophylaxis and that in some areas goitre was to be found without coexistent cretinism. A correlation between iodine prophylaxis and a decline in cretinism in Switzerland was shown by Wespi (35). Iodination of salt was introduced independently in
several Swiss cantons and the decline of deaf-mutism in each could be correlated
with the extent of salt iodination. However, this correlation was only time related
and other factors could have been held responsible. These deductions were subsequently criticized on the grounds that no cretins were born about the time that iodine
prophylaxis was introduced; indeed, all the cretins were born at least 10 years previously (36).

The controversy led to a double-blind controlled trial to assess the effectiveness
of iodine as a prophylactic for endemic cretinism. A single intramuscular injection
of iodinated oil had been shown to be an effective prophylactic for endemic goitre
(37), and it had a long duration of action. Four years after a single 4.0 ml dose, a
treated group had significantly higher serum protein-bound and urinary iodine excretion values and lower 24 hour radioiodine uptake than the untreated control group
(38–40). This made the use of intramuscular iodinated oil an ideal vehicle for a controlled trial in relation to endemic cretinism. The trial was carried out in the Jimi valley in the highlands of Papua New Guinea, an area with a high prevalence of
cretinism and goitre. On the occasion of a census, 16,500 people were enrolled in
the trial and alternate families were injected with either iodinated oil or saline solution, each member receiving 4 ml if aged 12 years or over and 2 ml if under 12 years
of age. The prevalence of cretinism in the subsequent follow-up over 6 years is
shown in Table 1. It was concluded that iodinated oil is effective in preventing endemic cretinism provided it is given prior to conception. It indicated that maternal
iodine deficiency during pregnancy leads to irreversible neurological damage to the
developing fetus (41,42).

A trial using iodinated oil was also carried out in Ecuador. All the inhabitants of
one village, Tocachi, were given iodinated oil and an adjacent village, La Esperanza, was used as the control. Subsequent follow-up of 217 children from Tocachi and

TABLE 1. *Outcome of iodized oil controlled trial*

	Mothers injected before conception		Mothers injected after conception	
	Iodized oil	Saline	Iodized oil	Saline
No of births	593	597	95	90
No of cretins	1	26	5	5
Prevalence of cretins per 1000 births	1.7	43.5	52.6	55.6

447 from La Esperanza found the former more advanced in neuromuscular development, but the results did not specifically report on cretinism (43,44).

A smaller study in Peru observed no significant difference in neuropsychiatric assessment between 46 children born to the oil-injected mothers and 35 controls (45). However, this trial also did not specifically mention cretinism. Further evidence on the importance of iodine in endemic cretinism arose from the observation that the disease was of recent onset in the Jimi valley of New Guinea. Following first contact with Europeans in 1953, there was a sharp rise in the prevalence of cretinism from approximately 0.1% pre-1953, rising in the late 1950s and early 1960s and reaching a peak of 15% of the children born in 1965. This increase in prevalence—due to an increase in incidence—was attributed to the substitution of locally produced salt by salt introduced by the Europeans. The salt produced prior to European contact was from saline pools in a volcanic area, analysis of which revealed a very high iodine content (46).

The above reports are concerned with trials where the "nervous" type of cretinism predominates. Iodinated oil has also been assessed as a prophylactic for the "myxedematous" type of cretinism on Idjwi island in Lake Kivu in Central Africa (47). The data on the effectiveness of iodine supplementation in preventing myxedematous endemic cretinism are not quite so convincing. The Idjwi island trial found four myxedematous cretins among 45 infants of mothers from the control villages but only one among 44 infants in the villages given intramuscular iodine. This one case was to a mother who received iodinated oil in the final month gestation (48). These several studies indicate that iodine deficiency leads to both forms of endemic cretinism.

SUBCLINICAL EFFECTS OF IODINE DEFICIENCY

Endemic cretinism shows a wide spectrum of severity of neurological deficit merging into normality. While it is now universally accepted that iodine given before conception can prevent the overt clinical manifestations of the syndrome, more recently interest has focused on the possibility that the effect of iodine may be of wider significance in preventing subclinical deficits of intellectual and motor performance.

Although the New Guinea trial was called to a halt in 1972 when the control group was given intramuscular iodinated oil, the cohort of children born into the trial between 1966 and 1972 has continued to be followed up and examined. In 1978 and 1982, measures of motor and cognitive function were incorporated into the assessment schedule. These included bead-threading and pegboard tests as measures of bimanual and unimanual dexterity, and the Pacific Design Construction Test (PDCT) developed by Ord and used in Papua New Guinea to select army recruits and young people for technical training (49). It was found that the children of mothers who received iodinated oil performed significantly better on the motor tests than did those of mothers who received no supplementary iodine. There was also a difference in the PDCT scores but this was not significant (50).

The results of the long-term follow-up of the two cohorts of children born into the controlled trial (51), although involving only a subset of the original trial group, confirm the previous observations (i.e., that iodinated oil was effective in preventing endemic cretinism provided it was given prior to conception). Not only was there a highly significant excess of definite and possible cretins in the control compared with the treated group, but there was also an excess of children in the control group who performed poorly on the cognitive and motor tasks. The designation as "poor performers" was made on an arbitrary criterion, namely a score in the lowest 10th percentile. All the definite cretins and all but one of the possible cretins performed poorly as judged by this criterion. The results are summarized in Fig. 1.

In the Ecuador trial, the children followed up were aged 2 to 9 years (44). These authors, using the Stanford-Binet intelligence scale, also observed a significant difference between the two groups of children, that is, those whose mothers had or had not received iodine. However, there were several methodological deficiencies. One village provided the test population and another the control so that the trial was not conducted blind; the number of children in the two groups was small and many were excluded from the assessment because they failed to cooperate or were suffering from severe malnutrition.

The Peruvian trial used the Gesell, Stanford-Binet and Brunet-Lezine assessments on children up to 5 years of age (45). Although the iodine-treated group showed marginally higher IQ scores than the iodine-deficient group, the differences were not statistically significant.

In a double-blind trial in Zaire, the Brunet-Lezine scale was used to assess children up to 2 years of age (52). The treated group performed significantly better than the untreated group.

The problem of comparison was addressed in a different manner in Java (53). Here the population of a village with a high goitre prevalence was compared with that of one with a low goitre prevalence. A battery of tests was directed at measuring intelligence as well as nonintelligence (motor skills, concentration, and perceptual capacity) factors. Although significant differences were observed in favor of the village with the low goitre prevalence, the presence of confounding variables detracted from the value of the study. For example, the village without goitre was closer to a major town, the main road, and the primary school.

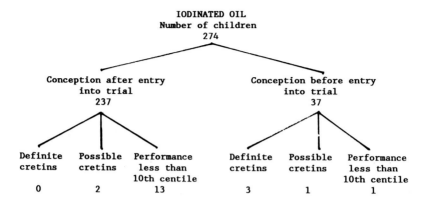

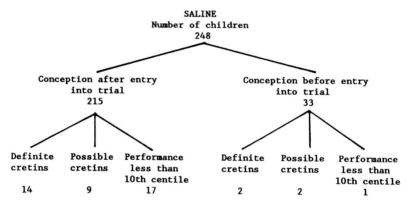

FIG. 1. Measures of outcome in test and control groups.

Although there may be criticism of the methodology of several of these studies, the overall indication is that there are subclinical deficits which are attributable to iodine deficiency.

Maternal iodine deficiency not only leads to endemic cretinism in the offspring but there is also a significant effect on mortality. The cumulative survival curves of children born into the iodinated (test) and saline (control) groups are shown in Fig. 2. There is a highly significant difference in 15-year cumulative survival rates in favor of the test group ($p = 0.002$, Lee Desu statistic). Unfortunately, information on the cause of death in individual cases could not be obtained.

Iodine is utilized by the thyroid to produce the hormones thyroxine, with four atoms of iodine (T_4), and triiodothyronine, with three atoms of iodine (T_3). In response to dietary iodine deficiency, serum T_4 levels become reduced but clinical euthyroidism is maintained because serum T_3 remains within the normal range ex-

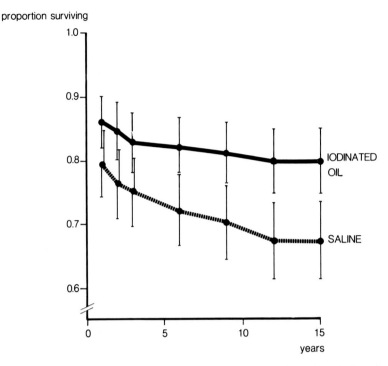

FIG. 2.   Cumulative survival rates of children whose mothers received either iodinated oil or saline (95% confidence limits).

cept in the face of extremely severe dietary iodine deficiency (54–56). Thus, serum T_4 is a marker of the severity of iodine deficiency.

In a series of follow-up examinations of children born to mothers whose thyroid status had been measured when the children were *in utero*, it was found that fetal wastage and clinical neurological damage was the rule when maternal serum T_4 was extremely low (57). Also, measures of cognitive and motor function in clinically normal children correlated with the level of maternal T_4 (58,59). Thus, the degree of iodine deficiency in the mother is associated with the level of neurological damage in the child.

In children and adolescents, there is some evidence that impaired mental functioning may be the consequence of iodine deficiency. Comparing mental and perceptual development in children from a severely iodine-deficient area in Spain with a control group matched by socioeconomic status and educational level, a significant difference was observed (60). Unfortunately, such comparisons of nonrandomized intervention and nonblind assessment must always be interpreted with great caution.

In summary, iodine deficiency leads to a variety of disorders of which goitre was the first to be recognized. Subsequently, it has been shown that maternal iodine deficiency leads to fetal wastage and increased infant and childhood mortality, clinical neurological abnormalities (deaf-mutism, spastic diplegia, and mental retardation), and subclinical deficits which may be made apparent with quantifiable measures of cognitive and motor functioning. Deficiency of iodine during childhood and adolescence may also give rise to suboptimal mental performance.

REFERENCES

1. Hetzel BS. Iodine deficiency disorders and their eradication. *Lancet* 1983;2:1126–9.
2. Kelly FC, Snedden WW. Prevalence and geographical distribution of endemic goitre. In: *Endemic Goitre* (World Health Organization Monograph Series no 44) Geneva: World Health Organization, 1960:27–233.
3. Hetzel BS. An overview of the prevention and control of iodine deficiency disorders. In: Hetzel BS, Dunn JT, Stanbury JB, eds. *The prevention and control of iodine deficiency disorders.* Amsterdam: Elsevier, 1987:7–31.
4. Chilean Iodine Educational Bureau. *Geochemistry of iodine.* London: Chilean Iodine Education Bureau, Stonehouse, Bishopsgate 1956.
5. Marine D, Kimball OP. The prevention of simple goiter in man. *Arch Intern Med* 1920;25:661–72.
6. Roche J, Lissitzky S. Etiology of endemic goitre. In: *Endemic goitre* (World Health Organization Monograph Series no 44) Geneva: World Health Organization, 1960:351–68.
7. Follis R. Recent studies on iodine malnutrition and endemic goiter. *Med Clin N Am* 1964; 48:1219–38.
8. Axelrad AA, Leblond C, Isler H. Role of iodine deficiency in the production of goiter by the Remington diet. *Endocrinology* 1955;56:387–403.
9. Perez C, Scrimshaw NS, Munoz HA. Technique of endemic goitre surveys. In: *Endemic goitre* (World Health Organization Monograph Series no 44) Geneva: World Health Organization, 1960: 369–84.
10. Clements FW. Health significance of endemic goitre and related conditions. In: *Endemic Goitre* (World Health Organization Monograph Series, no 44). Geneva: World Health Organization, 1960: 235–60.
11. Prosser T. *Account and method of cure of the bronchocele or Derby neck.* London, 1769.
12. Taylor S. Calcium as a goitrogen. *J Clin Endocrinol Metab* 1954;14:1412–22.
13. Day TK, Powell-Jackson PR. Fluoride, water hardness, and endemic goitre. *Lancet* 1972;1: 1135–8.
14. Gurevich GP. Quoted by Kelly FC, Snedden WW in Reference 2.
15. Webster B, Chesney AM. Studies in the etiology of simple goiter. *Am J Pathol* 1930;6:275–84.
16. Clements FW, Wishart JW. A thyroid blocking agent in the etiology of endemic goiter. *Metabolism* 1956;5:623–39.
17. Major RH. *Classic descriptions of disease.* Springfield, Illinois: Thomas, 1945.
18. Merke F. The history of endemic goitre and cretinism in the thirteenth to fifteenth centuries. *Proc R Soc Med* 1960;53:995–1002.
19. Cranfield PF. The discovery of cretinism. *Bull History Med* 1962;36:489–511.
20. Norris H. Notice of a remarkable disease analogous to cretinism existing in a small village in the west of England. *Medical Times (Lond)* 1947;17:257–8.
21. Farr W. *Vital statistics: memorial volume of selections from the reports and writings of William Farr.* London: Offices of the Sanitary Institute, 1885:57.
22. Curling T. Two cases of absence of the thyroid body and symmetrical swellings of fat tissue at the sides of the neck connected with defective cerebral development. *Medico-chirug Trans (Lond)* 1850;33:303.
23. Fagge CH. Sporadic cretinism occurring in England. *Medico-chirug Trans (Lond)* 1871;55:155–70.
24. Parker WR. An obsolescent variety of cretinism. *Br Med J* 1896;2:506–7.
25. Costa A, Cottino F, Mortara M, Vogliazzo U. Endemic cretinism in Piedmont. *Panminerva Medica* 1964;6:250–9.
26. Sardinian Royal Commission. Rapport de la commission crée parson majestie le roi de Sardaigne pour etudier le cretinisme. Turin: Imprimerie Royale, 1848.

27. Stott H, Bhatia BB, Lal RS, Rai KC. The distribution and cause of endemic goitre in the United Provinces. *Ind J Med Res* 1939;18:1059–85.
28. Greenwald I. The history of goiter in the Inca Empire: Peru, Chile, and the Argentine Republic. *Texas Rep Biol Med* 1957;15:874–89.
29. Gordon MB. Childhood myxedema or so-called sporadic cretinism in North America. *Endocrinology* 1922;6:225–54.
30. Gordon MB. Childhood myxedema (sporadic cretinism) in the United States. Transactions of the 3rd International Goiter Conference. Washington: Bernclipp Press 1938:114–29.
31. McCarrison R. Observations on endemic cretinism in the Chitral and Gilgit valleys. *Lancet* 1908;2:1275–80.
32. Pharoah POD, Geographical variation in the clinical manifestations of endemic cretinism. *Trop Geogr Med* 1976;28:259–67.
33. Pharoah POD, DeLange F, Fierro-Benitez R, Stanbury JB. Endemic Cretinism. In: Stanbury JB, Hetzel BS, eds. *Endemic goiter and endemic cretinism*. New York: Wiley, 1980:359–421.
34. Querido A, DeLange F, Dunn JT, et al. Definitions of endemic goiter and cretinism, classification of goiter size and severity of endemics and survey techniques. In: Dunn JT, Medeiros-Neto GA, eds. *Endemic goiter and cretinism: Continuing threats to world health*. Washington: Pan American Health Organization Scientific Publication no 292. 1974:267–72.
35. Wespi HJ. Abnahme der taubstummheit in der Schwiez als volge der kropfprophylaxe mit jordiertem kochsalz. *Schwiez Med Wochenschr* 1945;28:625–9.
36. Koenig MP, Veraguth P. Studies of thyroid function in endemic cretins. In: Pitt-Rivers R, ed. *Advances in thyroid research*. London: Pergamon Press, 1961.
37. McCullagh SF, Goitre control project. *Papua New Guinea Med J* 1959;3:43–7.
38. Clarke KH, McCullagh SF, Winikoff D. The use of an intramuscular depot of iodized oil as a long-lasting source of iodine. *Med J Aust* 1960;1:89–92.
39. Buttfield IH, Hetzel BS. Endemic goitre in Eastern New Guinea. *Bull WHO* 1967;36:43–62.
40. Buttfield IH, Hetzel BS. Endemic cretinism in Eastern New Guinea: Its relation to goitre and iodine deficiency. In: Hetzel BS, Pharoah POD, eds. *Endemic cretinism*. Institute of Human Biology, Papua New Guinea Monograph Series. Chipping Norton, New South Wales No 2, 1971:55–69.
41. Pharoah POD, Buttfield IH, Hetzel BS. Neurological damage to the fetus resulting from severe iodine deficiency during pregnancy. *Lancet* 1971;1:308–10.
42. Pharoah POD, Buttfield IH, Hetzel BS. The effect of iodine prophylaxis on the incidence of endemic cretinism. *Adv Exper Med Biol* 1972;30:201–21.
43. Ramirez I, Fierro-Benitez R, Estrella E, Gomez A, Jaramillo C, Hermida C, Moncayo F. The results of prophylaxis of endemic cretinism. *Adv Exper Med Biol* 1972;30:223–37.
44. Fierro-Benitez R, Ramirez I, Estrella E, Stanbury JB. The role of iodine in intellectual development in an area of endemic goiter. In: Dunn TJ, Medeiros-Neto GA, eds. *Endemic goiter and cretinism: continuing threats to world health*. Washington: Pan American Health Organization Scientific Publication No 292, 1974:135–42.
45. Pretell EA, Torres T, Zenteno V, Cornejo M. Prophylaxis of endemic goiter with iodized oil in rural Peru. *Adv Exper Med Biol* 1972;30:249–65.
46. Pharoah POD, Hornabrook RW. Endemic cretinism of recent onset in New Guinea. *Lancet* 1973;2:1038–41.
47. Thilly CH, DeLange FM, Camus M, Berquist H, Ermans AM. Fetal hypothyroidism in endemic goitre: The probable pathogenic mechanism of endemic cretinism. In: Dunn TJ, Medeiros-Neto GA, eds. *Endemic goiter and cretinism: continuing threats to world health*. Washington: Pan American Health Organization Scientific Publication No 292, 1974:121–8.
48. DeLange FM, Thilly C, Camus M, et al. Evidence for fetal hypothyroidism in severe endemic goitre. In: Robbins J, Braveman LE, eds. *Thyroid research*. Amsterdam: Excerpta Medica, 1976:493–6.
49. Ord IG. *Mental tests for pre-literates*. London: Ginn, 1971.
50. Connolly KJ, Pharoah POD. Fetal iodine deficiency and motor performance during childhood. *Lancet* 1979;2:1149–51.
51. Pharoah POD, Connolly KJ. A controlled trial of iodinated oil for the prevention of endemic cretinism: A long term follow-up. *Int J Epidemiol* 1987;16:68–73.
52. Thilly CH, Roger G, LaGasse R, et al. Fetomaternal relationship, fetal hypothyroidism, and psychomotor retardation. In: Ermans AM, Mbulamoko NM, DeLange F, Ahluwalia R, eds. *Role of cassava in the etiology of endemic goiter and cretinism* (IDRC 136e). Ottawa, Canada: International Development Research Centre, 1980.

53. Bleichrodt, N, Drenth PJD, Querido A. Effects of iodine deficiency on mental and psychomotor abilities. *Am J Phys Anthropol* 1980;53:55–7.
54. Patel Y, Pharoah POD, Hornabrook R, Hetzel BS. Serum triiodothyronine thyroxine and thyroid stimulating hormone in endemic goitre. A comparison of goitrous and nongoitrous subjects in New Guinea. *J Clin Endocrinol* 1973;37:783–9.
55. Pharaoh POD, Lawton NF, Ellis SM, Williams ES, Ekins R. The role of triiodothyronine (T$_3$) in the maintenance of euthyroidism in endemic goitre. *Clin Endocrinol* 1973;2:193–9.
56. Goslings BM, Djokomoeljanto R, Docter R, et al. Hypothyroidism in an area of endemic goitre and cretinism in Central Java, Indonesia. *J Clin Endocrinol Metals* 1977;44:481–90.
57. Pharoah POD, Ellis SM, Ekins RP, Williams ES. Maternal thyroid function, iodine deficiency, and fetal development. *Clin Endocrinol* 1976;5:159–66.
58. Pharoah POD, Connolly KJ, Ekins RP, Harding AG. Maternal thyroid levels in pregnancy and the subsequent cognitive and motor performance of the children. *Clin Endocrinol* 1984;21:265–70.
59. Pharoah P, Connolly K, Hetzel B, Ekins R. Maternal thyroid function and motor competence in the child. *Dev Med Child Neurol* 1981;23:76–82.
60. Bleichrodt N, Garcia I, Rubio C, Escobar GM, Escobar Del Rey F. Developmental disorders associated with severe iodine deficiency. In: Hetzel BS, Dunn JT, Stanbury JB, eds. The prevention and control of iodine deficiency disorders. Amsterdam: Elsevier, 1987:65–84.

DISCUSSION

Dr. Chandra: In iodine-deficient subjects we found that although ingestion of bacteria by neutrophils was normal, once the bacteria had been ingested the cells failed to kill them. Normally, nearly all bacteria are killed within about 2 hours of ingestion, whereas in samples from iodine-deficient patients it was only 45% to 50%. This could be corrected with iodine and thyroxine.

I have a question. What are the advantages or disadvantages of choosing iodized salt versus iodized oil injection for preventing neonatal hypothyroidism?

Dr. Pharoah: There has been no controlled trial on this. Iodized salt has been used in many countries with apparent success. In New Guinea, where all imported salt must be iodized by law, there have been no new cretins born in the previous high prevalence areas. There are, of course, other methods of supplementing dietary iodine intake, for example water or bread, and in the USA, iodized candy. Iodization of milk often occurs by accident because of the use of iodophor disinfectants in dairy farming. Iodized salt is fine if you have a good marketing distribution pattern, but if not, there may be difficulties especially in remote areas, which are where you see the disease anyway. If this kind of distribution problem occurs it is probably better to use iodized oil injections since one injection is sufficient for 5 years.

Dr. Chandra: There are several arguments against the widespread use of anything given by injection in large populations. It is very difficult to institute that kind of policy.

Dr. Chapparwal: In one of the Indian states, Maharashtra, iodized salt has been used since 1982. The Indian government has now decided to iodize the entire edible salt supply in the country by 1992. This decision was taken because iodine-deficient diets cause over 100 to 1000 stillbirths per year in Maharashtra alone, besides causing goiter and cretinism. The fear that excess iodine is harmful is unjustified, since the Japanese consume 2000 μg of iodine daily compared with a daily requirement of about 100 μg. The excess is excreted harmlessly. The cost of iodization works out as only Rs 1 per family per year.

Dr. Goyens: What are the pathophysiological mechanisms that could lead to the two totally different clinical entities in different parts of the world? We suggested that the destruction of the thyroid gland around birth, which characterizes the myxedematous variety (1), could be due, at least in part, to superimposed dietary trace element deficiencies depressing tissue resistance to oxygen and causing follicular cell death in an overstimulated but fragile thyroid.

Although we were not able to prove this, our data obtained in Kivu (Central Africa) were compatible with our hypothesis that selenium deficiency could contribute to the pathogenesis of myxedematous cretinism (2).

Dr. Pharoah: I think neurological cretinism is due to iodine deficiency in the mother in early pregnancy, resulting in insufficient maternal thyroid hormone. During the first 3 months of gestation, before the fetal thyroid is working, maternal thyroid hormone is essential for normal neurological maturation. Later on, when fetal thyroid function becomes important, thyroid deficiency results in a different sort of neurological damage.

Dr. Anke: Could we use the mineral supply to domestic animals to prevent iodine deficiency in humans?

Dr. Pharoah: Animal products in developing countries tend to have a high iodine content but people in rural areas often do not eat meat, or only very occasionally.

Dr. Goyens: Delange working in Central Africa in Kivu and Ubangi has shown that the balance between iodine and thiocyanate is the crucial factor in the etiology of endemic goiter and cretinism in that part of the world. The balance is more important than the iodine supply alone: when the I/SCN ratio falls below a critical level, either because of excessively low iodine intake or because of high thiocyanate production, goiter develops (3). Data on iodine intake or thiocyanate production in domestic animals in Central Africa are not available however.

Dr. Gabr: In some cases endemic goiter is associated with defective biosynthesis of thyroid hormone. High iodine intake can partly correct some of these biosynthesis defects. There is evidence now that iodine deficiency can affect cognitive functions in the absence of clinical cretinism or goiter. In communities where iodine deficiency is prevalent, iodination of salt is a most effective means of preventing this. I agree however that in those situations where there are transportation difficulties, or where there is an acute problem, the use of iodized oil is a practical solution.

Dr. Pharoah: I do not disagree with that. Each country has its own marketing pattern. No one solution is ideal for all situations.

Dr. Aggett: Can I ask a question of Professor Lombeck? In Germany, iodine supplementation of salt or foodstuffs is used, and yet there is still a relatively high incidence of goiter. Why is this?

Dr. Lombeck: Iodinization is not obligatory. You can buy normal or iodized salt as in Britain. By measuring urinary iodine excretion in different population groups, Professor Manz has shown recently that the iodine intake in Germany is lower than previously calculated. Our food habits have changed, and we now consume more ready-to-eat meals and less iodized salt. So we still have a problem of too low an iodine intake.

REFERENCES

1. Dumont JE, Ermans AM, Bastenie PA. Mechanism of thyroid failure in the Uele endemic cretins. *J Clin Endocrinol* 1963;23:847–60.
2. Goyens P, Golstein J, Nsombola B, Vis H, Dumont JE. Selenium deficiency as a possible factor in the pathogenesis of myxoedematous endemic cretinism. *Acta Endocrinol (Copenhagen)* 1987;114:497–502.
3. Ermans AM, Bourdoux P, Kinthaert J, et al. Role of cassava in the etiology of endemic goiter and cretinism. In: Delange F, Ahluwalia R, eds. *Cassava toxicity and thyroid: Research and public health issues.* Ottawa, Ontario: International Development Research Centre (IDRC-207e), pp. 9–16.

Trace Elements in Nutrition of Children—II,
edited by Ranjit K. Chandra, Nestlé Nutrition
Workshop Series, Vol. 23, Nestec Ltd.,
Vevey/Raven Press, Ltd., New York © 1991.

Fluoride Nutrition in Infancy—Is There a Biological Role of Fluoride for Growth?

Renate L. Bergmann and Karl E. Bergmann

Free University Berlin, Department of Pediatrics, and Federal Health Office, Berlin, Federal Republic of Germany

Fluoride is present in all soils, drinking waters, organisms, and foods at variable concentrations (Table 1). In many countries including West Germany, regulations require the fluoride concentration in drinking water to be below 1.5 ppm. In mineral waters, this value can be exceeded. If it is above 5 ppm, in our legislation a warning is required to limit the amount consumed. Worldwide, an estimated 300 million people consume fluoridated drinking water (0.6 to 1.2 ppm, depending on climate and season) to prevent tooth decay. This is not so in West Germany. More than 90% of the drinking waters in West Germany have a fluoride concentration below 0.25 ppm (3).

Fluoride intake in infancy largely depends upon foods consumed (Table 2), flu-

TABLE 1. *Fluoride content (ppm) of the human environment and of food in West Germany. Values are means (SD)*

	Usual content
Soil (5)[a]	100–300
Heavy clay (5)	–8300
Fresh water in West Germany (3)	0.1–0.3
Marine water (5)	1.2–1.4
Atmosphere	
unpolluted (5)	$< 0.05\ \mu g/m^3$
polluted city (4)	$1.93\ \mu g/m^3$
maximum allowed at workplace in West Germany (2)	$2500\ \mu g/m^3$
Vegetables (1)	0.03 (0.029)
Herbs (1)	0.63 (0.50)
Fruits (1)	0.027 (0.021)
Spices (1)	1.56 (2.19)
Cow's milk (1)	0.02 (0.01)
Canned food (1)	0.23 (0.48)
Meats (1)	0.18 (0.09)

[a]Numbers in brackets are references cited.

105

TABLE 2. *Fluoride concentration (ppm) in infant foods from West Germany*

	n	Mean	SD
Breast milk	23	0.003	0.002
Infant formulas	11	0.029	0.014
Strained fruits	18	0.061	0.032
Strained vegetables	16	0.078	0.052
Fruit juices	18	0.091	0.029
Meat-containing dinners	35	0.100	0.032
Poultry dinners[a]	10	0.303	0.298
Cereals	46	0.135	0.101

[a]Values after 1982.
From Bergmann KE, et al. (1,6).

oride concentration in drinking water, and fluoride supplements for caries prevention. It is lowest in the exclusively breast-fed infant under Western hygienic and living conditions. Fluoride intake of adults in Germany usually ranges between 0.4 and 1.0 mg/day (7–9, and unpublished data of the authors). It varies with fluoride concentration in drinking water (or mineral water), and consumption of tea and seafood. In the United States, because of drinking water fluoridation, the mean intake in young adults ranges from 0.9 to 1.9 mg/day (10).

More than 90% of ingested fluoride is absorbed (11). Retention depends upon age, fluoride content of the skeleton, and intake. In newborn infants, we found a retention of more than 90% of a single first fluoride dose of 0.25 mg (12). In adults, under steady-state conditions, usually more than 80% is excreted by the kidneys (11). Low pH values enhance fluoride absorption in the stomach and upper gastrointestinal tract in rats (13).

So far it has not been possible to remove fluoride from living organisms or their environment sufficiently to allow satisfactory investigation of its biological essentiality. Nor has fluoride deficiency affecting general health and functioning been observed in nature. However, the preventive effects of fluoride on dental decay have led several bodies to define fluoride as a beneficial trace element (14–16). While Nielsen (17) has denied that any of the available data justify the definition of fluoride as an essential nutrient, we thought that at least its importance for the formation of apatite *in vitro* (18) justified further exploration of its role in bone and tooth formation. The relationship between fluoride concentration and apatite formation in dilute supersaturated solutions has been further quantified for the concentrations observed *in vivo* by Varughese and Moreno (19). These authors suggested a role for fluoride in biological calcification. The 1983 communication by Farley et al (20) revealed that increasing the fluoride concentration within a physiological range in an embryonic chick bone cell or organ culture stimulated thymidine incorporation into bone-forming cells as well as stimulating cell proliferation and alkaline phosphatase activity, and it increased bone formation in embryonic calvaria. Similar observations have been published by Marie and Hott (21) on mouse embryonic cells.

Drinkard et al (22) found that fluoride stimulated the secretion of the low molecular weight proteins of the enamel matrix at concentrations in the physiological range. It also stimulated the activity of ion transport ATPase in cultivated bone forming cells (23). However, whether we are dealing here with mere *effects* or with a *biological role* of fluoride remains to be answered.

The scientific tools that can be used to explore a biological role of an element include reducing the dietary intake of the element under experimental conditions, and observing the effect of the element under conditions where natural exposure is very low. The observation that fluoride stimulates growth in young rats maintained on low fluoride intake in trace element sterile isolators (24,25) is suggestive of a global biological role of fluoride. The fluoride intake of the rats causing growth retardation can be estimated to be between 2 and 25 μg F per 100 kcal.

Our interest focuses on the question as to whether fluoride has any biological role in man apart from improving caries resistance.

ESSENTIALS OF STUDY DESIGN AND METHODS

On the basis of our own analyses which confirmed previously published data (26–28), we estimated that exclusively breast-fed infants had an average fluoride intake of about 3 μg per day or 0.3 to 8 μg per 100 kcal. This appeared to be of the order of magnitude where a careful study of growth was justified.

According to Gedalia et al (29), Hellström (30), and our own measurements (31,32), infants are born with appreciable amounts of fluoride in their skeleton, and these depend on the long-term fluoride exposure of the mother, and hence upon drinking water fluoride concentration. After scanning all available data on German drinking waters, we identified the north-eastern Bavarian city of Weiden as providing particularly low population exposure to fluoride. The area had values for drinking water fluoride of 0.02 to 0.16 ppm. To be certain that there was indeed a low population exposure, we also measured fluoride concentration in autopsy samples of rib bone collected by the pathologist (Professor Korb) at the community hospital, and in individual urine samples from the mothers and their infants who were eventually enrolled in our study (Table 3).

TABLE 3. *Fluoride concentration in autopsy samples (6th rib) from residents in Berlin, Weiden, West Germany (own measurements), and Rochester*

	F-conc in water (ppm)	n	Mean age	Mean F-conc in defatted bone ash (ppm)
Berlin 1984−85	0.2	41	65	638
Weiden 1985−86	0.07	59	65	442
Rochester 1950−51	0.06	64	60	978
Rochester 1975	1.0	17	70	2085

From Charen J, et al. (33).

In Germany, it is recommended that infants receive fluoride supplements of 0.25 mg per day with 500 IU of vitamin D in a tablet from birth. This is 80 to 100 times the amount ingested by young exclusively breast-fed infants. Some other countries recommend that fluoride supplementation should start only after the age of 6 months. This enabled us to assign 84 newborn infants randomly to either an early or a late fluoride supplementation group. An additional 25 infants were included, in whom parents selected fluoride from birth or who were assigned to late fluoride to compensate somewhat for the ones selecting fluoride. The impact of self-selection and non-random assignment was carefully evaluated (34) and could be disregarded. Our study group finally consisted of 109 infants who were exclusively breast-fed for at least 4 months. Fifty eight infants received a fluoride supplement from birth, 51 from 6 months onwards.

To permit the control of selection bias, all 1387 infants with birthweights greater than 2,500 g who were born during the recruiting period and on whom information was available to the maternity department were carefully recorded with their own and their parents' relevant variables to serve as the background population from which the cohort was drawn. The final analysis included models that weighted for differences between the background population and the cohort.

The problem of a potentially small influence of fluoride in the presence of other stronger factors was tackled by several steps, such as:

1. All measurements were taken extremely carefully in a standardized manner (35), mostly by the researcher himself.
2. The infants were seen nine times during the first year of life, and received a careful medical check-up. Fluoride and creatinine were measured in morning spot urine samples on four to six occasions per case. Fluoride was also determined in breast milk samples, in drinking and mineral waters, beverages and numerous food items of the infants by potentiometry after microdiffusion.
3. Only small deviations from projected age at measurement were allowed.
4. The urinary fluoride (μg/g creatinine) was unknown during the field work. The measurements could therefore be collected in a blinded manner with respect to this variable.
5. All *potential influences* on growth measured in this study were carefully evaluated for independent effects.
6. The modelling work applying GLIM (34) had to go through many steps, partly because we had to develop a way to describe growth in a more-dimensional manner. The final models only retained variables that had *consistent* and independent effects on a certain outcome, and which were *repeatedly* observed in different other models and under different assumptions of distribution and link function.

The models describing growth best and permitting the separation of fluoride influences from other factors most clearly utilized polygonal approximation for growth and fluoride intake at successive age intervals. An F value of 10 or greater with around 900 denominator degrees of freedom was the criterion of significance (corresponding to a *p* value of much less than 1%). For the more-dimensional statistical analyses, H. Busse, Federal Health Office, developed a modular system in GLIM to be applied by the authors; the most important analytical steps were performed by himself in close cooperation with the authors.

RESULTS

Urinary fluoride concentration of the mothers is considered to be a measure of habitual fluoride exposure. Table 4 contains means, standard deviations, and the range of values measured in our laboratory. When related to fluoride intake as estimated from diet history at birth, the individual means of fluoride concentration in urine (μg/g creatinine) were highly correlated to estimated intakes before delivery. The fluoride excretion values will be utilized as an index of habitual (including gestational) fluoride intake of the mother, which under steady-state conditions reflects her skeletal fluoride pool and thereby the prenatal exposure of the infant.

Fluoride concentrations in samples of mother's milk were low and did not vary systematically with duration of breast feeding (Table 5). Total fluoride intake of the infants from mother's milk and supplementary foods increased during the first 6 months of life (Table 6).

Table 7 shows the urinary fluoride concentration (μg/l) of the infants until 6

TABLE 4. *Fluoride concentration (ppm) in urine of breast-feeding mothers*

Weeks postpartum	n	Mean	SD	Max	Min
4	86	0.450	0.338	1.749	0.023
8	102	0.463	0.322	2.490	0.074
12	105	0.561	0.560	4.649	0.057
16	105	0.509	0.370	2.313	0.060
20	100	0.512	0.521	3.838	0.111
26	95	0.494	0.502	4.399	0.023

TABLE 5. *Fluoride concentration in breast milk during 6 months of lactation (in ppm)*

Weeks postpartum	n	Mean	SD	Max	Min
4	67	0.004	0.004	0.016	not detectable
8	82	0.003	0.003	0.012	not detectable
12	74	0.004	0.003	0.014	not detectable
16	81	0.004	0.003	0.016	not detectable
20	75	0.004	0.004	0.025	not detectable
26	65	0.003	0.003	0.012	not detectable

TABLE 6. *Mean fluoride intake (mg/day) of breast-fed infants in the first 6 months of life from breast milk, beikost, and supplements—as actually taken (51 infants without and 58 infants with F supplementation)*

Age in weeks	Breast-milk	Beikost	F tablets	Total intake	
				Without suppl.	With suppl.
0–4	0.0024	0.001	0.186	0.003	0.189
4–8	0.0022	0.001	0.237	0.003	0.240
8–12	0.0031	0.001	0.241	0.004	0.245
12–16	0.0031	0.003	0.237	0.006	0.243
16–20	0.0031	0.023	0.245	0.026	0.271
20–26	0.0023	0.048	0.240	0.050	0.290

TABLE 7. *Fluoride concentration in the urine of infants with (n = 58) and without (n = 51) fluoride supplements*

Age (weeks)	With F supplements		Without F supplements	
	Mean	SD	Mean	SD
4	0.084	0.099	0.013	0.022
8	0.096	0.098	0.011	0.027
12	0.197	0.242	0.015	0.034
16	0.153	0.176	0.013	0.019
20	0.195	0.211	0.025	0.037
26	0.213	0.169	0.071	0.074

months of age. It is different between the early and late fluoride groups and increases somewhat with the introduction of supplementary foods at around 20 weeks of age. Concentrations differ between groups by factors of 6 to 13, whereas total intakes differed by factors up to 80.

As an outcome variable, we present here body mass in infancy. Table 8 presents the means of our growth data in comparison with results of breast-fed boys from Iowa and Sweden (36,37) collected from families under good living conditions. Our data are in very close agreement with them. This means that children did not have gross deficiencies.

Figure 1 presents *attained body weights* of the infants in both the early and the late fluoride supplementation groups. The mean values are nearly identical. This does not necessarily imply that all influential factors are distributed identically in both groups. With individual values, there could well be a separation according to fluoride supplements. However, if there was any fluoride effect on attained body mass it could not be very large.

Figures 2 and 3 give a first impression of a potential difference in *growth rate* depending upon prenatal and postnatal fluoride exposure. During the first 4 months of

TABLE 8. *Percentiles (P) for body weight of boys in the Weiden study compared to breast-fed infants in USA and to infants in Sweden*

Age (weeks)	Weiden			USA and Sweden		
	10th P	50th P	90th P	10th P	50th P	90th P
0.5	3063	3500	4066	2924	3500	3982
4	3743	4386	4957	3482	4322	4787
8	4527	5292	6001	4463	5250	5923
12	5099	5961	6862	5264	5964	6911
16	5618	6615	7599	5758	6482	7647
20	6201	7245	8365	—	—	—
26	6814	7810	9038	6730	7740	9000
39	7825	9220	10271	7890	9080	10630
52	8848	10050	11114	8840	10160	11670

From Fomon SJ, et al. (36), and Karlberg and Taranger (37).

life—this was the period of exclusive breast feeding—infants with higher prenatal fluoride exposure grew faster than infants with lower prenatal exposure. Between 4 and 6 months (introduction of supplementary food), the differences were in the same direction although of smaller magnitude. After age 26 weeks (6 months)—this was when all infants received fluoride supplements—the differences reversed. A similar small effect could be observed when examining the timing of fluoride sup-

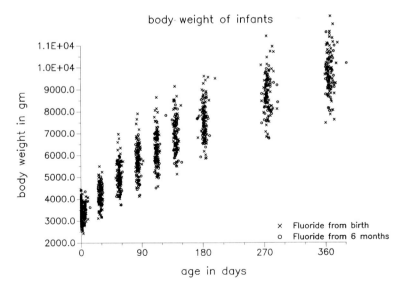

FIG. 1. Body weight of infants during the first year of life with early (from birth) and late (from 6 months) fluoride prophylaxis.

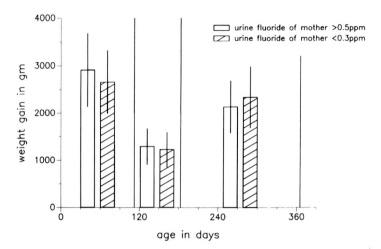

FIG. 2. Weight gain during the intervals birth to 112 days, 112 to 182 days, and 182 to 365 days of age in infants with higher prenatal fluoride exposure (urine fluoride of mother > 0.5 ppm) and lower prenatal fluoride exposure (urine fluoride of mother < 0.3 ppm). Urine fluoride of mother = fluoride concentration in samples of morning urine of the mother.

plements: the group which was supplemented later appeared to grow somewhat slower during the first 26 weeks.

The distribution of early and late fluoride supplements was independent of the fluoride excretion of the mother, as were the many other factors important for growth. More-dimensional analysis was applied to make groups and influences comparable and to submit them to *ceteris paribus* considerations.

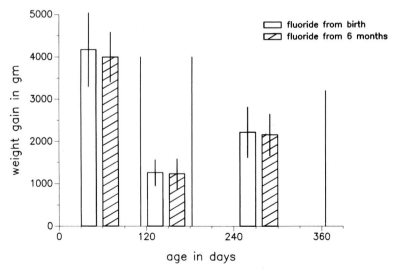

FIG. 3. Weight gain during the intervals birth to 112 days, 112 to 182 days, and 182 to 365 days of age in infants with early (from birth) or late (from 6 months) fluoride prophylaxis.

Prenatal Fluoride Exposure

Prenatal fluoride exposure proved to be a positive influence on weight gain. Its effect could be separated most clearly under Poisson distribution and link logarithm. The contribution to the fit was significant (F = 42) if attained weight during the first 6 months was considered (Table 9). It was also significant when considering growth rate during the whole of the first year of life. A significant improvement of fit was also apparent in other distributions and link functions, but Poisson and link logarithm fitted best. Under these conditions, we weighted our cohort to the background population for the purpose of generalization, and excluded the two infants with highest prenatal exposure and a particularly strong fluoride effect on growth to be on the safe side. The influence of prenatal fluoride exposure on weight gain was stronger in infants with early fluoride prophylaxis (Table 10). Gains in total body length (Table 11), and crown-rump length, were also significantly influenced by prenatal exposure. The impact of prenatal fluoride exposure on gain in head circumference and skinfold thickness was negligible.

TABLE 9. *Estimate of body weight in the first 6 months of life. More-dimensional analysis with GLIM (34) assuming Poisson distribution and logarithmic link*

Hypothesis	Deviance	Contrasted hypotheses	Degrees of freedom Nominator	Denominator	F value
1. HA3 + SEX + RES	54902				
2. HA3 + SEX + RES + MFL	51984	1:2	1	754	42.320

HA3 = Grand mean + AGE + $(AGE)^2$ + $(AGE)^3$; RES, residence; MFL, fluoride-to-creatinine concentration in urine of mothers.

TABLE 10. *Estimate of gain in body weight in the first year of life. More-dimensional analysis with GLIM (34) assuming Poisson distribution and logarithmic link*

Hypothesis	Deviance	Contrasted hypotheses	Degrees of freedom Nominator	Denominator	F Value
1. HAT + AK	32176				
2. HAT + AK + FLT	30954	1:2	1	925	36.5
3. HAT + AK + HAF	28360	2:3	8	917	10.5 (i.e., 8 × 10.5)
4. HAT + AK + F8	32018	1:4	1	925	4.5
5. HAT + AK + F8 + MFLF	30441	4:5	1	924	47.9
6. HAT + AK + F8 + MFL	31380	4:6	1	924	18.8

HAT = (polygonal approximation for growth rate during eight successive age intervals in the first year of life) in interaction with sex, + (birth measurements + parity + sex) + (mother's height + father's height + mother's age with parity) in interaction with sex; AK, age class 1, 0–6 months, age class 2, 7–12 months; FLT, number of fluoride tablets in preceding interval; HAF, polygonal approximation for number of fluoride tablets in each interval; F8, number of fluoride tablets from 6 through 9 months; MFLF, mother's urine fluoride-to-creatinine concentrations in infants with early fluoride prophylaxis; MFL, mother's urine fluoride-to-creatinine concentration, all infants.

TABLE 11. *Estimate of gain in body length in the first year of life. More-dimensional analysis with GLIM (34) assuming Poisson distribution and logarithmic link*[a]

Hypothesis	Deviance	Contrasted hypotheses	Degrees of freedom Nominator	Degrees of freedom Denominator	F Value
1. HAT + AK	15.52				
2. HAT + AK + FLT	15.08	1:2	1	925	26.8
3. HAT + AK + HAF	14.33	2:3	8	917	6.0 (i.e., 8 × 6)
4. HAT + AK + F8	14.85	1:4	1	925	41.0
5. HAT + AK + F8 + MFLF	14.46	4:5	1	924	25.2
6. HAT + AK + F8 + MFL	14.80	4:6	1	924	3.5

[a]Explanation of variables as in Table 10.

Postnatal Fluoride Exposure

Postnatal fluoride exposure of the order of magnitude contributed by beikost did not show any significant influence on growth. But the number of fluoride tablets consumed by the infant improved the fit significantly when estimating weight gain (F = 37), gain in total body length (F = 27), crown-rump length (F = 11), head circumference (F = 19), but not skinfold thickness (F = 2).

An internal structure of fluoride effects on growth could clearly be recognized, that is, pre- and postnatal fluoride exposure had combined effects, the strength of the fluoride effects differed between age intervals, and sex-specific differences could also be recognized. However, our cohort seemed too small to evaluate these interactions satisfactorily any further.

Slowing of growth rate at marginal or deficient intake is considered a relevant indicator for a biological role of a trace element. In the present study, fluoride could be shown to have a positive influence on growth rate of human infants when intake generally was low.

These findings, together with the biochemical effects of fluoride on cell proliferation, protein synthesis, and mineralization of bony structures, seem to suggest its classification as an essential trace element.

ACKNOWLEDGMENT

RLB was supported by a grant from the German Ministry of Research and Technology (BMFT 07047332) and from the German Research Foundation (DFG Be 624/2-1).

REFERENCES

1. Bergmann KE, Bergmann RL. Fluorid als Nahrungsfaktor. *Zahnärztl Mitt* 1987;77:2544–51.
2. Deutsche Forschungsgemeinschaft. Maximale Arbeitisplatzkonzentrationen und biologische Arbeitsstofftoleranzwerte 1989. Mitt. *XXIV* der Senatskommission zur Prüfung gesundheitsschädlicher Arbeitsstoffe. Weinheim: VCH Verlagsgesellschaft, 1989.

3. Eberle G, Wolter R. Fluoridkarte der Bundesrepublik Deutschland. *WIdO-Materialien* 1985; 25:31.

4. Erdmann W, Kettner H. Ergebnisse von Fluorid-Immissionsmessungen im Einflußbereich einer Aluminiumhütte. *Öff Gesundh-Wesen* 1975;37:29–32.

5. Michigan Office of Science and Technology. Report of the governor's task force on fluorides. Lansing: State of Michigan, December, 1979.

6. Bergmann KE, Bergmann RL, Turba H, Zwemke H. Fluoridgesamtaufnahme im ersten Lebensjahr. *Dtsch Zahnärztl Z* 1983;38: 145–7.

7. Oelschläger W, Feyler L, Schenkel H, Moser E, Seidel D. Das Nahrungsfluor in toxikologischer Hinsicht. Teil II: Die Fluorgehalte von Nahrungsmitteln pflanzlicher Herkunft und deren Beeinflussung durch erhöhte Fluoraufnahmen. *Staub-Reinhalt Luft* 1983;43:118–25.

8. Siebert G, Trautner K. Fluoride content of selected human food, pet food and related materials. *Z Ernährungswiss* 1985;24:54–66.

9. Schraitle R, Siebert G. Zahngesundheit und Ernährung. 4.8 Beitrag der Nahrung zur Fluoridversorgung. Vienna: Carl Hanser Verlag München, 1987:130–3.

10. Singer L, Ophaug RH, Harland BF. Dietary fluoride intake of 15–19-year-old male adults residing in the United States. *J Dent Res* 1985;64:1302–5.

11. Hodge HC, Smith FA. Fluoride. In: Bromer F, Coburn JW, eds. *Disorders of mineral metabolism.* New York: Academic Press, 1981:440–83.

12. Spelsberg A. Fluoride balances in newborn infants. Berlin: Free University of Berlin, 1990. Doctoral Thesis.

13. Whitford GM, Pashley DH. Fluoride absorption: The influence of gastric acidity. *Calcif Tissue Int* 1984;36:302–7.

14. American Academy of Pediatrics. Committee on Nutrition. Fluoride as a nutrient. *Pediatrics* 1972;49:456–60.

15. Committee on Dietary Allowances. *Recommended dietary allowances,* 9th ed. Washington: American Academy of Science, 1980.

16. Deutsche Gesellschaft für Ernährung. *Empfehlungen für die Nährstoffzufuhr.* Frankfurt am Main: Umschau Verlag, 1985.

17. Nielsen FH. Ultratrace elements in nutrition. *Annu Rev Nutr* 1984;4:21–41.

18. Newesely H. Changes in crystal types of low solubility calcium phosphates in the presence of accompanying ions. *Arch Oral Biol (Suppl)* 1961;6:174–80.

19. Varughese K, Moreno EC. Crystal growth of calcium apatites in dilute solutions containing fluoride. *Calcif Tissue Int* 1981;33:431–9.

20. Farley JR, Wergedal JE, Baylink DJ. Fluoride directly stimulates proliferation and alkaline phosphatase activity of bone-forming cells. *Science* 1983;222:330–2.

21. Marie PJ, Hott M. Short-term effects of fluoride and strontium on bone formation and resorption in the mouse. *Metabolism* 1986;35:547–51.

22. Drinkard CR, Crenshaw MA, Bawden JW. The effect of fluoride on the electrophoretic patterns of developing rat molar enamel. *Arch Oral Biol* 1983;28:1131–4.

23. Anderson RE, Kemp JW, Jee WSS, Woodbury DM. Effects of cortisol and fluoride on ion-transporting ATPase activities in cultured osteoblastlike cells. *In Vitro* 1984;20:847–55.

24. Schwarz K, Milne DB. Fluorine requirement for growth in the rat. *Bioinorganic Chem* 1972;1:331–8.

25. Schwarz K. Recent dietary trace element research, exemplified by tin, fluorine, and silicon. *Fed Proc* 1974:33:1748ff.

26. Ekstrand J, Boreus LO, de Chateau P. No evidence of transfer of fluoride from plasma to breast milk. *Br Med J* 1981;283:761–2.

27. Spak CJ, Hardell LI, De Chateau P. Fluoride in human milk. *Acta Paediatr Scand* 1983;72:699–701.

28. Esala S, Vuori E, Helle A. Effect of maternal fluorine intake on breast milk fluorine content. *Br J Nutr* 1982;48:201–4.

29. Gedalia I, Brzezinski A, Portuguese N, Bercovici, B. The fluoride content of teeth and bones of human foetuses *Arch Oral Biol* 1964;9:331–40.

30. Hellström I. Studies on fluoride distribution in infants and small children. *Scand J Dent Res* 1976;84:119–36.

31. Bergmann KE, Bergmann RL. Epidemiologische und ernährungsphysiologische Aspekte des Fluors. In: Gladtke E, Heimann G, Lombeck I, Eckert I, eds. *Spurenelemente.* Stuttgart: Georg Thieme Verlag, 1985:96–105.

32. Schraad F-J, Bergmann RL, Bergmann KE, Gawlik D, Gatschke W, Vogel M. Die Accretion von

Fluorid im Skelett während der Foetalperiode. *Dtsch Zahnärztl Z* 1984;39:965–7.

33. Charen J, Taves DR, Stamm JW, Parkins FM. Bone fluoride concentrations associated with fluoridated drinking water. *Calcif Tiss Int* 1979;27:95–9.
34. Healy MJR. *GLIM - An introduction*. Oxford: Clarendon Press, 1988.
35. Bergmann RL, Bergmann KE, Kollmann F, Maaser R. *Growth atlas*. Wiesbaden: Papillon Verlag, 1977:16,50,56.
36. Fomon SJ, Ziegler EE, Filer LJ, Anderson TA, Edwards BB, Nelson SE. Growth and serum chemical values of normal breastfed infants. *Acta Paediatr Scand (Suppl)* 1978;273:1–29.
37. Karlberg P, Taranger J. The somatic development of children in a Swedish urban community. *Acta Paediatr Scand (Suppl)* 1976;258:32.

DISCUSSION

Dr. Zlotkin: You didn't show any data on length catch-up, although you did for weight. Could you comment on that?

Dr. R. Bergmann: The catch-up in length was smaller than in weight. However, we found that the two groups were very different in many respects. It was therefore mandatory to model growth and the various other influences simultaneously, We have not yet developed a simple way to present this multidimensional model.

Dr. K.E. Bergmann: Careful more-dimensional analysis revealed that an independent statistically significant positive effect of pre- and postnatal fluoride exposure on length growth could clearly be separated from many other influences on growth.

Dr. Aggett: Concerning the intakes, there seemed to be a very large skew on the breast milk concentration data because they show a large standard deviation. Is this because some of your values were below the limit of detection?

Dr. R. Bergmann: Some of the mothers had fluoride supplements during gestation and lactation and these had higher breast-milk fluoride values than the others. The lowest values were within our range of detectability, which is 1 ppb.

Dr. Chandra: Do you have any explanation for the different growth rates in the supplemented and unsupplemented groups? How about the incidence of atopic disease or anemia?

Dr. R. Bergmann: I examined the children myself eight times during the first year and afterwards at six monthly intervals. I found no clinical differences between the groups except in one respect, which was that the infants with early fluoride supplementation more commonly had seborrheic or atopic dermatitis. There was, however, a difference in hemoglobin values. Infants in the early supplementation group had lower mean Hb at 6 months than those in the later supplementation group. The opposite was true at 1 year of age. These differences were a reflection of iron status, but they were not very large.

Dr. Chandra: I assume that the supplement you were giving was sodium fluoride? What was the level of zinc in it?

Dr. R. Bergmann: Yes, it was sodium fluoride. Dr. Rösick from the Hahn–Meitner Institute in Berlin has measured zinc in the preparation and found that the vitamin D tablets without fluoride contain 32 ng zinc and those with fluoride, 18 ng.

Dr. Aggett: Is there any possibility that fluoride may have been compensating for a partial iodine deficiency?

Dr. R. Bergmann: This I do not know. We did not investigate it. I do remember one child in the late supplementation group who looked like an iodine-deficient infant, but his thyroxine and thyrotropin values at age 6 months were normal.

Dr. K.E. Bergmann: We were looking for a presumably very small effect in the presence of other much stronger influences. This may be of fundamental importance in trace element research, especially if we are dealing with marginal deficiencies or excesses. The tool we applied in this study was more-dimensional modeling with GLIM, and the data set was first randomly divided into two subsets, one explorative and one confirmatory. GLIM is extremely flexible and will permit, for example, the comparison of different distribution assumptions on the fit of the model, as well as complete examination of any intercorrelations.

In our instance we feel comfortable with our findings because it was possible to separate the influences of fluoride exposure from other potential influences. Most of the assignment to early and late fluoride supplements occurred at random and the few nonrandom subjects did not differ from the others with respect to the relevant variables. The indicator of prenatal fluoride exposure (maternal fluoride excretion) was not known to the investigators during data collection so there was complete observer blinding with respect to this important variable. This enabled us to look at fluoride from two different points of view, both of which indicated a significant positive effect on growth. Separating other influences made the effect of fluoride stronger. There was a dose-response relationship for the number of fluoride tablets given by the mother. Omitting two cases with the strongest influence of fluoride somewhat weakened the relationship but it remained highly significant. Weighing the cohort for the differences in the population did not disrupt the results.

These factors make us feel comfortable that we are not dealing with a model artifact. Keeping everything constant except for urinary fluoride, the lowest prenatal fluoride exposure in this study during the first year of life leads to a weight gain about 1 kg less than in the highest prenatal fluoride exposure during the first year of life.

Trace Elements in Nutrition of Children—II,
edited by Ranjit K. Chandra, Nestlé Nutrition
Workshop Series, Vol. 23, Nestec Ltd.,
Vevey/Raven Press, Ltd., New York © 1991.

The Essentiality of Ultra Trace Elements for Reproduction and Pre- and Postnatal Development

Manfred Anke

Karl-Marx-Universität Leipzig, Sektion Tierproduktion und Veterinärmedizin, Wissenschaftsbereich Tierernährungschemie, Leipzig, German Democratic Republic

During the long passage of inorganic components of foodstuffs, water and air through the fauna, which lasted millions of years, the majority of these substances have probably become parts or activators of proteins, enzymes, hormones, or other parts of the body.

At present, two groups of essential elements can be distinguished. The first group comprises iron, iodine, copper, manganese, zinc, cobalt, selenium, and chromium. The deficiency symptoms caused by these elements in free-living animals and/or humans have been described all over the world.

Such evidence in animals and humans is controversial or not available for molybdenum and fluorine, which belong to the second category and are also essential trace elements. The same holds true for vanadium, silicon, nickel, arsenic, lithium, lead, and cadmium. According to the present level of knowledge, sufficient amounts of these elements occur in foodstuffs as well as in water (1). Thus no primary deficiency symptoms are to be expected in animals and humans. The detection of their essentiality is carried out by means of semisynthetic rations (2). The elements boron (3) and bromine (4), which may be essential elements for fauna, must probably also be assigned to this group. At present, there is no clear delimitation of essential trace elements from essential ultra trace elements. Frieden (5) only attributed iron, zinc, and copper to the essential elements and all the others to the ultra trace elements. For these reasons, we should continue to classify the practically important inorganic components of the diet as "bulk elements" (calcium, magnesium, phosphorus, potassium, sodium, sulphur, chloride) and "trace elements" (iron, zinc, copper, manganese, iodine, selenium, cobalt, chromium), and those elements which have been identified as essential only by means of synthetic rations and because they are components of essential parts of the body, but which occur in sufficient amounts in feed and foodstuffs, should be classified as "ultra trace elements." According to the present level of knowledge, fluorine, molybdenum, silicon, vanadium, nickel, arsenic, cadmium, lead, lithium, boron, and bromine might therefore be classified as ultra trace elements.

The available data on the biological essentiality of several trace elements for reproduction and the pre- and postnatal development are presented in this chapter. They are almost exclusively the results of animal experiments.

MOLYBDENUM

Molybdenum is a component of several enzymes in the flora and fauna (Table 1). Apart from nitrogenase, all molybdenum-dependent enzymes contain the same molybdenum factor, the organic basis of which is a pterin ring with a side chain containing a phosphate ester.

In spite of the fact that the presence of molybdenum has been clearly demonstrated in many enzymes, it has only proved possible to induce molybdenum deficiency in animals by high doses of tungsten, which has an antagonistic effect. Tungsten can replace 30% to 40% of the molybdenum in sulfite oxidase and thus inactivate it (7,8). Only the tenfold repetition of a molybdenum-deficient diet containing < 24 μg molybdenum/kg dry matter to growing, gravid, and lactating goats via a semi-synthetic ration was able to produce significantly reduced growth and reproductive performance in the molybdenum-deficient animals (Tables 2,3). The molybdenum-deficient goats had a significantly worse success rate of first inseminations, needed more services per gravidity, aborted more fetuses, and showed a significantly reduced life expectancy. The influence of intrauterine molybdenum deficiency on the development of fetal body weight remained insignificant. The molybdenum-deficient goats, however, delivered significantly more kids with a live weight of < 2.0 kg than control goats (10). At the end of the sucking period, the molybdenum-deficient kids weighed 22% less than the control animals on the 91st day of life. Due to the increased intake of the semi-synthetic ration, the difference

TABLE 1. *Molybdenum-containing enzymes of different origin*

Enzyme	Occurrence	Other prosthetic groups
Xanthine dehydrogenase	animal, plant, bacteria	FAD, Fe/S, MPT[a]
Aldehyde oxidase	animal	FAD, Fe/S, MPT
Nicotinic acid hydroxylase	bacteria	FAD, Fe/S, MPT, Se
Purine hydroxylase	A. nidulans	FAD, Fe/S, MPT
Sulfite oxidase	animal, plant, bacteria	Häm, MPT
Carbon monoxide dehydrogenase	bacteria	FAD, Fe/S, MPT
Assimilatory nitrate reductase	plants, microbes	FAD, Häm, MPT
Respiratory nitrate reductase	bacteria	Fe/S, MPT
Formic acid dehydrogenase	bacteria	Se, Fe/S, MPT
Nitrogenase	microbes	Fe/S

[a]Molybdopterin
From Rajagopalan KV (6).

TABLE 2. *The influence of molybdenum deficiency on reproductive performance and life expectancy*

Variable	Control animals	Mo-deficient animals	p
Success of first insemination (%)	69	57	< 0.05
Conception rate (%)	83	71	> 0.05
Services per gravidity	1.5	1.9	< 0.05
Abortions (%)	1.4	15	< 0.01
Kids per goat carrying to term	1.5	1.7	> 0.05
Died kids (%)	3	28	< 0.001
Died mothers (%)	25	61	< 0.001

From Anke M, et al. (9).

between the groups only became significant at the end of the sucking period. On the average, the milk of molybdenum-deficient goats contained double the amount of molybdenum in the semi-synthetic ration (9) (Table 4). The billy goats gained 27% less weight and the female goats 26% less weight than the control animals during the subsequent growth period.

In humans, there is a genetic defect which prevents sulfite oxidation. In children, this defect leads to serious cerebral injuries, disturbed mental development, dislocation of the optic lens, increased renal sulfite, and decreased sulfate excretion. Such children are not capable of synthesizing the molybdopterin complex. Molybdenum application does not overcome this damage (12–14).

The human embryo does not accumulate molybdenum (Table 5). Compared to other ultra trace elements, the human embryo stores extremely small amounts of molybdenum. These small amounts in the embryo, however, seem to be entirely sufficient to meet its intrauterine molybdenum requirements. In accordance with the

TABLE 3. *The influence of molybdenum deficiency on the pre- and postnatal development of kids*

Variable (n)	Control kids		Mo-deficient kids		p	%[a]
	$\bar{x}$	SD	$\bar{x}$	SD		
1st day of life (kg) (90;78)	3.1	0.78	2.9	0.77	> 0.05	94
91st day of life (kg) (50;43)	19.6	4.2	15.3	3.9	< 0.001	78
168 experimental days (g/day) (56;54) ♀	92	19	67	25	< 0.05	73
168 experimental days (g/day) (5;8) ♂	131	41	97	13	< 0.05	74

[a]Control kids ≙ 100%, deficient kids ≙ x%
From Anke M, et al. (10).

TABLE 4. *The influence of molybdenum deficiency on the molybdenum content of milk*
(µg/kg dry matter)

Stage of lactation	Control goats		Mo-deficient goats		p	%
	x̄	SD	x̄	SD		
Colostral milk (32;23)	61	61	35	26	> 0.05	46
Mature milk (76;48)	116	70	51	34	< 0.001	46

From Anke M (11).

TABLE 5. *Molybdenum concentration of the human embryo dependent on the*
stage of development (µg/kg dry matter) (n = 13)

	Month of pregnancy			p
	3–4	5	6–7	
x̄	174	152	145	> 0.05
s	51	52	38	

From Anke M, et al. (11).

findings of Schroeder et al. (15), and similar to kids and calves during the sucking
period, liver, kidneys, and ribs of babies up to the age of one year (Table 6) contained significantly less molybdenum than in later periods of life (9). This is due to
the fact that milk contains less molybdenum than the solid foodstuffs taken later (9).

Between 1 and 90 years, age and sex do not influence the molybdenum status significantly. The molybdenum concentration found in the human liver and other organs corresponds with that in the same organs of sheep, cattle, and pig (9).

The molybdenum requirement of fauna is < 100 µg/kg dry food substance. Since

TABLE 6. *The molybdenum content of the liver of humans dependent on age and sex*
(µg/kg dry matter)

Age (n)	Female		Male		p	%
	x̄	SD	x̄	SD		
0–1 year (10;10)	980	1150	1140	900	> 0.05	116
1–90 years (100;100)	2462	1260	2326	1080	> 0.05	94
p	< 0.001		< 0.01			
%	251		204			

From Anke M, et al. (11).

TABLE 7. *The molybdenum content of the diet taken by men and women in μg/kg dry matter and their molybdenum intake per day in μg (n = 14)*

	Female		Male			
	x̄	SD	x̄	SD	p	%
μg/kg dry matter	171	72	184	147	> 0.05	93
μg/day	47	9	65	13	< 0.05	72

From Anke M, et al. (16).

this requirement is always met, no primary molybdenum deficiency is to be expected. This statement is also true for fauna living in areas with molybdenum-deficient flora (9).

As demonstrated in investigations in Europe (Table 7), the calculated human molybdenum requirement of 25 μg/day is likely to be met under most conditions. Men as well as women consume about double the amount of the assumed molybdenum requirement. In summary, molybdenum is essential for animals and humans. Molybdenum deficiency does not occur.

FLUORINE

As early as 100 years ago, Erhardt (17) recommended that pregnant women and children during their second dentition should take fluorine pastilles. He had detected the densifying effect of fluorine on the dental enamel in dogs. This finding at first remained completely unnoticed. In the 1930s, the correlation between a low degree of caries and the occurrence of dental fluorosis (mottled enamel) was reported. The supplementation of drinking water with fluorine 1.9 mg F/1 was therefore suggested. This has been done in the USA from 1949 onwards, although objections to the procedure have been raised.

The essentiality of fluorine has been repeatedly investigated. Schroeder et al. (18) reported on slightly decreased growth and a reduced life expectancy of mice fed a fluoride-poor diet; Schwarz and Milne (19) also found a limited influence of fluoride deficiency on the growth of rats. The negative effect of fluoride-poor nutrition (0.1 to 0.3 mg F/kg) on the reproduction performance of mice observed by Messer et al. (20,21) was not confirmed by Tao and Suttie (22). Insufficient copper and iron in Messer's rations (21) was assumed to be the reason for the discrepant findings.

Fluoride deficiency experiments with growing, pregnant, and lactating goats, repeated twice, also failed to show a significant influence of fluoride-poor nutrition using a semi-synthetic ration which contained all other necessary components on growth. Both the reproduction and growth performance of the goats with a fluoride-poor diet (< 0.5 mg/kg dry matter) remained uninfluenced (Tables 8,9). Life expec-

TABLE 8. *The influence of fluorine deficiency on reproductive performance and life expectancy (n = 37;13)*

Variable	Control animals	F-deficient animals	p
Success of first insemination (%)	70	85	> 0.05
Conception rate (%)	89	92	> 0.05
Services per gravidity	1.4	1.5	> 0.05
Abortions (%)	0	8	> 0.05
Kids per goat carrying to term	1.3	1.2	> 0.05
Died kids (%)	3	0	> 0.05
Died mothers (%)	16	31	< 0.05

From Anke M, et al. (1).

TABLE 9. *The influence of fluorine deficiency on the pre- and postnatal development of kids*

Variable (n)	Control kids		F-deficient kids		p	%
	$\bar{x}$	SD	$\bar{x}$	SD		
1st day of life (kg) (42;16)	2.7	0.63	2.8	0.59	> 0.05	104
91st day of life (kg) (31;12)	15.6	2.2	15.4	4.2	> 0.05	99
168 experimental days (g/day) (15;9)	107	12	102	26	> 0.05	95

From Anke M, et al. (1).

tancy and milking performance, however, declined highly significantly, particularly after intrauterine fluorine depletion, when deaths regularly occurred during lactation. The mothers quickly lost weight and died. Their kids repeatedly suffered from skeletal damage in the hind legs, which did not occur in control kids.

Further repetitions of the experiments must clarify the influence of fluoride deficiency on the life expectancy of animals. In general there is at present no reliable evidence that fluorine is an essential nutrient. Most results obtained after fluoride supplementation are pharmacological effects (e.g., the positive results in the prophylaxis of dental caries and osteoporosis). Although a fluorine requirement for the biological mineralization involving the apatite may exist, it has not yet been experimentally demonstrated. Messer (23) therefore defined fluorine as "possibly essential". The fluorine deficiency experiments which will soon be finished point to the essentiality of fluorine.

VANADIUM

The effects of a vanadium-poor nutrition had already been investigated in rats and chicks by the beginning of the 1970s. Chicks given a diet containing 10 µg V/kg

TABLE 10. *The influence of vanadium deficiency on reproductive performance and life expectancy*

Variable	Control animals	V-deficient animals	p
Success of first insemination (%)	77	57	< 0.001
Conception rate (%)	89	85	> 0.05
Services per gravidity	1.4	2.0	< 0.01
Abortions (%)	0	27	< 0.001
Kids per goat carrying to term	1.5	1.1	< 0.001
Died kids (%)	9	41	< 0.001
Died mothers (%)	25	58	< 0.001

From Anke M, et al. (31).

grew badly. Their wing and tail feathers developed slowly (24). Rats on vanadium-poor rations showed improved growth (25) and better reproductive performance after vanadium supplementation (26). The influence of vanadium deficiency on the blood picture and iron metabolism of rats is controversial (25,27–30).

Because there were no definite results on the influence of a vanadium-poor nutrition, the effects of vanadium deficiency (1–9 μg V/kg diet) were investigated in growing, gravid, and lactating goats throughout their lifespan. The experiments were repeated seven times. Vanadium deficiency decreased the success of the first insemination, and increased the number of services per gravidity as well as the abortion rate significantly (Table 10). The number of kids per goat carrying to term and the life expectancy of the mothers and their offspring were also significantly reduced by the vanadium-poor nutrition. It was surprising that the pre- and postnatal development of the offspring remained completely unaffected by vanadium deficiency (Table 11) whereas milk production in vanadium-deficient goats was significantly reduced (by 9%).

The offspring of the vanadium-deficient goats frequently fell ill with skeletal damage in the forelegs. The goats suffered from joint pains and often changed their

TABLE 11. *The influence of vanadium deficiency on the pre- and postnatal development of kids*

Variable (n)	Control kids		V-deficient kids		p	%
	x̄	SD	x̄	SD		
1st day of life (kg) (93;50)	2.86	0.80	2.87	0.79	> 0.05	100
91st day of life (kg) (48;23)	17.2	4.0	16.4	4.6	> 0.05	95
168 experimental days (g/day) (53;33)	92	34	92	34	> 0.05	100

From Anke M, et al. (32).

FIG. 1. Newborn kid after intrauterine vanadium depletion.

position in order to relieve the strain on their legs. Finally, the metatarsal joints thickened and deformations of the fore extremities occurred (32).

After repeated intrauterine vanadium depletion, the kids of vanadium-deficient goats already had damage to the fore extremities at birth (Fig. 1).

The colostrum of control goats contained significantly more vanadium (8 μg/kg dry matter) than that of vanadium-deficient animals (1.4 μg/kg). These vanadium concentrations correspond to the vanadium content of the deficiency ration. The vanadium content of goat's milk is in good accordance with the vanadium content found by Byrne and Kosta (34) in two human colostral samples and also corresponds to the vanadium content of cow's milk (35,36).

Knowledge about the low vanadium content of the milk led to the assumption that the vanadium needed during the sucking period was stored in the skeleton during

TABLE 12. *The vanadium content of the milk of control and vanadium-deficient goats*
(μg/kg dry matter)

Kind of milk (n)	Control animals		V-deficient animals		*p*	%
	x̄	SD	x̄	SD		
Colostrum (6;7)	7.8	3.3	1.4	1.0	< 0.001	18
Mature milk (18;18)	3.1	1.8	2.4	1.1	> 0.05	77
p	< 0.001		< 0.05		—	
%	40		171			

From Anke M, et al (33).

TABLE 13. *The vanadium content of the ribs of control and vanadium-deficient kids and their mothers (μg/kg dry matter)*

Age (n)	Control kids		V-deficient kids		p	%
	x̄	SD	x̄	SD		
Kids (7;9)	83	13	96	18	> 0.05	116
Mothers (5;4)	210	49	84	13	< 0.001	40

From Anke M, et al. (33).

embryonic development. This was not true (Table 13). The ribs of the kids of control and vanadium-deficient goats contained the same amounts of vanadium on the first day of life. On the other hand, the ribs of adult vanadium-deficient goats contained significantly less vanadium than those of control goats and were therefore a good reflection of vanadium status. From these experiments it was thus impossible to clarify the role of vanadium in the body.

An influence of vanadium deficiency on the iron status and the blood picture could not be established (31). Although no vanadium-dependent enzymes have been detected up to now in mammals or birds, it seems likely that vanadium should be assigned to the essential elements, particularly in view of the damage to the fore extremities of the offspring of vanadium-deficient goats. The essentiality of vanadium for humans is assumed, but not demonstrated (26).

In summary, vanadium deficiency has only an insignificant effect on growth, whereas it reduced reproductive performance and life expectancy. Skeletal damage occurs in the fore extremities in vanadium-deficient goats.

NICKEL

Carbon monoxide dehydrogenase and methylcoenzyme-M-reductase of several species of bacteria, together with plant urease, are nickel-dependent enzymes (37).

Nickel-poor nutrition (< 100 μg/kg dietary dry matter) in ruminants and < 50 μg Ni/kg in monogastric species leads to disturbed reproduction performance (Table 14), reduced life expectancy (Table 14), and to growth depression among various species of fauna (Table 15) (38–44).

As a rule, minipigs (38,45), goats (46,47), and rats (43,42) with nickel-poor nutrition suffer from skin lesions and have shaggy coats. Pustules also occur on goats' udders (47), and individual cases of dwarfism have been observed (48). Nickel-deficient minipigs excrete more calcium than control animals in the urine; they have a lower calcium content in the skeleton (38,45).

Nickel-deficient rats incorporate magnesium into the skeleton instead of calcium (49). The disturbed calcium metabolism induces zinc depletion in goats (38,45,47)

TABLE 14. *The influence of nickel deficiency on reproductive performance and life expectancy*

Variable	Control animals	Ni-deficient animals	p
Success of first insemination (%)	70	55	< 0.05
Conception rate (%)	83	71	< 0.05
Services per gravidity	1.4	1.9	< 0.05
Abortions (%)	1	9	< 0.001
Died kids (%)	9	38	< 0.001
Died mothers (%)	24	43	< 0.01

From Anke M, et al. (48).

TABLE 15. *The influence of nickel deficiency on the pre- and postnatal development of kids*

Variable (n)	Control kids		Ni-deficient kids		p	%
	$\bar{x}$	SD	$\bar{x}$	SD		
1st day of life (kg)	3.1	0.77	2.8	0.80	< 0.05	90
91st day of life (kg)	19.1	4.2	16.3	3.8	< 0.001	85
168 experimental days (g/day)	99	33	88	42	< 0.05	89

From Anke M, et al. (41).

and rats (50). Nickel deficiency leads to reduced zinc incorporation into several organs and into milk. This has definitely been established by 65 zinc studies in goats and is due to lower zinc absorption (48). There are also interactions between nickel and iron. Rats with nickel-poor nutrition (51–56), as well as goats (47,57), suffer from anemia caused by a reduced hemoglobin and hematocrit-content. In another study it was found that intrauterine nickel deficiency also led to atrophy of the testicles, and to reduced sperm production and sexual libido in adult billy goats (48).

Nickel incorporation by embryos was investigated in humans and was found to be

TABLE 16. *Nickel concentration of the human embryo dependent on the stage of development ($\mu g/kg$ dry matter)*

	Month of pregnancy			$SD_{0.05}$	%
	3–4	5	6–7		
$\bar{x}$	3.573	1.620	1.646	1.226	45
s	931	690	316		

From Anke M, et al. (58).

extremely high compared to adults, with 3.573 Ni/μg/kg dry matter in the third and fourth months of pregnancy (Table 16). It decreased quickly during intrauterine development. Nickel seems to pass rapidly and in large amounts through the placenta. This finding is in accordance with the results obtained by Sunderman et al. (61) in rodents.

Ribs, kidneys, and liver of babies up to the age of 3 months contain significantly more nickel than they do between 1 and 90 years of age (Table 17). This agrees with the results obtained in kids and piglets (48). The nickel storage in the embryo and baby points to the biological essentiality of nickel during this period of development. However, this finding must also be interpreted in relation to the relatively low nickel content of mother's milk (Table 18). As a rule, goat's and cow's milk contain similar amounts of nickel as human milk (41). Plant and animal foodstuffs are usually much richer in nickel than human or goat's milk. During lactation, babies may meet a part of their nickel requirement from their intrauterine stores of nickel.

Baby food produced on a milk basis in the GDR contains less nickel than maternal milk (Table 19). Compared to the mean rations of adults, ready-to-serve baby food based on semolina, fruit, and meat have proven to be relatively nickel poor.

The nickel requirement of fauna including humans is < 500 μg Ni/kg dry matter.

TABLE 17. *The nickel concentration of different human organs by age and sex (μg/kg dry matter)*

Organ (n)	Babies		1–90 years			
	x̄	SD	x̄	SD	p	%
Ribs (18;184) ♀	5.046	2.962	1.980	1.360	< 0.001	39
♂			1.540	760	< 0.001	31
Liver (18;178)	966	699	647	458	< 0.01	67
Kidneys (20;184)	1.600	1.483	683	411	< 0.001	43

From Schneider H-J, et al. (59).

TABLE 18. *The nickel content of mother's milk*

	Week of lactation					
	8th		13th			
	x̄	SD	x̄	SD	p	%
Dry matter, μg/kg	283	137	333	223	> 0.05	118
Milk, μg/liter	33	16	39	26	> 0.05	118

From Anke M, et al. (48).

TABLE 19. *The nickel concentration of several baby foods in the GDR*
(μg/kg dry matter; n = 27)

	KiNa	Babysan	Milasan	Manasan	Ready-to-serve
x̄	47	51	92	106	158
s	58	34	46	32	147

From Anke M, et al. (60).

It may amount to < 100 μg/kg dry matter (48) and is met by all normal diets (57,58). Thus, no primary deficiency symptoms are to be expected.

In summary, there is clear evidence that nickel is essential for fauna.

ARSENIC

According to Frieden (5), the essentiality of arsenic is undisputed. Nielsen and Uthus (62) wrote: "In 1975 to 1976 the first findings showing that arsenic is essential came from two laboratories. The studies on arsenic essentiality were apparently carried out in each laboratory without the knowledge that similar studies were being carried out in the other laboratory. As a result of these investigations, signs of arsenic deprivation were described for chick, goat, minipig, and rat." The signs of deficiency for minipigs and goats were reviewed by Anke et al. (63–65) and those for chicks and pigs by Uthus et al. (66).

In spite of these findings, the functions of arsenic in animals and humans are far from certain. The results obtained in arsenic deficiency experiments repeated 12 times with growing, pregnant, and lactating goats are summarized as follows (67). Arsenic-poor nutrition (< 35 μg As/kg dietary dry matter) caused a significantly worse success rate of first insemination and a reduced conception rate in goats (Table 20). The arsenic-deficient animals needed more services per gravidity and

TABLE 20. *The influence of arsenic deficiency on reproductive performance and life expectancy*

Variable	Control animals	As-deficient animals	p
Success of first insemination (%)	75	57	< 0.01
Conception rate (%)	89	71	< 0.001
Services per gravidity	1.3	1.9	< 0.001
Kids per goat carrying to term	1.4	1.4	> 0.05
Abortions (%)	0.8	15	< 0.001
Died kids (%)	5.8	32	< 0.001
Died mothers (%)	24	48	< 0.001

From Anke M, et al. (67).

TABLE 21. *The influence of arsenic deficiency on the pre- and postnatal development of kids*

Variable (n)	Control kids		As-deficient kids			
	$\bar{x}$	SD	$\bar{x}$	SD	*p*	%
1st day of life (kg)	3.0	0.76	2.8	0.74	> 0.05	93
91st day of life (kg)	18.6	4.5	16.2	4.3	< 0.01	87
168 experimental days (g/day)	90	33	75	27	> 0.05	83

From Anke M, et al. (67).

aborted significantly more fetuses. The life expectancy of the goats and their off-spring was considerably decreased. Most goats died suddenly between the 17th and 35th day during the second lactation (65,67–69). No arsenic-deficient goat survived the second gravidity. Arsenic-deficient goats which did not get pregnant reached an age of more than 6 years (68). The ultrastructural changes induced by arsenic deficiency mainly affect the mitochondrial membranes of the heart and skeletal musculature (70,71).

The influence of arsenic deficiency on growth (Table 21) is less distinct. Kids showed significantly reduced growth only at the end of the lactation period. The milk of control and arsenic-deficient goats was arsenic-poor and contained less arsenic than the arsenic-deficient rations in both groups (Table 22). Kids accumulate large amounts of arsenic during the intrauterine period, which they utilize during the sucking period (Table 23). Compared to control kids, arsenic-deficient kids stored only very little arsenic.

Arsenic deficiency also reduced milk production in goats, and there was an increased fat content in the milk, although the protein remained unchanged (67).

The arsenic requirement of fauna has been calculated to be < 50 μg/kg dry food

TABLE 22. *Arsenic content of the milk of control and arsenic-deficient goats (μg/kg dry matter)*

Kinds of milk (n)	Control goats		As-deficient goats			
	$\bar{x}$	SD	$\bar{x}$	SD	*p*	%
Colostrum (4;7)	10	3.4	7.8	3.6	> 0.05	78
Mature milk (22;37)	24	21	15	8.3	< 0.05	62
p	> 0.05		< 0.05			
%	240		192			

From Anke M, et al. (67).

TABLE 23. *Arsenic content of several organs of kids of control and arsenic-deficient goats*
(μg/kg dry matter)

Organ (n)	Control kids		As-deficient kids		p	%
	x̄	SD	x̄	SD		
Kidneys (5;4)	737	819	16	10	> 0.05	2
Cardiac muscle (7;4)	130	235	15	9.3	> 0.05	12
Skeleton muscle (6;5)	97	84	36	42	> 0.05	37
Cerebrum (7;5)	49	40	21	12	> 0.05	43
Rib (3;2)	90	100	39	48	> 0.05	43
Lungs (7;2)	44	34	24	1.9	> 0.05	55

From Anke M, et al. (67).

matter (72). An arsenic requirement of adult humans of 6 μg per 1000 kcal or 12 to 25 μg per day has been derived from the results of animal experiments (73,74). The arsenic demand of animals and humans is met by dietary sources and water in the GDR (75,76).

In summary, the available results point to the essentiality of arsenic though no arsenic-dependent enzymes have been found up to now. Further experiments must confirm this statement.

CADMIUM

Cadmium belongs to the highly toxic elements. Due to its gradual accumulation in the kidneys with increasing age, it is particularly dangerous for long-living species of animals and humans (77). In spite of its highly noxious nature and the existence of only a few papers (78,79) which deal with the essentiality of this element, Smith (80) wrote: "Although these reports are not sufficient to establish definitively a specific function for cadmium, the metal is a good candidate for essentiality. The history of trace metal research should serve as a warning against taking too pessimistic a view on the possible essentiality of cadmium, because a number of other elements (notably selenium) whose toxicity alone was initially appreciated have been subsequently proved to be essential."

More evidence for the essentiality of cadmium is now available after tenfold repetition of cadmium deficiency experiments with growing, pregnant, and lactating goats and their offspring. Compared to control animals (300 μg Cd/kg dry feed matter), cadmium-poor nutrition (< 15 μg Cd/kg dry feed matter) reduced the success of the first insemination of the goats significantly (Table 24). The number of services as well as the abortion rate and the mortality of the mothers and their offspring increased significantly. After several experimental years, kids with intrauterine cadmium depletion repeatedly proved to be very lethargic, for example they were hardly able to keep their heads upright.

TABLE 24. *The influence of cadmium deficiency on reproductive performance and life expectancy*

Variable	Control animals	Cd-deficient animals	p
Success of first insemination (%)	73	46	< 0.001
Conception rate (%)	85	72	> 0.05
Services per gravidity	1.2	2.2	< 0.001
Kids per goat carrying to term	1.4	1.6	> 0.05
Abortions (%)	0	12	< 0.01
Died kids (%)	8.0	43	< 0.001
Died mothers (%)	30	41	< 0.05

From Anke M, et al. (81).

In 1985, nine kids of cadmium-deficient animals were at our disposal for the first time. All kids showed an acute muscular asthenia about 6 weeks after weaning from mother's milk. First they moved clumsily and stiffly. Later on, they became unable to move and could not stand. Finally, they were unable to raise their heads (Fig. 2) and died. After six of the nine cadmium-deficient kids had died, the three surviving animals (2 males, 1 female), which were also unable to move, were fed the control

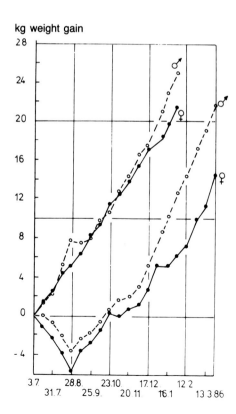

FIG. 2. Live weight gain of male and female control and Cd-deficient goats after weaning from mother's milk and the feeding of the control ration to the Cd-deficient kids.

FIG. 3. **A:** Billy goat suffering from Cd deficiency. **B:** Control billy goat.

ration of 300 μg Cd/kg. The animals slowly regained their mobility and gained weight (Fig. 3). The same syndrome of muscular asthenia was recorded in adult goats in 1987.

Cadmium deficiency had no significant effect on the growth of kids during the suckling period (Table 25). There was also no significant growth depression in kids bought after weaning and fed on a cadmium-deficient diet. But the cadmium-deficient goats produced 28% less milk than the control animals. Its fat content remained unaffected by the cadmium deficiency whereas its protein content increased significantly.

Ultrastructural analysis of liver, skeletal and cardiac muscle, and kidneys showed that cadmium-deficient goats had degenerative alteration to the mitochondria in liver and kidneys. Christolysis and vesicular distensions were detectable. These findings point to reduced protein synthesis and to increased protein mobilization from the musculature in lactating goats (81).

TABLE 25. *The influence of cadmium deficiency on the pre- and postnatal development of kids*

Variable	Control kids		Cd-deficient kids		p	%
	$\bar{x}$	SD	$\bar{x}$	SD		
1st day of life (kg)	3.0	0.76	2.8	0.74	> 0.05	93
91st day of life (kg)	18.6	4.5	16.2	4.3	> 0.05	97
168 experimental days (g/day)	90	33	75	27	> 0.05	83

From Anke M, et al. (81).

TABLE 26. *Cadmium concentration of the human embryo, by stage of development (μg/kg dry matter)*

| | \multicolumn{4}{c}{Month of pregnancy} | |
	2	3–4	5	6–7	%
x̄	2.546	764	562	454	18
SD	2086	589	302	87	
n	5	18	9	5	—

Cadmium is incorporated quickly and in relatively large amounts into the human embryo. During the further development, the cadmium content decreases continuously (Table 26). Skeleton and musculature contain little cadmium. Compared to other parts of the body, kidneys and liver of newborn babies contain the highest cadmium concentrations at birth (82).

The essentiality of cadmium cannot now be ruled out any longer. The cadmium requirement might amount to 20 μg/kg dry food substance. In one study the diet contained 68 μg/kg which certainly met this requirement (82). Primary cadmium deficiency symptoms are not to be expected in humans or animals (83) since the cadmium content of foodstuffs (84) is considerably higher than the assumed cadmium requirement. The practical importance of cadmium for fauna including humans is in its toxic effects (85,86).

LITHIUM

Investigations into the biological functions of lithium had already begun 125 years ago (87). However, lithium only became interesting when it was successfully used to treat several mental diseases and particularly patients with manic-depressive illness (88). The essentiality of lithium was tested relatively late. From 1976 onwards, Anke et al. (89–93) carried out lithium deficiency experiments with growing, gravid, and lactating goats. At the same time, Pickett and Hawkins (94,95) and Burt (96) began lithium deficiency experiments with rats. Both research teams found an effect of lithium-poor diet on reproduction and life expectancy in goats and rats. There were, however, differences between their findings as to the effect of lithium on growth. According to Mertz (97), however, these differences do not mean that there should be doubts about the essentiality of this element.

In spite of a normal heat, the first mating led to a significantly reduced insemination success in lithium-deficient goats (Table 27). Repeated services during the following ovulations improved the conception rate in these goats but without normalizing it. On an average, lithium-deficient goats needed 0.7 services more than the control animals. Fourteen percent of the goats with lithium-poor rations aborted. The results of the 12-year deficiency experiments show the effect of lithium defi-

TABLE 27. *The influence of lithium deficiency on reproductive performance and life expectancy*

Variable	Control goats	Li-deficient goats	p
Success of first insemination (%)	77	51	< 0.001
Conception rate (%)	86	74	< 0.05
Services per gravidity	1.28	1.97	< 0.001
Kids per goat carrying to term	1.55	1.58	> 0.05
Abortions (%)	1.0	14	< 0.001
Sex ratio ♀ = 1	1:1,61	1:0.70	< 0.001
Died kids (%)	6.0	14	> 0.05
Died mothers, first year (%)	7	41	< 0.001

From Arnold W (99).

ciency on reproduction (89–91,93,98). Pickett (96) reported that the conception times were 2 weeks longer in the first generation, that the size of the litter was 20% to 30% smaller in all generations, and that the survival up to one week was only 53% to 60% of that of controls. The influence of the lithium-poor diet on the sex ratio of the offspring is most surprising (Table 27). As a rule, goats without horns give birth to more male than female kids. This holds also true for control goats. Lithium-deficient goats, however, had more female kids. The reasons for this significantly abnormal sex ratio are unknown. The influence of lithium deficiency on the mortality of kids is noticeable; it does not, however, reach statistical significance. On the other hand, the life expectancy of lithium-deficient goats was reduced highly significantly. Forty-one percent of these animals had already died in the first year of trial.

The lithium-deficient goats usually ate less food than controls and gained less weight. This was also true for the intrauterine development of lithium-deficient kids, whose birth weight was reduced by 9% (Table 28). During the suckling period, the growth difference did not increase dramatically since the milk of lithium-deficient goats contains more lithium than is present in the low lithium (1.7 mg/kg

TABLE 28. *The influence of lithium deficiency on the pre- and postnatal development of kids*

Variable	Control kids		Li-deficient kids		p	%
	x̄	SD	x̄	SD		
1st day of life (kg)	2.86	0.76	2.60	0.70	< 0.01	91
91st day of life (kg)	17.4	4.4	14.8	4.3	< 0.001	85
168 experimental days	93	35	75	37	< 0.05	81

From Arnold W (99).

TABLE 29. *Lithium concentration of the milk of control and lithium-deficient goats (mg/kg dry matter)*

Day of lactation (n)		Control goats		Li-deficient goats		*p*	%
		x̄	SD	x̄	SD		
1st	(29;19)	5.2	3.8	3.4	1.8	> 0.05	65
14th	(25;16)	7.2	3.3	2.2	1.0	< 0.001	31
28th	(17;13)	8.8	4.0	2.7	1.9	< 0.001	31
56th	(16;13)	12	5.7	4.1	2.9	< 0.001	34

From Anke M, et al. (91).

dry) diet, though less than in the diet of control animals (Table 29). After weaning, when the low lithium semisynthetic ration was fed, the lithium-deficient goats gained 19% less weight than the control goats. This effect of the lithium-poor ration was not found by Pickett in rats (96).

The lithium-deficient goats produced 10% less milk, containing 22% less fat and 16% less protein than controls (99). Lithium deficiency had an effect on the activity of several enzymes, for example monoamineoxidase activity in liver tissue of lithium-deficient goats only reached 72% of the activity found in control goats (101).

The lithium content of the human embryo shows the same characteristics as nickel and cadmium. It decreases significantly from between the 3rd to 4th month of pregnancy and the 6th and 7th month (Table 30). The lithium content of mother's milk is not known. Cow's milk from the GDR contains substantial amounts of lithium (10 mg/kg dry matter), while different types of cheese and curd cheese have a considerably lower lithium content than milk. Much lithium is probably lost via whey when milk is turned into cheese. The same holds true for the lithium content of the baby food produced in the GDR, which contains < 1 mg Li/kg dry matter on average (Table 31).

TABLE 30. *Lithium concentration of the human embryo by stage of development (mg/kg dry matter)*

	Month of pregnancy			$SD_{0.05}$	%
	3–4	5	6–7		
x̄	6.9	2.1	1.9	4.5	28
SD	4.2	1.0	0.88		
n	5	5	4	—	—

From Bauman W, et al. (100).

TABLE 31. *The lithium concentration of several baby foods in the GDR*
(μg/kg dry matter)

	KiNa-new	Babysan	Milasan
x̄	0.39	0.64	0.61
SD	0.12	0.49	0.31
n	9	9	9

From Arnhold W (99).

The lithium intake of adults in the GDR varies between 231 and 568 μg Li/day in women and between 191 and 589 μg Li/day in men on average over weekly periods using results of four test teams of 14 persons. The different dry matter consumption and the site-specific differences of the lithium content in foodstuffs and beverages are responsible for the considerable variation range of the individual lithium intake (137 to 1449 μg Li/day in women, 147 to 1048 μg Li/day in men).

The "lithium requirement" of adults might amount to 200 μg/day (99). According to the data available (90,99,102–105) the lithium content of foodstuffs and beverages meets the assumed lithium requirement of the European fauna including humans.

LEAD, BORON, BROMINE

The essentiality of lead has mainly been investigated by Reichlmayr-Lais and Kirchgessner (106). They detected that rats on an extremely lead-poor diet (< 20 ppb Pb) had reduced hemoglobin, hematocrit, and mean corpuscular volume values. The erythrocyte count, however, was not affected. These extremely lead-depleted rats also showed growth depression.

In all lead-deficient animals, the blood iron level was markedly reduced, while the iron-binding capacity was increased. The iron content was also reduced in several tissues of lead-depleted rats. Lead deficiency reduces iron retention. It was possible to compensate for this effect by lead supplementation. In summary, it appears that lead must also be classified as an essential ultra trace element.

The biological essentiality of boron has mainly been investigated by Nielsen (107). A boron-poor diet caused growth depression in chickens. Cholecalciferol deficiency enhanced the need for boron and boron may interact with cholecalciferol metabolism, which in turn affects calcium, phosphorus, or magnesium metabolism. The effect of boron supplementation on the urinary excretion of calcium and magnesium in postmenopausal women also points to this (107).

Boron supplementation depressed the urinary excretion of phosphorus by magnesium-depleted, but not by magnesium-repleted, women. Boron supplementation also markedly elevated the serum concentrations of estradiol-17β and testosterone. Further investigations must clarify the biological essentiality of boron for humans and animals.

Large amounts of bromine occur in nature. The flora contains concentrations of this element which are typical of copper and which in some cases far exceed the copper concentrations. Plants contain about ten times more bromine than iodine. First deficiency experiments showed a surprisingly large effect of a bromine-poor diet on the conception and abortion rate as well as on milk production in goats. All these variables are significantly reduced. The growth of the bromine-deficient animals was decreased but not significantly so. The decline in hemoglobin, hematocrit and MCHC values in bromine-deficient goats was most impressive, but further investigations must confirm these findings (108). The bromine requirement might amount to < 1 mg/kg dry matter and this amount is assumed to be available in foodstuffs all over the world.

SUMMARY

According to the available experimental findings, it can be taken for granted that dietary intake of molybdenum, fluorine, vanadium, nickel, arsenic, cadmium, lithium, lead, boron, and bromine meets and exceeds the requirements of the fauna for reproduction and growth. Much information on the essentiality of these ultra trace elements is available, although this is not yet sufficient to prove it definitively. According to present knowledge, primary deficiency symptoms do not occur in humans or animals. However, secondary deficiency due to the influence of specific antagonists cannot be excluded. In the case of parenteral nutrition and of gene defects, particular attention must also be paid to the effect of ultra trace elements. Selenium was only considered a toxic element until its essentiality was detected.

REFERENCES

1. Anke M, Groppel B. Signifikanz der Essentialität von Fluor, Brom, Molybdän, Vanadium, Nickel, Arsen und Cadmium. *Zentralbl Pharm Pharmakother Lab Diagn* 1988;127:197–203.
2. Anke M, Groppel B, Kronemann H. Significance of new trace elements (like Si, Ni, As, V) for the nutrition of man and animal. In: Brätter P, Schramel P, eds. *Trace element analytical chemistry in medicine and biology*, vol 3. Berlin: Walter de Gruyter, 1984:421–36.
3. Nielsen FH, Boron B. In: Mertz W. ed. *Trace elements in human and animal nutrition*. 5th ed, Vol 2. Orlando: Academic Press, 1986:420–7.
4. Anke M, Groppel B, Arnhold W, Langer M. Essentiality of the trace element bromine. In: Brätter P, Schramel P, eds. *Trace element analytical chemistry in medicine and biology*, vol 5. Berlin: Walter de Gruyter, 1988:618–26.
5. Frieden E. *Biochemistry of the essential ultratrace elements*. New York: Plenum Press, 1984.
6. Rajagopalan KV. Molybdenum. In: Frieden E, ed. *Biochemistry of the essential ultra trace elements*. New York: Plenum Press, 1984:149–74.
7. Higgins ES, Richert DA, Westerfield WW. Molybdenum deficiency and tungstate inhibitions studies. *J Nutr* 1952;59:539–46.
8. Johnson JL, Rajagopalan KV, Cohen HJ. Molecular basis of the biological function of molyb-

denum. Effect of tungsten and xanthin oxidase and sulfite oxidase in the rat. *J Biol Chem* 1974;249:859–66.

9. Anke M, Groppel B, Kronemann H, Grün M. Die Versorgung von Pflanze, Tier und Mensch mit Molybdän. In: Anke M, ed. *Mengen- und Spurenelemente*, vol 3. Leipzig: Karl-Marx-Universität, 1983:22–36.
10. Anke M, Groppel B, Kronemann H, Grün M. Die biologische Bedeutung des Molybdäns für den Wiederkäuer. *Wiss. Z. Karl-Marx-Univ. Leipzig, Math.-Naturwiss. R.* 184;33:148–56.
11. Anke M, Groppel B, Kronemann H, Grün M. Molybdenum supply and status in animals and human beings. *Nutr Res* (Suppl) 1985;1:180–6.
12. Duran M, Beemer FA, van den Heiden C, et al. Combined deficiency of xanthine oxidase and sulfite oxidase: A defect of molybdenum metabolism or transport? *J Inher Metab Dis* 1978;1:175–8.
13. Johnson JL, Waud WR, Rajagopalan KV, Duran M, Beemer FA, Wadman SK. Inborn errors of molybdenum metabolism. Combined deficiencies of sulfite oxidase and xanthin oxidase in a patient lacking the molybdenum cofactor. *Proc Natl Acad Sci USA* 1980;77:3715–9.
14. Wadman SK, Duran M, de Bree PK, Beemer FA. Molybdenum cofactor deficiency. In: Gladtke E, et al., eds. *Spurenelemente*. Stuttgart: Georg Thieme Verlag, 1984:92–5.
15. Schroeder HA, Balassa JJ, Tipton IH. Essential trace metals in man: Molybdenum. *J Chron Dis* 1970;23:481–99.
16. Anke M, Groppel B, Krause U, Arnhold W, Langer M. Die Spurenelementaufnahme (Zink, Mangan, Kupfer, Molybdän, Jod und Nickel) Erwachsener in der DDR. In: Anke M, et al. (eds). *Mengen- und Spurenelemente* 1989;9:365–78.
17. Erhardt F. Memorabilien. *Heilbronn* 1974;8:359.
18. Schroeder HA, Mitchener M. Balassa JJ, Kanisowa M, Nason AP. Zirconium, niobium, antimony, and fluorine in mice. Effects on growth, survival, and tissue levels. *J Nutr* 1968;95:95–101.
19. Schwarz K, Milne D. Fluorine requirement for growth in the rat. *Bioinorg Chem* 1972;1:331–8.
20. Messer HH, Wong K, Wegner M, Singer L, Armstrong WD. Effect of reduced fluoride intake by mice on haematocrit values. *Nature (New Biol)* 1972;240:218–9.
21. Messer HH, Armstrong WD, Singer L. Fertility impairment in mice on a low fluoride intake. *Science.* 1973;177:893–4.
22. Tao S, Suttie JW. Evidence for a lack of an effect of dietary fluoride level on reproduction in mice. *J Nutr* 1976;106:1115–22.
23. Messer HH, Flurine. In: Frieden E, ed. *Biochemistry of the essential ultra trace elements.* New York: Plenum Press, 1984:55–87.
24. Hopkins LL, Mohr HE. The biological essentiality of vanadium. In: Mertz W, Cornatzer WE, eds. *Newer trace elements in nutrition.* New York: Marcel Dekker, 1971:195–213.
25. Strasia CA. Vanadium essentiality and toxicity in the laboratory rat. Ann Arbor: University of Michigan, 1971. Thesis.
26. Hopkins LL Jr., Mohr HE. Vanadium as an essential nutrient. *Fed Proc* 1974;33:1773–5.
27. Nielsen FH, Olbrich DA. Studies on a vanadium deficiency in chicks. *Fed Proc* 1973;32:929.
28. Williams DL. Biological value of vanadium for rats, chickens and sheep. Ann Arbor: Purdue University, 1973. Thesis.
29. Nielsen FH, Uhrich KE, Shuler TR, Uthus EO. Influence of vanadium deprivation on hematopoiesis and other biochemical parameters in iron-deprived and -adequate rats. In: Anke M, et al., eds. *Spurenelementsymposium*, No. 4. Leipzig: Karl-Marx-Universität, 1983:127–34.
30. Shuler TR, Nielsen FH. Interactions among vanadium, copper and sulphur amino acids affect liver trace element content. In: Mills CF, et al., eds. *Trace elements in man and animals*, vol 4. London: Commonwealth Agricultural Bureaux, 1984:382–4.
31. Anke M, Groppel B, Gruhn K, Kósla T, Szilágyi M. New research on vanadium deficiency in ruminants. In: Anke M, et al., eds. *New trace elements.* 5. Spurenelementsymposium. Leipzig: Karl-Marx-Universität 1986:1266–75.
32. Anke M, Groppel B, Kósla T, Gruhn K. Investigations on vanadium deficiency in ruminants. In: Hurley LS et al., eds. *Trace elements in man and animals*, vol 6. New York: Plenum Press, 1988.
33. Anke M, Groppel B, Kronemann H, Kósla T. Vanadium deficiency in ruminants. In: Mills CF, et al., eds. *Trace elements in man and animals*, vol 4. London: Commonwealth Agricultural Bureaux, 1985:275–9.
34. Byrne AR, Kosta L. Vanadium in foods and in human body fluids and tissues. *Sci Total Environ* 1978;10:17–21.
35. Söremark R. Vanadium in some biological specimens. *J Nutr* 1967;92:183–9.
36. Byrne AR, Kosta L, Ravnik V, Stupar J, Hudnik V. A study of certain trace elements in milk. *Pro-*

ceedings of Conference on Nuclear Activation Techniques in the Life Sciences. Vienna: JAEA, 1979;255.

37. Nielsen FH. Nickel. In: Mertz W, ed. *Trace elements in human and animal nutrition*, 5th ed. Vol 1. San Diego: Academic Press, 1987:245–73.

38. Anke M. Die Bedeutnung der Spurenelemente für die tierischen Leistungen. *Tag. -Ber., Akad Landw Wiss. DDR, Berlin* 1974;132:197–218.

39. Anke M, Henning A, Grün M, Partschefeld M, Groppel B, Lüdke H. Nickel - ein essentielles Spurenelement. 1. Mitt.: Der Einfluss des Nickelmangels auf die Lebendmasseentwicklung, den Futterverzehr und die Körperzusammensetzung wachsender Zwergschweine und Ziegen. *Arch Tierern* 1977;27:25–38.

40. Anke M, Partschefeld M, Grün M, Groppel B. Nickel - ein essentielles Spurenelement. 3. Mitt.: Der Einfluss des Nickelmangels auf die Fortpflanzungsleistung weiblicher Tiere. *Arch Tierern* 1978;28:83–90.

41. Anke M, Groppel B, Nordmann S, Kronemann H. Further evidence for the essentiality of nickel. In: Anke M et al., eds. 4. *Spurenelementsymposium*. Leipzig: Karl-Marx-Universität, 1983:19–28.

42. Schnegg FH, Kirchgessner M. Zur Essentialität von Nickel für das tierische Wachstum. *Z Tierphysiol Tierernähr Futtermittelkde* 1975;36:63–74.

43. Nielsen FH, Myron DR, Givand SH, Zimmerman TJ, Ollerich DA. Nickel deficiency in rats. *J Nutr* 1975;105:1620–30.

44. Spears JW, Hatfield EE, Forbes RM. Nickel for ruminants. II. Influence of dietary nickel on performance and metabolic parameters. *J Animal Sci* 1979;48:649–57.

45. Anke M, Grün M, Dittrich G, Groppel B, Hennig A. Low nickel rations for growth and reproduction in pigs. In: Hoekstra WG, ed. *Trace element metabolism in animals*, vol 2. Baltimore: University Park Press, 1974:716–8.

46. Anke M, Grün M, Partschefeld M. Nickel, ein neues lebensnotwendiges Spurenelement. *Arch Tierernähr* 1976;26:740–1.

47. Anke M, Kronemann H, Groppel B, Hennig A, Meissner D, Schneider H-J. The influence of nickel-deficiency on growth, reproduction, longevity and different biochemical parameters of goats. In: Anke M, ed. *Nickel 3. Spurenelementsymposium*. Leipzig: Karl-Marx-Universität, 1980:3–10.

48. Anke M, Groppel B, Kronemann H, Grün M. Nickel—an essential element. In: Sunderman FW Jr, ed. *Nickel in the human environment*. Oxford: Oxford University Press, 1974:339–65.

49. Kirchgessner M, Perth J, Schnegg A. Mangelnde Ni-Versorgung und Ca-, Mg- und P-Gehalte im Knochen wachsender Ratten. *Arch Tierernähr* 1980;30:805–10.

50. Schnegg A, Kirchgessner M. Zur Interaktion von Nickel mit Eisen, Kupfer und Zink. *Arch Tierernähr* 1976;26:543–9.

51. Schnegg A, Kirchgessner M. Veränderungen des Hämoglobingehaltes, der Erythrocytenzahl und des Hämatokrites bei Nickelmangel. *Nutr Metab* 1975;19:268–78.

52. Schnegg A, Kirchgessner M. Zur Absorption und Verfügbarkeit von Eisen bei Nickelmangel. *Int Z Vit Ernährungsforsch* 1976;46:96–9.

53. Schnegg A, Kirchgessner M. Zur Differentialdiagnose von Fe- und Ni-Mangel durch Bestimmung einiger Enzymaktivitäten. *Zentralbl Vet Med* 1977;24:242–7.

54. Kirchgessner M, Schnegg A. Eisenstoffwechsel im Nickelmangel. In: Anke M, ed. *Nickel. 3. Spurenelementsymposium*. Leipzig: Karl-Marx-Universität, 1980:27–31.

55. Nielsen FH, Myron DR. Effect of form of iron on the interaction between nickel and iron in rats: iron absorption. *Proc Natl Acad Sci USA* 1980;34:31–40.

56. Nielsen FH, Shuler TR, Zimmerman TJ, Collings ME, Uthus EO. Interaction between nickel and iron in the rat. *Biol Trace Element Res* 1979;1:325–35.

57. Anke M. Nickel als essentielles Spurenelement. In: Gladtke E, ed. *Spurenelemente*. Stuttgart: Georg Thieme Verlag, 1985:106–125.

58. Anke M, Grün M, Groppel B, Kronemann H. Nutritional requirements of nickel. In: Sarkar B, ed. *Biological aspects of metals and metal-related disease*. New York: Raven Press, 1983:89–105.

59. Schneider H-J, Anke M, Klinger G. The nickel status of human beings. In: Anke, ed. *Nickel. 3. Spurenelementsymposium*. Leipzig: Karl-Marx-Universität, 1980:277–83.

60. Anke M, Grün M, Groppel B, Kronemann H. Die Bedeutung des Nickels für den Menschen. *Zentralbl Pharm Pharmakother Lab Diagn* 1982;121:474–89.

61. Sunderman FW Jr, Shen SK, Reid MC, Allpass PR. Teratogenicity and embryotoxicity of nickel carbonyl in Syrian hamsters. In: Anke M, ed. *Nickel. 3. Spurenelement symposium*. Leipzig: Karl-Marx-Universität, 1980:301–7.

62. Nielsen FH, Uthus EO. Arsenic. In: Frieden E, ed. *Biochemistry of the essential ultra trace elements*. New York: Plenum Press, 1980:319–40.
63. Anke M, Grün M, Partschefeld M. The essentiality of arsenic for animals. In: Hemphill DD, ed. *Trace substances in environmental health*, vol 10. Columbia: University of Missouri, 1976:403–9.
64. Anke M, Grün M, Partschefeld M, Groppel B, Hennig A. Essentiality and function of arsenic. In: Kirschgessner M, ed. *Trace element metabolism in man and animals*, vol 3. Freising-Weihenstephan: Technical University of München, 1978:248–52.
65. Anke M, Groppel B, Grün M, Hennig A, Meissner D. The influence of arsenic deficiency on growth, reproductiveness, life expectancy and health of goats. In: Anke M, ed. *Arsen*. 3. Spurenelementsymposium. Leipzig: Karl-Marx-Universität, 1980:25–32.
66. Uthus EO, Cornatzer WE, Nielsen FH. Consequences of arsenic deprivation in laboratory animals. In: Lederer WH, ed. *Arsenic symposium, production and use, biomedical and environmental perspectives*. New York: Van Nostrand Reinhold, 1983:173–89.
67. Anke M, Krause U, Groppel B. The effect of arsenic deficiency on growth, reproduction, life expectancy and disease symptoms in animals. In: Hemphill DD, ed. *Trace substances in environmental health*, vol 21. Columbia: University of Missouri, 1987:533–50.
68. Anke M, Schmidt A, Groppel B, Kronemann H. Further evidence for the essentiality of arsenic. In: Anke M, ed. 4. Spurenelementsymposium. Leipzig: Karl-Marx-Universität, 1983;97–104.
69. Anke M, Schmidt B, Groppel B, Kronemann H. Importance of arsenic for fauna. In: Pais J, ed. *New results in the research of hardly known trace elements*. Budapest: Horticultural University, 1985:61–71.
70. Schmidt A, Anke M, Groppel B, Kronemann H. Histochemical and ultrastructural findings in As deficiency. In: Anke M, ed. *Mengen-und Spurenelemente*, vol 3. Leipzig: Karl-Marx-Universität, 1983:424–5.
71. Schmidt A, Anke M, Groppel B, Kronemann H. Effect of As deficiency on skeletal muscle, myocardium, and liver. A histochemical and ultrastructural study. *Exp Pathol* 1984;25:195–7.
72. Anke M. Arsenic. In: Mertz W, ed. *Trace elements in human and animal nutrition*, vol 2. Orlando: Academic Press, 1986;347–72.
73. Nielsen FH. Ultratrace elements in nutrition. *Annu Rev Nutr* 1984;4:21–41.
74. Anke M, Schmidt A, Krause U, Groppel B, Gruhn K, Hoffmann G. Arsenmangel beim Wiederkäuer. In: Anke M, ed. *Mengen- und Spurenelemente*, vol 6. Leipzig: Karl-Marx-Universität, 1986:225–45.
75. Krause U. The site-specific arsenic supply of ruminants in the GDR. In: Anke M, ed. *New trace elements*. 5. Spurenelementsymposium. Leipzig: Karl-Marx-Universität, 1986:856–63.
76. Krause U, Anke M. Arsenversorgung von Mensch und Tier. *Zentralbl Pharm Pharmokother Lab Diagn* 1988;127:363–4.
77. Friberg L, Piscator M, Nordberg GF, Kjellström T. *Cadmium in the environment*, 2nd ed. Cleveland: CRC Press, 1974.
78. Schwartz K, Spallholz JE. The potential essentiality of cadmium. In: Anke M, Schneider H-J, eds. *Cadmium*. 2. Spurenelementsymposium. Leipzig: Karl-Marx-Universität, 1977:188–9.
79. Anke M. Discussion of the potential essentiality of cadmium. In: Anke M, Schneider H-J, eds. *Cadmium*. 2. Spurenelementsymposium. Leipzig: Karl-Marx-Universität, 1977:192–4.
80. Smith HA. Cadmium. In: Frieden E, ed. *Biochemistry of the essential ultratrace elements*. New York: Plenum Press, 1984:341–66.
81. Anke M, Groppel B, Schmidt A. New results on the essentiality of cadmium in ruminants. In: Hemphill DD, ed. *Trace substances in environmental health*, vol 21. Columbia: University of Missouri, 1987:556–66.
82. Anke M, Kronemann H, Groppel B, Riedel E. Die biologische Bedeutung kleinster Kadmiummengen für die Fauna. *Wiss Z Karl-Marx-Universität Leipzig, Math.-Naturwiss R* 1984; 33:157–65.
83. Masaoka T, Anke M, Kronemann H, Grün M. The cadmium status of animal and man. In: Anke M, ed. *New trace elements*. 5. Spurenelementsymposium. Leipzig: Karl-Marx-Universität, 1986: 979–89.
84. Kronemann H, Anke M, Grün M. Der Kadmiumgehalt der Nahrungsmittel in der DDR. *Zentralbl Pharm Pharmakother Lab Diagn* 1982;121:556–9.
85. Kostial K. Cadmium. In: Mertz W, ed. *Trace elements in human and animal nutrition*, 5th ed, vol 2. Orlando: Academic Press, 1986:319–45.
86. Hienzsch E, Schneider H-J, Anke M, Hennig A, Groppel B. The cadmium, zinc, copper, and manganese level of different organs of human beings without considerable Cd-exposure in dependence

on age and sex. In: Anke M, Schneider H-J, eds. *Kadmiumsymposium 2.* Leipzig: Karl-Marx-Universität, 1978:276–82.

87. Salm-Horstmar, Fürst ZU. Uber die Notwendigkeit des Lithiums und Fluorkaliums zur Fruchtbarkeit der Gerste. *J Prakt Chem* 1961;84:140–51.
88. Cade JFJ. Lithium salts in the treatment of psychotic excitement. *Med J Aust* 1949;2:349–56.
89. Anke M, Groppel B, Grün M, Kronemann H, Riedel E. Effects of Li-poor rations in ruminants. In: Szentmihályi S, ed. *Proceedings of the International Conference of Feed Additives.* Budapest, 1981:245–8.
90. Anke M, Grün M, Groppel B, Kronemann H. The biological importance of lithium. In: Anke M, Schneider H-J, eds. *Mengen- und Spurenelemente,* vol 1. Leipzig: Karl-Marx-Universität 1981:217–39.
91. Anke M, Groppel B, Kronemann H, Grün M. Evidence for the essentiality of lithium in goats. In: Anke M, ed. *Lithium.* 4. Spurenelementsymposium. Leipzig: Karl-Marx-Universität, 1983: 1983–65.
92. Anke M, Groppel B, Grün M, Kronemann H, Riedel E. Die biologische Bedeutung des Lithiums. *Wiss Z Karl-Marx-Universität Leipzig, Math.-Naturwiss. R,* 1983;32:260–70.
93. Anke M, Groppel B, Kuhnert E, Angelow L. Der Einfluss des Lithiums auf Futterverzehr, Wachstum und Verhalten von Schwein und Rind. In: Anke M, ed. *Mengen- und Spurenelemente,* vol 4. Leipzig: Karl-Marx-Universität, 1984:537–44.
94. Pickett EE, Hawkins JL. Determination of lithium in small animal tissues at physiological levels by flame emission photometry. *Anal Biochem* 1987;112:213–9.
95. Pickett EE. Evidence for the essentiality of lithium in the rat. In: Anke M, ed. *Lithium.* 4. Spurenelement-Symposium. Leipzig: Karl-Marx-Universität, 1983:66–70.
96. Burt J. Lithium. Columbia: University of Missouri, 1982. Thesis.
97. Mertz W. Lithium. In: Mertz W, ed. *Trace elements in human and animal nutrition,* vol 2. Orlando: Academic Press, 1986:391–7.
98. Szentmihályi S, Anke M, Regius A. The importance of lithium for plant and animal. In: Pais J, ed. *New results in the research of hardly known trace elements.* Budapest: Horticultural University, 1984:136–51.
99. Arnhold W. Die Versorgung von Tier und Mensch mit dem lebensnotwendigen Spurenelement Lithium. Promotion A. Leipzig: Karl-Marx-Universität, 1989.
100. Baumann W, Stadie G, Anke M. Der Lithiumstatus des Menschen. In: Anke M, ed. *Lithium.* 4. Spurenelementsymposium. Leipzig: Karl-Marx-Universität, 1983:180–5.
101. Szilágyi M, Anke M, Szentmilhályi S. The effect of lithium deficiency on the metabolism of goats. In: Pais J, ed. *New results in the research of hardly known trace elements.* Budapest, Horticultural University 1984:167–72.
102. Szentmihályi S, Regius A, Lokay D, Anke M. Der Lithiumgehalt der Vegetation in Abhängigkeit von der geologischen Herkunft des Standortes. In: Anke M, ed. *Lithium.* 5. Spurenelementsymposium. Leipzig: Karl-Marx-Universität, 1983:18–24.
103. Regius A, Pavel J, Anke M, Szentmihályi S. Der Lithiumgehalt der Futter- und Nahrungsmittel. In: Anke M et al, eds. *Lithium.* 4. Spurenelementsymposium. Leipzig: Karl-Marx-Universität, 1983:45–51.
104. Tölgyesi G. Die Verbreitung des Lithiums in ungarischen Böden und Pflanzen. In: Anke M, ed. *Lithium.* 4. Spurenelementsymposium. Leipzig: Karl-Marx-Universität, 1983:39–44.
105. Lambert J. Lithium content in the grassland vegetation. In: Anke M, ed. *Lithium.* 4. Spurenelementsymposium. Leipzig: Karl-Marx-Universität, 1983:32–8.
106. Reichlmayr-Lais AM, Kirchgessner M, Lead. In: Frieden E, ed. *Biochemistry of the essential ultra trace elements.* New York: Plenum Press, 1984:367–87.
107. Nielsen FH. Nutritional significance of the ultra trace elements. *Nutr Rev* 1988;46:337–41.
108. Anke M, Groppel B, Arnhold W. Further evidence for the essentiality of bromine in ruminants. In: Anke M, ed. 6. *Spurenelementsymposium.* Leipzig: Karl-Marx-University, Friedrich- Schiller-Universität Jena 1989:1120–31.

DISCUSSION

Dr. Chandra: I want to make two comments relating to our work on cadmium and zinc and their effects on the immune response. If you feed rodents three levels of cadmium—5, 50, and 500 ppm—it is the intermediate group that has the optimal immune response. Both low and high groups have deficient responses. The same applies to other heavy or "toxic" elements.

The second point relates to interactions among various trace elements. We know, for example, that the amount of dietary zinc is very critical when evaluating the effect of cadmium.

Dr. Marini: The values you have given us are average values. Did you estimate concentrations in different tissues—brain, heart, etc? We know that treatment with lithium during pregnancy can be dangerous. There are several examples of women with mental diseases getting pregnant while on lithium treatment and having offspring with Ebstein's anomaly, a very rare condition normally. Maybe there are different concentrations in different tissues.

Dr. Anke: We did not analyze lithium concentration in different embryonic tissues, we analyzed the complete embryo. We did, however, analyze various enzymes separately. Monoamino-oxidase (MAO) for example, which is most important in the field of pharmacology in relation to depression, had 50% less activity in lithium-deficient animals. I cannot say what this effect means, but this is a developing field.

Dr. Mertz: When I listen to Dr. Anke's presentation I think of the consequences of these fascinating studies for us in the audience—pediatricians, internists, nutritionists. I am reminded of the time a little more than 30 years ago when Klaus Schwarz made the discovery that selenium is an essential element. That was almost 10 years after the nutrition community was convinced that with the discovery and identification of vitamin B_{12} we knew everything. Selenium was at that time considered a poison and a carcinogen. We are in a similar position today with some of the new trace elements. Some of the discoveries have been independently confirmed; others await confirmation. There are great challenges. In the cases of lithium, epidemiologists have correlated its concentration in drinking water with risk of coronary heart disease and with admission to mental hospital, while a recent report, already confirmed, reveals a requirement for lithium for the propagation of certain lymphocytes *in vitro* in the absence of calf serum. Dr. Anke has also told us that our lithium intake may possibly be marginal.

Dr. Anke: Lithium intake in the GDR varies between 230 and 560 µg per day in women, and between 200 and 600 µg per day in men. Nobody knows whether 200 µg per day is enough.

Trace Elements in Nutrition of Children—II,
edited by Ranjit K. Chandra, Nestlé Nutrition
Workshop Series, Vol. 23, Nestec Ltd.,
Vevey/Raven Press, Ltd., New York © 1991.

Update of Iron Needs and Iron Deficiency in Pediatrics

Martti A. Siimes

Department of Pediatrics, University of Helsinki, SF-00290 Helsinki, Finland

Iron deficiency may develop in infants and children even though the newborn is fairly well-loaded with iron at birth. The reasons for this are complex. The iron concentration in the circulation is high since the hemoglobin concentration is elevated at birth. In addition, tissue iron content is also high at birth. Although both of these reserves are available for further iron needs, primarily to produce hemoglobin, and only small amounts of iron are lost from the body in the absence of bleeding, iron deficiency is a relatively common condition in infants and small children. The purpose of this chapter is to discuss iron needs in small children with excessive intakes of iron and in those with marginal intakes. The latter is often associated with the development of iron deficiency.

SMALL CHILDREN WITH EXCESSIVE INTAKE OF IRON

Infants may receive iron from iron-supplemented infant milk formulas, iron-fortified baby foods, or medicinal iron. Many iron-supplemented formulas contain 6–12 mg of iron/liter. Use of such milk usually leads to an iron intake of about 1 mg/kg·day. Several studies show that this feeding results in effective prevention of iron deficiency (1–3) and probably also in excessive intake of iron. Similar amounts of iron may also be obtained from iron-fortified baby foods if they are used daily. Medicinal iron, usually in the form of small tablets, is commonly used, primarily in low-birthweight infants during the first year of life, since nutritional sources of iron are not able to guarantee optimal iron availability, particularly in infants with birth weight below 1.5 kg.

Even if iron intake is excessive, there may be a large variation in iron needs in individual infants. For instance, full-term infants of average birth weight may weigh between 8 and 12 kg at age 1 year. This variation in weight has a surprisingly strong influence on individual iron needs. The calculations in Table 1 show that the annual increment of hemoglobin iron is about +65 mg in the infant with a weight of 8 kg and nearly three times as much (+175 mg) in an infant weighing 12 kg at age 1

TABLE 1. *Kinetic calculation of the influence of weight growth on hemoglobin iron requirement in two full-term infants*

	Infant 1	Infant 2
Weight (kg)		
At birth	3.5	3.5
At age 1 year	8.0	12.0
Hemoglobin iron (mg)		
At birth	150	150
At age 1 year	215	325
Increment per year	+ 65	+ 175

year. The 65 mg can easily be mobilized from tissue iron stores and dietary iron. However, to accumulate 175 mg of iron, the iron availability from the diet may be a rate-limiting factor. Thus iron absorption from foods must be much more effective in the latter case since the extra need for iron is unlikely to be compensated by increased dietary intake, which would require a nearly threefold increase in daily food consumption. This means that to prevent the development of iron deficiency the larger baby must be able to increase his iron absorption. If he is unable to do so, even if he has a relatively high iron intake, iron deficiency may develop. This discussion emphasizes the fact that it is not only low-birthweight infants but also full-term infants who grow unusually fast who have increased need for iron.

Accordingly, one might anticipate that those infants with the least growth would be protected from the development of iron deficiency and that those with the fastest growth would almost always end up with evidence of iron deficiency. However, this is not necessarily the case when iron is readily available in the diet and when the infants are healthy (4). It is of interest that not only full-term infants but also the smallest prematures are able to increase their rates of iron absorption in order to compensate for the greater need for iron during rapid growth if adequate iron is available in the diet.

A similar phenomenon which is an important determinant of individual iron needs is a potential change in the hemoglobin level within the normal limits. It appears that hemoglobin concentration shows a tracking phenomenon in healthy subjects (i.e., a high, average, or low normal level of hemoglobin concentration is seen systematically if one individual is carefully followed). However, this tracking phenomenon develops during early infancy. Thus tracking is rarely evident if the hemoglobin concentrations are compared in infants between birth and 1 year of age, and therefore newborns with a $+2$ SD level of hemoglobin may in some cases have a -2 SD level of hemoglobin concentration at 1 year of age, or vice versa (Table 2). Consequently, infants with a low normal concentration of hemoglobin at birth and a high normal concentration at age 12 months have a considerably greater need for iron than do infants with a high normal concentration at birth and a low normal con-

TABLE 2. *Hemoglobin concentration (g/liter) in infants on prolonged iron supplementation and iron deficiency excluded by laboratory criteria[a]*

Age (months)	− 2 SD	Mean	+ 2 SD
0.5	134	166	198
1	107	139	171
2	94	112	130
4	103	122	141
6	111	126	141
9	114	127	140
12	115	127	139

[a]MCV below 71 fl, serum iron saturation below 10%, and serum ferritin below 10 μg/liter.
From Saarinen UM, and Siimes MA (5).

centration at age 12 months. The change in hemoglobin tracking can have a major influence on the variation in iron needs among individuals, as emphasized in Table 2.

The considerations described above may explain in part why healthy infants occasionally develop evidence of iron deficiency even if they have been fed appropriately. For instance, the results of a recent study from Austria fit this hypothesis (6). The authors followed healthy term infants in a longitudinal study from 15 to 365 days of age. The infants were fed according to their current feeding recommendations. Nevertheless, about 5% of the infants developed anemia and about 10% developed low serum ferritin concentrations. Although the prevalence of iron deficiency anemia and depletion of the iron stores were lower than in previous studies, the infants developed iron deficiency even if they were fed optimally.

SMALL INFANTS WITH MARGINAL IRON INTAKE

Although human milk contains relatively small quantities of iron, which seems to decrease even further through lactation, infants who are exclusively breast-fed rarely appear to develop evidence of iron deficiency if breast feeding is not prolonged beyond 6 months (7; see also the chapter by Lönnerdal, *this volume*). This is due to the better availability of human milk iron in conditions where human milk is the only food.

Some infants continue to receive human milk as the only source of iron even after 6 months of age. If these infants are started on iron-fortified baby foods, their laboratory criteria of iron nutrition improves rapidly (8). This may be evidence for a high bioavailability of iron under these conditions. This is in contrast to a relatively low availability of iron from baby foods when they are given to breast-fed infants who have also been introduced earlier to cow's milk products (9).

TABLE 3. *Influence of dietary factors on iron status at 1 year of age[a]*

	Iron sufficiency ($n = 26$)	Iron deficiency ($n = 25$)
Dietary inadequacies (overall diet)	35%	80%
Full cow's milk before age 6 months	12%	40%
Intake of over 900 ml/day of cow's milk	16%	40%
Insufficient solids	16%	40%

[a]History of iron-sufficient and iron-deficient infants is compared.
[b]$p < 0.05$.
From Morton RE, et al. (11).

The growing weanling becomes vulnerable to iron deficiency when the neonatal stores have been consumed unless the diet contains enough iron and/or vitamin C (10). The use of ascorbic-acid-rich foods and meat products decreases the likelihood of iron deficiency (10). It should be emphasized that early weaning to cow's milk results in increased risk of early iron deficiency. Recently, a study dealing with etiological factors in iron deficiency concluded that the preceding use of cow's milk was one of the strongest determinants of the later development of iron deficiency (Table 3) (11).

IRON DEFICIENCY IN SMALL CHILDREN

Diagnosis of iron deficiency can be made by several alternative approaches. If hemoglobin concentration indicates anemia in an otherwise healthy child, one may start iron medication and watch for a response in hemoglobin concentration. This may be the most reliable single criterion of iron deficiency anemia. Following the reticulocytosis peak, hemoglobin concentration rises at an average of 0.25 to 0.4 g/dl·day (12). The reticulocytosis, usually occurring 7–10 days after initiation of iron medication, may also be used as an independent criterion of therapeutic response.

The diagnosis of iron deficiency is further supported by other simple tests, including mean corpuscular red blood cell volume (MCV) or red blood cell morphology (Table 4). MCV is a practical tool since its technical and biological variation is small. Further, its decrease is a sensitive indicator of iron deficiency. An additional advantage of MCV is that it is often available as a side product of hemoglobin analysis. Thus mild iron deficiency is probable if a child has both hemoglobin concentration and MCV at the low-normal range (9) (Fig. 1). Red blood cell morphology is not usually a sensitive tool for detecting children with mild iron deficiency anemia, but it is a simple and practical method in cases with moderate or severe anemia.

TABLE 4. *Indications of iron deficiency during infancy and childhood*

Age (years)	Hemoglobin (g/liter) lower limit	MCV (fl) lower limit
0.5–2	110	70
2–5	110	73
5–9	115	75
9–12	120	76
12–14 (females)	120	77
12–14 (males)	125	76
14–18 (females)	120	78
14–18 (males)	130	77

Diagnosis of iron deficiency anemia can also be made by more sophisticated and expensive methods. These include serum iron, total iron binding capacity (TIBC), and ferritin concentration. A practical way is to calculate transferrin iron saturation from serum iron as a percentage of TIBC. In healthy infants the saturation remains well above 10%, and in children and adults, above 16%. The mean values in healthy populations are usually around 30%. Low values are indications of iron deficiency and probably of ongoing sideropenic erythropoiesis. Some laboratories measure transferrin concentration rather than TIBC. The transferrin values can equally well be used to calculate transferrin iron saturation. If serum iron is determined, the blood sample should be drawn in the morning to avoid the problems caused by diurnal variation in serum iron concentration. The concentration of serum ferritin is a measure of tissue iron stores and is independent of serum iron and transferrin saturation. Serum ferritin concentration is high at birth, rises further soon after birth, and then gradually decreases during the first 4–6 months down to low levels (10–140 μg/liter) which are maintained throughout childhood (9). Values below 10 μg/liter indicate very limited iron storage. Several types of diseases may disturb serum ferritin concentration. In particular, infections, inflammation, and liver problems result in temporarily high ferritin concentrations. In societies where lead poisoning is common, the erythrocyte protoporphyrin test may be useful in detecting cases with either lead poisoning or iron deficiency anemia.

Thus, even today, a laboratory diagnosis of mild iron deficiency anemia may not always be easy. However, regardless of the selection of the diagnostic method, it is necessary for the physician to diagnose the *cause* of iron deficiency anemia as well as treating the patient with iron.

There are two approaches to the treatment of iron deficiency anemia. If one is able to give iron tablets on an empty stomach or with juice or water prior to a meal, a relatively small dose of iron may be used (2–3 mg/kg·day, divided into two or three doses). However, in most cases it is more practical to give the tablets at the same time as a meal. In these cases, more iron is needed to achieve the same re-

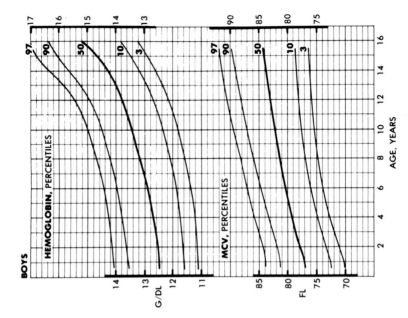

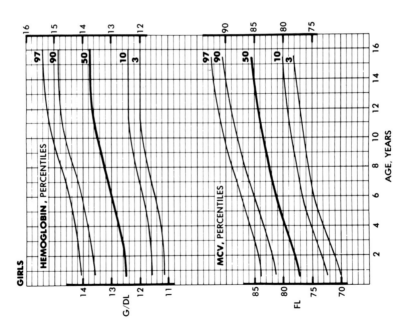

FIG. 1. Hemoglobin concentration and mean corpuscular volume (MCV) in infants and children. From Dallman PR and Siimes MA (17).

sponse (5–6 mg/kg·day). Furthermore, these larger doses may be associated with gastrointestinal complications which are avoided by the use of small doses. Occasionally, if the composition of the meal is the reason for iron deficiency anemia, absorption of iron may not be optimal if given during the meal. Personally, I prefer to give a small dose prior to the meal.

IRON DEFICIENCY AND INFANT DEVELOPMENT

Animal experiments show that iron deficiency anemia in infants is associated with decreased concentrations of nonheme iron in the brain (13). Further, the data show that brain iron deficiency developing in infancy is not completely corrected even if proper iron medication is given (13). In recent years an increasing amount of evidence has accumulated from human studies indicating that iron deficiency, particularly in infancy, may cause developmental problems which are long-lasting even though the subjects are treated with iron.

Behavioral effects of iron deficiency and its treatment were studied in a double-blind randomized community-based investigation of 191 Costa Rican infants with various degrees of iron deficiency (14). The infants with iron deficiency anemia showed lower mental and motor test scores, and these findings persisted among the majority of the initially anemic infants with severe or chronic iron deficiency even after iron treatment. The authors conclude that iron therapy that is adequate for correcting anemia is insufficient to reverse behavioral and developmental disturbances in many infants (15). In another study iron-deficient anemic children were given iron therapy. The children showed no difference in mean mental development score at baseline compared with a well-matched control group (15). On later follow-up the behavioral rating data revealed differences between the anemic and control groups, the controls being rated more responsive. The data suggest that failure to show improvement in scores in the anemic group after treatment may indicate some irreversible behavioral deficit. It appears that not only lower scores in cognitive functions but also noncognitive disturbances are observed in infants with iron deficiency. These may also be associated with limited physical activity and working capacity, as reviewed by Lozoff (16). If so, these complications and long-lasting effects may have a major importance in developing countries, in most of which iron deficiency is extremely common.

REFERENCES

1. Reeves JD. Iron supplementation in infancy. *Pediatr Rev* 1986;8:177–84.
2. Stekel A, Olivares M, Cayazzo M, Chadud P, Llaguno S, Pizarro F. Prevention of iron deficiency by milk fortification. II. A field trial with a full-fat acidified milk. *Am J Clin Nutr* 1988;47:265–9.
3. Hertrampf E, Cayazzo M, Pizarro F, Stekel A. Bioavailability of iron in soy-based formula and its effect on iron nutriture in infancy. *Pediatrics* 1986;78:640–5.
4. Siimes MA, Järvenpää A-L. Prevention of anemia and iron deficiency in very low-birth-weight infants. *J Pediatr* 1982;101:277–9.

5. Saarinen UM, Siimes MA. Developmental changes in red blood cell counts and indices of infants after exclusion of iron deficiency by laboratory criteria and continuous iron supplementation. *J Pediatr* 1978;92:412–6.
6. Pietschnig B, Haschke F, Vanura H, Heil M, Camaya Z, Schuster E, Schilling R. Nutritional iron status of infants fed according to current recommendations. *Klin Padiatr* 1986;198:484–8.
7. Siimes MA, Salmenperä L, Perheentupa J. Exclusive breast feeding for 9 months: Risk of iron deficiency. *J Pediatr* 1984;104:196–9.
8. Siimes MA, Salmenperä L. The weanling: iron for all or one. *Acta Paediatr Scand (Suppl)* 1989;361:103–8.
9. Dallman PR, Siimes MA, Stekel A. Iron deficiency in infancy and childhood. *Am J Clin Nutr* 1980;33:86–118.
10. Dallman PR. Iron deficiency in the weanling: a nutritional problem on the way to resolution. *Acta Paediatr Scand* 1986;323:59–67.
11. Morton RE, Nysenbaum A, Price K. Iron status in the first year of life. *J Pediatr Gastroenterol Nutr* 1988;7:707–12.
12. Lanzkowsky P. Problems in diagnosis of iron deficiency anemia. *Pediatr Ann* 1985;14:622–3.
13. Dallman PR, Siimes MA, Manies EC. Brain iron: persistent deficiency following short-term iron deprivation in the rat. *Br J Haematol* 1975;31:209–15.
14. Lozoff B, Brittenham GM, Wolf AW, et al. Iron deficiency anemia and iron therapy effects on infant developmental test performance. *Pediatrics* 1987;79:981–95.
15. Deinard AS, List A, Lindgren B, Hunt JV, Chang PN. Cognitive deficits in iron-deficient and iron-deficient anemic children. *J Pediatr* 1986;108:681–9.
16. Lozoff B. Behavioral alterations in iron deficiency. *Adv Pediatr* 1988;35:331–59.
17. Dallman PR, Siimes MA. Percentile curves for hemoglobin and red cell volume in infancy and childhood. *J Pediatr* 1979;94:26–31.

Trace Elements in Nutrition of Children—II,
edited by Ranjit K. Chandra, Nestlé Nutrition
Workshop Series, Vol. 23, Nestec Ltd.,
Vevey/Raven Press, Ltd., New York © 1991.

Concentrations, Compartmentation, and Bioavailability of Trace Elements in Human Milk and Infant Formula

Bo Lönnerdal

Department of Nutrition, University of California, Davis, California 95616, USA

An adequate supply of essential trace elements is necessary to assure normal growth, health, and development of newborn infants. Recent studies have shown that even in the absence of overt deficiency signs, suboptimal trace element status can compromise the immune function (1) and thus affect an infant's capacity to resist infections during this vulnerable period.

Human milk is viewed as a norm when deciding on the appropriate level of a nutrient to use in infant formulas. However, since the bioavailability of many nutrients is higher from human milk than from many other infant diets, the concentration of a nutrient in formulas must be increased by a "safety factor" to result in an amount of absorbed nutrient similar to that available from human milk. Bioavailability studies are needed to assess properly the magnitude of the safety factor. The absorption of nutrients such as the trace elements can be determined with a high degree of accuracy by using isotopes. To better understand the mechanisms behind the differences in trace element bioavailability among various diets, characterization of the components in the diet that bind and affect the absorption is necessary. With such knowledge, the composition of a formula may be changed to improve the bioavailability of an element instead of requiring further supplementation.

CONCENTRATIONS OF TRACE ELEMENTS IN INFANT DIETS

Iron

The concentration of iron in human milk shows a declining pattern during lactation; colostrum may contain as much as 0.5–0.8 mg/liter, while mature milk contains about 0.2–0.3 mg/liter (2). Similar levels have been found in several populations, and the most likely explanation is that neither maternal iron status (3) nor dietary intake of iron (4) appear to affect the level of iron in human milk. This

153

lack of effect may be explained by receptor-mediated regulation of iron uptake into the mammary gland (5), which can ensure an adequate supply of iron to the breast-fed infant even when the mother is anemic. This mechanism may not be efficient in all instances; for example, low milk iron levels have been found in lactating women who consumed high levels of coffee during pregnancy and lactation (6).

The level of iron in infant formula varies considerably; label claims range from a high level of 12 mg/liter in iron-supplemented U.S. formulas, to 6–7 mg/liter in most European formulas, to 1 mg/liter in unfortified formulas. It has been noted, however, that when the actual iron level of formula is analyzed, an even greater variation is found (7). The fortification compound used in infant formula is usually ferrous sulfate, whereas products for older infants contain a variety of iron compounds (8,9).

Zinc

Early in lactation, the zinc concentration in human milk may be 10 times higher than that in mature milk. Levels of 5–10 mg/liter are found in colostrum, while mature milk contains 1–2 mg/liter (10). As with iron, there appears to be little, if any, effect of maternal zinc status or intake on milk zinc concentration (11–13). This suggests regulation of the transport of zinc into milk by some unknown mechanism. This mechanism, however, may be defective in some women, as several mothers who were breast-feeding their prematurely born infants have been found to have low milk zinc levels (14). Since the mothers had no signs of zinc deficiency and the milk had normal levels of other nutrients and trace elements, the uptake mechanism for zinc appeared to be specifically affected.

Infant formulas are usually fortified with zinc to a level of 4–5 mg/liter. Large variations in formula zinc levels have been reported, however (7). Inorganic salts such as zinc chloride or zinc sulfate are usually used as fortification compounds.

Copper

The concentration of copper in human milk is somewhat higher in colostrum, which contains 0.3–0.4 mg/liter, than in mature milk, with 0.1–0.2 mg/liter (10). Most infant formulas contain slightly higher values, around 0.4–0.6 mg/liter which is largely derived from supplemental copper, as cow's milk is low in copper (15).

Manganese

There is no pronounced change in the manganese level of human milk; concentrations range from 4 to 6 μg/liter (16). Infant formulas based on cow's milk usually contain levels of 30–50 μg/liter, but occasionally manganese is added to formulas, resulting in manganese levels as high as 1000 μg/liter (7,17). Soy protein is naturally high in manganese, and soy formulas usually contain around 300 μg of manganese/liter (18).

COMPARTMENTATION OF TRACE ELEMENTS IN MILKS AND FORMULAS

Lipids

Milks and formulas can be separated into various compartments by centrifugation. A fat layer will then be formed which can be removed and analyzed for trace elements. Lipids from human milk have thus been shown to contain 30%, 18%, 20%, and 20% of iron, zinc, copper, and manganese, respectively (19–22). Lower percentages are found for cow's milk (23). For these milks, the fat layer is largely composed of triglycerides and contains little protein. The trace elements, however, are largely integral components of the membrane proteins surrounding the lipids (21). Examples of this would be iron in xanthine oxidase and zinc in alkaline phosphatase (21,24). It should be noted that larger amounts of trace elements in human milk are present in the fat than in cow's milk, despite a higher amount of lipid and protein in cow's milk fat. This suggests that the trace elements are specifically incorporated into some fat globule membrane components in human milk but not to the same extent in cow's milk.

When infant formulas are separated by centrifugation, the flotation layer contains a large proportion of protein (25). Vegetable oils in formulas do not contain any membranes, and the presence of protein is due to the use of emulsifiers in formula. These emulsifiers tend to form lipid–protein aggregates which have a lower density and subsequently will form a flotation layer after centrifugation. To what extent these aggregates remain in the gastrointestinal tract of infants, or if they affect trace element absorption, is not known. Typically, 20–40% of the trace elements in infant formula associate with this protein–lipid complex (22,26,27). It is reasonable to believe that the trace elements are bound to casein in cow's milk formula, as this protein has a preference to aggregate with lipids in the presence of emulsifiers.

Casein/Insoluble Proteins

Casein in human milk, cow's milk, and cow's milk formula will sediment when subjected to centrifugation, due to the higher density of the casein micelles. Similarly, insoluble or partially soluble proteins in soy formula will form a sediment following centrifugation. This sedimented material contains 60–80% of the total amount of trace elements in formula. If one assumes that the lipid–protein layer consists largely of casein and insoluble soy proteins, casein/insoluble proteins in formula will contain 80–95% of the total trace element content. Naturally, this has strong implications for the bioavailability of trace elements, as these proteins need to be solubilized in order to make the trace elements available for absorption (see below). The larger percentage of trace elements already present in the whey of whey-predominant formula as opposed to casein-predominant formula prior to digestion may explain the higher bioavailability of some trace elements from whey-predominant formula (28).

Whey/Soluble Proteins

The remaining portion of milks and formulas after removal of fat and casein/insoluble protein represents soluble proteins and low-molecular-weight compounds. Human milk whey contains lactoferrin that binds iron (19) and manganese (22), and serum albumin that binds zinc and copper (29). It has also been proposed that lactoferrin binds zinc in human milk (30,31). This is due to the fact that lactoferrin and serum albumin elute at the same position in several chromatographic techniques, so that zinc bound to serum albumin is erroneously identified as being bound to lactoferrin (29). Some studies in experimental animals have failed to demonstrate an effect of lactoferrin on zinc absorption (32). In addition, it has been shown by electrophoresis and Western blotting that iron and manganese, but not zinc, bind to human lactoferrin under physiological conditions (33).

A relatively small proportion of the trace elements in cow's milk and infant formula is associated with whey proteins (22,26,27). Low-molecular-weight components, predominantly citrate, bind trace elements in both human milk and cow's milk, but the relative proportion is higher in human milk (24,34,35). This is likely to be due to the higher concentration of casein in cow's milk, which binds trace elements with a high affinity (36,37). Zinc binding by several other ligands in human milk has been proposed but later shown to be incorrect. Picolinic acid is one example; this compound was tentatively identified as a zinc-binding ligand in human milk (38). Chromatography of this putative ligand with zinc demonstrated, however, that the zinc-binding ligand in human milk did not elute at the same position as the picolinic acid–zinc complex, thus failing to show identity (39). In addition, Rebello et al. (40) analyzed picolinic acid in human milk by high-performance liquid chromatography and found negligible concentrations, inadequate to chelate any significant concentrations of zinc. Seal and Heaton (41) have also shown in experimental animals that if picolinic acid were a zinc-binding ligand in human milk, it would enhance the absorption of zinc, but even more so enhance the excretion of zinc because of its high binding constant to zinc. Thus picolinic acid would cause a net loss of zinc rather than stimulating the bioavailability of zinc. The latter finding may explain why some investigators have shown a stimulating effect of picolinic acid in some experimental models that measured uptake only. Formulas are usually supplemented with salts containing trace element ligands such as citrate, and a certain proportion of trace elements in formulas will be bound to these ligands.

BIOAVAILABILITY OF TRACE ELEMENTS FROM INFANT DIETS

Iron

Many studies have attempted to assess the bioavailability of iron from various infant diets. The results have been highly variable, due in part to a very high variability in iron absorption among human subjects. Other methodological problems include the method of isotopic labeling of the diet, the dose size used, and finally, the formulation of the diet tested.

Radioisotopes have been used in only a few studies on human infants (42–44). In general, a high bioavailability of iron from human milk has been found, although absorption values showed a wide range. A reference dose of ferrous sulfate with ascorbic acid, which is used in similar studies in adults, was not utilized to assess each infant's inherent capacity to absorb iron, probably to minimize radiation exposure. Thus, intersubject variation may have obscured the results. In addition, extrinsic labeling with ^{59}Fe was used in these studies. It has been shown that this method does not label iron-binding compounds in human milk in proportion to their capacity to bind the "native" element (24,45). Therefore, a larger than "normal" labeling of lactoferrin was achieved, possibly suggesting that the bioavailability of iron from human lactoferrin is high. The size of the dose given also affects the degree of absorption. In many instances a small meal size was used to facilitate the feeding. It has been shown, however, that iron absorption is much higher from a small volume than from a more regular meal-size portion, possibly due to a higher proportion of gastric acid and proteolytic enzymes to the amount of protein given (46). Finally, the infant diet tested was often quoted as infant formula, but in reality was dilute, heat-treated cow's milk rather than the current processed infant formulas. The applicability to commercial formulas presently being marketed is therefore somewhat questionable.

Human adult subjects have also been used to assess iron absorption from infant diets (47,48). These studies also suffer from many of the drawbacks described above. Another problem is that in some studies the amount of iron added to formula or human milk was clearly excessive, which in itself reduces iron absorption.

Studies in experimental animals that have lactoferrin in their milk, such as the suckling pig and weanling mouse, suggest a high bioavailability of iron bound to lactoferrin (49,50). However, in these studies bovine lactoferrin was used, which is somewhat different from the lactoferrin of other species. Recently, receptors for lactoferrin have been described in the intestinal mucosa of rabbits (51), mice (52), and rhesus monkeys (52). In the case of the infant rhesus monkey, the receptor was found to be highly specific and iron absorption was facilitated only by human or rhesus lactoferrin (which are very similar and cross-react immunologically), while no effect was observed for bovine lactoferrin or human transferrin (53). The difference in binding appears to be explained by differences in the carbohydrate side chains among these molecules. It was subsequently found that partially digested lactoferrin was also able to deliver iron to the receptor (33). A relatively large proportion of human lactoferrin is known to survive passage through the infant's gut in an intact or only partially digested form (54). Thus the stability of human lactoferrin, coupled with the presence of intestinal lactoferrin receptors, may explain the high bioavailability of iron from human milk. The lack of binding affinity of bovine lactoferrin to the receptor may also explain the lack of effect on iron absorption of supplementing infant formula with bovine lactoferrin (55).

There may, however, be several other milk constituents that contribute to the differences observed among various diets. For example, cow's milk is high in calcium, four to five times higher than human milk and two to three times higher than infant formula, which may have a negative effect on iron absorption. Barton et al. (56) have shown in a rat model that iron uptake from human milk was higher than from cow's milk, but that supplementation of human milk with calcium to the same level as in cow's milk resulted in a significantly lower iron uptake, now similar to cow's milk. It is also possible that casein in cow's milk, which is known to bind iron (36), can have a negative effect on iron absorption, as with zinc (see below). In a recent study in infant rhesus monkeys, in which we successfully labeled human milk and formula extrinsically, and used a reference dose and a realistic meal size, we found that iron absorption was high from both human milk and whey-predominant formula (46). Supplementation of the formula with human or bovine lactoferrin did not affect iron absorption. It is possible that a lack of inhibitory factors (such as casein and calcium), coupled with the presence of low-molecular-weight ligands such as citrate, lead to a high degree of iron absorption and that lactoferrin does not cause any enhancement beyond this level of absorption. Citrate, which is present in human milk and formulas in high concentration, has been shown to solubilize iron and enhance its absorption (57,58) as well as increase water flux across the intestinal mucosa (59), possibly causing a "solvent-drag" effect. In addition, supplementation of formula with ascorbic acid has a stimulatory effect on iron absorption, in particular from soy formula (60).

Zinc

The absorption of zinc from various infant diets is strongly dependent on their composition. Similar results have been obtained from human studies and experimental animals and there appears to be little species variation. Other factors that contribute to the relative ease of performing zinc absorption studies are that extrinsic labeling with an isotope has been shown to be valid (26,61) and that there is relatively little subject-to-subject variation (62).

Indications of a higher bioavailability of zinc from human milk than from cow's milk or formula were obtained from observations on patients with acrodermatitis enteropathica, who have a genetic disorder of zinc metabolism and become zinc-deficient when weaned (63); and from data on plasma zinc and growth of formula-fed infants compared to breast-fed infants (64,65). Direct support for this hypothesis was obtained from zinc absorption studies in suckling rats (26) as well as in human adults (66,67). Zinc absorption was found to be high from human milk, lower from cow's milk–based formula, and lowest from soy formula. Subsequent studies demonstrated that casein in cow's milk formula has a negative effect on zinc absorption and, as a consequence, that zinc absorption is higher from whey-predominant than from casein-predominant formula (28). It is not yet known whether the negative effect of bovine casein on zinc absorption is due to the presence of negatively charged, phosphorylated residues in the polypeptide backbone of the molecule (68) or to the presence of colloidal calcium phosphate within the casein micelle (69). It was also strongly suggested that phytate in soy formula has an inhibitory effect on zinc absorption (28). Removal of phytate by enzymatic or precipitation methods was found to improve zinc absorption from soy formula considerably when studied in infant rhesus monkeys (70). It is possible that some fermentation or further processing of soy protein isolate or soy formula may also have a positive effect, as it has been shown that only partial dephosphorylation of phytic acid has a pronounced beneficial effect on zinc absorption (71).

In the light of the pronounced differences in zinc bioavailability found for infant diets, it is sometimes difficult to explain why a low level of zinc in some formulas is not associated with zinc deficiency in infants (72,73). There are two possible explanations for this: (1) the signs of milder forms of zinc deficiency are difficult to diagnose and measurement of plasma zinc alone may not detect a deficiency; and (2) there may be homeostatic mechanisms compensating for low amount of zinc in the diet, in a manner analogous to what is known to occur for iron absorption. While the first explanation remains plausible, two recent studies support homeostatic regulation of zinc absorption. Ziegler et al. (74) have shown in human infants, using a stable isotope of zinc and the balance technique, that zinc absorption is higher and zinc excretion is lower when infants are fed a formula low in zinc than when they are fed a "normal" level of zinc. In a study on rhesus monkeys in which females had been fed a diet marginal in zinc throughout pregnancy and lactation, offspring had significantly higher zinc absorption than infants born to mothers fed a control diet (75). It should be noted that although some indicators of zinc status, such as immune competence, were affected in the marginal zinc group, plasma zinc was not affected, supporting the first explanation above. Thus it appears that an infant with impaired zinc status can upregulate zinc absorption. It is not known, however, to what extent this can occur or how it varies among individuals.

Copper

Few studies have addressed the bioavailability of copper to human infants. In part, this may be due to the lack of convenient isotopes, radioactive or stable, but also to a lack of cases of copper deficiency in term infants. Copper deficiency is known to occur in premature infants (76) but is then virtually always associated with feeding cow's milk or unsupplemented formula. In such instances, the considerably lower stores of copper in such infants at birth, combined with rapid growth and a diet very low in copper, can precipitate copper deficiency, which is often accompanied by anemia (77). The use of copper supplementation of formulas should prevent this from occurring, and it has been shown that even modest supplementation is effective (72,78).

Dietary components that affect zinc absorption appear to have similar effects on copper absorption from infant diets, at least as assessed by the suckling rat pup model (27). Copper bioavailability was high from human milk and cow's milk formula, lower from cow's milk, and lowest from soy formula. It should be noted that the absorption of copper from a so-called "premature formula" was lower than from human milk or from a milk formula for term infants. This may be due to the higher protein level of such formulas, causing incomplete protein digestion and copper utilization. The level of copper supplementation chosen in such products, however, should compensate for this slight negative effect.

Manganese

Little is known about the absorption of manganese in human infants. Studies in suckling rats show that a high proportion of dietary manganese is absorbed and retained at young age (79). In the adult, a large proportion of initially absorbed manganese is excreted via the bile (81). It is possible that the low output of bile in the early neonatal period will prevent manganese excretion (80). Another possibility is that some high-affinity sites in the body will bind manganese and thus prevent it from being excreted (82). The absorbed manganese is retained primarily by muscle and bone, but a relatively large proportion is bound in the brain. With increasing age, less manganese is retained by the brain and other tissues and the net retention is considerably lower. The significant proportion of manganese retained by the brain at a young age causes some concern for potential manganese toxicity, as it has been shown in human adults that the primary site for manganese toxicity is the extrapyramidal system in the brain (83). However, although manganese toxicity has been suggested in children with high hair manganese levels (84,85), there is little evidence that this is related to the choice of diet at young age.

The large proportion of manganese bound to lactoferrin in human milk appears to be well absorbed (22). Uptake of manganese bound to lactoferrin is also mediated by lactoferrin receptors in the small intestine, although it has been shown that the affinity for the receptor is higher for the lactoferrin–iron complex than for lactoferrin–manganese (33). It is likely, however, that other forms of manganese are also well absorbed. Manganese absorption does not appear to be saturable at a young age (86), and consequently, manganese in "free" form or loosely associated to low-molecular-weight complexes is taken up by diffusion. It is therefore not surprising that manganese absorption is high from all diets investigated. In our rat pup model, manganese absorption from various infant diets varied between 60 and 90%, with soy formula being lowest and human milk and cow's milk formula highest (79). Because of the high level of manganese in soy formula and the low level in human milk, the same volume of soy formula would provide 25 times as much absorbed manganese as human milk. In the human adult, similar differences were found among the infant diets, but absorption levels were much lower, ranging from 1 to 9% (87). Thus it appears that the higher concentration of manganese in soy formula is "compensated" for by a lower bioavailability.

Premature infants are of particular concern regarding manganese nutrition. When fed human milk, their manganese intake will be very low and they are therefore usually in negative manganese balance (88). Premature formula, however, is relatively high in manganese, 100–200 μg/liter, and infants fed such formulas are in positive manganese balance. Since a high proportion of manganese in this formula (18–42%) is absorbed, it is possible that this level of manganese may be excessive. On the other hand, the amount of manganese retained from such formulas is in agreement with current estimates of manganese requirements. However, as stated previously, our knowledge about the absorption and requirements of manganese is still limited.

TRACE ELEMENT INTERACTIONS

The similarity among several of the trace elements with regard to physicochemical properties (i.e., the configuration and coordination of these cations with water in solution) leads to the possibility of them competing with each other for absorption sites/pathways. In effect, if one trace element is supplemented at a generous level, it may inhibit the absorption of another trace element. Since wide variations in trace element levels in infant formulas have been demonstrated (7), this potential risk may exist for formula-fed infants.

Interaction between iron supplements and zinc uptake was shown in adult humans by Solomons and Jacob (89). This experiment was, however, performed with pharmacological levels of zinc to enable the investigators to measure changes in plasma zinc. The levels of iron were also very high, and it is unclear if this study is of any relevance to infant nutrition. A long-term study on iron supplementation of infants failed to show any effect on zinc status, as assessed by plasma zinc (90). This index of zinc status may, however, be inadequate to detect any adverse effect on zinc status. Better measurements of zinc status, such as plasma or erythrocyte metallothionein measurements (91), are needed to detect better any adverse effects on zinc status. It is also possible, as mentioned previously, that adaptive responses to zinc depletion have corrected the situation. This may explain why some investigators have found lower plasma zinc levels in young infants fed formula with iron supplementation than in infants fed unsupplemented formula (92), while others have not. Another possible explanation for the lack of an effect is that iron supplements given with a meal do not affect zinc absorption, while an effect can be seen when the two elements are given as salts in a water solution (93). Although zinc and copper are known to interact with each other, the ratios between these two elements in infant formulas appear to be far from the levels used in the studies in experimental animals that have shown such an interaction (94).

Iron and manganese have been shown to interact with each other (95,96). There are two possible scenarios that may be of relevance to infants. First, iron-deficient infants are likely to have much higher than normal iron absorption, and it is known that manganese absorption will also be dramatically increased in this situation (97,98). Thus an iron-deficient infant given a diet high in manganese may be susceptible to manganese toxicity. This is of particular concern, as legumes and cereals are high in manganese but contain little absorbable iron (unless fortified). Second, human milk is very low in manganese, and infants are often found to be in negative manganese balance (88). Thus, if such infants are given iron supplements, manganese excretion may be increased, exacerbating the situation.

The potential problem of trace element interaction has received little attention to date with regard to infant nutrition. Part of this is likely to be due to our lack of sensitive indicators of impaired zinc, copper, and manganese status. Hopefully, the awareness of this possibility will lead to a balanced approach when setting limits for supplementation of infant formulas with trace elements (18), thus avoiding the potential risk.

REFERENCES

1. Chandra RK, Dayton DH. Trace element regulation of immunity and infection. *Nutr Res* 1982; 2:721–30.
2. Siimes MA, Vuori E, Kuitunen P. Breast milk iron—a declining concentration during the course of lactation. *Acta Paediatr Scand* 1979;68:29–31.
3. Lönnerdal B. Effect of maternal iron status on iron in human milk. In: Hamosh M, Goldman AS, eds. *Human lactation 2: maternal and environmental factors.* New York: Plenum Press, 1986: 363–70.
4. Siimes MA, Salmenperä L, Perheentupa J. Exclusive breast-feeding for 9 months: risk of iron deficiency. *J Pediatr* 1984;104:196–9.
5. Sigman M, Lönnerdal B. Identification of a transferrin-receptor mediating iron uptake into rat mammary tissue plasma membranes (abstract). *Fed Proc* 1987;46:438.
6. Munoz LM, Lönnerdal B, Keen CL, Dewey KG. Coffee consumption as a factor in iron deficiency anemia among pregnant women and their infants in Costa Rica. *Am J Clin Nutr* 1988;48:645–51.
7. Lönnerdal B, Keen CL, Ohtake M, Tamura T. Iron, zinc, copper, and manganese in infant formulas. *Am J Dis Child* 1983;137:433–7.
8. Morck TA, Lynch SR, Skikne BS, Cook JD. Iron availability from infant food supplements. *Am J Clin Nutr* 1981;34:2630–4.
9. Hurrell PF. Bioavailability of different iron compounds used to fortify formula and cereals. In: Stekel A, ed. *Iron nutrition in infancy and childhood.* Nestlé Nutrition Workshop Series, vol 4. New York: Raven Press, 1984:95–118.
10. Vuori E, Kuitunen P. The concentrations of copper and zinc in human milk. *Acta Paediatr Scand* 1979;68:33–7.
11. Moser PB, Reynolds RD. Dietary zinc intake and zinc concentrations of plasma, erythrocytes and breast milk of postpartum lactating and non-lactating women: a longitudinal study. *Am J Clin Nutr* 1983;38:101–8.
12. Krebs NF, Hambidge KM, Jacobs MA, Oliva-Rasbach J. The effects of a dietary zinc supplement during lactation on longitudinal changes in maternal zinc status and milk zinc concentration. *Am J Clin Nutr* 1985;41:560–70.
13. Lönnerdal B. Effects of maternal dietary intake on breast milk composition. *J Nutr* 1986; 116:499–513.

14. Atkinson SA, Whelan D, Whyte R, Lönnerdal B. Abnormal zinc content in human milk: risk for development of nutritional zinc deficiency in infants. *Am J Dis Child* 1989;143:608–11.
15. Lönnerdal B, Keen CL, Hurley LS. Iron, copper, zinc and manganese in milk. *Annu Rev Nutr* 1981;1:149–74.
16. Vuori E. A longitudinal study of manganese in human milk. *Acta Paediatr Scand* 1979;68:571–3.
17. Stastny D, Vogel RS, Picciano MF. Manganese intake and serum manganese concentration of human milk-fed and formula-fed infants. *Am J Clin Nutr* 1984;39:872–8.
18. Lönnerdal B. Trace element absorption in infants as a foundation to setting upper limits for trace elements in infant formulas. *J Nutr* 1989;119:1839–45.
19. Fransson G-B, Lönnerdal B. Iron in human milk. *J Pediatr* 1980;96:380–4.
20. Fransson G-B, Lönnerdal B. Zinc, copper, calcium and magnesium in human milk. *J Pediatr* 1982;101:504–8.
21. Fransson G-B, Lönnerdal B. Iron, copper, zinc, calcium and magnesium in human milk fat. *Am J Clin Nutr* 1984;39:185–9.
22. Lönnerdal B, Keen CL, Hurley LS. Manganese binding proteins in human and cow's milk. *Am J Clin Nutr* 1985;41:550–9.
23. Fransson G-B, Lönnerdal B. Distribution of trace elements and minerals in human and cow's milk. *Pediatr Res* 1983;17:912–5.
24. Lönnerdal B. Iron in breast milk. In: Stekel A, ed. *Iron nutrition in infancy and childhood*. Nestlé Nutrition Workshop Series, vol 4. New York: Raven Press, 1984:95–118.
25. Rudloff S, Kunz C, Lönnerdal B. Chromatographic and electrophoretic pattern of cow's milk and cow's milk based formulas (abstract). *FASEB J* 1988;2:A652.
26. Sandström B, Keen CL, Lönnerdal B. An experimental model for studies of zinc bioavailability from milk and infant formulas using extrinsic labelling. *Am J Clin Nutr* 1983;38:420–8.
27. Lönnerdal B, Bell JG, Keen CL. Copper absorption from human milk, cow's milk and infant formulas using a suckling rat pup model. *Am J Clin Nutr* 1985;42:836–44.
28. Lönnerdal B, Cederblad Å, Davidsson L, Sandström B. The effect of individual components of soy formula and cow's milk formula on zinc bioavailability. *Am J Clin Nutr* 1984;40:1064–70.
29. Lönnerdal B, Hoffman B, Hurley LS. Zinc and copper binding proteins in human milk. *Am J Clin Nutr* 1982;36:1170–6.
30. Ainscough EW, Brodie AM, Plowman JE. Zinc transport by lactoferrin in human milk. *Am J Clin Nutr* 1980;33:1314–5.
31. Blakeborough P, Salter DN, Gurr MI. Zinc binding in cow's milk and human milk. *Biochem J* 1983;209:505–12.
32. Blakeborough P, Gurr MI, Salter DN. Digestion of the zinc in human milk, cow's milk and a commercial baby food: some implications for human infant nutrition. *Br J Nutr* 1986;55:209–17.
33. Davidson LA, Lönnerdal B. Specificity of the intestinal lactoferrin receptor. In: Barth CE, Schlimme E, eds. *Milk proteins in human nutrition*. Darmstadt, West Germany: Steinkopf Verlag, 1989:76–82.
34. Lönnerdal B, Stanislowski AG, Hurley LS. Isolation of a low molecular weight zinc binding ligand from human milk. *J Inorg Biochem* 1980;12:71–8.
35. Martin MT, Licklider KF, Brushmiller JG, Jacobs FA. Detection of low molecular weight copper (II) and zinc (II) binding ligands in ultrafiltered milks—the citrate connection. *J Inorg Biochem* 1981;15:55–65.
36. Hegenauer J, Saltman P, Ludwig D, Ripley L, Ley A. Iron-supplemented cow milk. Identification and spectral properties of iron bound to casein micelles. *J Agric Food Chem* 1979;27:1294–301.
37. Harzer G, Kauer H. Binding of zinc to casein. *Am J Clin Nutr* 1982;35:981–7.
38. Evans GW, Johnson PE. Characterization and quantitation of a zinc-binding ligand in human milk. *Pediatr Res* 1980;14:876–80.
39. Hurley LS, Lönnerdal B. Picolinic acid as a zinc binding ligand in human milk: An unconvincing case. Letter to the Editor. *Pediatr Res* 1981;15:166–7.
40. Rebello T, Lönnerdal B, Hurley LS. Picolinic acid in milk, pancreatic juice, and intestine: inadequate for role in zinc absorption. *Am J Clin Nutr* 1982;35:1–5.
41. Seal CJ, Heaton FW. Chemical factors affecting the intestinal absorption of zinc in vitro and in vivo. *Br J Nutr* 1983;50:317–24.
42. Garby L, Sjölin S. Absorption of labelled iron in infants less than three months old. *Acta Paediatr Scand (Suppl)* 1959;117:24–8.
43. Heinrich HC, Gabbe EE, Whang DH, Bender-Götze Ch, Schäfer KH. Ferrous and hemoglobin ^{59}Fe

absorption from supplemented cow milk in infants with normal and depleted iron stores. *Z Kinderheilk* 1975;120:251–8.

44. Saarinen UM, Siimes MA, Dallman PR. Iron absorption in infants: high bioavailability of breast milk iron as indicated by the extrinsic tag method of iron absorption and by the concentration of serum ferritin. *J Pediatr* 1977;91:36–9.
45. Lönnerdal B, Glazier C. An approach to assessing trace element bioavailability from milk in vitro: extrinsic labeling and proteolytic degradation. *Biol Trace Element Res* 1989;19:57–69.
46. Davidson LA, Lönnerdal B. Bioavailability of iron from infant formula supplemented with human or bovine lactoferrin (abstract). *FASEB J* 1989;3:A1246.
47. McMillan JA, Landaw SA, Oski FA. Iron sufficiency in breast-fed infants and the availability of iron from human milk. *Pediatrics* 1976;58:686–91.
48. McMillan JA, Oski FA, Lourie G, Tomarelli RM, Landaw SA. Iron absorption from human milk, simulated human milk, and proprietary formulas. *Pediatrics* 1977;60:896–900.
49. Fransson G-B, Thoren-Tolling K, Jones B, Hambraeus L, Lönnerdal B. Absorption of lactoferrin-iron in suckling pigs. *Nutr Res* 1983;3:373–84.
50. Fransson G-B, Keen CL, Lönnerdal B. Supplementation of milk with iron bound to lactoferrin using weanling mice. I. Effects on hematology and tissue iron. *J Pediatr Gastroenterol Nutr* 1983;2:693–700.
51. Mazurier J, Montreuil J, Spik G. Visualization of lactotransferrin receptors by ligand blotting. *Biochim Biophys Acta* 1985;821:453–60.
52. Hu W-L, Mazurier J, Sawatski G, Montreuil J, Spik G. Lactoferrin receptor of mouse intestinal brush border. Binding characteristics of membrane-bound and Triton X-100 solubilized forms. *Biochem J* 1988;249:435–41.
53. Davidson LA, Lönnerdal B. Specific binding of lactoferrin to brush border membrane: ontogeny and effect of glycan chain. *Am J Physiol* 1988;254:G580–5.
54. Davidson LA, Lönnerdal B. Persistence of human milk proteins in the breast-fed infant. *Acta Paediatr Scand* 1987;76:733–40.
55. Fairweather-Tait SJ, Balmer SE, Scott PH, Minski MJ. Lactoferrin and iron absorption in newborn infants. *Pediatr Res* 1988;22:651–4.
56. Barton JC, Conrad ME, Parmley RT. Calcium inhibition of inorganic iron absorption in rats. *Gastroenterology* 1983;84:90–101.
57. Gillooly M, Bothwell TH, Torrance JD, et al. The effects of organic acids, phytates, and polyphenols on the absorption of iron from vegetables. *Br J Nutr* 1983;49:331–42.
58. Hazell T, Johnson IT. In vitro estimation of iron availability from a range of plant foods: influence of phytate, ascorbate and citrate. *Br J Nutr* 1987;57:223–33.
59. Rolston DDK, Moriarty KJ, Farthing MJG, Kelly MJ, Clark ML, Dawson AM. Acetate and citrate stimulate water and sodium absorption in the human jejunum. *Digestion* 1986;34:101–4.
60. Gillooly M, Torrance JD, Bothwell TH, et al. The relative effect of ascorbic acid on iron absorption from soy-based and milk-based infant formulas. *Am J Clin Nutr* 1984;40:522–7.
61. Flanagan PR, Cluett J, Chamberlain MJ, Valberg LS. Dual-isotope method for the determination of human zinc absorption: the use of a test meal of turkey meat. *J Nutr* 1985;115:111–22.
62. Arvidsson B, Björn-Rasmussen E, Cederblad Å, Sandström B. A radionuclide technique for studies of zinc absorption in man. *Int J Nucl Med Biol* 1978;5:104–9.
63. Moynahan EJ. Acrodermatitis enteropathica. A lethal inherited human zinc-deficiency disorder. *Lancet* 1974;ii:399–400.
64. Walravens PA, Hambidge KM. Growth of infants fed a zinc supplemented formula. *Am J Clin Nutr* 1976;29:1114–21.
65. Hambidge KM, Walravens PA, Casey CE, Brown RM, Bender C. Plasma zinc concentrations of breast-fed infants. *J Pediatr* 1979;94:607–8.
66. Casey CE, Walravens PA, Hambidge KM. Availability of zinc: loading tests with human milk, cow's milk, and infant formulas. *Pediatrics* 1981;68:394–6.
67. Sandström B, Cederblad Å, Lönnerdal B. Zinc absorption from human milk, cow's milk and infant formulas. *Am J Dis Child* 1983;137:726–9.
68. Greenberg R, Groves ML, Dewer HJ. Human β-casein: amino acid sequence and identification of phosphorylation sites. *J Biol Chem* 1984;259:5132–8.
69. Kiely J, Flynn A, Singh H, Fox PF. Improved zinc bioavailability from colloidal calcium phosphate-free cow's milk. In: Hurley LS, Keen CL, Lönnerdal B, Rucker RB, eds. *Trace elements in man and animals—TEMA 6.* New York: Plenum Press, 1988:499–500.

70. Lönnerdal B, Bell JG, Hendrickx AG, Burns RA, Keen CL. Effect of phytate removal on zinc absorption from soy formula. *Am J Clin Nutr* 1988;48:1301–6.
71. Lönnerdal B, Sandberg A-S, Sandström B, Kunz C. Inhibitory effects of phytic acid and other inositol phosphates on zinc and calcium absorption. *J Nutr* 1989;119:211–4.
72. Higashi A, Ikeda T, Uehara I, Matsuda I. Effect of low-content zinc and copper formula on infant nutrition. *Eur J Pediatr* 1982;138:237–40.
73. Vigi V, Chierici R, Osti L, Fagioli F, Rescazzi R. Serum zinc concentration in exclusively breastfed infants and in infants fed an adapted formula. *Eur J Pediatr* 1984;142:245–7.
74. Ziegel EE, Serfass RE, Figueroa-Colón R, Nelson SE, Edwards BB, Hook RS, Thompson JJ. Effect of low zinc intake on absorption and excretion of zinc by infants studied with ^{70}Zn as extrinsic tag. *J Nutr* 1989;119:1647–53.
75. Lönnerdal B, Keen CL, Hendrickx AG, Golub MS, Gershwin ME. The influence of dietary zinc and iron on zinc absorption/retention in pregnant rhesus monkeys and their infants (abstract). *FASEB J* 1989;3:A456.
76. Cordano A. Copper deficiency in clinical medicine. In: Hambidge KM, Nichols Jr BL, eds. *Zinc and copper deficiency in clinical medicine.* New York: SP Medical and Scientific, 1978: 119–26.
77. Shaw JCL. Copper deficiency and non-accidental injury. *Arch Dis Child* 1988;63:448–55.
78. Hatano S, Aihara K, Nishi Y, Usui T. Trace elements (copper, zinc, manganese, and selenium) in plasma and erythrocytes in relation to dietary intake during infancy. *J Pediatr Gastroenterol Nutr* 1985;4:87–92.
79. Keen CL, Bell JG, Lönnerdal B. The effect of age on manganese uptake and retention from milk and infant formulas in rats. *J Nutr* 1986;116:395–402.
80. Miller ST, Cotzias, GC, Evert HA. Control of tissue manganese: initial absence and sudden emergence of excretion in the neonatal mouse. *Am J Physiol* 1975;229:1980–4.
81. Papavasiliou PS, Miller ST, Cotzias GC. Role of liver in regulation, distribution and excretion of manganese. *Am J Physiol* 1966;211:211–6.
82. Ballatori N, Miles E, Clarkson TW. Homeostatic control of manganese excretion in the neonatal rat. *Am J Physiol* 1987;252:R842–7.
83. Papavasiliou PS. Manganese and the extrapyramidal system. In: Alexander PA, ed. *Electrolytes and neuropsychiatric disorders.* New York: SP Medical and Scientific, 1978:187–225.
84. Pihl RO, Parkes M. Hair element content in learning disabled children. *Science* 1977;198:204–6.
85. Collipp PG, Chen SY, Maitinsky S. Manganese in infant formulas and learning disability. *Ann Nutr Metab* 1983;27:488–94.
86. Bell JG, Keen CL, Lönnerdal B. Higher retention of manganese in suckling than in adult rats is due to maturational differences in manganese uptake by rat small intestine. *J Tox Env Health* 1989;26:387–98.
87. Davidsson L, Cederblad Å, Lönnerdal B, Sandström B. Manganese absorption from human milk, cow's milk and infant formula in humans. *Am J Dis Child* 1989;143:823–7.
88. Atkinson SA, Fraser D, Lönnerdal B. Manganese intakes and excretion in premature infants fed mothers' milk or formula (abstract). *FASEB J* 1989;3:A1246.
89. Solomons NW, Jacob RA. Studies on the bioavailability of zinc in humans: effect of heme and nonheme iron on the absorption of zinc. *Am J Clin Nutr* 1981;34:475–82.
90. Yip R, Reeves JD, Lönnerdal B, Keen CL, Dallman JP. Does iron supplementation compromise zinc nutrition in healthy infants? *Am J Clin Nutr* 1985;42:683–7.
91. Morrison JN, Bremner I. Effect of maternal zinc supply on blood and tissue metallothionein I concentrations in suckling rats. *J Nutr* 1987;117:1588–94.
92. Craig WJ, Balbach L, Harris S, Vyhmeister N. Plasma zinc and copper levels of infants fed different milk formulas. *J Am Coll Nutr* 1984;3:183–6.
93. Sandström B, Davidsson L, Cederblad Å, Lönnerdal B. Oral iron, dietary ligands and zinc absorption. *J Nutr* 1985;115:411–4.
94. Hurley LS, Keen CL, Lönnerdal B. Aspects of trace element interactions during development. *Fed Proc* 1983;42:1735–9.
95. Thomson ABR, Olatunbosum D, Valberg LS. Interrelation of intestinal transport system of manganese and iron. *J Lab Clin Med* 1971;78:643–55.
96. Hallberg L, Rossander L, Brune M, Lönnerdal B, Sandström B. Inhibition of iron absorption in man by manganese and zinc. In: Hurley LS, Keen CL, Lönnerdal B, Rucker RB, eds. *Trace elements in man and animals—TEMA 6.* New York: Plenum Press, 1989:233–4.

97. Chandra SV, Shukla GS. Role of iron deficiency in inducing susceptibility of manganese toxicity. *Arch Toxicol* 1976;35:319–25.
98. Davidsson L, Cederblad Å, Lönnerdal B, Sandström B. Manganese retention in man: a method for estimating manganese absorption in man. *Am J Clin Nutr* 1989;49:170–9.

DISCUSSION

Dr. Bergmann: When I came back to Germany from the United States in 1973 I thought that iron deficiency must occur very commonly in Germany. However, when I did a study and measured iron and hemoglobin values in German infants and children, I found that iron-deficient indices were extremely rare. Most German so-called "adapted" infant formulas were whey-predominant, in contrast to those available in the United States at that time, so maybe this was one of the reasons for the lower incidence of iron deficiency. I also computed total iron intake during the first year of life, assuming that 10% of iron was biologically available, and reckoned that most infants should have iron deficiency anemia by 1 year of age. There is therefore a difference between what we actually observe and what should be expected to occur on the basis of absorption studies.

Dr. Lönnerdal: Peter Dallman and co-workers did a study in California in 1982–3, looking at infants who had received formula for a long period of time. They also found a very low incidence of iron deficiency. The only cases they found were in infants who had had repeated infections. There was no correlation with diet. There was thus a difference in the incidence of iron deficiency in this American study from what had been reported before. All the infants in Dallman's study were receiving the so-called "modern" infant formulas.

Dr. Haschke: Studies carried out in infants using stable isotopes indicate that iron retention is in the region of 5–10%. Should we have lower iron fortification levels in infant formulas in future?

Dr. Lönnerdal: Yes, I think that 12 mg/liter is excessive. I even think that we have a fairly large safety margin with the 7 mg/liter used in Europe. It is possible that 3–4 mg/liter is adequate with the changes in formula composition that have taken place in the past decade. No evaluation of these lower levels has been done. It may be that sufficient compensation occurs in the absorption mechanisms to allow the same retention with less fortification, and at the same time reduce the possible interfering effects on other trace elements (e.g., copper).

Dr. Gabr: We have a lot of thalassemia in Egypt, and high levels of iron fortification might be harmful for children with this condition. Thalassemia is also prevalent in Sicily. I should like to ask Dr. Marini about the levels of iron fortification in Italian formulas.

Dr. Marini: There is no special rule in Italy. Formulas are available with 12 mg/liter, 7 mg/liter, and no iron fortification. In thalassemia, the iron overload provided by repeated transfusions is so great that the amount present in the formula is of secondary importance, although of course there is no reason at all to give any extra iron to these babies.

I have a comment. Dr. Lönnerdal described the effects of iron administration on the hemoglobin level during pregnancy. I think one should be very cautious in interpreting data on hemoglobin levels in pregnancy because of the increased blood volume. This might be one reason why some people who have tried to correct Hb during pregnancy when there was a good preconceptional value have reported adverse effects on the fetus. Maybe in some cases iron administration during pregnancy can be harmful. On the other hand, a study from South Africa showed that iron administration during pregnancy may be helpful during lactation.

Another point is that we have been talking mainly about anemia as a consequence of iron deficiency, but there are other effects. There is evidence of muscle enzyme impairment and deregulation of catecholamine excretion. We have done a study in preterm infants in which we gave different levels of iron supplementation, using two formulas, one with 12 mg/liter and the other with 7 mg/liter. We followed these babies for a year. At 6 months the iron ferritin values in the babies fed 12 mg/liter formula were only marginally higher, and the Hb level was the same. At 9–12 months the babies receiving more iron, although still having similar Hb and cardiac output, showed a diminished cardiovascular load (lower heart rate and heart rate × mean systemic arterial pressure product). They also had lower VMA excretion. Thus the amount of iron in the formula cannot be evaluated simply in terms of the hematological findings.

Dr. Lönnerdal: I did not want to make too much of an issue of the hemoglobin values. I only said that there was one study indicating that maternal iron status as assessed by Hb did not affect milk iron. I agree that Hb is not a good measure. But there are studies in Nigeria in which transferrin saturation was examined in severely iron-deficient women and in those who had received sufficient iron supplementation to saturate transferrin. There were no differences in milk iron in these two groups. My point was that iron status does not seem to affect milk iron.

Dr. R. Bergmann: If calcium has such a big influence on iron absorption, what about premature formulas? They are very high in calcium.

Dr. Lönnerdal: I think this is a potential concern. I have not personally been involved in studies in this area, but Hallberg and co-workers have shown a significant effect of calcium on iron absorption in human adults. If we see this in adults, we should expect a more pronounced effect in infants.

Dr. Hambidge: I question whether this is really important. Premature formulas are given only up to about 36 weeks post-conception, and iron absorption at this early stage is not a very important issue.

Dr. Chandra: Do you foresee any problem with the high manganese content of soy formulas? Are there any studies to show that this may have adverse consequences?

Dr. Lönnerdal: I think one should be concerned about manganese, but because soy formula is naturally high in Mn it is apparently difficult to do much about it.

Dr. Hambidge: I am surprised by the high fractional absorption of manganese in your animal models. In the adult human there is only 1–10% absorption depending on the type of formula, while absorption in premature infants has been reported to be 16%. There is a lot of difference between your data from animal models and data for humans.

Dr. Lönnerdal: These data were from suckling rat pups and absorption was very high, about 80% at a young age, but decreasing later. The problem we are facing is that soy formula is very high in Mn, containing about 300 ppb compared to 50 ppb in cow's milk and < 10 ppb in human milk. If we look at the percentage retention at 24 hours it is higher from human milk and cow's milk formula than from soy formula, but the absolute retention is about 25 times greater from soy formula than from breast milk. We have no evidence that this is true for human infants, but the metabolic fate of manganese once it has entered the body is very different at different stages of development. In the young pup the liver accumulates manganese and later releases it for distribution to the body tissues, particularly the brain. Later in life, the liver still takes up Mn, but the brain holds on to much less and clearance is considerably greater. Thus the possible scenario would be that the young infant could retain a large part of the ingested manganese which could adversely affect the developing brain, the primary site of Mn toxicity.

We have two potential concerns for manganese. We have iron-deficient infants who might be given high levels of manganese in formula. We know that when iron absorption is upregulated because of iron deficiency, exactly the same thing happens to Mn absorption, which may then become excessive. The other concern is with breast-fed infants receiving a very low Mn intake. If such infants are given iron drops, there is interference with Mn absorption and the possibility of inducing Mn deficiency.

Dr. Aggett: We have performed serial balance studies of metabolism of manganese in term infants at 1, 2, and 3 months of age. Six infants were studied. The data are summarized in Table 1. The net intestinal absorption and maximum apparent retention of manganese by these infants is relatively constant throughout this period. They showed no evidence of the increased intestinal absorption and whole body retention that has been observed in studies of suckling mice and rats.

We also conducted a randomized crossover study, again using the balance approach, of metabolism and manganese in infants fed a soy-based formula with and without its customary iron fortification. We wished to test the hypothesis that the iron fortification altered the metabolism of manganese. However, analysis of the data showed no evidence of this; they were confounded by a marked time effect. Table 2 summarizes our findings. In this study the manganese intake provided by the soy-based formula was five to six times that of those being fed a cow's milk–based formula. It could be seen that between the first and second studies there was a marked fall in the net intestinal absorption and maximum retention of manganese. Thus, although the study was not specifically designed to investigate this possibility, these data suggest that the metabolism of manganese alters during human infancy in a similar way to changes observed in suckling mice and rat pups.

Dr. Ament: As far as deficiency is concerned, apart from growth failure, what do you expect to find?

Dr. Aggett: In the original description of manganese deficiency, the diagnosis of manganese deficiency was retrospective. The volunteer concerned did not respond specifically to manganese supplements. He merely went to a normal hospital diet and it was only later that calculations suggested that the experimental diet had been deficient in manganese. I think the only corroborative evidence that it might have been manganese deficiency has been subsequent studies of depletion in young male volunteers in whom an evanescent skin rash developed along with a fall in circulating cholesterol concentrations. However, after these volunteers were put back on the manganese supplement, their cholesterol levels did not return to normal, thereby raising the possibility that this fall may have been a feature of the diet itself rather than of manganese deficiency (1).

TABLE 1. *Manganese balance during the first 3 months of life in infants fed a cow's milk–based formula*[a]

Age (months)	Intake	Net intestinal absorption	Maximum apparent retention
1	0.64 (0.01)	0.49 (0.12)	0.14 (0.20)
2	0.49 (0.12)	0.36 (0.10)	0.11 (0.11)
3	0.46 (0.09)	0.32 (0.08)	0.15 (0.14)

[a]Mean: SD; μmol/kg·day.

TABLE 2. *Manganese balances in infants fed a soy-based infant formula*[a]

Postnatal age (weeks)	Intake	Net intestinal absorption[b]	Maximum apparent retention[b]
First study			
Mean 16	3.33 (0.34)	1.00 (0.45)	0.98 (0.43)
Range 12–21	2.93–3.74	0.48–1.65	0.48–1.60
Second study			
Mean 19	2.46 (0.45)	− 0.04 (0.4)	− 0.04 (0.4)
Range 16–24	1.78–3.25	− 0.49–0.45	− 0.49–0.45

[a]Mean: SD; μmol/kg·day.
[b]Denotes net intestinal or whole body loss.

Dr. Mertz: As far as I am concerned, we have not yet shown definitively that manganese deficiency or toxicity occurs in humans. We know from the naturally occurring deficiency states in animals what to look for, so it is unlikely that we have overlooked anything.

Dr. Lombeck: When looking for clinical symptoms of manganese deficiency in humans we should remember the main symptoms of patients with prolidase deficiency. This is a recessively inherited defect in which patients suffer from various skin lesions, particularly leg ulcers. Seventy-five percent are mentally retarded. They excrete massive amounts of iminodipeptides. I found that in addition to a marked reduction in prolidase activity, activity of arginase (another mangano enzyme) was markedly reduced in erythrocytes. Plasma manganese values were normal. I speculate that there must be a manganese cofactor common for both these mangano enzymes. In patients with suspected manganese deficiency we should look for similar clinical symptoms and estimate prolidase and arginase activity.

Dr. Chandra: What are the biochemical and clinical features of suspected manganese toxicity?

Dr. Hambidge: Excess manganese given to rats can cause cholestatic liver disease in addition to the classic extrapyramidal central nervous system manifestations. Are there any effects on the immune system?

Dr. Chandra: The effects of deficiency of manganese are similar to that of magnesium. In 20–25% of animals given either a deficient or an excess amount of manganese, we see tumors of the thymus and features of a thymoma. In the blood there is the picture of chronic myeloid leukemia. Why only a minority of animals develop this is not clear.

Dr. Ament: Manganese excess will cause cholestasis and hepatocellular injury. Therefore, liver failure secondary to manganese excess causes a combined picture of cholestasis and hepatitis.

Dr. Zlotkin: What will be the effects on trace element nutrition of the recent recommendations of various authorities to increase the fiber intake of the diet?

Dr. Mertz: We have done extensive studies on the effects of phytate and different fiber fractions on the bioavailability of minerals and trace elements in adults but not in children. The interpretation of these studies was that the effects of reasonable levels of phytate and fiber on iron and zinc status are relatively minor. The term "reasonable" would cover not only the intakes from typical Western diets, but the reduced-fat diets recommended by several health authorities. I cannot speak for the pediatric age group.

Dr. Zlotkin: These comments highlight the fact that not enough research has been done on the effects of dietary fiber in this age group.

Dr. Haschke: Nobody has yet mentioned that there is increasing concern about iron overload. We are now aware that 1:400 Caucasian infants will develop hemochromatosis later in life, so we have to start thinking about high iron intakes in these infants. Hemochromatosis does occur in Scotland. It is not known how much and it is possible that some cases are missed. On the basis of experience in Salt Lake City, Brisbane, and Brittany, where the incidence approaches 1 in 400, we could expect more because of the similar origins of the population. In Scotland there is an additional problem of alcoholic hepatitis and liver disease. It is not always possible to investigate such patients with determinations of hepatic iron content. Some work which has come from Brisbane suggests that the accumulation of iron in patients with hemochromatosis is progressive throughout childhood and that by relating the iron content of a liver biopsy to the patient's age, one can derive an iron-age index from which those with inappropriately high hepatic iron contents can be identified and evaluated further for the possibility of hemochromatosis (2). Hemochromatosis seems to have originated in Scandinavia and swept across with the Norsemen to Scotland and to Brittany; later migration has taken it to the North American Midwest and Salt Lake City and to Australia. So these may be fairly small "colonies" of people who have kept some genetic homogeneity.

Dr. Singh: Does hemochromatosis have any effect on immunity?

Dr. Chandra: In hemochromatosis we are dealing with a state of chronic overload, but infections are not a big problem in these patients. Morbidity and mortality are due mostly to liver and cardiac failure and to diabetes mellitus. I think that there are a lot of holes in the hypothesis that iron deficiency protects against infection and iron excess increases the risk. The only exception is in patients with severe kwashiorkor who have very low levels of transferrin. In these children one must be cautious about giving iron because there is some evidence that parenteral iron may provoke septicemia. This applies only to the first few days of nutritional rehabilitation, because transferrin is rapidly restored.

Dr. Mertz: What about the observation of Golden in Jamaica that high iron stores are correlated with diminished survival in malnutrition?

Dr. Goyens: Golden and co-workers observed that plasma ferritin is increased in severely malnourished children, particularly in those who die (3). Their observation tended to support the proposition that there was a high body burden of iron in malnutrition in Jamaica. Similar conclusions have been drawn by Fondu and co-workers in Kivu in central Africa (4). Iron accumulation in tissues might be attributable to slow release because of reduced synthesis of transferrin and other iron-binding proteins in kwashiorkor. Iron is a major biological generator of free radicals. These authors suggest that high levels of iron, associated with a low-selenium status resulting in reduced glutathione peroxidase activity and inadequate protection from lipid peroxidation, together with low levels of vitamin E, may result in fatal generation of free radicals.

Dr. Ament: I should like to know the opinion of the group about chromium deficiency. How important is it to supplement TPN solutions with chromium?

Dr. Mertz: There have been various reports of chromium deficiency. The need for chromium and its essentiality is well established in my opinion, but it is questionable whether a substantial number of new cases will now occur. The very low intravenous requirement for chromium is usually met by the natural chromium content of the fluids used. Many intravenous preparations in the United States are now supplemented with chromium.

Dr. Ament: I run a home parenteral nutrition program for adults and children, and I have 100 patients on parenteral nutrition at any one time, some of whom have been with me for over a decade. I have never seen features of chromium deficiency, although we are always looking for it.

Dr. Mertz: My guess is that the physiological requirement of chromium is about 1 μg/day, and I would say that unless you use very highly purified solutions, this amount will probably be furnished naturally.

REFERENCES

1. Friedman BJ, Freeland-Graves JH, Bales CW, Mehmardi F, Shorey-Kutschke RL, Willis RA, Crosby JB, Trickett PC, Houston SD. Manganese balance and clinical observations in young men fed a manganese deficient diet. *J Nutr* 1987;117:133–43.
2. Bassett ML, Halliday JW, Powell LW. Value of hepatic iron measurements in early human chromatosis and determination of the critical iron level associated with fibrosis. *Hepatology* 1986;6: 24–9.
3. Golden MHN, Ramdath D. Free radicals in the pathogenesis of kwashiorkor. *Proc Nutr Soc* 1987;46:53–68.
4. Fondu P, Harriga-Muller C, Mozes N, Nève J, Van Steirteghem A, Mandelbaum IM. Protein-energy malnutrition and anemia in Kivu. *Am J Clin Nutr* 1978;31:46–56.
5. Jeejeebhoy KN, Chu, RC, Marliss EB, Greenberg GR, Bruce-Robertson A. Chromium deficiency, glucose intolerance, and neuropathy reversed by chromium supplementation, in a patient receiving long-term total parenteral nutrition. *Am J Clin Nutr* 1977;30:531–8.
6. Freund H, Atamian S, Fischer JEP. Chromium deficiency during total parenteral nutrition. *JAMA* 1979;241:496–8.
7. Brown RO, Forloines-Lynn S, Cross RE, Heizer WD. Chromium deficiency after long-term total parenteral nutrition. *Dig Dis Sci* 1986;31:661–4.

Trace Elements in Nutrition of Children—II,
edited by Ranjit K. Chandra, Nestlé Nutrition
Workshop Series, Vol. 23, Nestec Ltd.,
Vevey/Raven Press, Ltd., New York © 1991.

Zinc and Copper Concentrations in Moroccan Children with Protein-Energy Malnutrition

M. Lahrichi, L. Chabraoui, *A. Balafrej, and †A. Baroudi

*Laboratoire de Biochimie, Hôpital d'Enfants, Rabat, Morocco; *Laboratoire de Biochimie, Faculté de Médecine et de Pharmacie, Rabat, Morocco; and †Service de Pédiatrie II, Hôpital d'Enfants, Rabat, Morocco*

Although much is known about various clinical and metabolic features of protein-energy malnutrition (PEM), studies of trace elements are relatively recent. These investigations were prompted by the characteristic features of PEM. For example, the extensive involvement of the skin in PEM has some resemblance to the dermatologic features of acrodermatitis enteropathica, a syndrome of partial malabsorption of zinc (1); the alterations in neuromuscular function may suggest copper deficiency (2); and the occurrence of cardiomyopathy, peripheral myopathy, and erythrocyte macrocytosis may in part be due to selenium deficiency (3,4).

There are significant changes in serum and cellular concentrations of various trace elements in PEM, and it is to be expected that the recovery phase would require additional amounts of trace elements for the synthesis of new tissue. We report here the results of red blood cells (RBCs) and serum zinc and copper in healthy children and in children suffering from PEM. This is the first such investigation in Morocco.

METHODS

Patients

Our study involved two population groups. The first group consisted of hospitalized patients ($n = 46$) suffering from PEM. Their age was between 6 and 60 months. Comprehensive data for each patient were obtained, including history, clinical findings, and the nature of the diets before and during hospital admission. The distinction between kwashiorkor ($n = 15$) and marasmus ($n = 31$) was established by clinical criteria. The second group consisted of a control population of healthy children in the same age range.

Analytical Procedures

All tubes, pipettes, and syringes were acid-rinsed. Blood was drawn 12 h after the last feed both in the patients and in the healthy controls. After centrifugation at 3500 rpm for 5 min, the plasma was separated and analyzed or stored at −40°C. The hemolysate was prepared as follows. When the plasma was withdrawn, the white blood cells and platelets were removed. The red blood cells were then washed three times with physiological saline. After each wash, the supernatant and the upper cells were removed. The aliquot obtained was diluted 1:2 in physiological saline. The hematocrit was measured by centrifugation. The red blood cells then hemolyzed with demineralized water.

Plasma zinc and copper were determined by atomic absorption spectrometry (AAS). Red blood cell zinc and copper were measured spectrometrically by inductively coupled plasma (ICP) (Laboratoire du Centre de Médecine Préventive, Vandoeuvre les Nancy, France). Serum albumin was analyzed by the bromocresol green reaction.

RESULTS AND COMMENTS

Zinc

Red Blood Cell Zinc

Results of RBC zinc determination in healthy subjects and in those with kwashiorkor and marasmus are shown in Table 1. The results obtained in healthy children are similar to those obtained by other authors, with an average of 140 μmol/liter (5). The variation observed was due to analytical variations and to physiological variables such as age, sex, and weight.

In the malnourished children the RBC zinc values were considerably reduced: 48.6 μmol/liter in children with kwashiorkor and 41.2 μmol/liter in marasmics. The difference observed between kwashiorkor and marasmus was not statistically significant.

TABLE 1. *Red blood cell zinc (μmol/liter): mean and range*[a]

Healthy	Kwashiorkor	Marasmus
140.2	48.6	41.2
135.2–145.8	29.6–69.4	17.4–70.6
(*n* = 30)	(*n* = 15)	(*n* = 31)

[a]Reference range: 135–145 μmol/liter (5).

Warren in 1969 (6) and Cheek in 1970 (7) have noted an important decrease in muscle and liver zinc. However, when the same data are expressed per DNA unit (3), it is apparent that all cytoplasmic constituents are reduced to the same extent in malnourished patients in both liver and muscle. These data illustrate the difficulties in interpreting the gross tissue contents of trace elements. Other authors found a reduction in white cell zinc in zinc-deficient swine (8).

As zinc is linked, for the most part, to soluble proteins in the cell, such as enzymes, one could speculate that the decrease is secondary to the reduced metabolic activity and protein turnover. On the other hand, in kwashiorkor the frequent presence of infection induces the synthesis and release of interleukins which cause redistribution of trace elements from the plasma to the tissues. It is of interest that no differences have been found in brain between control and malnourished children (9).

Serum Zinc

The values obtained in healthy children (Table 2) are similar to those found in previously published reports (10–13). There was, however, an important decrease in malnourished children. Golden (3) also found this to be the case. Because of the difficulty in obtaining appropriate controls, we also used the children as their own controls. After feeding for 3 weeks, we observed an important increase in serum zinc: 68% in patients with kwashiorkor and 80% in marasmics. All patients who had an initial concentration ≤10 μmol/liter (80% of the patients) showed an increase, beginning as early as the first week but becoming of major importance after 3 weeks.

Serum albumin used as a marker had the same kinetic. The relation between zinc and albumin was $r = 0.74$. Other proteins, such as retinol binding protein, also have the same kinetics (3). In contrast, the content of RBC or hair zinc only increases after 3 months (14). It seems that plasma zinc reflects an intake of zinc in the short term, while RBC or hair levels reflect long-term intakes (15). Serum zinc concentration could be the best biochemical indicator of zinc status (3). Zinc deficiency can be demonstrated by observing the effects of supplementation, as we have shown in this study.

TABLE 2. *Serum zinc on admission (μmol/liter): mean and range*[a]

Healthy	Kwashiorkor	Marasmus
14	4.70	7.88
10.7–14.3	2.81–7.40	3.30–9.8
(n = 30)	(n = 8)	(n = 32)

[a]Reference range: 10–18 μmol/liter (10–13).

Zinc and Infectious Diseases

In our study we sought for a relationship between zinc and infectious diseases. All patients who had a zinc concentration of about 7 μmol/liter or less had an infectious disease. However, such a relationship between serum zinc concentrations and infections does not demonstrate cause and effect.

There are clinical similarities between malnutrition and acrodermatitis enteropathica, a disease caused by partial malabsorption of zinc. They both feature anorexia, diarrhea, skin excoriations and breakdown, immunoincompetence with fungal infections, and an altered affect. Chandra has developed this topic in his chapter (*this volume*).

Copper

RBC Copper

RBC copper concentration in the healthy control group was 10 μmol/liter (Table 3). This level is similar to other published data (5). In kwashiorkor and marasmus the values were decreased significantly (Table 3).

Warren has shown a decrease in liver copper (6). Muscle copper is also decreased in PEM (Table 4) (9,16). As with zinc, the degree of fall is in keeping with the reduction in soluble protein. However, there is a difference in the findings between

TABLE 3. *RBC copper (μmol/liter): mean and range[a]*

Control	Kwashiorkor	Marasmus
9.74	2.16	3.56
7–10	0.35–5.65	1.53–5.18
(*n* = 30)	(*n* = 18)	(*n* = 26)

[a]Reference range: 10 μmol/liter (5).

TABLE 4. *Copper concentrations in liver and muscle of children who died from PEM (μmol/g tissue)*

	Control	Marasmus	Marasmic Kwashiorkor	Kwashiorkor
Liver	2.19	1.68	—	0.76
Muscle	1.29	1.08	1.67	0.57

From Lehman BH, et al. (9).

kwashiorkor and marasmus, the concentrations being lower in kwashiorkor. In this disease there is a reduction in the circulating levels of hepatic export proteins (albumin, transferrin, retinol binding protein, prealbumins, etc.) (2,9). In marasmus these proteins tend to be better preserved (3).

Serum Copper

The values obtained in healthy controls were around 15 μmol/liter (Table 5), similar to other published values (4,10,11). During PEM there was a decrease in serum copper, especially in kwashiorkor. Similar results have been obtained by various other workers (17–22) (Table 6).

After re-feeding we observed an increase of about 160% and 40% respectively, in children with kwashiorkor and marasmus. All the patients who had an initial concentration <13 μmol/liter showed an increase (50% of patients). These values must be interpreted in relation with ceruloplasmin. This protein is a hepatic export protein and is reduced in conditions such as kwashiorkor. However, ceruloplasmin is also an acute phase reactant secreted in response to inflammatory stress (23,24). Thus variation in hepatic function, the type and severity of infections, and the ability of the body to synthesize the mediators of inflammatory responses are the most important determinants of circulating copper levels. Our results may suggest a decrease in

TABLE 5. *Serum copper (μmol/liter): mean and range*[a]

Controls	Kwashiorkor	Marasmus
15	9.58	15.35
12–18	5.83–14.33	6–25.92
($n = 30$)	($n = 8$)	($n = 31$)

[a]Reference range: 12–25 μmol/liter (4,10,11).

TABLE 6. *Average plasma or serum copper concentrations in malnourished children (μmol/liter)*

Country	Kwashiorkor	Marasmus	Control	Reference
Chile		21.7	14.1	(17)
Jamaica	11.6	21.4	17.1	(18)
Egypt	11.7	13.5	14.9	(19)
Nigeria	13.7	—	28.6	(20)
India	8.9	22.5	18.9	(21)
Pakistan	20.3	20.8	22.9	(22)
Morocco	9.6	15.4	15	

copper during PEM. But to assess the effect of malnutrition on copper status it is necessary to have a biological index that reflects copper status without the confounding effect of other pathogenic processes. The RBC enzyme copper/zinc superoxide dismutase (Cu SODA) has been used (25,26). Using this enzyme, Golden (3) found that of 39 malnourished children 25% had values above 2 SD and 9% had values above 3 SD, below those of a control group. There was no difference between kwashiokor and marasmus. There was also no relationship between Cu SODA and any particular clinical feature on admission, in particular skin lesions, anemia, and hair changes.

CONCLUSION

We studied RBC and serum zinc and copper concentrations. In healthy patients the levels were similar to previously published data. The intersubject differences observed are due to analytical and physiological variations. In malnourished children the RBC zinc and copper values were lower than in the healthy controls. However, more research is necessary to confirm if there is really a fall in these trace elements in the tissues. Serum zinc and copper were also lower in comparison with the values in healthy children. These values increase after 3 weeks of feeding, though there is considerable interpatient variability.

From this and other considerations, it appears likely that there is a deficiency of these elements, probably due to an inadequate intake during the development of PEM. But we do not know what exactly is the role of this inadequate intake in the pathogenesis of PEM, nor do we know the effects of altered body composition on normal zinc and copper metabolism.

REFERENCES

1. Golden BE, Golden MHN. Plasma zinc and the clinical features of malnutrition. *Am J Clin Nutr* 1979;32:2490–4.
2. Gordano A, Beartl JM, Graham GG. Copper deficiency in infancy. *Pediatrics* 1966;26:326–30.
3. Golden MHN, Golden BE, Bennett FI. In: Chandra RK, ed. *Trace elements in nutrition of children.* Nestlé Nutrition Workshop Series, vol 8. New York: Raven Press, 1985:185–204.
4. Vinton NE, Dakhtrom KA, Strobel CT, Ament ME. Macrocytosis and pseudoalbinism: manifestations of selenium deficiency. *J Pediatr* 1987;111:711–7.
5. Denis A, Bureau F, Duhamel JF, Drosdowsky M. Les oligo-éléments en pédiatrie. *ISB* 1985; 11:55–63.
6. Warren PJ, Hansen JDL, Lehman BH. The concentration of copper, zinc and manganese in the liver of African children with kwashiorkor and marasmus (abstract). *Proc Nutr Soc* 1969;28:6–7A.
7. Cheek BD, Hill DE, Cordano A, Graham GG. Malnutrition in infancy: changes in muscle and adipose tissue. *Pediatr Res* 1970;4:135–44.
8. Aggett PJ, Crofton RW, Hilton PJ, Thompson RPH. Plasma leucocyte and tissue zinc concentrations in young zinc deficiency pigs. *Pediatr Res* 1983;17:433–40.
9. Lehman BH, Hansen JDL, Warren PJ. The distribution of copper, zinc and manganese in various regions of the brain and in other tissues of children with protein calorie malnutrition. *Br J Nutr* 1971;26:197–202.
10. Lockitch G, Halstead AC, Wadsworth L, Quigeley G, Reston L, Jacobson B. Age and sex specific pediatric reference intervals and correlations for zinc, copper, selenium, iron, vitamins A and E and related proteins. *Clin Chem* 1988;34:1625–8.

11. Hatano S, Aihara K, Nishi Y, Usni T. Trace elements (copper, zinc, manganese and selenium) in plasma and erythrocytes in relation to dietary intake during infancy. *J Pediatr Gastroenterol Nutr* 1985;4:87–92.
12. Guerrier G, Bienvenu F, Graveriau D, Noiret A, Lahet CH, Carron R, Cotte J. Etude du zinc sérique dans une population de consultants en allergologie infantile. *Rev Fr Allergol* 1987;27:7–11.
13. Dorner K. Routine determination of copper and zinc in serum and urine for the determination of qualified reference values in childhood. *J Clin Chem Clin Biochem* 1980;18:713–4.
14. Krebs NF, Hambidge KM, Walravens PA. Increased food intake of young children receiving a zinc supplement. *Am J Dis Child* 1984;138:270–3.
15. Golden MHN, Jackson AA, Golden BE. Effect of zinc on thymus of malnourished children. *Lancet* 1977;ii:1057–9.
16. McDonald I, Warren PJ. The copper content of the liver and hair of African children with kwashiorkor. *Br J Nutr* 1961;15:593–6.
17. Castillo Duran C, Fisberg M, Valenzuela A, Egana JI, Uay R. Controlled trial of copper supplementation during recovery from marasmus. *Am J Clin Nutr* 1983;37:898–903.
18. Golden BE, Golden MNH. Zinc and copper nutriture in and during recovery from severe malnutrition. *W Ind Med J* 1983 (suppl); 29.
19. Khalil M, Kabiel A, El Khateb M. Plasma and red cell water and elements in protein calorie malnutrition. *Am J Clin Nutr* 1974;27:260–7.
20. Eolozien JC, Udeozo IOK. Serum copper, iron and iron binding capacity in kwashiorkor. *J Trop Pediatr* 1970;6:60–4.
21. Gopalan C, Reddy V, Mohan VS. Some aspects of copper metabolism in protein calorie malnutrition. *J Pediatr* 1963;63:646–9.
22. Zain BK, Haquani AH, Iffat un Nisa. Serum copper and zinc levels in PCM. *Trop Pediatr Environ Child Heath* 1978;24:198–9.
23. Engler R. Proteines de la reaction inflammatoire. *Ann Biol Clin* 1988;46:336–42.
24. Goldstein IM, Kaplan HB, Weissmann G. Ceruloplasmin: an acute phase reactant that scavenges oxygen derived free radicals in C reactive protein and the plasma protein response to tissue injury. *Ann NY Acad Sci* 1982;389:368–78.
25. Bettger WJ, Fish TJ, O'Dell BL. Effects of copper and zinc status on erythrocyte stability and superoxide dismutase activity. *Proc Soc Exp Biol Med* 1978;158:279–82.
26. McCord JM, Fridovich I. Superoxide dismutase. *J Biol Chem* 1969;244:6049–55.

DISCUSSION

Dr. Aggett: Could you give us some data on the patients? What were your criteria for defining kwashiorkor and marasmus?

Dr. Lahrichi: The population consisted of hospitalized children with malnutrition aged between 6 months and 5 years. Classical criteria were used to differentiate between marasmus and kwashiorkor. Edema was the essential feature for the diagnosis of kwashiorkor.

Dr. Chandra: How can one assess the prevalence of true zinc deficiency in hypoproteinemic states? We know that zinc is bound to many proteins, and if these protein levels are low, as in kwashiorkor, zinc levels may merely reflect hypoproteinemia.

Dr. Hambidge: We do not have all the information we need to say how much a change in serum albumin will affect the zinc level. In our experience with hepatic disease it appears that hypoalbuminemia does not have a detectable effect until serum albumin falls below 3 g/dl. Knowing how to adjust zinc levels for changes in serum albumin is, however, not the only difficulty in interpreting plasma zinc data.

Dr. Zlotkin: We have published results from a study in preterm infants where we measured albumin and zinc. Albumin levels below 2 g/dl were common in these infants, but serum zinc was in the normal range for full-term infants. *In vitro* there is excess binding capacity for zinc on albumin, and there are also other proteins and amino acids in the serum that bind zinc, including histidine-rich glycoprotein, α_2-macroglobulin, transferrin, cysteine, and histidine.

Dr. Goyens: During a discussion in the previous Nestlé Nutrition Workshop on trace elements in Münich (1985), I presented some data from Zaire concerning serum zinc levels in marasmic kwashiorkor. On admission to the hospital, serum zinc levels were very low, similar to the levels reported by Dr. Lahrichi. When we treated these patients with the usual rehabilitation diet, increasing the energy and protein intake but without supplying specific trace mineral supplements, we observed no change in the serum zinc levels. These increased after we had given zinc supplementation; however, they also increased after we had given copper supplementation of 300 μg/kg·day without any supplementary zinc. Thus copper supplementation apparently caused a redistribution of the zinc, which was clearly available but apparently not mobilized.

Trace Elements in Nutrition of Children—II,
edited by Ranjit K. Chandra, Nestlé Nutrition
Workshop Series, Vol. 23, Nestec Ltd.,
Vevey/Raven Press, Ltd., New York © 1991.

Trace Metals in Parenteral Nutrition

Marvin Ament

*Division of Pediatric Gastroenterology, Marion Davies Children's Clinic, Los Angeles,
California 90024, USA*

The human body is recognized to contain at least 60 minerals (1). Trace elements
are those minerals present in tissue in picogram to microgram quantity per gram of
wet tissue (2–4). Of the 95 naturally occurring elements, 26 are recognized as performing essential functions in humans. The 15 minerals considered to be trace elements are iron, zinc, copper, manganese, nickel, cobalt, molybdenum, selenium,
chromium, iodine, fluorine, tin, silicon, vanadium, and arsenic (2). Trace elements
are said to be essential if their deficiency consistently results in impairment of function (5). Trace element deficiency may produce both specific and nonspecific effects. Conversely, an excess of a trace metal, arising either through a failure of
intrinsic control mechanisms or through excessive exposure, may produce toxicity,
which may be apparent immediately or be latent and of potential significance in the
long term (6). Trace metals, whether in human tissues, serum, or urine, undergo
pronounced alterations in response to infection, stress, malignancy, hormones, and
drugs (7–12).

In humans, only iron, zinc, copper, chromium, selenium, iodine, and cobalt have
been shown to be necessary. Although isolated cases of what has been presumed to
be vanadium and molybdenium deficiency have been described, further cases or
studies need to be done to confirm these (13,14).

Trace elements circulate as protein-bound complexes that are not always in free
equilibrium with tissue stores. For example, the exchangeable plasma copper is
present in very small amounts bound to albumin (15). In contrast, the major form of
circulating copper, ceruloplasmin, is not freely exchangeable (16). Therefore, circulating levels of a trace element may not reflect the availability of an element for
nutritional needs. During periods of deficient supply, tissue stores of a trace element
may not be available to meet needs. If they are incorporated in enzyme proteins,
they do not exchange with the free pool of trace elements. Second, during periods
of tissue buildup or anabolism there is net flow of trace elements into cells so that
cellular stores cannot be mobilized. It is obvious that during catabolism the converse
is true.

During nutritional support, a positive zinc balance occurs with protein synthesis.
The plasma levels fall and deficiency will result unless exogenous zinc is given.

Clinical deficiency of a trace element cannot be predicted by a simple demonstration of a low blood level because the action of the trace elements depends on other factors, such as age, metabolic and nutritional states, and the availability of agonists and antagonists.

Another example of this is the fact that some degree of selenium deficiency can be overcome by providing vitamin E. It has been shown that children with symptomatic selenium deficiency, such as in Keshan disease, have levels of plasma selenium no lower than in children with phenylketonuria receiving artificial diets, yet the latter do not show a clinical deficiency (17). Patients who may not have overt clinical deficiency of trace elements may still show disordered function in body processes because of the deficiency.

We need to recognize that the route of excretion of most trace elements, except for chromium, is through the gastrointestinal tract. This should make us aware that abnormal gastrointestinal losses may increase the requirements in patients with disease of the gastrointestinal tract. In addition, patients who have renal disease in most instances will require the same amount of trace elements as those who do not, because they are excreted through the gastrointestinal tract rather than through the renal tract.

IRON

Iron is an essential constituent of prophyrin-based compounds bound to protein, such as hemoglobin and myoglobin. Smaller amounts of tissue iron associated with enzymes and mitochondria have significant metabolic functions. Iron is found in storage or transport forms bound to protein as ferritin and transferrin (18). Hemosiderin is a protein form of storage iron. The amount of iron that is found in the ferritin versus the hemosiderin form depends on the iron concentration. When body iron concentrations are lower, more iron is bound to ferritin, and when body concentrations are high, hemosiderin is the predominant storage form of iron (19).

Very little iron is excreted from the body: 0.2–0.5 mg/day is typically excreted in the feces (20), 0.2 mg in the urine (21), and a variable amount in sweat (22). In normal men, losses average 0.6–1.0 mg/day. In women, menstrual losses increase iron losses by an additional 0.5–0.8 mg/day or more. In normal humans, iron stores are governed by control of absorption from the gastrointestinal tract. A substantial amount of iron absorption occurs in the duodenum. Therefore, patients who receive parenteral nutrition but who still consume food and/or take iron supplements may still be able to receive the greater portion of their iron needs via the digestive tract. Individuals who eat little and who do not tolerate oral supplements may do better with intravenous iron.

Losses of iron occur from the gastrointestinal tract when it is inflamed. Iron may also be lost from bile drainage (23). Frequent laboratory tests in the hospital and outside may lead to iron depletion, so the need for iron in patients on parenteral nutrition may be increased if they undergo frequent venesection. The assessment of iron requirement is difficult. The best means of assessing it is to assay the iron content of bone marrow. Another method is to evaluate stainable hemosiderin in the marrow. Ferritin concentrations in plasma are high in patients with inflammation and liver disease, so they are not a fair indicator of iron stores in these conditions (24). Iron dextran injection will also cause a rise in circulating ferritin levels (25). Measurement of serum transferrin and serum iron are commonly used to assess the iron status of the body. The problem with these determinations is that they are unreliably low when infection and malnutrition induce protein synthesis and alter the body's distribution of iron. In an infection, iron released from erythrocytes is taken up by macrophages and is transferred to transferrin. In the presence of inflammation, macrophages do not release iron; thus circulating serum iron levels and saturation are reduced. When patients are malnourished, transferrin synthesis falls, so circulating iron levels are reduced. Therefore, in the presence of malnutrition and infection, there are no very simple means of getting a good assessment of iron status.

Normal males require 1 mg of absorbed iron per day; menstruating females, 2 mg/day. Patients who are receiving total parenteral nutrition (TPN) may require even more iron, depending on whether or not they have abnormal losses and have frequent venesections. One study found that up to 25 mg of iron per week given to patients on TPN reduced the need for blood transfusion. Only when there is a recognized deficiency of iron in tissues can the administration of intravenous iron truly make the iron available to the tissues. If a patient has reduced macrophage transfer despite normal stores, or reduced transferrin levels because of malnutrition, additional iron will make no difference in terms of the iron reaching the necessary tissues.

Patients hospitalized and receiving parenteral nutrition for less than 30 days may not need iron added to their solutions. They may have sufficient stores. If patients are recognized to be deficient, 1–2 mg of iron per day in the form of iron dextran may be added to the parenteral nutrition solutions. This dosage can be increased by an additional 1–2 mg/day in women. Patients on home TPN may have iron added at the rate of 1–2 mg/day and their serum iron monitored at yearly intervals.

ZINC

Zinc is essential for the function of more than 70 enzymes from different species. Examples of such enzymes are carbonic anhydrase, carboxypeptidase, alkaline phosphatase, oxydoreductases, transferases, ligases, hydrolases, lysases, and isomerases. In the presence of zinc deficiency, there is a marked effect on nucleic acid metabolism, therefore influencing protein and amino acid metabolism. Zinc is a major constituent of DNA polymerase, reverse transcriptase, RNA polymerase, RNA synthetase, and the protein chain elongating factor (26). In the presence of zinc deficiency, growth arrest occurs. Many functions which are dependent on protein synthesis are suppressed by zinc deficiency (27). These, obviously, include growth, cellular immunity, and fertility (28,29). In addition, hair growth, wound healing, and plasma protein levels may be affected. Zinc is found through all the soft tissues of the body as well as in blood cells and teeth (30). Zinc is bound to protein firmly and during the deficiency state the concentration of zinc in tissues does not change in a major way (31). Endogenous stores of zinc are mobilized in the fasting state, but in the presence of anabolism, do not meet the body's needs. This is because the net movement of zinc is into the tissues during anabolism and not out of it. Zinc that directly enters the circulation via the parenteral route is bound by albumin or an α-2-macroglobulin and carried to the liver (30). Zinc is excreted mainly in the feces, with a smaller amount in the urine (21,31). Urinary excretion is not influenced by intake. Significant losses of zinc are said to occur in the tropics; however, losses of zinc are thought to diminish with deficiency (32).

Diarrhea and stomal and fistula losses are major routes of increased or abnormal losses of zinc from the body (33–35). Patients who are hypercatabolic may also have increased losses of zinc in the urine (36). Zinc is taken up by the liver and other tissues. An infection results in increased uptake of zinc by the liver (37). The assessment of zinc status and requirements may be difficult. The most typical way to determine zinc status is to measure the circulating plasma concentrations because it is a method of analysis that can readily be obtained in most communities. Although hair zinc content is low when there is low-grade chronic deficiency, this type of determination is not readily available in most communities. Leukocyte enzyme levels are a reliable indicator of zinc deficiency, but this is not a measurement obtained easily (38).

Zinc Requirements

Investigators believe that patients receiving parenteral nutrition should receive a minimum of 2.5 mg of zinc per day if no diarrhea is present. In the presence of diarrhea and major gastrointestinal losses, the requirements of zinc may increase substantially. Determination of zinc in small intestinal fluid has shown values as high as 12 mg/liter and in some as high as 17 mg/liter. Patients who receive parenteral nutrition and are having large losses from the intestinal tract have to be given more than the maintenance levels.

Infants have a unique property when compared to adults—they are growing. They therefore require maintenance levels plus additional zinc for growth. The preterm infant has the greatest requirement of zinc, because it is especially during the last trimester that the infant's zinc is transferred from the mother to the infant. It has been said that about 0.5–0.75 mg of zinc per day is taken up during the last 3 weeks of gestation and the first 3 weeks of postnatal life. Some investigators have reported a requirement of as much as 300 μg/kg·day to maintain balance. In older children, 50 μg/kg·day has been said to maintain serum concentrations and to promote growth (39,40). Our experience of the use of 100 μg/kg·day shows that level to be unnecessarily high.

Recently, some investigators have shown that there are dramatic alterations in serum zinc concentrations before and after major operative trauma (41). These studies have shown that serum zinc concentration drops markedly 6 h after operation in both supplemented and unsupplemented patients. It gradually returns to near normal without exogenous supplies of zinc. Provision of therapeutic doses of zinc was unable to prevent the abrupt dip of serum zinc level (42). In a study of 99 adult patients receiving controlled total parenteral nutrition, Tagaki showed that administration of 3.9 mg/day of zinc was adequate to prevent plasma zinc concentrations from falling and could maintain them in the normal range. None of the patients who received this dose of zinc developed signs or symptoms of zinc deficiency or showed abnormally elevated plasma zinc concentrations. In none of the patients studied did the erythrocyte concentration of zinc move out of the normal range (43). Therefore, erythrocyte zinc levels are not a sensitive indicator of body zinc status.

Infants may require even larger amounts of zinc on a milligram/kilogram basis because of their growth. In immature infants at the time of birth, there is a greater need for zinc in those who require parenteral nutrition (44). James and MacMahon found that infants require as much as 300 μg/kg·day to maintain balance (46). At least 100 μg/kg·day should be given to infants beyond the first 6 months of life (47,48). After adolescence, 50 μg/kg·day should be sufficient, provided that the patient does not have any extraneous losses (44–46).

COPPER

The typical human body contains approximately 75 mg of copper, of which 2% turns over daily (49). This means that approximately 1.5 mg of copper is needed each day. In normal human beings, 25–40% of copper that is taken in food and drink is absorbed. The rate of absorption is regulated by the intestinal mucosa. Copper is excreted via the bile into the intestinal tract (48). The absorption of copper throughout the intestinal tract is regulated in part by sulfur-rich proteins in the mucosal cells. These proteins are either identical with or closely related to the threonine moiety of metallothionein. Following administration of copper into the bloodstream, it becomes complexed with albumin and free amino acids and is transported to the liver. This fraction of plasma copper (so-called direct-reacting copper) normally makes up 10% or less of the total copper in plasma. The rest is firmly bound to ceruloplasmin. Although many of the key functions of this protein are unknown, we do know that it catalyzes oxidative reactions and transports copper to tissues. Protein fraction, or apoceruloplasmin, is synthesized in the liver, where copper is added to form the holoprotein. Ceruloplasmin reaches a maximum in plasma 24-h after a dose of copper is given. Intravenous copper is not accumulated by extrahepatic tissue until after its appearance in ceruloplasmin; tissues tend to take up ceruloplasmin copper in preference to cupric iron. Ceruloplasmin is more efficient in restoring cytochromic oxidase activity than is cupric chloride.

Copper is a part of a variety of enzymes, including cytochrome *c* oxidase, superoxide dismutase, dopamine B-hydroxylase, monomine oxidase, and lysyloxidase (49). Major manifestations of copper deficiency are shown through the consequences of ceruloplasmin and lysyloxidase deficiencies, although some have described abnormalities in catecholamine metabolism. Ceruloplasmin is intimately related to iron metabolism (50). Ceruloplasmin is an iron oxidase. When red cells are broken down, the iron released is ingested by macrophages. It is ultimately released by the macrophages and comes down as transferrin for transport to iron-storing and iron-requiring tissues. Iron storage in the liver also is in equilibrium with transferrin. Ceruloplasmin oxidizes ferrous iron and supports the transfer of iron from stores to transferrin (51). The vitamin riboflavin reduces the iron to the ferrous form in order to cross the cell membrane. After this has occurred, it is reoxidized to the ferric form to bind to transferrin (52). As a result of copper deficiency, a secondary iron deficiency develops.

Two of the body's supportive proteins, collagen and elastin, are dependent on the copper-containing enzyme lysyloxidase for their formation. In the copper deficiency state, poorly formed collagen and elastin are synthesized or are reduced in production (53). This can result in poor wound healing and weakening of tissues. Because of this, patients with Menke's disease are susceptible to aneurysm formation. The most commonly recognized deficiency of copper is secondary leukopenia (54).

The greatest concentrations of copper are in the liver and brain, with smaller amounts in the heart, kidney, spleen, and skeleton (55). Two thirds of the body's copper are found in the liver and the brain. Most of the copper circulates in the blood bound to ceruloplasmin; a small amount is found in albumin (56). The albumin-bound copper is the true transport copper which exchanges with tissue. In normal individuals, the body copper is controlled by absorption and biliary secretion (57,58). Formally, copper absorption is enhanced by deficiency and is depressed by ascorbic acid, cadmium, and phytates in the diet. Interestingly, zinc inhibits copper absorption by promoting intestinal metallothionein synthesis. It is this increased metallothionein production which binds copper and prevents its transfer to the circulation when the body has normal or excessive amounts of copper present (59). Balance studies show that the dietary requirement is in the range 2–5 mg/day. Of this amount, approximately one third is absorbed (0.6–1.6 mg/day) (60). Other studies have shown that 1.2 mg/day is more than adequate (61). Excretion in the bile amounts to 0.5–1.3 mg of copper per day. There is no enterohepatic circulation of copper (60). Only 10–60 μg/day is excreted in the urine. Infusion of copper intravenously does not increase its losses (61). Small amounts of copper may be lost in the perspiration each day, probably around 0.34–0.58 mg/day (62). Diarrhea increases copper losses but not in proportion to the volume of diarrhea. Liver disease and reduced liver function reduces the amount of copper that is lost from the body. Cholestasis markedly reduces the amount of copper lost. Corticosteroids in excess increase urinary copper excretion, whereas deficiency results in the converse (63). Trauma results in major increases in urinary copper excretion, just as it does for other trace metals. Studies have shown that the mean urinary copper excretion rate rises to 256 μg/day (64).

Copper in the circulation is bound to albumin. Other amino acids that are bound to copper are histidine, threonine, and glutamine. Copper is taken up by the liver and bone marrow. Copper in the liver is incorporated into ceruloplasmin and is released into the circulation or excreted into the bile. Within the bone marrow, it is incorporated into erythrocuprine and released in the red cells. Ceruloplasmin has been recognized as donating copper for incorporation into enzymes, such as superoxide dismutase, lysyl oxidase, and cytochrome oxidase (65).

Plasma copper is obviously reduced in copper deficiency and is affected by a variety of factors that alter the serum concentration of ceruloplasmin. Protein-energy malnutrition results in a decrease in serum ceruloplasmin level; nephrosis also results in reduced levels of copper (66). Infections, inflammatory conditions, and Hodgkin's disease all increase the level of serum copper. Oral contraceptives also increase plasma copper levels. Studies have shown the range of plasma copper in patients taking oral contraceptives to increase to 300 ± 7 μg/dl. This represents an increase from the normal range of 118 ± 2 μg/dl in women who are not taking oral contraceptives.

Measurement of copper in hair is not a reliable index of deficiency of this element, since hair is not a major site of deposition of copper (67). A typical Western diet supplies 2–4 mg of copper per day, and with this intake copper deficiency has never been seen in an adult.

During pregnancy, the major portion of the fetus's copper is obtained during the last 10 weeks of gestation (68). During the first month of life, a premature or term infant will typically retain 100–130 μg/kg·day. Malnourished infants have been shown to require anywhere from 40 to 135 μg/kg·day to correct their deficiencies.

Studies in adult patients receiving parenteral nutrition have shown that a minimum of 0.3 mg/day was necessary to meet their requirements, as long as they did not have abnormal gastrointestinal losses. Patients with diarrhea required at least 60% more. Patients who have large stoma losses should receive additional copper besides that deemed necessary for normal maintenance. Patients with abnormal liver function may require as little as 0.10 mg/day (61). In critically ill patients, it is recommended that at least 0.50 mg/day be provided (69). In infants, the intravenous requirement for copper ranges between 10 and 50 μg/kg·day (70). Some investigators have shown that a dosage of 50 μg/kg·day resulted in a reversal of leukopenia and neutropenia within a period of 5 days, and a normalization of the plasma copper level in a comparable period of time. Anemia need not be present at the same time as leukopenia and neutropenia. A greater deficiency of copper may be required for this to take place (71). Copper deficiency may also be responsible for scurvy-like changes in long bones. The typical bony changes include osteoporosis and metaphyseal and soft tissue calcification. These changes are essentially those of scurvy. Patients who receive parenteral nutrition should no longer become copper-deficient if physicians pay attention to the total needs of their patients (72). Our child patients, who receive 100 μg/kg·day, have serum copper levels in the normal range.

CHROMIUM

Chromium is similar to the other essential trace elements; it is a transition element in the periodic table. The fact that this element is able to form coordination compounds and chelates is a characteristic that makes essential metals available in living systems (73). Chromium is recognized in our diet in two forms, as inorganic chromium (Cr^{3+}) and in a biologically active molecule. The biologically active molecule seems to be a dinicotinachromium $3+$ complex, which is coordinated with amino acids to stabilize the molecule (74).

Studies done in the 1950s and 1960s showed that there was an insulin potentiating factor found in brewer's yeast, which when fed to rats produced glucose tolerance. Chromium was recognized as the active ingredient in the glucose tolerance factor and was reported to be essential for optimal function of insulin in mammalian tissue (75). It has been shown that the glucose tolerance factor which has been extracted from brewer's yeast binds to and potentiates insulin (76). Chromium has not yet been shown to function in enzyme systems or in metalloprotein complexes and/or related structures. The exact role of chromium and how it functions have not been elucidated. It is uncertain how well chromium is absorbed in humans (77). It is thought that organically complexed chromium is more immediately available for metabolic needs, but inorganic chromium requires incorporation into biologically active molecules.

Chromium binds competitively to transferrin; this suggests that it may be transported and stored with ferric iron (78). Whereas chromium affects glucose disposal, there is no evidence that iron does. Chromium is released into the blood along with insulin following a glucose challenge (79). Surprisingly, this release has not been as evident in subjects with abnormal glucose tolerance (77). Ninety-five percent of chromium excretion takes place in the urine and averages less than 1 μg/day (80,81).

Chromium seems to be a very safe trace metal, even in pharmacologic doses. A dose of 250 μg given to malnourished, chromium-deficient children apparently showed no side effects (82). Human chromium deficiency has been difficult to document. Most studies that have been done have been in individuals with abnormal glucose intolerance and/or elevated lipid levels. Because chromium levels have often been difficult to measure, it has been very hard in many instances to interpret results of studies. Chromium is distributed throughout the human body and its concentration declines with age (83). This therefore correlates with the fact that glucose tolerance decreases with age. It would seem logical that if chromium deficiency is responsible for decreased glucose tolerance, then supplementation might improve this (84). A well-controlled study in elderly adults showed that supplementation of the diet with brewer's yeast improved glucose tolerance while no improvement was obtained with the use of a yeast that was free of chromium.

Excretion of chromium is into the urine, and urinary losses are enhanced by glucose loading in diabetic subjects (85). Smaller amounts are lost in the stool. Losses of chromium in healthy adults amount to between 5.9 and 10.0 μg/day (86). Measurement of chromium status is difficult. Normal ranges from some laboratories indicate that no detectable chromium may be considered to be normal. It is therefore hard to understand at what level deficiency truly occurs. It is said that hair chromium declines in situations associated with deficiency (87). Some people believe that the only way to assess chromium deficiency is to demonstrate normal glucose clearance responding to chromium supplementation.

The true chromium requirements have not been determined. Data are woefully lacking in this area. There is a literature report of one adult patient requiring between 10 and 20 μg/day. In a study of infants, a requirement of 0.14–0.2 μg/kg·day was determined. Studies need to be done to improve our understanding of our needs for chromium. Kien et al. (88) reported a 6½-year-old boy who received chromium-free total parenteral nutrition for a period of 16 months, but still maintained serum chromium levels that were four times the upper limit of normal. This was following an interval of over 2 years in which he received 3 μg/day of chromium in chromic chloride. His unsupplemented TPN solution contained 4 μg/day. This investigator concluded that chromium contamination of standard parenteral nutrition fluid may prevent biochemical evidence of low chromium status (89). Physicians should be cautious of supplementing their solutions with chromium in view of these observations. Our experience has been that unsupplemented TPN solutions provide negligible chromium. However, we have not recognized glucose intolerance in any of our children on long-term TPN who have subnormal chromium levels, and none have developed peripheral neuropathy.

MANGANESE

Manganese was reported to be an essential trace metal in animals in the early 1930s. Although knowledge of the metabolism and enzymatic functions of manganese has increased, its significance in humans is still not clearly defined. The adult human body contains 10–20 mg of manganese (90). Unlike copper, manganese is not accumulated in the liver before birth (91,92). In animals, regulation of the manganese levels occurs primarily through excretion rather than through regulation of absorption. Absorbed manganese is excreted through the intestine via bile, which is its main regulatory route. It is recognized that manganese retention in very young animals is considerable. It is also recognized that manganese retention may be depressed by the addition of iron to the diet (93).

Manganese functions biochemically either as a cofactor activating a large number of enzymes which form metal enzyme complexes, or as an integral part of metalloenzymes, in which the metal is built rather firmly into a metalloprotein. A group of enzymes that seem to be involved in manganese deficiency are the glycosal transferases. These enzymes are activated by manganese as a co-factor and are required for synthesis for glucoseaminoglycans (94). Manganese-containing metalloenzymes are found primarily in the mitochondria. The two manganese metalloenzymes are pyruvate carboxylase and manganese superoxide dismutase.

A deficiency of manganese in animals results in abnormalities of cartilage growth. It may also be necessary for the action of vitamin K in adding the carbohydrate component of prothrombin to the prothrombin protein. A case has been described in which vitamin K could not correct prothrombin levels until the patient was given manganese. A human patient has been recorded with manganese deficiency. This followed the inadvertent omission of manganese salt from a vitamin-K-deficient purified diet that he was receiving as a volunteer under metabolic ward conditions. This patient developed hypercholesterolemia, weight loss, transient dermatitis, occasional nausea and vomiting, changes in hair and beard color, and slow growth of beard and hair (95).

The human body contains 12–20 mg of manganese, mainly present in the mitochondria (96). As indicated earlier, only 3–4% of an oral dose of manganese is absorbed and it is very efficiently excreted by the intestine. Lesser amounts are excreted in pancreatic juice and through the intestinal wall. Little manganese is excreted in the urine. Manganese in the circulation is bound to a beta globulin, transferrin. It is taken up by the mitochondria and more slowly by the nuclei. Intake in excess of need leads to excretion through the gastrointestinal tract (97).

Dietary requirements are said to be between 2 and 3 mg/day (98). The amount retained is between 50 and 400 μg/day. The requirement for patients on parenteral nutrition has still not been well established. Shils, in a study of various commercially produced parenteral nutrition solutions, showed that the amount of manganese in preparations tested varied among manufacturers and lots (99). He showed that some of the additives in the solutions were high in manganese, particularly potassium, phosphate, and magnesium sulfate. The calculated manganese content in TPN formulations varied from 8.07 to 21.75 μg per total daily volume. These values agreed with those obtained from the analysis of the actual TPN solutions. Although many components of TPN solutions are contaminated with manganese, the contamination is relatively small and represents a small fraction of the lower limit of the suggested daily intravenous intake for stable adult TPN patients, of 0.15–0.8 mg.

The potential daily supply for infants receiving TPN is unlikely to exceed 0.7–1 μg/kg on an intake of 2 g/kg of amino acids and 110 kcal/kg the recommended dosage being 2–10 μg/kg body weight. When there is persistent biliary obstruction, excretion of manganese may be impeded. Therefore, monitoring of blood levels is indicated if supplementary manganese is being contemplated or given. Our long-term pediatric patients had normal manganese levels in their plasma, despite the fact that no manganese was added to the solutions. This indicates that the natural contamination was sufficient to meet their needs.

Although there are no data concerning manganese toxicity in patients treated with TPN, liver damage has been described in self-induced hypermanganesemia, with a liver manganese of 2.17 mg/dl, the normal value cited being 0.11 mg/dl. Chronic industrial manganese poisoning mostly affects the brain, producing extrapyramidal symptoms; in these cases, blood and urine manganese levels were increased to 3.6 and 16.0 μg/dl, respectively, normal values being 2.0 and 0.1–0.2 μg/dl. Blood manganese four times greater than the highest level of normal values may be accompanied by signs of liver damage. (98).

MOLYBDENUM

Molybdeum is an essential constituent of xanthine oxidase, aldehyde oxidase, and sulfite oxidase. The activities of these enzymes decline in experimental deficiency. Xanthine oxidase activity in the blood of humans and in the tissues of animals living in a high-molybdenum geochemical province of the Soviet Union is significantly increased. In that population, uric acid levels in blood and urine are raised and the incidence of gout is very high. This is much below the 10–15 mg/day associated with gout in the Soviet Union. Human liver and kidney have the highest concentrations of molybdenum (99).

Molybdenum in the diet is absorbed as molybdate in its hexavalent form and is easily absorbed from salts and from vegetables. Excretion is mainly in the urine, but urinary excretion rises as sulfate intake or endogenous sulfate production increases. It has been found that patients with diseases such as Crohn's disease causing large volume diarrhea may have excessive molybdenum losses in their stool (99). The minimum requirements for molybdenum are unknown. Limited balanced studies have shown that between 48 and 96 μg/day may be required. Larger supplementation may be required in the patient with additional gastrointestinal losses. Normally, patients with acute stress-like illnesses may have greater requirements. Intravenous data in children are not available. A single case of molybdenum deficiency has been recognized. The patient developed a coma-like syndrome that was reversed with 300 μg of molybdenum per day (100).

SELENIUM

More than a generation ago, it was recognized that selenium prevented dietary liver necrosis in the rat (101). Subsequent to this, other selenium-responsive conditions were recognized in a variety of animal diseases. All of these conditions occurred when there was low soil selenium content and they were prevented by supplementing animal rations with selenium. In the late 1960s, pure selenium deficiency, defined as a pathological clinical condition occurring in the presence of adequate vitamin E, was produced in animals in the laboratory. Pure selenium deficiency in chicks caused pancreatic degeneration (102). Growth retardation, partial alopecia, aspermatogenesis, and cataracts were manifestations of selenium deficiency in rats (103–105). The selenium content of food depends on the soil in which it is produced.

Another factor that determines food selenium content is its content of protein. Selenium is typically found in protein fractions of foods; therefore, plants such as fruits and vegetables are poor sources of selenium. Meats are reliable sources of this element. In the United States, the daily dietary selenium intake is 60–216 μg (106,107). In the areas of China where Keshan disease occurs, selenium intake is less than 30 μg/day (105). In the late 1970s some therapeutic and formula diets were found to provide less than 5 μg of selenium in the daily intake (108,109,113). In some parts of the world, selenium intake is quite high and intakes have been reported up to 500 μg/day without any toxicity (110).

Food selenium is largely in the form of amino acids, such as selenomethionine (111). Selenomethionine and sodium selenite, the inorganic form, have similar potencies for preventing selenium deficiency states. Both promote tissue glutathione peroxidase when administered to selenium-deficient individuals. Selenomethionine causes a greater rise in blood and tissue selenium levels, probably because selenium is incorporated into the primary structure of tissue proteins in place of methionine. Selenium in this form becomes available to the organism only after catabolism of the seleno amino acid. This form of selenium may serve as an unregulated storage or buffer pool of the element, providing endogenous selenium when dietary supply is interrupted. There is no other recognized storage form of selenium in the body. The absorption of selenium from the body appears to be under no physiological control. More than 90% of a given dose of selenium is absorbed, even when toxic levels are given. Reports in humans indicate that selenomethionone and selenite are absorbed nearly completely (112). It appears that humans regulate their selenium content through excretion.

Selenium and vitamin E are interrelated in their actions. A deficiency of one can be partially corrected by giving the other. Glutathione peroxidase is an enzyme made up of four subunits, each containing selenocysteine as in integral part of the molecule (113). In association with superoxide dysmutase, it controls the levels of superoxide and peroxide in the cell. This, in turn, affects lipid peroxidation of polyunsaturated fatty acids in cell membranes. Vitamin E is the second line of defense that controls the formation of hydroperoxides in the fatty acid residues of phospholipids, a process that depends on the antioxidant role of the vitamin and also involves its entering into a structural relation with membrane phsopholipids (114).

Intracellular lipid hydroperoxides may be reduced by glutathione oxidase to hydroxy acids. There are four biological reactions that produce superoxide: (1) enzyme reactions, such as those involving xanthine oxidases and galactose oxidase; (2) metabolic pathways, such as the hexose monophosphate shunt and oxidated reactions mediated by cytochrome P450; (3) interaction of dioxygen with the electron transport chain in the mitochondria; and (4) phagocytosis, where a burst of oxidative metabolism is associated with generation of NADPH by the hexose monophosphate shunt, which in turn is used by the NADPH oxidase to generate superoxide. The excess superoxide is controlled by superoxide dismutase and glutathione peroxidase. Therefore, bacterial killing is unlikely to be affected by selenium deficiency.

Selenium is bound to albumin, and after being processed by red cells circulates in association with betalipoprotein (122). It is taken up by tissues of the body and is incorporated into proteins and glutathione peroxidase. Fecal excretion accounts for almost 60% of losses and the urinary excretion the remainder (123,124).

Plasma selenium and glutathione peroxidase levels are sensitive to selenium intake and can be used to assess the need for this trace element. It has not been clearly determined how selenium conditions the need for vitamin E in humans. The exact selenium requirements per day have not been determined. Some metabolic studies in humans suggest a minimum intake of 20 μg/day, others have estimated the need to be as high as 54 μg/day (123).

Patients receiving parenteral nutrition may develop selenium deficiency with associated muscle pain and weakness. This may be manifested by elevations of serum creatine kinase, and electromyographic evidence of myositis and nonspecific membrane irritability. Reversal of the myositis and normalization of serum creatine kinase can occur in less than 2 weeks. Patients with selenium deficiency may be asymptomatic but have elevated transaminases and creatine phosphokinase. Pain and muscle weakness have been observed in both children and adults, and pseudoalbinism has been described. A unique characteristic of patients on TPN with selenium deficiency is the presence of macrocytosis without anemia. Such a finding has been described in adults as well as children. Decreased skin pigmentation has also been seen in both children and adults. Thirty-five percent of children and 75% of adults who received long term parenteral nutrition at UCLA Medical Clinic were found to have manifestations of selenium deficiency prior to the institution of selenium supplementation. Reversal of pseudoalbinism, darkening of skin and pigmentation, and reversal of macroytosis occurred in all following supplementation of TPN solutions with selenium. Children were repleted with 2 μg/kg·day and adults with 100 μg/kg·day for 2–4 weeks, followed by maintenance selenium levels in children of 0.5–1 μg/kg·day and 40 μg/day for adults. Periodic monitoring of serum levels should be done to avoid toxicity. All individuals found to be selenium deficient had normal vitamin E status and none were shown to have increased hemolysis of red blood cells (115–121).

Well-planned and well-executed balance studies of trace metal requirements of infants and children are lacking. Current recommendations are often based on extrapolation of knowledge gained from studies of enteral absorption. Knowledge is the least reliable for the immature infant and term neonate.

REFERENCES

1. Ulmer DD. Trace elements. *N Engl J Med* 1977;297:318–21.
2. Underwood EJ. *Trace elements in human and animal nutrition*, 4th ed. New York: Academic Press, 1977.
3. Li TK, Vallee BL. The biochemical and nutritional role of trace elements. In: Wohl MG, Goodhart RS, eds. *Modern nutrition in health and disease*. Philadelphia: Lea & Feiger, 1978:377.
4. Anspaugh LR, Robison WL. Trace elements in biology and medicine. *Prog Atom Med* 1971; 3:63–138.
5. Mertz W. Some aspects of nutritional trace element research. *Fed Proc* 1970;29:1482–8.
6. Mendel LB, Bradley HC. Experiment studies on the physiology of the molluscs: second paper. *Am J Physiol* 1905;14:313–27.
7. Beisel WR. Trace elements in infectious processes. *Med Clin North Am* 1976;60:831–49.
8. Biesel WR, Pekarek RS. Acute stress and trace element metabolism. *Int Rev Neurobiol* 1972; suppl 1: 53–82.
9. Schwartz MK. Role of trace elements in cancer. *Cancer Res* 1975;35:3481–7.
10. Schrauzer GN. Inorganic and nutritional aspects of cancer. *Adv Exp Med Biol* 1978;91:323–44.
11. Henkin RI. Trace elements in endocrinology. *Med Clin North Am* 1976;60:779–97.
12. Becking GC. Trace elements and drug metabolism. *Med Clin North Am* 1976;60:813–30.
13. Golden MHN, Bolden BE. Trace elements. *Br Med Bull* 1981;37:31–6.
14. Abumrad NN, Schneider AJ, Steel D, et al. Amino acid intolerance during prolonged total parenteral nutrition (TPN) reversed by molybdenum (abstract). *Am J Clin Nutr* 1981;34:618.
15. Bush JA, Mahoney JP, Gubler CJ, et al. Studies on copper metabolism; transfer of radio-copper between erythrocytes and plasma. *J Lab Clin Med* 1956;47:898–906.
16. Sternlieb I, Morell AG, Tucker WD, et al. The incorporation of copper into ceruloplasmin in vivo: studies with copper-64 and copper-67. *J Clin Invest* 1961;40:1834–40.

17. Diplock AT. Metabolic and functional defects in selenium deficiency. *Phil Trans R Soc Lond B* 1981;294:105–17.
18. Finch CA, Hubers H. Perspectives in iron metabolism. *N Engl J Med* 1982;306:1520–28.
19. Shoden A, Gabrio BW, Finch CA. The relationship between ferritin and hemosiderin in rabbits and man. *J Biol Chem* 1953;204:823–30.
20. Dubach R, Moore CV, Callender S. Studies in iron transportation and metabolism. IX. The excretion of iron as measured by the isotope technique. *J Lab Clin Med* 1955;45:599–615.
21. Robinson MF, McKenszie JJ, Thomason CD, et al. Metabolic balance of zinc, copper, cadmium, iron, molybdenum and selenium in young New Zealand women. *Br J Nutr* 1973;30:195–205.
22. Foy H, Kondi A. Anaemias of the tropics; relation to iron intake, absorption and losses during growth, pregnancy and lactation. *J Trop Med Hyg* 1957;60:105–18.
23. Morgan EH, Walters MN. Iron storage in human disease. Fractionation of hepatic and splenic iron into ferritin and hemosiderin with histochemical correlations. *J Clin Pathol* 1963;16:101–7.
24. Lipschitz DA, Cook JD, Finch CA. A clinical evaluation of serum ferritin as an index of iron stores. *N Engl J Med* 1974;290:1213–16.
25. Wan Kk, Tsallas G. Dilute iron dextran formulation for addition to parenteral nutrient solutions. *Am J Hosp Pharm* 1980;37:206–10.
26. Vallee BL, Falchuk KH. Zinc and gene expression. *Phil Trans R Soc Lond B* 1981;294:185–97.
27. Prasad AS. *Zinc in human nutrition.* Boca Raton, FL: CRC Press, 1979:1–80.
28. Golden MHN, Golden BE, Harland PSEG, et al. Zinc and immunocompetence in protein-energy malnutrition. *Lancet* 1978;1:1226–27.
29. Fernandes G, Nair M, Onoe K, et al. Impairment of cell-mediated immunity functions by dietary zinc deficiency in mice. *Proc Natl Acad Sci USA* 1979;76:457–61.
30. Richards MP, Cousins RJ. Isolation of intestinal zinc: proposed function in zinc absorption (abstract). *Fed Proc* 1977;36:1106.
31. Kirchgessner M, Roth HP, Weigand E. Biochemical changes in zinc deficiency. In: Prasad AS, ed. *Trace elements in human health and disease,* vol 1. New York: Academic Press, 1976:189–225.
32. Prasad AS, Schulert AR, Sandstead HH, et al. Zinc, iron and nitrogen content of sweat in normal and deficient subjects. *J Lab Clin Med* 1963;62:84–9.
33. Abdu-Hamdan DK, Migdal SD, Whitehouse AS, et al. Disparate urinary zinc (Zn) handling in response to Zn infusion and amino acids (abstract). *Kidney Int* 1979;16:818.
34. Smith KT, Cousins RJ. Quantitative aspects of zinc absorption by isolated, vascularly perfused rat intestine. *J Nutr* 1980;110:316–23.
35. McClain CJ. Zinc metabolism in malabsorption syndromes. *J Am Coll Nutr* 1985;4:49–64.
36. Main AN, et al. Clinical experience of zinc supplementation during intravenous nutrition in Crohn's disease. Value of serum and urine zinc measurement. *Gut* 1982;23:984–91.
37. Beisel WR, Perarek RS, Wannemacher RW Jr. The impact of infectious disease on trace-element metabolism of the host. In: Hoekstra WG, Suttie JW, Ganther HE, et al, eds. *Trace element metabolism in animals,* vol 2. Baltimore: University Park Press, 1974:217–40.
38. Whitehouse RC, Prasad AS, Rabbani PI, et al. Zinc in plasma, neutrophils, lymphocytes, and erythrocytes as determined by flameless atomic absorption spectrophotometry. *Clin Chem* 1982;28:475–80.
39. James BE, MacMahon RA. Balance studies of 9 elements during complete intravenous feeding of small premature infants. *Aust Pediatr J* 1976;12:154–62.
40. Ricour C, Duhamel JF, Gros J, et al. Estimates of trace element requirements of children receiving total parenteral nutrition. *Arch Fr Pediatr* 1977;34 (suppl 7): 92–100.
41. Fawaz F. Zinc deficiency in surgical patients: a clinical study. *JPEN* 1985;9:463–9.
42. Jiang ZM, Yang NF, Jiao KS, Zhu Y, Fei LM, Tseng H. Postoperative fall in serum zinc concentrations unaffected by intravenous zinc therapy. *JPEN* 1985;9:196–9.
43. Takagi Y, Okada A, Itakura T, Kawashima Y. Clinical studies on zinc metabolism during total parenteral nutrition as related to zinc deficiency. *JPEN* 1986;10:195–202.
44. Widdowson EM, Dauncey J, Shaw JCL. Trace elements in foetal and early postnatal development. *Proc Nutr Soc* 1974;33:275–84.
45. James BE, MacMahon RA. Balance studies of 9 elements during complete intravenous feeding of small premature infants. *Aust Pediatr J* 1976;12:154–62.
46. Shaw JCL. Trace elements in the fetus and young infant. I. Zinc. *Am J Dis Child* 1979; 133:1260–8.

47. Arakawa T, Tamara T, Igarashi Y, et al. Zinc deficiency in two infants during total parenteral alimentation for diarrhea. *Am J Clin Nutr* 1976;29:197–204.
48. Hambidge KM, Walravens PA. Trace elements in nutrition. *Pract Pediatr* 1975;1:17.
49. Mason KE. A conspectus of research on copper metabolism and requirements in man. *J Nutr* 1979;109:1979–2066.
50. Evans JL, Abraham PA. Anemia, iron storage and ceruloplasmin in copper nutrition in the growing rat. *J Nutr* 1973;103:196–201.
51. Osaki S, Johnson DA, Freiden E. The possible significance of the ferrous oxidase activity of ceruloplasmin in normal human serum. *J Biol Chem* 1966;241:2746–51.
52. Golden MHN. Trace elements in human nutrition. *Hum Nutr Clin Nutr* 1982;36C:185–202.
53. O'Dell BL. Roles for iron and copper in connective tissue biosynthesis. *Phil Trans R Soc Lond B* 1981;294:91–104.
54. Cordano A, Baertl JM, Graham GG. Copper deficiency in infancy. *Pediatrics* 1964;34:324–6.
55. Hamilton EI, Minsky MJ, Cleary JJ. The concentration and distribution of some stable elements in healthy human tissues from the United Kingdom. *Sci Total Environ* 1972;1:341–74.
56. Gubler CJ, Lahey ME, Cartwright GE, et al. Studies on copper metabolism; transportation of copper in blood. *J Clin Invest* 1953;32:405–14.
57. Bremner I. Absorption, transport and storage of copper. In: *Biological roles of copper*. CIBA Foundation Symposium No 79. Amsterdam: Excerpta Medica, 1980:23–48.
58. Own CA. Absorption and excretion of ^{64}Cu-labelled copper by the rat. *Am J Physiol* 1964;207:1203–6.
59. Hall AC, Young BW, Bremner I. Intestinal metallothionein and the mutual antagonism between copper and zinc. *J Inorg Biochem* 1979;11:57–66.
60. Cartwright GE, Wintrobe MM. Copper metabolism in normal subjects. *Am J Clin Nutr* 1964;14:224–32.
61. Shike M, Roulet M, Kurian R, et al. Copper metabolism and requirements in total parenteral nutrition. *Gastroenterology* 1981;81:290–7.
62. Jacob RA, Sandstead HH, Munoz JM, et al. Whole body surface loss of trace metals in normal males. *Am J Clin Nutr* 1981;34:1379–83.
63. Henkin RI. On the role of adrenocorticosteroids in the control of zinc and copper metabolism. In: Hoekstra WG, Suttie JW, Ganther HE, et al. eds. *Trace element metabolism in animals*, vol 2. Baltimore: University Park Press, 1974:647–51.
64. Askari A, Long CL, Murray RRL, et al. Zinc and copper balance in the severely injured patient (abstract). *Fed Proc* 1979;38:707.
65. Bremner I, Mills CF. Absorption, transport and tissue storage of essential trace elements. *Phil Trans R Soc Lond B* 1981;294:75–89.
66. Kovalsky VV. The geochemical ecology of organisms under conditions of varying contents of trace elements in the environment. In: Mills CF, ed. *Trace element metabolism in animals*, vol 1. Edinburgh: Churchill Livingstone, 1970:385–97.
67. Hambidge KM. Increase in hair copper concentration with increasing distance from the scalp. *Am J Clin Nutr* 1973;26:1212–5.
68. Jacobson S, Western PO. Balance study of twenty trace elements during total parenteral nutrition in man. *Br J Nutr* 1977;37:107–26.
69. Phillips GD, Garnys VP. Parenteral administration of trace elements to critically ill patients. *Ann Intensive Care* 1981;9:221–5.
70. Mertz W, Roginski EE, Schwartz K. Effects of trivalent chromium complexes on glucose uptake by epididymal fat tissue of rats. *J Biol Chem* 1961;236:318–22.
71. Sriram K, O'Gara JA, Strunk JR, Peterson JK. Neutropenia due to copper deficiency in total parenteral nutrition. *JPEN* 1986;10:530–2.
72. Tokuda Y, Yokoyama S, Tsuti M, Sugital T, Tajima T, Mitomi T. Copper deficiency in an infant on prolonged total parenteral nutrition. *JPEN* 1986;10:242–4.
73. Rollinson CL, Rosenbloom WE. In: Bailar JC, Jr, ed. *Coordination chemistry*. New York: Kirschner, 1969:103–24.
74. Toepfer WW, Mertz W, Polansky MM, Roginski EE, Wolf WR. Synthetic organic chromium complexes and glucose tolerance. *J Agr Food Chem* 1977;25:162–5.
75. Schwarz K, Mertz W. Chromium (III) and the glucose tolerance factor. *Arch Biochem Biophys* 1959;85:292–5.

76. Evans GW, Roginski EE, Mertz W. Interaction of the glucose tolerance factor (GTF) with insulin. *Biochem Biophys Res Comm* 1973;50:718–22.
77. Mertz W. Chromium occurrence and function in biological systems. *Physiol Rev* 1969; 49:163–203.
78. Sargent R, Lim TH, Gensen RL. Reduced chromium retention in patients with hemochromatosis, a possible basis for hemochromatotic diabetes. *Metabolism* 1979;28:70–9.
79. Glinsman WH, Feldman FJ, Mertz W. Plasma chromium after glucose administration. *Science* 1966;152:1243–5.
80. Guthrie BE, Wolf WR, Veillon C, Mertz W. In: Hemphill DC, ed. *Trace substances in environmental health XII.* Columbia: University of Missouri Press, 1978.
81. Veillon C, Wolf, WR, Guthrie BE. Determination of chromium in biological materials by stable isotope dilution. *Anal Chem* 1979;51:1022–4.
82. Hopkins LL Fr., Ransome-Kuti O, Majaj AS. Improvement of impaired carbohydrate metabolism in malnourished infants. *Am J Clin Nutr* 1968;21:203–11.
83. Schroeder HA, Balassa JJ, Tipton IH. Abnormal trace metals in man—chromium. *J Chron Dis* 1962;15:941–64.
84. Freed BA, Pinchofsky G, Nasr N, et al. Normalization of serum glucose levels and decreasing insulin requirements by the addition of chromium to TPN (abstract). *JPEN* 1981;5:568.
85. Schroeder HA. The role of chromium in mammalian nutrition. *Am J Clin Nutr* 1968;21:230–44.
86. Hambidge KM. Chromium nutrition in the mother and the growing child. In: Mertz W, Cornatzer WE, eds. *Newer trace elements in nutrition.* New York: Marcel Dekker, 1971:169–94.
87. Jeejeebhoy KN, Chu RC, Marliss EB, et al. Chromium deficiency, glucose intolerance and neuropathy reversed by chromium supplementation in a patient receiving longterm total parenteral nutrition. *Am J Clin Nutr* 1977;30:531–8.
88. Underwood EJ. *Trace elements in human and animal nutrition,* 4th ed. New York: Academic Press, 1977.
89. Freund H, Atamin S, Fischer JE. Chromium deficiency during total parenteral nutrition. *JAMA* 1979;241:496–8.
89a. Kien CL, Veillon C, Patterson KY, Farrell PM. Mild, peripheral neuropathy but biochemical chromium deficiency during 16 months of "chromium-free" total parenteral nutrition. *JPEN* 1986;10:662–4.
90. Schroeder HA, Balassa JJ, Tipton IH. Essential trace metals in man: manganese, a study in homeostasis. *J Chron Dis* 1966;19:545–71.
91. Widdowson EM, Chan H, Harrison GE, Milner RDG. Accumulation of Cu, Zn, Mn, Cr, and Co in the human liver before birth. *Biol Neonate* 1972;20:360–7.
92. Casey DE, Robinson MF. Copper, manganese, zinc, nickel, cadmium and lead in human fetal tissue. *Br J Nutr* 1978;39:639–46.
93. Gruden N. Suppression of transduodenal manganese transport by milk diet supplemented with iron. *Nutr Metab* 1977;21:305–9.
94. Leach RM Jr. In: Prasad A, ed. *Trace elements in human health and disease,* vol 2. New York: Academic Press, 1976:235–47.
95. Lustig S, Pitlik SD, Rosenfeld JB. Liver damage in acute self-induced hypermagnesemia. *Arch Intern Med* 1982;142:405–6.
96. Cotzias GC. Manganese in health and disease. *Physiol Rev* 1958;38:503–32.
97. Greenberg DM, Copp DH, Cuthbertson EM. Studies in mineral metabolism with the aid of artificial radioactive isotopes. *J Biol Chem* 1943;147:749–57.
98. Kurkus J, Alcock NW, Shils ME. Manganese content of large-volume parenteral solutions and nutrient additives. *JPEN* 1984;8:254–7.
99. Abumrad NN. Molybdenum—is it an essential trace metal? *Bull NY Acad Med* 1984;60:163–71.
100. Abumrad NN, Schneider AJ, Steel D, et al. Amino acid intolerance during prolonged total parenteral nutrition reversed by molybdate therapy. *Am J Clin Nutr* 1981;34:2351–9.
101. Schwarz K, Foltz CM. Selenium as an integral part of factor 3 against dietary necrotic liver degeneration. *J Am Chem Soc* 1957;79:3292–3.
102. Thompson JN, Scott ML. Impaired lipid and vitamin E absorption related to atrophy of the pancrease in selenium-deficient chicks. *J Nutr* 1970;100:797–809.
103. Sprinker LH, Harr JR, Newberne PM, Whanger PD, Weswig PH. Selenium deficiency lesions in rats fed vitamin E-supplemented rations. *Nutr Rep Int* 1971;4:335–40.

104. Keshan Disease Research Group: Observations on effect of sodium selenite in prevention of Keshan disease. *Chinese Med J* 1979;92:471-6.
105. Keshan Disease Research Group. Epidemiologic studies on the etiologic relationship of selenium and Keshan disease. *Chinese Med J* 1979;92:477-82.
106. Levander O A. In: *Proceedings of the Symposium on Selenium-Tellurium in the Environment.* Pittsburgh: Industrial Health Foundation, 1976:26-53.
107. Olson OE, Palmer IS. Selenium in foods consumed by South Dakotans. *Proc Acad Sci* 1978;57:113-21.
108. Lombeck I, Kasperek K, Harcisch HD, et al. The selenium state of children. *Eur J Pediatr* 1978;129:213-34.
109. Zabel NL, Harland J, Gormican AT, Ganther HE. Selenium content of commercial formula diets. *Am J Clin Nutr* 1978;31:850-8.
110. Sakuari H, Tsuchiya K. A tentative recommendation for the maximum daily intake of selenium. *Environ Physiol Biochem* 1975;5:1207-18.
111. Olson OE, Novacek, EJ, Whitehead EI, Palmer IS. Investigations on selenium in wheat. *Phytochemistry* 1970;9:1181-8.
112. Thomson CD, Burton CE, Ronbinson MF. On supplementing the selenium intake of New Zealanders. I. Short experiments with large doses of selenite or selenomethionine. *Br J Nutr* 1978;39:579-87.
113. Rotruck JT, Pope AL, Gather HE, et al. Selenium: biochemical role as a component of glutathione peroxidase. *Science* 1973;179:588-90.
114. Diplock AT, Lucy J A. The biochemical modes of action of vitamin E and selenium: a hypothesis. *FEBS Lett* 1973;29:205-10.
115. Lane HW, Barroso AO, Englert DA, Dudrick ST, MacFadyen B S. Selenium status of seven chronic intravenous hyperalimentation patients. *JPEN* 1982;6:426-31.
116. Baptista RJ, Bistrian BR, Blackburn FL, Miller DG, Champagne CD, Buchanan L. Suboptimal selenium status in home parenteral nutrition patients with small bowel resections. *JPEN* 1984; 8:542-5.
117. Fleming CR, McCall JJ, O'Brien JF, Forsman R W, Ilstrup DM, Petz J. Selenium status in patients receiving parenteral nutrition. *JPEN* 1984;8:258-62.
118. Watson RD, Cannon RA, Kurland GS, Cox KL, Frates C. Selenium responsive myositis during prolonged home total parenteral nutrition in cystic fibrosis. JPEN 1985;9:58-60.
119. Dahlstrom KA, Ament ME, Medhin MG, Meurling J. Serum trace elements in children receiving longterm parenteral nutrition. *J Pediatr* 1986;109:625-30.
120. Vinton NE, Dahlstrom KA, Strobel CT, Ament ME. Macrocytosis and pseudoalbinism; manifestations of selenium deficiency. *J Pediatr* 1987;111:711-7.
121. Vinton NE, Ament ME, Dahlstrom KA, Strobel CT. Treatment of selenium deficiency in stable longterm total parenteral nutrition patients. JPEN (in press).
122. Underwood EJ. Selenium. In: *Trace elements in human and animal nutrition,* 4th ed. New York: Acadmic Press, 1977:246-302.
123. Levander OA, Sutherland V, Morris VC, et al. Selenium balance in young men during selenium depletion and repletion. *Am J Clin Nutr* 1981;23:2662-9.
124. Stewart RD, Griffiths NM, Thomson CD, et al. Quantitative selenium metabolism in normal New Zealand women. *Br J Nutr* 1978;40:45-54.

DISCUSSION

Dr. Mertz: It is the final concentration of elements in fluids that really counts, not how much is added. It is risky to make recommendations for additions because that would require that we know what is in the original, which we don't. Therefore, it would be very desirable for every parenteral nutrition unit to have its own analytical setup, although this may not always be possible.

Dr. Ament: I agree. That is why I showed what really was in the solution versus what we thought we were adding to the solution. We thought we were only adding zinc and copper, as they were the only additives we knew we were giving, but when we analyzed the solution we found all these other trace metals. That is why zinc levels in the patients' blood were higher than we had calculated. Aluminum contamination is an important historical example of the accidental provision of trace metals in TPN solutions, with serious consequences. We have our own parenteral fluid quality control system, but I realize that this isn't always feasible.

Dr. Stockhausen: I'm surprised that you found symptoms of selenium deficiency in your infants even though serum selenium was not very low. There must be other reasons.

Dr. Ament: These children had been on parenteral nutrition for a very long time, in some cases for 3 or 4 years, so we think the time factor was important. Vitamin E levels in these patients were all normal and we found no other factors predisposing to the clinical signs. When we supplemented the solutions with selenium this was the only change we made. However, the liver function tests did not return to normal completely, so some of the patients may have had other reasons for the liver abnormalities.

Dr. Lombeck: It is not clear what selenium compound we should use: selenite, selenate, or selenomethionine. The investigation of this is an important task that you should undertake in your parenterally fed patients, correlating the data with the input of amino acids, especially methionine, fatty acids, and vitamins.

With regard to the assessment of selenium status it is necessary to measure not only the selenium content of plasma and whole blood, but also the urinary excretion of selenium and the activity of glutathione peroxidase in plasma and erythrocytes.

Finally, I have a query about supplementation dose. You first supplemented the patients with 3 μg/kg selenium and later with 1 μg/kg. I think that for long-term parenteral nutrition even the latter dose is high. It corresponds to an oral intake of 2.5 μg/kg, assuming an absorption rate of 40%. This is more than most healthy children get. Do you postulate a higher need in these TPN patients?

Dr. Ament: I think 1 μg/kg is the correct maintenance dose for selenium. Patients with Crohn's disease and chronic diarrhea have an excess loss of selenium in intestinal contents.

Dr. Zlotkin: I have some data to emphasize the point that it is always important with parenteral nutrition to consider possible nutrient interactions. We studied 14 infants in TPN, 12 preterm, at a mean postnatal age of 22.6 days. None had diarrhea and they were maintained on parenteral nutrition only . We used a crossover study design to examine the influence of cysteine and histidine intake on urinary zinc excretion. Each infant received two formulations with either low histidine/no cysteine, no cysteine/high histidine, high cysteine/high histidine, or high cysteine/low histidine. Zinc intake was kept as constant as possible. We found that urinary zinc excretion in the group receiving no cysteine/low histidine was significantly lower than in the other three groups. So there seemed to be an interaction between the amino acid intake and the excretion of zinc. There was a positive correlation between urinary zinc excretion and urinary cysteine excretion. Thus the intakes of specific amino acids must be considered when zinc dosages are calculated (1).

Dr. Ament: Despite normal calcium, phosphorus, and magnesium nutrition, we still have a problem of osteopenic bones in our long-term patients on parenteral nutrition. Does anyone feel that this may be secondary to some other deficiency?

Dr. Mertz: This is a very promising field of enquiry. Fluoride, copper, zinc, and silicon could all be added to the list.

Dr. Bergmann: Fluoride in pharmacological doses, 100 μg/kg·day or even higher, may be tried.

Dr. Ament: In one adult patient of mine who had been on parenteral nutrition for over a decade, severe osteoporosis of the spine responded to intravenous fluoride. The spine appeared to become recalcified and all bone pain in the back disappeared. Interestingly, the pelvic bones did not recalcify.

REFERENCES

1. Zlotkin SM. Nutrient interactions with total parenteral nutrition: effect of histidine and cysteine intake on urinary zinc excretion. *J Pediatr* 1989;114:859–64.

Trace Elements in Nutrition of Children—II,
edited by Ranjit K. Chandra, Nestlé Nutrition
Workshop Series, Vol. 23, Nestec Ltd.,
Vevey/Raven Press, Ltd., New York © 1991.

Trace Elements and Immune Responses

Ranjit Kumar Chandra

*Memorial University of Newfoundland, Janeway Child Health Centre,
St. John's Newfoundland, A1A 1R8, Canada*

Although nutrition and immunology are both old disciplines, an understanding of their interactions is a recent phenomenon. In the last two decades, several studies have confirmed the consistent changes in the immune system seen in protein-energy malnutrition and other nutritional deficiencies (1–12).

Clinical malnutrition is a complex syndrome in which deficiencies of several individual nutrients are included. Thus it is important to examine the influence of each nutrient on various aspects of immunocompetence. The prevalence worldwide of trace element deficiencies and of infectious disease has prompted examination of the role of these nutrients in host defense mechanisms. The known role of several trace elements in key metabolic and cellular functions suggests that they would exert an important influence on immune responses. This has been amply verified in recent investigations in humans and laboratory animals (13,14).

In this selective review, I advance the concept that a progressive reduction in nutrient intake and body stores of many trace elements results in impaired immunocompetence that in turn increases the risk of infection. On the other hand, excessive amounts of trace elements also impair immune responses and could be detrimental to health.

MECHANISMS OF HOST PROTECTION

A number of protective factors shield humans from microbial invasion. These include the physical barriers of skin and mucous membranes, mucus and cilia on epithelial surfaces, phagocytes including polymorphonuclear leukocytes and macrophages, complement system, immunoglobulin and antibodies, and cell-mediated immune responses (Table 1) (12). The two main components of antigen-specific immune protection, humoral immunity and cell-mediated immune responses, interact synergistically with several nonspecific factors of host resistance, such as complement and phagocytosis, to restrain the invasion and multiplication of microorganisms and/or to eliminate them. The relative importance of various components of host defenses depends on the nature, dose, and route of antigen expo-

TABLE 1. *Host protective factors*

Antigen-specific
   Antibodies
   Cell-mediated immunity
Antigen-nonspecific
   Skin
   Mucous membrane
   Cilia
   Mucus
   Phagocytes
   Complement system
   Lysozyme
   Interferon
   Others

sure. Humoral immune responses consist of specific antibodies that recognize and react with antigens and the complement system. B-lymphocytes, which mature in the bone marrow, respond to appropriate antigenic stimulation by proliferation and differentiation into plasma cells. These in turn synthesize and secrete antibodies into lymph and serum. Antibodies are immunoglobulins and have a wide range of specificity for different antigens. In humans, there are five major classes of immunoglobulins (Ig), designated as IgG, IgA, IgM, IgD, and IgE. Their basic structure is similar, but they differ in the type of amino acid heavy chain, molecular weight, and function. A deficiency of B-lymphocytes is associated with bacterial and viral infections.

The second antigen-specific mechanism, cell-mediated immunity, relies primarily on cells, such as thymus-dependent T-lymphocytes rather than molecules such as immunoglobulins in humoral immunity. When T-lymphocytes are exposed to antigens, usually by accessory cells, such as phagocytic macrophages, metabolic changes occur at the cell surface and inside the cell. In addition to cell division or transformation, clones of cells are formed that carry receptors specific to the sensitizing antigen. Upon re-exposure to the same antigen, T-lymphocytes bearing the appropriate antigen receptor release soluble lymphokines. These, with the aid of other cells (e.g., macrophages), can destroy the antigen. Delayed cutaneous hypersensitivity testing is a useful tool for assessing cell-mediated immunity *in vivo*. Defective cell-mediated immunity is associated with infectious diseases caused by certain pathogenic bacteria, mycobacteria, viruses, fungi, and parasites.

Immunoregulatory mechanisms determine the type and pace of immune response generated on exposure to an antigen. The three principal cell types involved in immunoregulation are T- and B-lymphocytes and macrophages. T-lymphocytes are a heterogeneous group of cells that mediate cellular immune responses, such as delayed hypersensitivity, allograft and xenograft rejection, and destruction of virus- and bacteria-infected cells, and of cancer cells. T-lymphocytes also regulate the responses of other immunocompetent cells. The different subsets of T-cells are recognized by the presence of "differentiation antigens" with the help of monoclonal antibodies. Helper-inducer T-cells facilitate antibody production by plasma cells and modulate interactions between lymphocytes and accessory cells through the release of lymphokines. Cytotoxic-suppressor T-cells destroy target cells or provide negative feedback to inhibit antibody response or down-regulate inflammatory response. Of the antigen-nonspecific mechanisms of defense, much work has focused on the front-line role of phagocytosis, a nonspecific process of ingesting foreign material. In human beings, there are both circulatory phagocytes, which include monocytes and granulocytes (neutrophils, eosinophils, basophils) and "fixed" phagocytes, primarily macrophages or large scavenger cells. The latter are important in the initial processing of an antigen for its recognition by T- and B-lymphocytes. Phagocytosis is facilitated by opsonins that coat particles before ingestion. Opsonization depends on both antibodies and the complement system that is a complex set of proteins and is the primary humoral mediator and amplifier. Antibody and other molecules can activate the cascade of complement enzymes. Activation of complement promotes varied functions, such as phagocytosis, viral neutralization, and lysis of virus-infected cells.

IMMUNOCOMPETENCE IN PROTEIN-ENERGY MALNUTRITION

To examine the impact of trace element nutrition on immune responses, it is important to emphasize that isolated deficiencies of single nutrients are extremely rare in humans. On the other hand, the clinical syndrome of protein-energy malnutrition (PEM) affects at least 100 million persons worldwide and is often complicated by deficiencies of iron, trace elements, and vitamins. Morbidity is increased (Fig. 1). Thus it is useful first to understand the effects of PEM on immune responses (1,9). The most consistent effects of PEM on immunocompetence include absent or reduced delayed cutaneous hypersensitivity response to common microbial antigens, decreased number of thymus-dependent T-lymphocytes, reduced bactericidal capacity of neutrophils, lower mucosal secretory IgA antibody titer, and depressed complement system. Lymphoid involution is a significant finding. Death from starvation

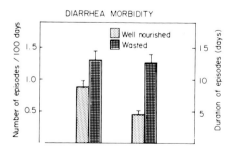

FIG. 1. Morbidity due to diarrheal disease in well-nourished and malnourished children.

results in profound thymic atrophy to the extent that it may be difficult to locate the organ. The thymus of undernourished children is usually small on x-ray examination; in those patients who die of kwashiorkor or marasmus, the thymus weighs less than one third of the normal organ. Similar changes are seen in the lymph nodes. In the thymus, the normally clear distinction between densely packed cortex and the sparse medulla is ill-defined and Hassall's corpuscles appear degenerated, enlarged, and crowded together. This appearance is distinct from that of the thymus in primary defects of the immune system. The histologic changes in the thymus are most marked in those patients who show lymphopenia before death. In the spleen, the periarteriolar cuff of lymphocytes is less prominent; in the lymph node, germinal centers are scanty and small; there is a reduction in the number of small lymphocytes and plasma cells.

Cell-mediated immunity is impaired. This is reflected in changes in delayed skin reactions, lymphocyte subpopulations, and *in vitro* responses. Cutaneous tests, using commonly encountered recall antigens (such as candidin, trichophytin, streptokinase-streptodornase, mumps, tetanus, diphtheria, and purified protein derivative of tuberculin) evaluate the memory response dependent on T-lymphocytes and inflammatory cells and are generally depressed in patients with PEM, even in those with mild forms (Fig. 2). There is a reduction in the proportion and absolute number of circulating thymus-dependent T-lymphocytes, identified by their ability to form rosettes with sheep red blood cells, and some correlation between the severity of PEM and T-cell number, although the underlying mechanisms(s) is/are not clear: changes in surface membrane proteins [including the putative receptor(s) for sheep red blood cells] or the presence of inhibitors, such as C-reactive protein, IgE, microbial products, and α-fetoprotein, lympholysis due to elevated levels of free cortisol, impaired maturation and differentiation of T-cell precursors, and reduction of pre-T-cells due to impaired cellular multiplication. Our recent studies with monoclonal antibodies and a cell-sorting technique have demonstrated that there is a marked numerical and functional deficiency of T4-helper cells, whereas T8 cytotoxic/suppressor cells are affected to a lesser extent. These changes in functionally distinct T-lymphocyte subpopulations are probably important. Coculture experiments show

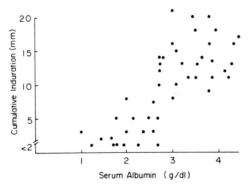

FIG. 2. Correlation between delayed hypersensitivity and serum albumin concentration. Skin tests were performed using seven different antigens, and the cumulative induration was measured as the maximum diameter of induration for each site.

that T-cell help is deficient in PEM. Lymphocyte proliferation response to mitogens may be reduced particularly when cell cultures are set up in autologous sera. Plasma of malnourished, often infected patients contains inhibitory factors and may also lack essential supporting factors for cell proliferation. It is essential to plot dose-respone curves since optimal concentrations of mitogen to produce maximum stimulation may vary for different cell preparations. Interferon synthesis is reduced, particularly in young children. The production of leukocyte migration inhibition factor is normal and that of macrophage migration inhibition factor is normal or slightly reduced. Interleukin-2 synthesis is decreased.

The concentrations of serum immunoglobulins are generally elevated or within the normal range in PEM. Antibody titers after immunization with tetanus and diphtheria toxoids, poliovirus, measles, pneumococcal polysaccharide, and keyhole-limpet hemocyanin are normal in PEM. However, some T-cell-dependent antigens may not induce antibody response to the same extent in PEM as in the healthy state. Antibody affinity is decreased. The concentrations of secretory IgA and mucosal antibody responses are decreased relative to total protein and albumin content in moderately severe PEM. Secretory IgA antibody response to live attenuated measles and poliovirus vaccines is reduced in malnourished children. Antibody was detected less frequently, the time of its first appearance was delayed, and the maximum level was significantly lower.

The impairment of the secretory immune system may have several possible consequences. It may contribute to prolonged and severe illness in which recovery depends on an adequate local antibody response. Replication and shedding of the pathogen may be prolonged, increasing the period of infectivity. Reduced mucosal immunity may also permit systemic spread, explaining in part the frequent occurrence of gram-negative septicemia in malnutrition. The complement system shows suboptimal function. In PEM, serum concentrations of almost all complement components are reduced. Children with PEM show a slight delay and reduction in the mobilization of monocytes in traumatic Rebuck skin windows and in response to bacillus Calmette-Guérin (BCG). Chemotaxis of polymorphonuclear neutrophil leukocytes may be slightly sluggish *in vitro*, but given enough time, this function becomes normal unless infection is present. There are several deficits in the postphagocytic metabolic burst of oxidative and glycolytic activity, and the intracellular killing of ingested bacteria is reduced.

IRON

The interactions of iron, immunity, and infection is a topic of intense debate and controversy. *In vitro*, iron is required by most bacteria for their growth and multiplication. This is achieved by the development of iron-chelating siderophores. Clinical data, however, do not support the concept of "iron nutritional immunity," meaning that iron deficiency protects against infection (15,16). In experiments conducted on laboratory animals, both deficiency and excess of iron result in increased

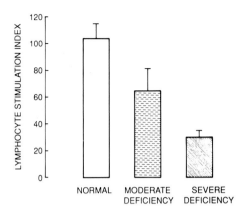

FIG. 3. Lymphocyte transformation response to phytohemagglutinin in children with isolated moderate and severe iron deficiency.

susceptibility to infection. In humans, mucocutaneous candidiasis and herpes simplex occur more frequently in iron-deficient than among iron-replete subjects. Chronic iron overload, as seen in hemochromatosis, results in death usually due to cardiac and hepatic failure, and only rarely due to pneumonia. Similarly, in thalassemia and sickle cell anemia, infections are associated with functional or surgical splenectomy and do not correlate with the degree of transferrin saturation.

Iron deficiency impairs cell-mediated immunity (Fig. 3) as well as neutrophil function. T-cell number is reduced slightly and lymphocyte response to mitogens is decreased. Intracellular killing of bacteria is decreased. In contrast, there is a minimum effect of iron deficiency on the complement system and antibody production. The cellular and molecular basis of immunologic changes in iron deficiency has been the subject of much investigation. Iron is essential for the activity of ribonucleotidyl transferase enzyme that is critical for DNA synthesis and cell proliferation. Iron-binding lactoferrin has bactericidal properties and interacts with neutrophils to kill bacteria. Myeloperoxidase depends on the presence of iron for optimum function, including bacterial killing.

ZINC

Infection is a life-threatening event in children with acrodermatitis enteropathica. Similar observations have been made in laboratory animals fed zinc-deficient diets and challenged with a variety of microorganisms such as *Salmonella, Listeria,* and coxsackie virus B. These findings and the recognized role of zinc in several important enzymes led to studies on zinc and immune responses.

Zinc deficiency produces a reversible atrophy of lymphoid tissues, such as the thymus. The changes are most pronounced in cortical areas of the thymus and the thymus-dependent areas of the spleen and lymph nodes. The observed rapid increase in thymus size in children with PEM treated with zinc may not be applicable universally, since the prevalence of zinc deficiency among malnourished individuals varies enormously from one population group to another.

The causes of lymphoid atrophy in zinc deficiency can lie in several factors. First, zinc deficiency reduces cellular multiplication and thus decreases the number of T- and B-lymphocytes being produced during the normal resting phase and during antigen stimulation. Second, zinc deficiency results in low levels of serum thymic inductive factors, and consequently, the maturation and release of thymocytes is impaired (Fig.4). Third, zinc deficiency is associated with an elevation of free-cortisol concentration, which may have a lympholytic effect. Finally, it is possible that zinc deficiency causes shifts in pools of lymphocytes in various tissue compartments and in lymphocyte traffic to various organs, as has been shown in PEM. Zinc deficiency can result in a reduced lymphocyte count. There is a significant reduction in the proportion of T4+ helper cells, with improvement in the number after zinc therapy. Low thymopoietin levels, associated with zinc deficiency, increase after zinc treatment, and there is an increase with T-lymphocyte number.

Lymphocyte stimulation response to mitogens and antigens is markedly depressed in zinc deficiency in experimental animals and man. In eight patients with acrodermatitis enteropathica and low serum zinc, the lymphocyte stimulation response to phytohemagglutinin was reduced; zinc therapy restored skin responses as well as lymphocyte proliferation (17). Delayed cutaneous hypersensitivity is impaired in zinc deficiency. Golden et al (18), in a study of 10 children with PEM, performed skin testing with *Candida* antigen on both arms of each child. One arm was treated with a local application of an ointment that contained 1% zinc sulfate, and the control arm with the same ointment base without zinc sulfate. It was reported that the arm with zinc sulfate application showed a much larger response, which was suggested to be due to local absorption of zinc and its positive effect on cell-mediated immunity. The amount of the difference between the test arm and the control arm correlated negatively with the plasma zinc concentration. A close look at the size of the reported reactions shows, however, that even on the control arm two subjects showed a reaction of about 5 mm induration, which cannot be considered negative, and another three subjects showed a reaction of about 3 to 4 mm induration, which would not be classified as "anergy." We have not been able to confirm these findings (Table 2) (13). This may be due to the lower prevalence of zinc deficiency in association with PEM observed in most parts of the world compared with

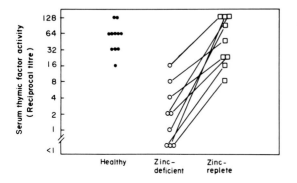

FIG. 4. Serum thymic factor activity in zinc deficiency and after treatment.

TABLE 2. *Effect of local application of zinc sulfate ointment, systemic zinc therapy, or general protein-calorie supplements on delayed cutaneous hypersensitivity response to* Candida

Treatment	Number of respondents	Size of induration (mm) (mean ± SD)
Local zinc sulfate		
Before therapy	1/20	2.0 ± 0.9
After therapy	2/20	2.5 ± 1.2
Systemic zinc therapy		
Before therapy	1/20	1.6 ± 0.7
After therapy	6/20	4.1 ± 1.6
Protein-calorie supplements		
Before therapy	5/50	1.8 ± 1.1
After therapy	29/50	5.3 ± 1.7

the Jamaican report. Björksten et al (19) also found low serum zinc levels and depressed delayed cutaneous hypersensitivity in patients with Down's syndrome. With dietary therapy there was an increase in serum zinc levels and the skin response also improved significantly. They suggested that the increased susceptibility to infection in Down's syndrome may in part be due to zinc deficiency.

Studies in children with acrodermatitis enteropathica showed that the major abnormalities in immune responses are in T-lymphocytes and neutrophil functions. There is a reduction in thymulin activity, proliferation of lymphocytes in the presence of mitogens, delayed cutaneous hypersensitivity, and neutrophil chemotaxis. All these changes are easily reversed on zinc supplementation for 6–8 weeks. Whereas clinical studies suggest that the B-cell system of antibody synthesis is not affected by zinc deficiency, experiments in laboratory animals fed moderately zinc-deficient diet indicate that the differentiation and function of B-cells may also be affected.

High concentrations of zinc inhibit neutrophils (20). Our data on the effect of increasing zinc concentration in culture medium on oxygen consumption and bactericidal activity of neutrophils are shown in Table 3 and are reported elsewhere. The depressive effect of high concentrations of zinc on phagocytosis and microbicidal

TABLE 3. *Effect of increasing zinc concentration* in vitro *on neutrophil function*

Zinc concentration (μM)	Oxygen consumption (%)	Bacterial killing (%)
2	100	97
20	64	81
40	39	73
60	27	61

TABLE 4. *Plasma zinc levels, and polymorphonuclear (PMN) leukocyte function[a]*

Time of sample	Plasma zinc (μg/dl)	Chemotactic migration[b] (PMNs per 10 HPF)[c]	Ingestion of bacteria (no./100 PMNs)	Bactericidal capacity (% viable bacteria)
Baseline	83.0 ± 9.2[d]	632 ± 101[d]	493 ± 47[d]	3.1 ± 1.1[e]
During zinc administration (weeks)				
2	101.1 ± 12.7[e]	585 ± 99[e]	386 ± 51[f]	3.9 ± 1.4[e]
4	181.5 ± 21.1[d]	355 ± 86[d]	272 ± 36[d]	4.6 ± 1.9[e]
6	199.7 ± 18.5[d]	292 ± 57[d]	251 ± 40[d]	3.8 ± 2.1[e]
Follow-up after cessation of zinc supplement (weeks)				
2	167.4 ± 20.3[d]	401 ± 71[d]	198 ± 43[d]	4.5 ± 2.3[e]
10	90.3 ± 10.0[d]	576 ± 114[d]	459 ± 56[d]	2.7 ± 1.2[e]

[a]Values are given as mean ± SE.
[b]HPF indicates high-power field.
[c]Results are shown for migration at 120 min. Similar differences were observed at 60 and 180 min.
[d]$p < 0.01$ for differences between baseline or follow-up figures and values obtained during zinc administration.
[f]$0.5 < p < 0.1$.
[e]NS, $p > 0.1$.

activity (Table 4) could be due to blocking the membrane receptor(s), changing the membrane fluidity, an effect on the cellular microskeleton, or by an antagonistic effect on Ca^{2+} transport across the membrane. In addition, changes in membrane lipoproteins may be important. The effects of increased quantities of zinc result also in decreased platelet aggregation, poor histamine release by mast cells, and diminished oxygen consumption by neutrophils in association with diminished phagocytosis and bactericidal activity. Lymphocyte stimulation response is impaired in healthy subjects given zinc supplements of 300 mg daily (Fig. 5) (20).

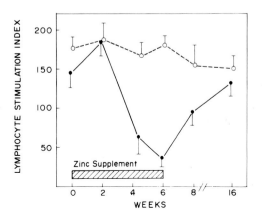

FIG. 5. Lymphocyte stimulation response to phytohemagglutinin in 11 healthy young men given 150-mg zinc supplements twice daily for 6 weeks (●) and in matched controls given a placebo (○).

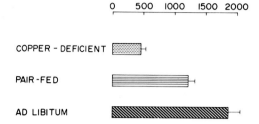

FIG. 6. Antibody-producing cells in the spleen of copper-deficient rats and pair-fed and ad libitum controls.

COPPER

Clinical deficiency of copper is extremely rare, although it may occasionally occur in association with PEM. Deficiency of copper is associated with an increased incidence of infection, as seen in patients with Menkes' kinky-hair syndrome (21). Pneumonia and other infections are a frequent cause of death in persons with this condition. Animals deficient in copper also show increased susceptibility to bacterial pathogens, such as *Salmonella* and *Listeria*, but not to the same extent for coxsackie virus infection. In laboratory animals the function of the reticuloendothelial system is depressed, and the microbicidal acitivity of granulocytes is reduced. This has been attributed to the role of copper in superoxide dismutase and cytochrome *c* oxidase enzyme systems. We have shown an impaired antibody response to heterologous red blood cells and low levels of thymic hormone activity in copper-deficient animals when compared with pair-fed controls (Fig. 6) (22). This depression of antibody response correlates with the low levels of ceruloplasmin.

SELENIUM

In human beings, there are a few nutritional circumstances associated with selenium–vitamin E deficiency. They include the following: (1) ingestion of commercial formulas high in polyunsaturated fats and low in vitamin E and selenium, especially in low-birth-weight infants: (2) in populations where the selenium content of the soil is poor (e.g., Keshan region of China and some areas of New Zealand), (3) prolonged intravenous hyperalimentation with no selenium, and (4) kwashiorkor. The role of selenium in the prevention of infectious illness in human beings is at present not clear. However, cardiomyopathy seen in Keshan disease may be due to activation of viruses in selenium-deficient immunologically incompetent host.

Most of the current data on selenium and immunity are derived from animal studies. In chicks fed a diet deficient in selenium and vitamin E, the humoral immune response was depressed. In swine, the presence of concomitant selenium and vitamin E deficiency resulted in increased severity and frequency of clinical signs and the extent of enteric lesions. Enhancement of vaccine-induced immunity against malaria in Swiss Webster mice by the addition of selenium (2.5 g/liter) in drinking water was seen. Decreased glutathione peroxidase activity of phagocytic cells of Se-deficient animals has been observed, and this was shown to be associated with decreased microbicidal activity *in vitro*.

IODINE

There are very few studies that have examined the possible role of iodine nutrition in host defense. Iodine by the interaction of iodine neutrophil peroxidases is an important bactericidal mechanism. It has been suggested that the halide-superoxide oxidative system operative *in vivo* in activated neutrophils is modulated by the amount of thyroid hormone that supplies the iodine molecule. Thus it is not surprising that in hypothyroid patients of Hashimoto's disease, the bactericidal capacity of neutrophils is decreased and is restored after treatment with thyroid hormone (23). Recent observations among endemic iodine deficiency areas reveal that both lymphocyte and neutrophil functions may be decreased, even among asymptomatic subjects with euthyroid state. There is a clear need for further work in this area.

OTHER TRACE ELEMENTS

Cobalt has been linked to antibody synthesis and phagocytic activity of neutrophils and macrophages. The presence of divalent cobalt, along with antigen-antibody complexes, induces spread of macrophages on a glass surface. Increased phagocyte uptake of albumin-coated paraffin oil particles by human neutrophils and rabbit alveolar macrophages in the presence of ionic cobalt has been reported. Deficiency of transcobalamin II, the carrier protein for vitamin B_{12}, is associated with low IgG levels. A modest increase in the intake of cadmium enhances antibody response and protects against experimental infection, whereas the effect of toxic doses is to depress the immune system and increase the susceptibility to infections. We have postulated that this may, in part, be due to the zinc-depleting effect of cadmium. Prolonged feeding of cadmium can lead to diminished formation of neutralizing antibody, decreased number of rosette-forming B-cells in the spleen and bone marrow, and reduced IgM and IgG formation by splenic lymphocytes after primary and booster inoculations with sheep red blood cells. The mitogenic response of splenic lymphocytes is decreased. Cell-mediated immunity and phagocyte function are depressed after exposure to cadmium. Arsenic has been shown to inhibit the production of interferon and antibodies. Boron deficiency in chicks results in a syndrome that resembles human arthritis. Intraperitoneal injections of boron analogs in rats and mice inhibited experimentally induced inflammatory arthritis. It also enhanced cyclic AMP activity.

CONCLUSIONS

Both deficiencies and excesses of trace elements influence various components of the immune system and thereby alter susceptibility to infection and other diseases (24–26). The extent of immunologic impairment depends on the type of nutrient involved, its interactions with other essential nutrients, severity of deficiency, presence of concomitant infection, and age of the subject. Isolated deficiencies of trace elements are rare, with the exception of iron. In general, trace element deficiencies impair immune responses and enhance the risk of serious infection.

On the other hand, the deleterious effects of excessive intake of trace elements and on immune responses should be recognized. For each trace element, there is both a lower and an upper safe limit for optimum physiological functions, and the immune system is a sensitive barometer of trace element nutriture. Thus test of immune responses, among other methods, can be used to titrate the physiological requirements of individual trace elements (14).

REFERENCES

1. Chandra RK, Newberne PM. *Nutrition, immunity and infection. Mechanisms of interactions.* New York: Plenum Press, 1977.
2. Chandra RK. *Immunology of nutritional disorders.* London: Edward Arnold, 1980.
3. Beisel WR. Single nutrients and immunity. *Am J Clin Nutr* 1982;35:417–63.
4. Keusch G, Wilson CS, Waksal SD. Nutrition, host defenses, and the lymphoid system. *Arch Host Def Mech* 1983;2:275–359.
5. McMurray DN. Cell-mediated immunity in nutritional deficiency. *Prog Food Nutr Sci* 1984; 8:193–228.
6. Chandra RK, ed. *Nutrition and immunology.* New York: Alan Liss, 1988.
7. Bendich A. Antioxidant vitamins and immune responses. In: Chandra RK, ed. *Nutrition and immunology.* New York: Alan Liss, 1988:125–48.
8. Watson RR, ed. *Nutrition, disease resistance and immune function.* New York: Marcel Dekker, 1984.
9. Gershwin ME, Beach RS, Hurley LS. *Nutrition and immunity.* New York: Academic Press, 1984.
10. Bendich A, Chandra RK, eds. *Micronutrient effects on immune functions.* New York: New York Academy of Sciences, 1990.
11. Chandra RK. Numerical and functional deficiency in T-helper cells in protein energy malnutrition. *Clin Exp Immunol* 1983;51:126–32.
12. Chandra RK, ed. *Primary and secondary immunodeficiency disorders.* Edinburgh: Churchill Livingstone, 1983.
13. Chandra RK, Puri S. Trace element modulation of immune responses and susceptibility to infection. In: Chandra RK, ed. *Trace elements in the nutrition of children.* New York: Raven Press, 1985;87–101.
14. Chandra RK. Micronutrients and immune functions: an overview. *Ann NY Acad Sci* 1990; 156:9–16.
15. Vyas D, Chandra RK. Functional implications of iron deficiency. In: Stekel A, ed. *Iron nutrition in infancy and childhood.* New York: Raven Press, 1984:45–59.
16. Hershko C, Peto TEA, Weatherall DJ. Iron and infection. *Br Med J* 1988;296:660–4.
17. Chandra RK. Acrodermatitis enteropathica; zinc levels and cell-mediated immunity. *Pediatrics* 1980;66:789–91.
18. Golden MHN, Golden BE, Harland PSEG, Jackson AA. Zinc and immunocompetence in protein-energy malnutrition. *Lancet* 1978;i:1226–8.
19. Björksten B, Back O, Gustavavson KH, et al. Zinc and immune function in Dowen's syndrome. *Acta Paediatr Scand* 1980;69:183–7.

20. Chandra RK. Excessive intake of zinc impairs immune responses. *JAMA* 1984;252:1443–6.
21. Pedroim F, Bianclin F, Vgazio AL, Burgio GR. Immunodeficiency and steely hair. *Lancet* 1975;i:1303.
22. Vyas D, Chandra RK. Thymic factor activity lymphocyte stimulation response and antibody-forming cells in copper deficiency. *Nutr Res* 1983;3:343–50.
23. Farid NR, AU B, Woodford G, Chandra RK. PMN function in hypothyroidism. *Hormone Res* 1976;8:247–53.
24. Chandra RK. Nutrition, immunity and infection. Present knowledge and future directions. *Lancet* 1983;i:688–91.
25. Chandra RK. Nutrition immunity and infection. Basic considerations and practical significance. *Nutrition* 1989;5:297–302.
26. Chandra RK. Nutritional regulation of immunity and risk of infection in old age. *Immunology* 1989;67:141–7.

DISCUSSION

Dr. Zlotkin: In your experiments you appear to have primarily investigated extremes (i.e., extreme deficiency versus extreme excess). Could you make a comment about the effect on immune responses of marginal status of some of the trace metals?

Dr. Chandra: There are data to suggest that marginal deficiencies impair selected aspects of immunity. For example, rodents fed various levels of zinc begin to show changes in immune responses without any clinical signs of zinc deficiency or change in growth pattern. In general, mitogen responses, thymic hormone activity, interleukin-2 production, and NK cell activity are particularly sensitive to zinc status. In humans, serum thymulin activity is a sensitive and specific parameter of zinc intake. However, there are no nutrient-specific tests for other trace elements.

Dr. R. Bergmann: Do you know of any study on the role of trace elements in allergic disease?

Dr. Chandra: I know of no studies that have looked specifically at this question and come up with good data. However, trace elements and fatty acids have important metabolic relationships, and in at least two types of skin disorders, atopic eczema and psoriasis, it has been claimed that a beneficial effect results from a change in the fatty acid intake. It is possible that this could be mediated by some effect of trace elements acting through fatty acid metabolism. Secondly, changes in immunoregulatory T lymphocytes in trace element deficiency may lead to altered IgE production.

Dr. Chapparwal: What is the effect of immunization procedures in infants who have protein-energy malnutrition and trace element deficiency?

Dr. Chandra: In infants with severe malnutrition it may be advisable to delay immunization with live vaccines. In all other cases immunization is to be recommended. Even though the antibody responses may be suboptimal, at least some protective effect is achieved. The degree of protection depends on the type of vaccine. For example, malnutrition has little effect on the efficacy of tetanus immunization because tetanus toxoid is a very strong immunizing agent. This is particularly true after booster doses. On the other hand, response to BCG vaccine is compromised by malnutrition, and this may have been one reason for the failure of the multimillion-dollar trial of BCG vaccination in south India.

Dr. Gabr: From our own experience TAB vaccination is not affected by malnutrition, and antibody response to polio-3 is poor only in the most severely malnourished cases.

Dr. Chapparwal: We still have a high rate of infant mortality in India, and respiratory infections account for a large proportion of this. Is this due to compromised immune function?

Dr. Chandra: Environmental conditions play a very important role. Certain nutrients play an important part in specific mucosal immunity, as also in the bacterial binding to epithelial cells. We recently published data (1) to show that moderate vitamin A deficiency in children was associated with a twofold increase in the number of bacteria that bound to nasopharyngeal mucosal cells. Among infants who developed respiratory syncytial virus infection, those with the highest morbidity tended to have the lowest serum retinol levels, although serum values were all within the normal range.

Dr. Aggett: Could you comment on the possibility that Keshan disease or cardiomyopathy of selenium deficiency is related to the incidence of intercurrent infection, especially viral infections?

Dr. Chandra: Serum samples obtained from Chinese patients with Keshan disease, who are either selenium deficient or who have excess selenium, often show evidence of recent viral infection. Second, it is possible to produce in mice a syndrome that looks like the cardiomyopathy of Keshan disease by a combination of selenium deficiency and coxsackie virus B3 infection, whereas on their own these agents produce very little damage.

Dr. Lombeck: Chinese peasants live under special conditions in remote areas. The soil is leached out; water supply is local. No one knows if there are toxins, parasites, bacteria, or other agents in the water. It is common to fertilize crops with human feces. Nutrition is very different from ours, with 10% of energy from fat and 70–80% from carbohydrates. Because of the hard work, energy intakes are high in some areas, perhaps as high as 4000 kcal/day. In many regions the fat intake is mainly from rape seed oil with a very high erucic acid content of 40–50%. It remains to be determined whether this very high erucic acid intake can cause cardiac lipidosis or whether it may lead, in combination with reduced glutathione peroxidase activity, to an irreversible change in the myocardium. In hospitals in different parts of China I have seen many children with cardiac diseases of unknown origin.

Dr. Ament: I question whether selenium deficiency is the only factor in Keshan disease. We have done cardiac evaluation in adults and children with selenium deficiency and have not found abnormalities. We think there must be some other factor operative in addition to selenium deficiency.

REFERENCE

1. Chandra RK. Increased bacterial binding to respiratory epithelial cells in vitamin A deficiency. *Brit Med J* 1988;297:834–5.

Trace Elements in Nutrition of Children—II,
edited by Ranjit K. Chandra, Nestlé Nutrition
Workshop Series, Vol. 23, Nestec Ltd.,
Vevey/Raven Press, Ltd., New York © 1991.

Assessment of Trace Element Status: General Considerations

Dr. Chandra: For the last part of our workshop, we shall discuss a very important and certainly a very practical area in nutrition, i.e., the assessment of trace element status. We have talked about deficiencies and excesses and requirements, but when the question arises of how you define "deficiency," and what are the ways in which we can think of requirements from a physiological basis, we are stuck. There are many varied opinions, only some of which are based on actual information; all of us have theories and conjectures. From my own point of view as a clinician and investigator in this field, it is crucial to have some discussion and perhaps a consensus on what we believe to be the methods by which we can assess trace element status reliably. Obviously we have better information for some trace elements than for others, and for some age groups than for others.

Dr. Lönnerdal: I have fairly limited experience with using *animal models to assess trace element status.* I think that we should always have a sound skepticism when using animal models. We can use them as long as we make sure that they really show what we are looking at. Let me elaborate a little on that. Animal models can give important suggestions for directions to look at things, just as Dr. Anke showed us in experimental animals, because we have a situation in which we can virtually eliminate one trace element and we can add excesses in a way that we could never do in the human situation. We have rare human models, such as acrodermatitis enteropathica. There is also the possibility that human genetic mutants may help us in assessing trace element status. But it is difficult even in that situation to address some of the issues that we can in the animal model. How do we know that we do not have a marginal zinc deficiency, a marginal copper deficiency, and so on? It is very difficult. So I think the animal models can allow us to produce a clear-cut situation, in which we can really assess the effects on particular enzymes, on particular immune functions, etc., and then we can follow it up in the human situation.

I have had some experience assessing bioavailability. In one experiment we wanted to assess the bioavailability of zinc in four different infant diets: human milk, cow's milk formula, whole cow's milk, and soy formula. In adult rats there were some differences in the uptake of zinc from the different diets. Zinc bioavailability from soy formula was lower than from human milk, but there was not a large difference, around 4% to 8%, and it is difficult to assess small differences. We also tried the zinc-deficient adult rat, since that concept has been used in, for example, iron bioavailability studies in iron-deficient rats (i.e., the hemoglobin repletion assay). This approach can sometimes be more sensitive, but we did not find a very good correlation between data points, and we think that there are many other problems with the zinc-deficient adult rats. We also tried weanling rats which have been used earlier, and we found some differences in zinc bioavailability. Then we used infant suckling rats, and we have been using them subsequently. In the suckling rats there were significant differences between the diets. My personal opinion is that once the rat has been weaned and goes on a solid diet it develops a very efficient machinery for utilizing nutrients from all kinds of diets. That is one aspect.

The other aspect is that animals are usually on a very crude diet as compared to humans. For this reason I do not think that the adult rat is a good model for looking at zinc absorption. In the suckling rat pup, however, we have documented that what we are looking at is very similar to what we would see in the human. The results of zinc absorption from identical diets in the suckling rat pups are very similar to those in infant monkeys. So when we go to higher primates we have similar results to those from rodents. We also see the same differences in human adults as we do in infant rhesus monkeys, but the differences are more pronounced in the infant animals. So I think that as we can show this we can rest assured that we will have some applicability of our data to humans. This applies to zinc, but it has to be confirmed for each element; for manganese I think we have a similar situation, but for iron the rodent is not a good model. It does not handle ferric iron and ferrous iron in the same way, and it has a quite different iron requirement on a body-weight basis. So, if we take some precautions I think animal models can give us indications, and in some cases even strong support, for what we subsequently can follow-up in human infants and children.

Dr. Chandra: Did you have any measures of zinc adequacy in terms of function?

Dr. Lönnerdal: Not in our bioavailability studies. This has been done, though, in the rhesus monkey studies in which a marginal zinc deficiency was induced. A lot of functional measures were made in those studies, but my particular interest has been in the bioavailability aspects and in membrane transport of trace elements. However, they looked at immune function as correlated to tissue stores of zinc, etc.

Dr. Lombeck: As a comparison for the results in patients with acrodermatitis enteropathica, we investigated the zinc absorption of adults in the fasting state. The absorption rate amounted to between 58% and 77%. In your data there was a difference between the mean values of the monkeys (60%) and that of the humans (30%).

Dr. Lönnerdal: The infant monkeys received the incubated dose after 4 hours of fasting, by which time the stomach is virtually clean. The human subjects were fasted overnight. In all cases we gave a fairly large dose of the liquid diet, not a trace dose, that is, we gave reasonable meals. To the human adults we gave about 400 ml of diet with the isotope, and to the infant monkeys we gave about 20 ml of diet.

Dr. Hambidge: During the course of this meeting, there have already been numerous references to the *limitations of sample analyses in the assessment of human trace element status*. This is of special concern in the human, for whom access to sample materials is severely restricted. However, it has become abundantly clear, for example, in the case of zinc, that this approach can be severely limited in value even when there is no restriction on the availability of tissue samples.

Table 1 provides a very simplistic and incomplete overview of relatively available samples that have been analyzed in order to try to assess human trace element status. It will be noted that several of the trace elements that are considered to be essential micronutrients for humans are not included in Table 1. In my opinion, there is no reliable information at this time to indicate that we can achieve an assessment of nutritional status with respect to these elements by analyses of any of the samples included in Table 1. For example, though unusually low plasma concentrations of manganese have been reported in association with certain diseases, it is unclear whether this finding signifies some degree of manganese deficiency.

Plasma or serum concentration can provide useful information on nutritional status with respect to iron, copper, and selenium, and also for more severe degrees of zinc deficiency. It is not, however, the most useful index of either iron or selenium status. Whole blood analyses can be equally useful for selenium and perhaps for copper, but not for zinc. Separation of erythrocytes does not, in general, provide any advantage over whole blood and plasma analyses. Considerable attention has been accorded to neutrophils, monocytes, mixed leukocytes and/or platelets in the assessment of zinc nutrition. However, the value of any of these cell types in the assessment of zinc status is far from universally accepted. Moreover, the separation procedures are too cumbersome to allow use of this approach for population survey studies. Urine excretion of zinc is affected by recent dietary zinc intake, but there is little to suggest that urine zinc excretion rates will provide a reasonably sensitive index of zinc nutritional status. This sample has proved useful, however, in field studies of iodine status.

My early experience with hair analyses in the assessment of zinc status left me with very little doubt that in some circumstances hair zinc concentrations did reflect zinc nutritional status. Moreover, it appeared that hair zinc could be depressed with even mild zinc deficiency states. However, I also learned to appreciate the difficulties associated with the interpretation of hair zinc data. It has, therefore, been with considerable interest that I have noted Rosalind Gibson's more recent and apparently quite effective use of hair analyses in studies pertaining to zinc nutritional status. It was by analyses of hair for zinc that she recently identified a subgroup of school-aged children who responded to zinc supplementation with a significant in-

TABLE 1. *Assessment of trace element status in humans*

	Iron	Zinc	Copper	Selenium	Iodide
Plasma	+ +	±	+	+ +	±
Whole blood	−	−	+	+	−
Erythrocytes	−	−	−	+	−
Leukocytes	−	±	−	−	−
Platelets	−	±	−	−	−
Urine	−	±	−	−	+
Hair	−	±	−	−	−

crease in growth velocity (1). Without use of hair analyses she would not have identified this subgroup. It seems that, whatever the magnitude of the difficulties in interpretation of data, we cannot totally ignore the potential value or use of hair analysis in selected circumstances in the assessment of zinc status.

Despite many limitations, measurement of the concentration of zinc in plasma or serum is still more useful than the measurement of zinc in any other readily available samples. It is, however, pertinent and important to illustrate some of the difficulties associated with the interpretation of plasma zinc data.

In our recently reported study of the effects of zinc supplementation on growth of infants and toddlers with inorganic failure to thrive, the 6 months of supplementation with zinc did not lead to any detectable change in plasma zinc concentrations compared with the placebo-treated group (2). Initially these levels were within the normal range, supporting the concept that plasma zinc is not sufficiently sensitive to changes in zinc status to be useful in the detection of mild zinc-deficiency states. The mean concentrations for both the zinc-supplemented and the placebo-treated children were, however, quite low with respect to our normal mean. This can be explained by the fact that it was impossible to standardize collections to a pre-breakfast time. There are substantial variations in normal plasma zinc concentrations across a 24-hour period. It has become increasingly clear that these changes are related primarily to meals, with an average decline of approximately 15% in plasma zinc following the first meal of the day, and a cumulative decline over the daytime hours, given a typical meal pattern which is considerably greater than that (3). When on sabbatical leave in my program, Professor Janet King undertook a study in which normal volunteers were fed isocaloric meals at precisely 6-hr intervals across the 24-hr period (King and Hambidge, unpublished data). The preliminary interpretation of the data derived from this study indicates that all of the changes across a 24-hr period can be attributed to changes in metabolism related to the consumption of food.

We need to be aware that standardization of sample-collection time to a specific hour of the day prior to breakfast does not entirely obviate the variation associated with meals. In another recent study (4), we found that the pre-breakfast 0700-hr plasma zinc concentration depended to a significant extent on both the size and the time of the last meal or meals taken the previous evening.

Another cause of variation in results for plasma or serum zinc determinations is the duration for which samples are left after collection and before separation of serum or plasma (5). There is a linear increase in plasma zinc concentration across this time interval so that values obtained on the same sample that is left for 2 hours is 6% higher than the value obtained when separation is performed after 10 minutes. The findings in this study indicated that at least 80% of reported differences between serum and plasma concentrations of zinc can be attributed to the fact that for serum samples clot retraction is allowed to occur for an hour or two prior to separation. Incidentally, this change in concentration prior to separation is specific for zinc. We have not seen a similar phenomenon for major minerals or for copper. This suggests that there is a component of the zinc present in the erythrocyte membrane or within the red cell which is released very freely into the circulation after collection.

It is not only the *in vitro* changes that are specific for zinc. The decline in plasma zinc following a meal is not mimicked by any other element that has been investigated. The magnitude of the decline is similar to that observed for phosphorus but the decline in the latter occurs much sooner than does the net efflux of zinc from the plasma compartment (King and Hambidge, unpublished data). We are interested in determining the destination of the zinc involved in this net efflux from the plasma compartment, which may well provide important insight into the role of zinc in intermediary metabolism. Thus, though these investigations have emphasized the problems associated with using zinc concentrations in the circulation to assess zinc nutritional status, they may have provided interesting data that may help to provide new insight into the biological role and the metabolism of this micronutrient.

Dr. Chandra: On the basis of what you have presented and of your published experience, plasma levels of zinc remain a practical method to assess deficiency, given all the problems in terms of collection, storage, estimation, effects of recent meal, and of age, and various physiological states such as pregnancy.

Dr. Hambidge: We could add to these limitations others, such as circulating hormone levels. There are a lot of factors that make the interpretation of circulating zinc levels extremely complex. Most plasma concentrations of zinc are not useful for the marginal zinc-deficiency state which is the one with which we want to identify.

Dr. Dorner: Can you comment on the different zinc loading tests for the assessment of zinc status? Are they reliable?

Dr. Hambidge: I have not considered zinc loading tests as a useful way of assessing zinc status. To my knowledge such tests have been used primarily as a semiquantitative way of measuring zinc absorption. Zinc absorption may reflect differences in zinc status, but even with quantitative measurements, this is not a means of assessing status.

Dr. Bergmann: We have measured serum zinc concentration in about 60 healthy children of diabetic parents during a glucose tolerance test. It may be of interest that it drops after a glucose load. Perhaps the carbohydrates taken at breakfast produced this effect in your example.

Dr. Lahrech: What is your opinion about zinc concentration in nails? Is it easy to perform, and is it significant?

Dr. Hambidge: I think the nails probably have the same kind of limitations as hair, and maybe a few more limitations as well. It is certainly difficult to be sure the sample is clean.

Dr. Anke: We measured the capacity to reflect zinc status in different kinds of animals and in different tissues of these animals, and we found that it is most difficult to estimate well zinc status in animals by using the tissues.

Dr. Hambidge: This applies in particular to skeletal muscle which accounts for about 60% of total body zinc. The zinc concentration in muscle did not change with zinc deficiency. I would like to ask whether Dr. Chandra has seen any changes in zinc concentration or change in the concentration of any other trace element in the immune system with changes in dietary intake.

Dr. Chandra: We have looked at granulocytes as have other people; alterations in lymphocyte zinc levels precede those in neutrophils. I feel this has only a marginal benefit over serum values.

Dr. Lombeck: Hair zinc values are not always easy to interpret. Besides the well described age dependency we found in an epidemiological study of 474 kindergarten children from North Rhine-Westphalia, that the children with frequent upper respiratory tract infections (more than six infections/year) showed significantly lower zinc values than those with fewer infections. It is far from clear whether the zinc content is low because the children suffer from many infections or whether they suffer from frequent infections because of low zinc status. Concerning hair selenium: selenium intoxication clearly shows up in hair like arsenic intoxication. Also in endemic areas with low selenium intake hair selenium values are low. At the moment it is not clear if hair selenium reflects also moderate low or moderate high selenium states.

Dr. Hambidge: I did not include hair analysis for selenium in the table because it does not appear to offer any advantage over whole blood and plasma selenium and glutathion peroxidase activity.

Dr. Chandra: Your observations on low hair zinc and increased incidence of infections are interesting. I want to emphasize that morbidity data should be collected every two weeks otherwise their validity is extremely limited.

Dr. Bergmann: We tried to find out whether there was any relationship between zinc in hair and growth rate. If we took all of the values that were available after standardizing for age and gender we did not find any significant correlation. However, if we only took the values below 70 ppm in hair, then after standardizing for age and gender, we found a significant positive correlation between hair zinc and growth rate. And it was an indicator of growth of lean body mass that correlated closest with hair zinc concentration and its changes below 70 ppm, the value that was utilized by Dr. Hambidge in 1972 as the cut-off point for zinc deficiency.

Dr. Ament: I would like to comment about selenium in the hair. The hair selenium content correlates very well with the plasma levels. In a study that was presented this morning we were able to show sequential changes in the plasma and in the hair, over a period of time, the hair and plasma levels correlated closely.

Dr. Mertz: I would like to mention the subject of speciation with regard to the tissues under investigation. It is possible that when you measure a 20% decline in the total tissue, it is really a 100% decline of a small, special fraction of the tissue. Many people have tried to fractionate trace elements in serum by ultrafiltration and other methods, but not much was gained by these efforts. I wonder whether new attempts of speciation with our modern methods and increased knowledge might not be a way to improve our diagnostic capability.

Dr. Hambidge: I think that it is a good point and it may well be true. I would also mention, however, the kind of test that we all need today is one that we can use very easily for population surveys. And for this purpose it has to be kept as simple as possible.

Dr. Oster: I want to make a comment on the determination of zinc in plasma from the analytical point. In plasma, zinc concentrations are always higher than in serum.

This is true at least for Germany. The sample containers for plasma measurements contain zinc as a contaminant together with the anticoagulant. If you measure the zinc in serum the contamination problem is much easier to control.

Dr. Zlotkin: My comments will be by definition quite general because I think one could spend an entire symposium talking about *functional measures of trace mineral status.* I think it is an extremely important subject, for reasons that are apparent to everyone here. We might start by asking the question: does the measurement of trace minerals in urine and serum in some way reflect stores in the body? So often our assumption is that concentrations of trace minerals in urine, serum, or hair are somehow a reflection of the functionally active pool for that mineral. I will discuss major problems in the interpretation of this type of data.

I would like to discuss the role of trace minerals as co-factors in initiating and maintaining enzyme activity. In theory, enzyme activity will be adversely affected if stores are depleted and levels in body pools are also depleted. That is the theory. In practice, however, for most of the trace minerals in humans, either we do not have enough information on the effect of trace minerals on specific enzymes, or we have not found the right enzyme to measure. That is not always the case. Glutathione peroxidase is an example of a good correlation between a serum concentration of a trace mineral and a specific enzyme activity. There is an excellent correlation in humans between plasma selenium concentrations and glutathione peroxidase activity. There are perhaps one or two other examples that I shall discuss in a moment, but unfortunately for the majority of the trace mineral-dependent enzymes the correlation between concentration and activity is poor.

The other problem I should mention is that what is true in an animal model is not necessarily true in a human situation. For example, zinc is known to be a co-factor for a large number of enzymes. In various animal models one can demonstrate a functional deficit (i.e., decreased enzyme activity) in a situation where there is also a deficit both in the storage of zinc and in the plasma concentration of zinc. Let me give another example to show that one cannot simply extrapolate from animal experiments to humans. Two species, rats and guinea pigs, were put on zinc-deficient diets. The plasma levels of zinc in the guinea pigs, 6.3 versus 17.9, and the rats, 4.7 versus 18.4, were significantly lower in the animals receiving the zinc-deficient diet. Angiotensin 2, an angiotensin-converting enzyme, is zinc-dependent in both species. Although there was no difference in the plasma levels of angiotensin 2, there was a significant decrease in the activity of the enzyme in the zinc-deficient animals. So here, in two animal species, one can demonstrate the effect of a deficiency on enzyme function. In a human study, Dr. R. Gibson of Guelph, Ontario, Canada, induced marginal zinc deficiency in volunteers by depleting the diet of zinc. She measured serum zinc in the population and described a significant difference between the depletion and repletion periods. Of particular importance was the finding that angiotensin-converting enzyme was unaffected. Thus, although this was a good marker of zinc deficiency in guinea pigs and rats, marginal zinc deficiency in the human was not reflected in angiotensin activity.

Alkaline phosphatase is another zinc-dependent enzyme. In a study of patients who were acutely zinc-deficient, there was a very good correlation between serum zinc and serum alkaline phosphatase. However, there are also examples in the literature of populations with normal serum zinc levels and decreased alkaline phosphatase activity. The overall picture is confusing. Some published data suggest that there is a correlation, but there are several papers that suggest there is no correlation.

I would like to discuss copper and the use of superoxide dismutase as an indication of copper status. In a study that examined a malnourished population in South America, there was a significant change in the plasma copper concentration before and after refeeding. There was also a significant change in ceruloplasmin and in superoxide dismutase. This and other studies in humans have shown that superoxide dismutase is a relatively good functional indicator of copper status. This relationship has also been demonstrated in various animal models of copper deficiency. There is a significant positive relationship between plasma copper and superoxide dismutase activity. This relationship is one of the only reproducible examples of a measurable functional effect of a marginal trace mineral deficiency.

Dr. Chandra: In the case of adult male, serum testosterone levels and thymulin activity may indicate a marginal zinc deficiency.

Dr. Zlotkin: This was not meant to be a comprehensive review of all the trace mineral dependent enzymes that have been suggested as potential markers of trace mineral status. My sense is that at this time no one would feel confident in presenting a manuscript that would simply show enzyme activity without showing other parameters of trace mineral status. I think the day will come when there will be a functional measure which one can present without having to present simultaneously serum zinc, urine zinc, neutrophile zinc or 10 other measures. But that day has not arrived.

Dr. Aggett: I think that there is a need to try to define or understand what we are trying to achieve in determining ''trace element status.'' This is one of those convenient shorthand terms which is sometimes used a little uncritically. In the context of most usage, people are trying to consider whether or not the individual population under study is suffering from a deficient or excessive supply of an element, or, whether or not they are at risk of developing a deficiency or toxicity syndrome. There any many compositional and functional assays which will provide information suggestive of deficient or toxic exposure. Nonetheless, as has been discussed elsewhere, we know that some static compositional assays such as plasma zinc and copper concentrations, are subject to a variety of other pathophysiological influences which render their interpretation difficult.

I would like to raise the posssibility that with an improved understanding of the systemic metabolism of trace elements and of the homeostatic responses to adequate and inadequate supplies, it may be possible to monitor these processes and to use the information to assess ''status.''

It is becoming increasingly evident that we need to be concerned with measuring ''status'' at the marginal area between adequate intakes and the inadequate or excessive intakes of the elements.

I would like to illustrate this point by reference to the schematic representation of the spectrum of trace element status shown in Table 2. Essentially this derives from the outline described by Dr. Mertz in this workshop. At the gross extremes of this spectrum it can be seen that the clinical features of toxicity and excess have a similar extreme outcome, namely death. Within these extremes there are phases where subjects will show the features of deficiency or excess, often these are non-specific, but if the observer is aware of the possibility that elemental excess or deficiency is involved in the pathogenesis of these features, then the diagnosis can be made. At these ends of the spectrum systemic homeostasis of the elements has been unable to conserve or acquire sufficiently to avoid deficiency or excrete and suitably sequestrate sufficiently to avoid toxicity, and it is probable that compositional and functional assays of the nutrient will be abnormal.

Moving more towards the center of this spectrum one comes to a stage where it is envisaged that there are no obvious clinical features. Indeed, there may be no abnormalities of compositional assays but there may in fact be functional abnormalities which in turn indicate disturbed metabolism of the nutrient itself and of other nutrients. All of these aforementioned abnormalities develop when systemic homeostasis of the element has been overwhelmed.

Our current approaches to assessing trace element status fall within these extremes of the spectrum which I have outlined. Steadily, as more insight is gained into the function of elements, more sensitive functional assays of nutritional status are becoming available. Thus, for example, superoxide dismutase activity in certain tissues such as erythrocytes is more sensitive than circulating plasma copper or ceruloplasmin concentrations are in detecting a possible deficiency of copper, though of course its value is limited by the long half-life of erythrocytes. In due course it may well transpire that cytochrome C oxidase activity may be more sensitive than measuring that of superoxide dismutase, and that it can be measured in a compartment with a short turnover time (e.g., platelets). However, though these approaches are generating for many elements more sensitive indicators of deficiency, the point remains that once such abnormalities are present, it is quite apparent that deficiency has developed.

TABLE 2. *A spectrum of trace element status*

Death	
Inadequate homeostasis	Toxicity; abnormal clearance/compartmentation; disease
Compensatory homeostasis	Homeostasis adequate; normal clearance and/or compartmentation
Excess	Stores full
Adequacy	Good health
Deficiency	Stores depleted
Compensatory homeostasis	Vital function(s) protected
Inadequate homeostasis	Functional defects; metabolism of other nutrients disrupted; disease
Death	

When one is assessing excessive exposure to elements it may well be that determining their content in key tissues would be a more sensitive indicator of overexposure than they are of impending deficiency. It may well be that there is a greater tolerance for marginally high exposure than there is for inadequate intakes. Clearly, if one is trying to assess "marginal status," then the ideal methods have yet to be developed. For none of the essential trace elements has the vital pool of the element that is most sensitive to inadequate and/or excessive supply been identified. Furthermore, the identity of this pool may differ between deficiency and toxicity states. Nonetheless, although these metabolic compartments have not been characterized, and we cannot measure them, we may be able to measure the systemic adaptations which these compartments initiate when exposed to excessive or inadequate supplies of the relevant elements. I therefore would like to suggest that one of the important strategies in the development of assessing trace element "status" is to be able *to characterize more effectively the systemic adaptations of metabolism.* Essentially this means being able to determine the gastrointestinal uptake and transfer of elements, renal excretion and conservation, hepatobilliary excretion, sequestration in tissues, and so on, and simultaneously trying to identify and determine any mediators or regulators of these responses which can be assayed as indicants of metabolic adaptation, and thus by implication status.

The usefulness of such approaches are now becoming apparent in the studies of the metabolism of sodium and of calcium. As with trace metals, compositional assays have been of relatively little value in detecting marginal "status" for either of these elements. However, the measurement of atrial natriuretic peptide, aldosterone, vasopressin, etc., are providing valuable ways of detecting systemic reaction to sodium overload or deficiency, and the concomitant changes in water balance; and, it is apparent that assays of parathormone, osteocalcin, calcitonin, and calcitriol can be used in similar circumstances for monitoring of the adequacy or otherwise of calcium supply and of systemic efforts to maintain the plasma-ionized calcium concentrations. Similarly, the use of isotopic labels of calcium has enabled the exploration of calcium metabolism by determination of elemental fluxes through the compartments.

We deduce from changes in plasma and urinary zinc concentrations and copper concentrations in catabolic, anabolic, and stress states, that these states change the flow of these elements in and out of tissues and the circulation. The flux of zinc has been studied in human volunteers on normal and high intakes (6), and Chesters' use of such flux studies to investigate in pigs the hypozincemia associated with zinc deficiency or with endotoxin stress has shown clear differences in the two metabolic states (7). This study used albumin labelled with zinc, but he pointed out that the speciation of zinc used in such studies of flux may be important because one cannot presume that all bound forms of the element are similarly sensitive to the risk of deficiency or excess.

Some specific proteins have been identified which appear to be specifically involved in the metabolism of trace elements. Such proteins include those involved in transport processes and those involved in the sequestration, either for storage or "detoxification" of the elements. The latter appear to be the more useful as is exemplified by the use of ferritin in assessments of iron status. Measuring plasma ferritin concentrations as a circulating index of the reticulo-endothelial stores of iron is an established practice, but even so, many have become cautious about interpreting single plasma ferritin concentrations without reference to the patient's pathophysiological condition and other indicators of iron metabolism.

A similar situation is now developing for the use of metallothionein in the interpretation or assessment of zinc metabolism. In rat models, Bremner and colleagues demonstrated that metallothionein was not synthesized in zinc deficiency (8). It was shown that metallothionein induction was increased with increasingly adequate zinc supply, and that plasma concentrations of metallothionein corresponded to those in the liver. When it was apparent that metallothionein concentrations increased with stress but were reduced with true zinc deficiency, a means became available of using this mediator of zinc homeostasis as an indicator of zinc status, in as much as the hypozincemia of zinc deficiency was found to be associated with low plasma metallothionein levels in zinc-deficient rats, whereas the hypozincemia of stress was associated with elevated metallothionein levels. However, technical difficulties have limited the extension of this work to humans, and disappointingly further experience of Bremner's group with animal models has shown that with more marginal states of zinc deprivation and other nutritional perturbations, the interpretation of these values are less reliable. However, such setbacks should not deter us from trying to elucidate better the regulatory and mediatory mechanisms of systemic homeostasis of elements: such information is essential both for determining status and for assessing nutritional requirements more accurately.

Dr. Brätter: At this workshop I learned new facts concerning trace elements, and I also noticed some gaps in knowledge. I think that progress in trace element metabolism research depends essentially on further progress in analytical chemistry.

Dr. Mertz: The National Bureau of Standards in Washington has now issued the total diet standard reference material for trace elements that everybody can use for dietary studies. And they will also issue very soon a reference serum which will be certified for normal levels of several trace elements.

Dr. Chandra: Can you tell us if the use of a chelating agent and estimation of urinary copper excretion is of any value for evaluating copper status?

Dr. Aggett: I have no direct experience except for the diagnostic method used in copper overload with Wilson's disease.

Dr. Lombeck: We observed fatal copper intoxication in some German infants who were bottle fed. Water with a pH below 6.5 was transported through copper pipes into households leading to a high copper content of the "drinking" water (up to 3–10 mg/liter). The clinical picture was compatible with liver disease: hyperbilirubinemia, increased transaminases, and finally cirrhosis and liver failure. Copper values in the plasma were usually normal, whereas urinary copper excretion can be increased. In those children who were diagnosed early enough and where water supply was changed, transaminases decreased within days and the children recovered.

Dr. Gabr: I am worried about deficiency as well as about toxicity. For example, the wide use of oral rehydration solutions which are now produced locally in every developing country. A malnourished child with diarrhea might receive a large amount of salt which may contain toxic contaminants, including heavy metals.

REFERENCES

1. Gibson RS, Vanderkooy PDS, MacDonald AC, Goldman A, Ryan BA, Berry M. A growth limiting mild zinc deficiency syndrome in some Southern Ontario boys with low height percentiles. *Am J Clin Nutr* 1989;49:1266–73.
2. Walravens PA, Hambidge KM, Koepfer DM. Zinc supplementation in infants with a nutritional pattern of failure to thrive: a double-blind controlled study. *Pediatrics* 1989;83:532–8.
3. Hambidge KM, Goodall M, Stall C, Pritts J. Postprandial and daily changes in plasma zinc. *J Trace Elem Electrolytes Health Dis* 1989;3:55–7.
4. English JL, Hambidge KM, King JC, Kern DL, Pritts JL, Stall CD. The effect of evening meals on pre-breakfast plasma zinc concentrations (abstract). *Fed Proc* 1988;2:A635.
5. English JL, Hambidge KM. Plasma and serum zinc concentrations: Effect of time between collection and separation. *Clin Chim Acta* 1988;175:211–6.
6. Babcock AK, Henkin RI, Aomodt RL, Foster DM, Berman M. Effects of oral zinc loading on zinc metabolism in humans II: In vivo kinetics. *Metabolism* 1982;31:335–47.
7. Chesters JK, Will M. Measurement of zinc flux through plasma in normal and endotoxin-stressed pigs and the effects of zinc supplementation during stress. *Br J Nutr* 1981;46:111–8.
8. Bremner I, Mehra RK, Sato M. Metallothionein. In: Kagi JHR, Kojina Y (eds). *Proceedings of the 2nd International Meeting on Metallothionein and the Low Molecular Weight Metal Binding Proteins.* Basel: Birkhauser Verlag; 507–18.

Subject Index

A

Absolute requirement
    dietary requirement distinction, 11
    general considerations, 1–2
    and supplementation trials, 2
Absorption efficiency, 3, 11
Acrodermatitis enteropathica
    immunocompetence, 206–208
    in pregnancy, 30
    and protein-energy malnutrition, 176
Adaptations of metabolism, 47–48, 70,
        159, 224
Albumin, 179
Alkaline phosphatase, 64, 221–222
Allergic disease, 213
Aluminum
    blood level monitoring, 24–25
    bone disease, 17–18
    metabolism, 15–16
    sources of, 19–22
    tissue levels, 16
    toxicity, 15–23
Aluminum-containing phosphate binders,
        15
Aluminum cookware, 19–20
Amino acids, 60–61
Aminosyn, 61
Anemia, 18
Anencephaly, 35
Angiotensin-converting enzyme, 221
Animal models, 215–216, 221
Anionic elements
    homeostatic control, 7–8
    serum level variations, 12
Arsenic, 130–132
Ascorbic acid, 10
Assessment issues, 216–226

B

B-lymphocytes
    function of, 202–203
    and zinc, 208

Balance studies
    quality of, 10–11
    zinc requirements, 70
Bioavailability, 153–171, 215–216
Body weight, fluoride, 110–113
Bone disease, aluminum, 17–18
Boron
    biological essentiality, 138–139
    and immunocompetence, 211
Breast milk
    fluoride, 109–111
    selenium, 79–90
    zinc, 51–54, 63–64
Bromine, 138–139
Brunet-Lezine scale, 98

C

Cabbage diet, 93
Cadmium
    and immunocompetence, 211
    zinc ratio, 39, 47, 143–144
Calcium, and iron, 158, 167
Calcium salts, 21
Cardiomyopathy, 214
Casein, 155–156, 159
Cationic elements
    homeostatic control, 7–8
    serum level variations, 12
Cell-mediated immunity
    iron deficiency effect, 206
    in protein-energy malnutrition, 204
Ceruloplasmin, 177, 185–186
Chromium
    adequate intake range, 8–9
    parenteral nutrition, 187–189
Chromium deficiency, 170–171, 188
Citrate, 158
Cobalt, 211
Cohn fractionation process, 21
Copper
    adequate intake range, 8–9
    ascorbic acid interactions, 10

227